Special Warfare: Special Weapons

The Arms & Equipment of the
UDT and SEALS from 1943 to the present

Produced with the co-operation of the UDT-SEALS Museum

By Kevin Dockery

EMPEROR'S PRESS
Chicago, Illinois

The fortifications put in place on top of a SEAL billet in Vietnam during the Tet Offensive of 1968. At the lower right of the photo can be seen an M1 steel helmet laying on top of an M69 armor vest. Next to the vest is a set of web gear including at least one canteen. On top of the sandbags can be seen the buttplate of a loaded M60 machine gun. Next to the M60, leaning against the crate of ammunition, is a Stoner 63A light machine gun with a 150 round belt drum in place for use. Leaning against the wall just to the left of the sandbags is an M14 rifle with a 20 round magazine locked into place. The bandoleers appear to be additional 7.62mm ammunition in stripper clips for the M14 and additional M14 magazine are laying on top of the wall. Belts of 7.62mm ammunition for the M60 and 5.56mm belts for the Stoner are both draped over the wall. At the base of the M14 are the black fiberboard tubes holding high explosive ammunition for the M29 81mm mortar, the top portion of which can be seen just to the right of the center foreground of the picture.
PHOTO CREDIT: UDT-SEAL MUSEUM

Special Warfare: Special Weapons

© Emperor's Press

All rights reserved. No part of this publication may be reproduced, stored in a retrieval system, or transmitted in any form, or by any means, electronic, mechanical, photocopying, recording, or otherwise without the prior written permission of Emperor's Press and the author.

Printed and Bound in the United States of America

ISBN 1-883476-00-3

The Emperor's Press
5744 West Irving Park Road
Chicago, Illinois 60634 U.S.A.
(773) 777-7307

Table of Contents

Credits and Acknowledgements
Page 4

Chapter One: Knives
Page 6

Chapter Two: Pistols
Page 22

Chapter Three: Submachineguns
Page 56

Chapter Four: Shotguns
Page 98

Chapter Five: Rifles
Page 120

Chapter Six: Grenades
Page 168

Index
Page 190

This book and others to follow in this field are dedicated to the memory of Dr. Edward C. Ezell, Ph.D. who encouraged me to continue my writing, guided me, and told me I had paid my dues.

Help from a great many individuals and organizations went into the creation of this book and the items described between these pages. Because of the nature of their work, many of these individuals did not want to see their name in print. For others, the passage of time has rendered them anonymous.

The Author's personal and heartfelt thanks are extended to both the above and the following individuals, organizations, and institutions;

AAI Corporation, Hunt Valley, Maryland
Elaine Abbrecht
ARES, Inc, Port Clinton, Ohio
Beretta U.S.A. Corp
LTCM Roy Boehm, USN (Ret.)
Michael Boynton
Richard Brozak
Colt Firearms Division, Hartford, Connecticut
Federal Bureau of Alcohol, Tobacco, and Firearms
    - Ed Owens, Jr.
Great Lakes Arsenal, Ray, Michigan
    - Vincent Tessier
Heckler & Koch, Inc. Sterling, Virginia
    - Mr. Jim Schatz
Ian Hogg
Harry Humphries
Kerry N. Kinder & Family
Knight Armament Company
    - Mr. C. Reed Knight, Jr.
    - Mr. Eugene Stoner
CMDR Richard Marcinko, USN (Ret.)
CPT Ryan McCombie, USN (Ret.)
Greg McPartlin
LCDR Stanley "Pete" Meston, USN (Ret.)
Militec Corporation, Arlington Virginia
    - Mr. Russel A. Logan
Mission Knives, Inc.
    - Mr. Richard A. Schultz
Frank Moncrief
Naval Historical Center
    - Dr. Dean C. Allard
    - Dr. William F. Dudley
    - Mr. Henry A. Vadnais, Jr.
    - Dr. Norman Cary
    - Mrs. Kathy Lloyd

    - Mr. Mark Wertheimer
    - Mr. Frank V. Thompson
Naval Sea Systems Command
    - Mr. Richard E. Brown
    - Mr. Homer Detrich
Naval Surface Warfare Center, Crane, Indiana
    - Mr. Larry Nash
    - Mr. Mike Anderson
    - Mr. Jim Scott
Sage International, Ltd.
    - John M. Klein
Jim Shults
CMDR Larry Simmons, USN (Ret.)
Smith & Wesson, Springfield, Massachussets
    - Ken Jorgensen
Smithsonian Institution, Museum of American History
    - Dr. Edward C. Ezell
Dante S. Stephensen
CWO4 Thomas Swearengen, USMC (Ret.)
LTCM Frank F. Thornton, USN (Ret.)
UDT-SEAL Museum, Fort Pierce, Florida
    - Jim Watson QMCS, USN (Ret.)
    - H.T. Aldhizer, III
    - Don Balzarini
United States Special Operations Command, PAO
US Army Ordnance Museum, Aberdeen Proving Grounds
CPT Richard Woolard, USN (Ret.)
Darryl Young

And to the men of the Teams, past, present, and future.

A member of UDT-21 proudly displays a t-shirt with his unit's emblem after coming ashore in Denmark during NATO exercise Northern Wedding 82. He is armed with a Vietnam era XM177E2 fitted with a China Lake blank adapter. At his left shoulder is a Mark 1 Ka-bar with a cast aluminum pommel dating from World War II. The story of the UDT's came to an end within a year of this pictures being taken. In 1983, all UDT's were decommissioned and became SEAL Teams or SDV Teams.
Photo credit: US Navy

Knives

A PAL RH-35 version of the USN Mark 1 knife. This particular variant has an aluminum pommel and a well-worn blade.
PHOTO CREDIT: KEVIN DOCKERY

"The large number of Mark 1's produced during World War II resulted in a number of cutlers making the Mark 1, each one modifying the design slightly to meet his own manufacturing methods. But though the details of the knife may have been different (the pommels were made of aluminum, plastic, flat steel, even wood), and the handles were in slightly different shapes, the general style of the knife remained the same."

TECHNICAL DATA—Mk 1 Ka-Bar
KNIFE PATTERN—Short-blade bowie
BLADE TYPE—Single edge clip point
EDGE TYPE—V-grind, double edge bevel
POINT TYPE—Saber
TANG TYPE—Narrow full hidden tang w/pinned shaped metal pommel
BLADE MATERIAL—Carbon steel
BLADE FINISH—Blued or parkerized
HANDLE MATERIAL—Compressed leather washers
SHEATH MATERIAL—Gray plastic w/internal web reinforcing, steel chape, gray canvas hanger with 1 snap loop keeper
WEIGHTS
KNIFE—0.42 lb (0.19 kg)
SHEATH—0.25 lb (0.11 kg)
DIMENSIONS
KNIFE—10.13 in (25.7 cm)
BLADE—5.25 in (13.3 cm)
CUTTING EDGE—5 in (12.5 cm)
BLADE THICKNESS (MAXIMUM)—0.166 in (4.22 mm)
BLADE WIDTH (MAXIMUM)—1.09 in (2.8 cm)
SHEATH—10.74 in (27.3 cm)

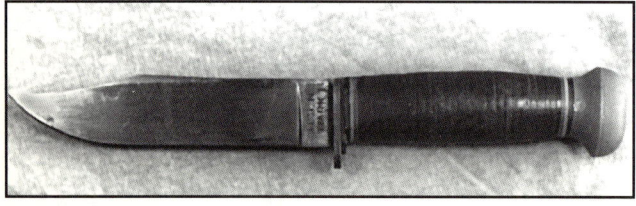

The USN Mark 1 knife, commonly used by the UDTs during World War II. The stacked-leather washer handle is visible in this well-used specimen. This particular specimen also has a cast-aluminum pommel. Other examples of the Mark 1 had plastic or metal pommels in flat and rounded shapes.
PHOTO CREDIT: KEVIN DOCKERY

Special Weapons

One of mankind's oldest tools was also the only weapon used by the UDTs in their earliest years during World War II. To the men of the Teams, a good knife was a necessity, and they carried one with them constantly. Even when a swimmer wasn't wearing much more than his swim trunks, face mask, and fins, on a belt around his waist would be a knife in its sheath.

Mk 1 Ka-Bar

The first issue knife to the early UDTs was the U.S.N. Mark 1, standard throughout the Fleet. From the official drawing of the Mark 1 dated November 1943, the design called for a 5.125 inch blade with a shaped aluminum pommel over a stacked leather washer grip with a small, flat steel guard. The flat-ground single edge blade of the Mark 1 greatly resembles the general style of hunting knife that was popular in the civilian market at the time. The shaped metal pommel was also a part of popular commercial knives during the 1940's. It may be that the design of the Mark 1 wasn't influenced by commercial knives as much as it was just much easier to make a knife for the Navy that the civilian cutlers were already tooled up for.

On the ricasso (the flat area on the blade between the guard and where the cutting edge begins) of the Mark 1's blade is stamped U.S.N. MARK 1. On the opposite side of the blade is usually the maker's name. The large number of Mark 1's produced during World War II resulted in a number of cutlers making the Mark 1, each one modifying the design slightly to meet his own manufacturing methods. But though the details of the knife may have been different (the pommels were made of aluminum, plastic, flat steel, even wood), and the handles were in slightly different shapes, the general style of the knife remained the same. Two very different kinds of sheaths were found on the Mark 1, though only one was well accepted by the UDTs.

The first type of sheath on the Mark 1 was a traditional-

A group of UDT swimmers on an island in the Pacific during World War II. All three of the men are armed with M1 carbines, the man on the right having two carbine magazine pouches on his M1936 pistol belt. Each of the pouches holds two of the standard 15-round carbine magazines. Both the man on the far right and far left are wearing inflatable life belts above their M1936 pistol belts. The man on the far left is holding a pair of swim fins in his right hand and has a small green rubber/glass diving mask used by the UDT hanging around his neck, just below his chin. This same man has a Mark 1 Ka-Bar knife hanging from his pistol belt just in front of his right leg. The UDT man in the center of the picture has a native machete or parang knife slipped through his pistol belt.
PHOTO CREDIT: UDT-SEAL MUSEUM

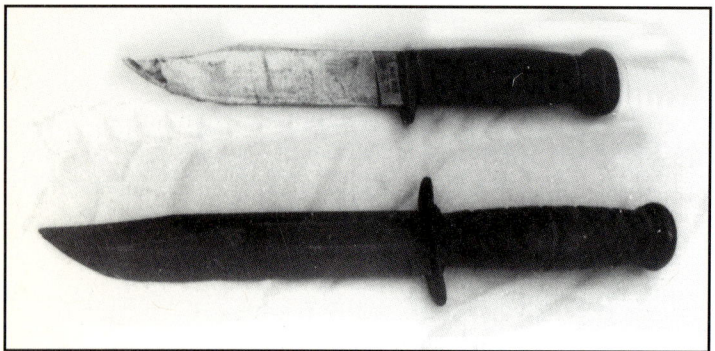

Two of the three Navy issue UDT/SEAL knives that received mark identifiers. At thew top is a PAL RH-35 Mark 1 with an aluminum pommel. The well-worn blade of this Mark 1 specimen has lost most of its dark finish through use, leaving the blade bright. The lower knife is a Camillus manufactured Mark 2. This one is almost new– most of the bluing is intact.
PHOTO CREDIT: KEVIN DOCKERY

"Where the blade of the Mark 1 had a flat grind extending from the back to the edge, the Marine knife's blade had flat, parallel sides to within a few inches of the tip and an edge grind that didn't come up to the mid point of the blade. A fuller was also ground into each side of the blade to help strengthen and lighten it."

TECHNICAL DATA—Mk 2 Ka-Bar
KNIFE PATTERN—Bowie
BLADE TYPE—Single edge clip point w/short back edge, shallow fuller
EDGE TYPE—V-grind, double edge bevel
POINT TYPE—Saber w/back edge
TANG TYPE—Narrow full hidden tang w/peened flat metal pommel
BLADE MATERIAL—Carbon steel
BLADE FINISH—Blued or parkerized
HANDLE MATERIAL—Compressed leather washers with 5 deep grooves
SHEATH MATERIAL—Gray plastic w/internal web reinforcing, steel chape, gray canvas hanger with 1 snap loop keeper
WEIGHTS
KNIFE—0.63 lb (0.29 kg)
SHEATH—0.29 lb (0.13 kg)
DIMENSIONS
KNIFE—12 in (30.5 cm)
BLADE—7 in (17.8 cm)
CUTTING EDGE (PRIMARY)—6.81 in (17.3 cm)
CUTTING EDGE (SECONDARY)—2.25 in (5.7 cm)
BLADE THICKNESS (MAXIMUM)—0.163 in (4.14 mm)
BLADE WIDTH (MAXIMUM)—1.19 in (3.0 cm)
SHEATH—13.25 in (33.7 cm)

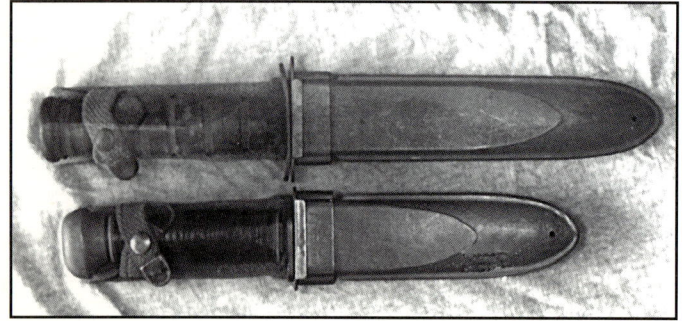

The two most common knives used by the UDTs during World War II. At the top is the Mark 2 knife with a flat-steel pommel while below it is a Mark 1 knife with a cast aluminum pommel. Both of the knives are sheathed in the gray plastic scabbards found on most of the Navy contract knives. The Mark 2, also commonly called a Ka-Bar, remained in common use in the UDTs and the later SEAL Teams until well after World War II. Examples of the Mark 2 are still seen in use in the SEAL Teams today, though in much smaller numbers than before.
PHOTO CREDIT: KEVIN DOCKERY

style folded brown leather sheath with a snap-type keeper. As the Mark 1 was intended to be a general issue knife, it was thought that the leather sheath would be satisfactory throughout the Navy. This was quickly proved false as the sheath was found to quickly deteriorate, no matter how well-kept, in the hot and humid conditions of the Pacific. For the men of the UDT, the leather sheath would be quickly rendered useless by the constant and extended immersion in salt water it received on operations and during training. A fiber-reinforced gray plastic scabbard was designed and issued for the Mark 1. The new scabbard was well received by the men of the UDTs as well as many of the Fleet sailors.

A drawback of the Mark 1 was the reported weakness of the blade. Tapering from the base to the point, the Mark 1 had a light and handy blade but not one of the strongest design. Being issued Navy wide, the Mark 1 was subject to some serious misuse, especially when being used as a pry-bar to open boxes and cases. The small sized blade was also considered by many to be too short for effective use as a combat/fighting knife.

There was also the problem of wartime production to be considered. It was not the best use of material to have several types of knives made for different service units that did much the same work. The thousands of knives needed by the Navy should also meet the requirements of the Marine Corps, since the two services worked so close together.

Mk 2 Ka-Bar

Camillus Cutlery Company had submitted a knife to the Marine Corps in December 1942. The design was of a multipurpose tool that would also serve well as a fighting knife. The knife was adopted as USMC item # 1219C2c and put into production. In general, the knife had a great deal in common with the Mark 1 design. The handles of both knives were made up of stacked leather washers with an attached metal pommel and the guard was a simple metal stamping.

The Camillus knife had a seven-inch blade with a clip point sharpened on the back edge. The metal pommel was a flat-metal affair suitable for pounding, specially in the later pinned models. The leather handle was oval in cross-section and had five grooves turned into it as an aid in gripping the knife.

Where the blade of the Mark 1 had a flat grind extending from the back to the edge, the Marine knife's blade had flat, parallel sides to within a few inches of the tip and an edge grind that didn't come up to the mid point of the blade. A fuller was also ground into each side of the blade to help strengthen and lighten it.

All in all, the knife was everything the Marine Corps wanted in a combat/utility blade and was later adopted by the Navy as the Mark 2. First manufactured only by Camillus, the Marine knife was duplicated by a number of other manufacturers. Union Cutlery was one of these producers and they already manufactured a line of knives under the trade name KA-BAR. Knives supplied to the Marine Corps from Union Cutlery were marked U.S.M.C. on one side of the ricasso and KA-BAR on the opposite side. The name Ka-Bar stuck in popular use and has been used interchangeably with the Navy Mark 2 designation.

During the war, many thousands of the Ka-Bar and Mark 2 designs were produced by at least five different makers. These makers all would put their own markings on the blade as well as have slight differences in the overall knife due to their own manufacturing methods. Several design changes were also dictated by the Marines and the Navy after field experience with the weapon. The three different methods of attaching the pommel cap are the most obvious. The first Mark 2s and Ka-Bars had the pommel cap held on by a flush mounted threaded nut. Later pommels were peened in place and finally held in place with a cross pin through the tang. All of the steel parts of the knives were either matte blued or, most commonly, parkerized with a dull gray phosphate coating.

The marking of the blade for the Mark 2 also changed during the war, being moved from the ricasso to the flat metal guard. The popular story is that stamping the ricasso weakened the blade but that was not the case. According to the people at Union Cutlery, the Mark 2 design was so popular that it was eventually demanded by all the services, including the Coast Guard. Instead of putting whatever designation was required onto the blade, and scrapping a blade that was mis-marked, markings were moved to the easily handled guard. Even mis-marked guards could be used if necessary by obliterating the markings with chisel cuts, something that would have been excessive if done to the blade.

Except for the very earliest issue blades, the Navy Mark 2 was given out sheathed in a gray-plastic scabbard similar to the model used in the later production Mark 1s. Part of the popularity and success of the Mark 2 was due to the excellent design of the scabbard, the plastic and canvas construction proving very resistant to damage from exposure to the elements. The scabbards were not produced by the various cutlery firms that were making the knives. A single contractor, the Beckwith Manufacturing Company, B.M. Co. is the marking on the back of the chape, made the scabbards and supplied them to the various cutlery companies.

Though the scabbard did not suffer greatly in a moist environment, the blades of both the Mark 1 and Mark 2 were not so resistant. Being made of carbon steel, the knife blades would very soon rust after exposure to the water. Even the metal fittings on the scabbards were susceptible to corrosion. The most exposed of all the thousands of Mark 2 knives used during the war were those used by the UDTs. Even the Marine Corps with their specialty in amphibious operations only spent enough time actually in the water as was needed to get to the landing beach. The UDTs performed their missions almost constantly in the water. To help minimize the corrosion, Union Cutlery produced a modified Mark 2 especially for the UDTs, called the Bright Mark 2.

The first model of the special UDT knives had no fuller ground into the blade and all the metal parts of the knife were bright chromed. Since the UDTs were under orders not to expose themselves to direct combat with the enemy, they were considered far to valuable to risk in such a manner, the brilliant shiny appearance of the knives was

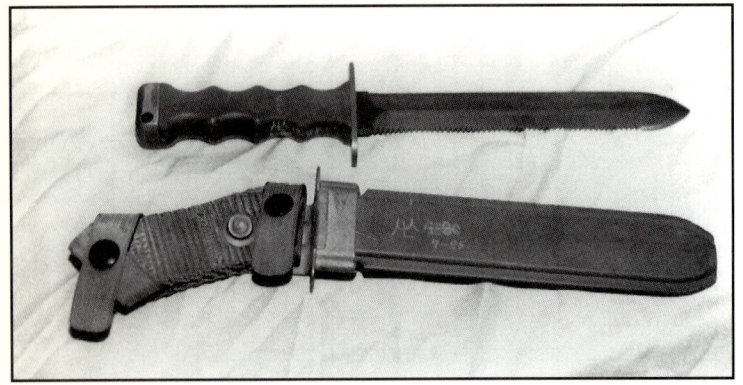

The nonmagnetic SCUBA swimmer's knife shown with its special sheath. The twin-edged blade of the knife can be plainly seen with the saw-toothed edge facing the scabbard. The unusual marking on the scabbard, also seen inside the second finger groove of the knife handle, indicates that this item was tested and found to be totally nonmagnetic. The large rivet just above the first keeper strap is the pivot point between the scabbard and the nylon cloth hanger.
PHOTO CREDIT: KEVIN DOCKERY

"...the Nonmagnetic SCUBA Swimmers Knife is made of exotic alloy and has no detectable magnetic signature."

A UDT swimmer preparing to enter the water in the 1960's. Wearing a minimum of equipment, inflatable life vest, t-shirt, trunks, and canvas/rubber coral shoes, this swimmer also has a quick-release belt around his waist securing a Mark 2 knife. As is commonly done in the teams, this swimmer has taped a Mark 13 day/night signal flare to the scabbard of his Mark 2.
PHOTO CREDIT: KEVIN DOCKERY

TECHNICAL DATA—Nonmagnetic SCUBA Swimmer's Knife
KNIFE PATTERN— Long blade dagger
BLADE TYPE—Double edged w/rear rake saw back
EDGE TYPE—Hollow ground w/wide 0.19 in (4.83 mm) double edge bevel
POINT TYPE—Double edge spear
TANG TYPE—Full hidden tapered tang w/pinned flat steel pommel
BLADE MATERIAL—Haynes Alloy No. 25 (Copper-chromium-tungsten-nickel)
BLADE FINISH—Gray oxide
HANDLE MATERIAL—Molded glass fiber w/sharp 20 lpi molded checkering on flats and 4 finger grooves, all metal fittings are 310 Stainless alloy
SHEATH MATERIAL—Glass fiber laminate w/nylon hanger riveted to chape extension, two 2-piece snap button nylon keepers, metal chape w/copper-beryllium alloy retainer springs, all metal fittings are 310 Stainless alloy
WEIGHTS
KNIFE—0.68 lb (0.31 kg)
SHEATH—0.36 lb (0.16 kg)
DIMENSIONS
KNIFE—12 in (30.5 cm)
BLADE—7.31 in (18.6 cm)
CUTTING EDGE (PRIMARY)—7 in (17.8 cm)
CUTTING EDGE (SECONDARY)—1.38 in (3.5 cm) tip edge 5.88 in (14.9 cm) 9 tpi Saw back
BLADE THICKNESS (MAXIMUM)—0.158 in (4.01 mm)
BLADE WIDTH (MAXIMUM)—
SHEATH—12.88 in (32.7 cm)

Special Weapons

not a drawback. The "flat-sided" Bright UDT knife was made in very limited numbers and is quite rare today. Though still made in limited numbers, the "production" Bright UDT knife was made with a standard, fullered blade and a pinned pommel.

Another unique feature of the special UDT knife was the leather grip. Where in the standard Mark 2 and Marine Ka-Bar, the leather handle had a number of grooves cut into it, the UDT knife had a smooth grip. Removing the grooves cut down on the exposed surface area of the grip and helped to limit seawater absorption into the leather. A heavy varnish was applied to the leather during manufacture to also help protect the grip from the water.

Though several makers produced the Mark 2 during World War II, and in prodigious numbers, only the Union Cutlery Company made the special UDT Bright Mark 2. In 1945, at the end of the war, Union Cutlery had made about 1 million Mark 2 knives. Out of that number, it is thought that only a thousand or less of the special UDT knives were made, perhaps only a few hundred. At the war's end, no more of the plastic Mark 2 scabbards were produced, the numbers available being thought sufficient for future needs.

For the rest of the 1940's and through the 1950's, the UDTs continued using the Mark 2 and remaining Mark 1s as the general issue knife. The small number of special UDT Bright Mark 2s were quickly absorbed into the growing Teams. The rare chromed Bright Mark 2 became a cherished possession of the WWII veteran Officers and senior Petty Officers who remained in the postwar UDTs. The vast number of World War II manufactured Mark 2 knives in the Navy inventories were easily able to fill the needs of the UDTs for some time.

Nonmagnetic SCUBA Swimmer's Knife

Early in the 1960's, a new knife was required for special use by the Navy. Explosive Ordnance Disposal (EOD) missions were often performed by UDT divers as part of their beach-clearing operations. Underwater mines with magnetically-influenced fuzes had become much more common by the late 1950's and were an EOD problem by the 1960's. The standard clearing procedure of blowing the mines in place was complicated by the need for a swimmer to closely approach the mine to emplace the destruction charge. The equipment for such a swimmer had to be completely nonmagnetic and usually nonferrous. Special nonmagnetic breathing equipment and other diving gear was available for EOD missions that would help increase the safety of the swimmer. But the Mark 1 and 2 knives were made of carbon steel and unsuitable for specialized EOD use.

A procurement contract was issued by the Navy in February 1961 and by April 1962 a new type of knife was ready for issue. Developed by the US Navy Bureau of Weapons and the Imperial Knife Company of Providence Rhode Island, the Nonmagnetic SCUBA Swimmers Knife is made of exotic alloy and has no detectable magnetic signature.

The initial problem with making such a knife was in coming up with a material that was nonmagnetic, and yet could be hardened sufficiently to hold a sharp edge without being too brittle for field use. A nonferrous alloy, Haynes Number 25, was chosen to make up the blade of the new knife. Haynes Number 25 is a mixture of copper, chromium, tungsten, and nickel. After a process that included cold-rolling, machining, grinding, and a five-hour, 1000 degree F. heat treatment, the hardness of the finished blades were at a Rockwell-C of 53-54. The blades were able to hold a worthwhile working edge but the material was still considerably more brittle than an equivalent steel blade.

Additional fittings for the knife and scabbard were of glass-fiber plastic and 310 stainless steel. 310 stainless steel has a high chromium and nickel content giving the alloy strong resistance to corrosion and no magnetic signature. Retaining springs inside of the scabbard were made of a copper-beryllium alloy. All the remaining components of the knife and scabbard were either nylon or reinforced plastic.

Due to the relatively high individual cost of a finished knife (over $100 dollars in 1962) as well as the brittleness of the blade, the Nonmagnetic SCUBA Swimmers Knife was kept for special-issue only. Each blade was consecutively serial numbered and marked with the year of manufacture. All production of the nonmagnetic knife was carried out by the Imperial Knife Company with the initial production lot being 280 knives and scabbards. Only about 1,100 of the nonmagnetic knives were produced in the early 1960's and the knife has remained available for issue well into the 1990's.

As the SEALs and UDTs entered into action in the Vietnam War, the Mark 2 knife remained the standard issue blade. Sufficient numbers of the Mark 1 knife remained in the supply system to issue the knife to the men who preferred the smaller blade. For diving operations, any commercially available quality stainless steel diver's knife was considered interchangeable with a Team-issued blade. Operators in the UDT and especially the SEALs were given a great deal of flexibility in choosing whatever knives they preferred to carry. An individual could purchase and carry any blade with which he felt comfortable. With the level of training and professionalism in the Teams, none of the men would have carried an excessively complex blade or one that could not be counted on.

When a sheath knife is carried during a dive, its primary purpose is to cut the swimmer free of any entanglements he might encounter. Because of this, it was specified that the diver's knife be securely attached to a web belt or one of the diver's legs and not to any piece of jettisonable equipment such as a weight belt. Making certain that the knife always stayed with an operator through any situation made it an excellent place to carry another required piece of emergency gear, the day/night flare.

In many of the post World War II photos of UDT or SEAL operators, a Mark 13 day/night flare can be seen securely taped or strapped to the scabbard of a Mark 2 knife. On some occasions, an individual may have two Mark 13's attached to his knife's scabbard. This procedure

TECHNICAL DATA—Mk 3 (NSN 1095-00-391-1056)
KNIFE PATTERN— Short blade bowie
BLADE TYPE—Single edge deep clip point w/sharp clip and forward rake saw back
EDGE TYPE—V-grind, double edge bevel
POINT TYPE—Deep concave clip point
TANG TYPE—Full hidden tang w/heavy flat steel pommel
BLADE MATERIAL—Carbon steel
BLADE FINISH—Matt blue
HANDLE MATERIAL—Polycarbonate plastic w/embossed checkering
SHEATH MATERIAL—Polycarbonate plastic w/nylon frog, metal belt hanger, 2-piece snap button loop keeper, metal spring clip chape
WEIGHTS
KNIFE—0.62 lb (0.28 kg)
SHEATH—0.32 lb (0.15 kg)
DIMENSIONS
KNIFE—10.88 in (27.6 cm)
BLADE—6 in (15.2 cm)
CUTTING EDGE (PRIMARY)—5.25 in (13.3 cm)
CUTTING EDGE (SECONDARY)—2.5 in (6.4 cm) 11 tpi Saw back edge 1.75 in (4.4 cm) Clip point back edge
BLADE THICKNESS (MAXIMUM)—0.166 in (4.22 mm)
BLADE WIDTH (MAXIMUM)—1.23 in (3.1 cm)
SHEATH—12.5 in (31.8 cm)

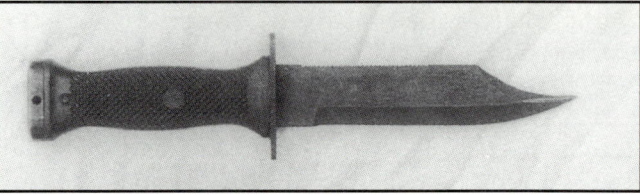

The third of the three Navy issue UDT/SEAL knives that received a Mark identifier. This Mark 3 Mod 0 was manufactured by the Ontario Knife Company.
PHOTO CREDIT: KEVIN DOCKERY

"The pattern of the Mark 3 was an adaptation of the AKM-47 bayonet design used in the Soviet Union."

TECHNICAL DATA—SwissChamp Swiss Army knife
KNIFE PATTERN— Multiblade folding knife
NUMBER OF BLADES/TOOLS 2 blades, 25 tools
CUTTING BLADE TYPE—Single edge spear point
EDGE TYPE—flat grind w/double edge bevel
OTHER BLADES/TOOLS—Corkscrew, jewelers screwdriver, wood chisel, 3/32 in flat screwdriver, awl, 1/4 in flat screwdriver, bottle opener, wire stripper, 1/8 in flat screwdriver, can opener, #1 Philips screwdriver, magnifying glass, pliers w/serrated center, small wire cutter, scissors, wood saw, fish hook disgorger, fish scaler, inch/metric scale, fine file, nail cleaner, hacksaw, ball-point pen, toothpick, tweezers.
MATERIAL—Stainless steel
FINISH—Bright polished
HANDLE/SCALE MATERIAL—Black plastic scales
POUCH MATERIAL—Leather
WEIGHTS
KNIFE—0.42 lbs (0.191 kg)
POUCH—0.14 lbs (0.062 kg)
DIMENSIONS
OVERALL FOLDED/OPEN—3.63/6.25 in (9.2/15.9 cm) (large blade open) 6.44 in (16.4 cm) (pliers open)
CUTTING BLADE—2.5 in (6.4 cm)
WIDTH—1 in (2.5 cm) deep, 1.25 in (3.2 cm) wide
POUCH—2.5 x 4.5 in (6.4 x 11.4 cm)

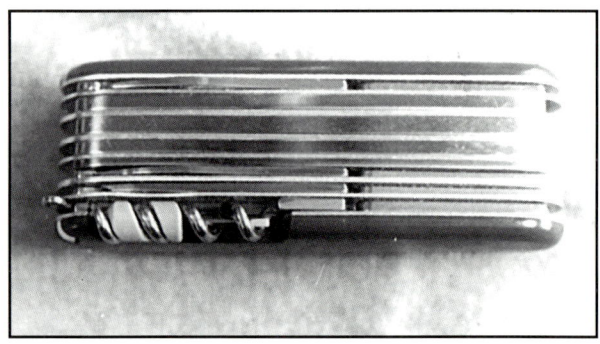

The bottom side of the SwissChamp pocket knife. At the top of the picture, hinged at the center of the knife, is the reamer blade for enlarging holes in various materials. At the bottom of the picture is the corkscrew with a removable flat mini-screwdriver threaded into it. Directly above the corkscrew is the wood chisel blade, also hinged at the center of the knife. Above the wood chisel is the small flat screwdriver blade. The curved white piece at the left end of the bottom of the knife is the removable toothpick. Lastly, the protrusion at the left side of the knife, above the corkscrew, is the attachment point for the key ring or lanyard line.
PHOTO CREDIT: KEVIN DOCKERY/KERRY KINDER

is still followed as Mark 13's or other signals can be seen attached to the sheathes of knives worn by today's SEALs.

During the Vietnam War, a great number of non-issue knives were carried by the SEALs. Some operators would take little or no interest in which specific knife they carried. The issue Mark 2 was quite satisfactory for these men and the blade saw good service in their hands. Other SEALs had different tastes and some of these men would carry two or more knives on operations. In the case of men carrying multiple knives, very often one would be a folding pocketknife such as the military issue Camillus all-purpose S1760, an all-metal, four bladed pocketknife stamped U.S. on one side.

Blades issued by other branches of the Service were also popular with the SEALs, such as the Air Force's Camillus Pilot Survival knife. Commercial combat knives such as Randalls and Gerber Mark IIs were carried, along with the occasional custom blade made to a SEAL's specifications. Probably the most personal knives carried were the "used" gift blades, given to an operator from a friend or relative who had carried the knife in an earlier conflict.

The SEALs received training in hand-to-hand combat that included fighting with and against a knife. Though it was rare, SEALs were much more likely to use a knife as a weapon in combat than almost any other US military unit. In general, if an enemy sentry required quiet dispatching, the weapon of choice would be a suppressed firearm rather than a blade. But the SEALs were always ready to make use of the weapons that they had immediately at hand.

During the 1970's and the post-Vietnam cutbacks, the SEALs and UDTs saw the same austerity program as the other services. As they had during the last several decades, the Mark 2 and occasional Mark 1 fulfilled the cutlery needs of the Teams. With the increase in emphasis on the SEALs and other Special Operations units in the 1980's, manpower in the Teams increased and so did the demand for new equipment.

Mk 3

A replacement for the dwindling stocks of Mark 2 knives was desired and a number of replacements examined. From the Naval Weapons Support Center in Crane, Indiana came a design for a new knife that was finally accepted as the Mark 1 Mod 0 Combat Knife on 21 October, 1982. The pattern of the Mark 3 was an adaptation of the AKM-47 bayonet design used in the Soviet Union. One result of this adoption was that the Mark 3 knife had a very deep, concave clip point giving the blade a sharp, upswept tip. The intent of the tip was to ease the penetration of the knife into a target. But the combat knife was also to be a utility blade and such blades were used for prying materials apart and digging into the ground when necessary. The tip style of the Mark 3 was very weak for this kind of work and was a drawback of the pattern

Part of the initial pattern for the Mark 3 included an insulated wire cutter built into the scabbard. By inserting a stud on the scabbard tip through a hole in the blade, a

The Mark 3 combat knife outside of its sheath. The deep clip point is very visible in this photograph as is also the serrated back edge. The forward-facing serrations cut on the push stroke of the knife are primarily intended for severing rope and other fibrous materials.
PHOTO CREDIT: KEVIN DOCKERY

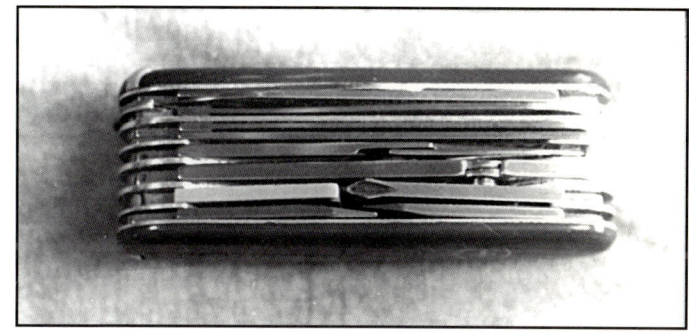

The SwissChamp, this illustration showing the main side of the pocket knife with its many blades folded. At the top left is the small pen blade, top right is the large knife blade. Next down hinged at the left is the nail/metal file blade with its hacksaw edge on the inside. The next two blades, both hinged on the left side are first the wood saw, and then the combination fish scaler and fish hook disgorger with an inch/metric rule engraved on the sides. Fourth up from the bottom is the scissors, hinged on the left side. Next down from the scissors is the folding pliers also hinged on the left side. The pliers have a nut-driver center section and a small wire cutter edge. The small gray piece, second from the bottom on the left side, is the magnifying glass, powerful enough to use for starting fires in the bright sun. Hinged on the right side, across from the magnifying glass, is the number 1 phillips screwdriver. At the bottom of the knife, on the left side, is the large, flat screwdriver blade. The large screwdriver blade also has a bottle opener and a notch for stripping wire. Across the bottom from the large screwdriver blade is the can opener, hinged on the right side. The can opener also has a medium, flat screwdriver blade on its tip. The small gray protrusion on the upper right end of the knife is the ball point pen that slips out from under the side of the pocketknife. Slightly visible at the bottom, right side of the SwissChamp is the tweezers that also fit under the side plate.
PHOTO CREDIT: KEVIN DOCKERY/KERRY KINDER

Knives

TECHNICAL DATA—Leatherman
KNIFE PATTERN— Multiblade folding tool
NUMBER OF BLADES/TOOLS 1 blade, 9 tools
CUTTING BLADE TYPE—Single edge clip point
EDGE TYPE—Hollow grind w/double edge bevel
OTHER BLADES/TOOLS—Awl, 3/8 in flat screwdriver blade, 1/4 in flat screwdriver blade, can/bottle opener, #1 Philips screwdriver, flat jewelers screwdriver, coarse/fine file, needle-nosed pliers w/cutters, serrated center opening, inch/cm scale on handles
MATERIAL—Stainless steel
FINISH—Satin
HANDLE/SCALE MATERIAL—Stainless w/no scales
POUCH MATERIAL—Leather w/snap cover
WEIGHTS
KNIFE—0.33 lb (0.15 kg)
POUCH—0.0.07 lb (0.03 kg)
DIMENSIONS
OVERALL FOLDED/OPEN—4.0/8.0 in (10.2/20.4 cm) maximum
6.25 in (15.9 cm) open to pliers
CUTTING BLADE—5.13 in (13 cm)
WIDTH—1.06 in (2.7 cm) folded
1.84/5.13 in (4.7/13 cm) open to pliers
POUCH—4.25 x 1.25 x 1.25 in (10.8 x 3.2 x 3.2 cm)

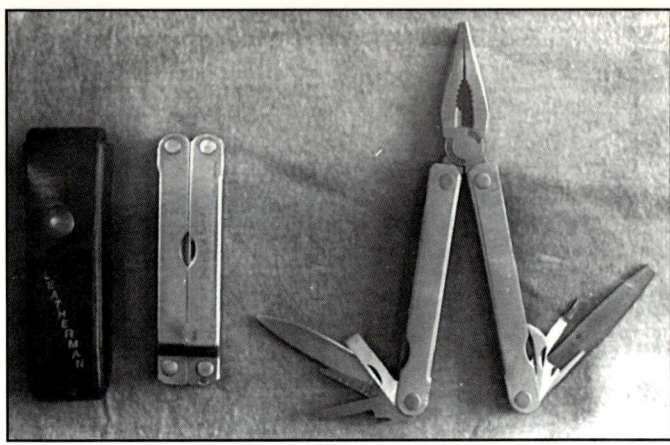

The leatherman tool, from the right, unfolded, folded for carrying, and the belt pouch for the tool. In the unfolded position, the needle-nosed pliers portion of the tool is ready for use with the wire cutter visible just below the nut driver portion of the pliers jaws. On the left side of the tool is the knife blade, reamer, medium flat screwdriver, and large flat screwdriver. On the right side of the tool is the file, with a fine and coarse side, the small flat screwdriver, the number 1 phillips screwdriver, and the can opener blade. On the inside of the handles are engraved both an inch and a metric scale.
PHOTO CREDIT: KEVIN DOCKERY

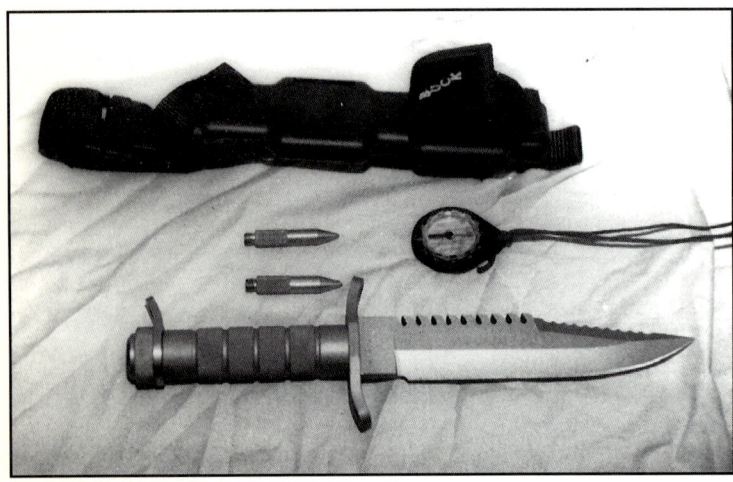

The Buckmaster knife showing its scabbard and the two removable anchor pins. The pins and lensatic compass can be carried in the removable pouch shown attached to the scabbard. The large protrusion just below the pommel cap of the Buckmaster is a removable lug for the attachment of a line or carabiner ring.
PHOTO CREDIT: KEVIN DOCKERY

TECHNICAL DATA—SEAL Buckmaster
KNIFE PATTERN— Hollow grip, long blade bowie
BLADE TYPE—Single edge w/serrated edge sharp clip, saw back
EDGE TYPE—Hollow ground w/double bevel edge, Flat ground partial serrated chisel edge clip, rear rake, very coarse saw back
POINT TYPE—Spear point w/serrated back edge
TANG TYPE—Partial stub welded to hollow handle w/ removable threaded o-ring sealed flat steel pommel
BLADE MATERIAL—Stainless steel
BLADE FINISH—Matt
HANDLE MATERIAL—Thick walled stainless steel tubing with 5 deep grooves and sharp knurling between grooves
SHEATH MATERIAL—Polycarbonate plastic w/nylon frog, quick-release buckle nylon belt hanger, 1 snap button keeper strap, metal spring clip chape, removable nylon parts pouch w/ velcro strap, integral sharpening stone on sheath back, multiple belt loops on sheath body
WEIGHTS
KNIFE—1.39 lbs (0.63 kg) w/o spikes or lanyard ring
1.57 lbs (0.71 kg) complete
SHEATH—0.56 lb (0.5 kg) w/o pouch, compass or lanyard
0.64 lb (0.29 kg) w/pouch, compass, lanyard
DIMENSIONS
KNIFE—12.56 in (31.9 cm)
BLADE—7.63 in (19.4 cm)
CUTTING EDGE (PRIMARY)—7.75 in (19.7 cm)
CUTTING EDGE (SECONDARY)—2.5 in (6.4 cm) Serrated clip edge, 2.88 in (7.3 cm) 4 tpi Saw back, 2 in (5.1 cm) installed knurled base guard spikes (2)
BLADE THICKNESS (MAXIMUM)—0.287 in (7.29 mm)
BLADE WIDTH (MAXIMUM)—1.5 in (3.8 cm)
SHEATH—13.38 in (34 cm) w/belt loop closed

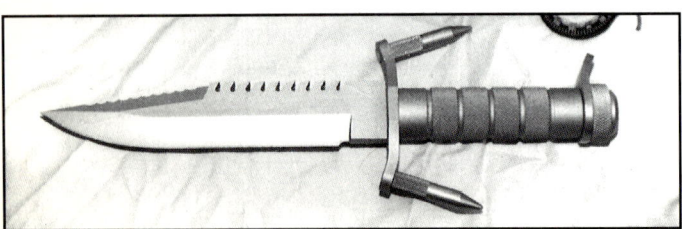

The Buckmaster knife with the anchor pins threaded into the cross guard.
PHOTO CREDIT: KEVIN DOCKERY

scissor-type wire cutter could be made. This idea can be directly traced to the AKM bayonet in use by Soviet forces. Though considered a good idea, the wirecutter provision further complicated and weakened an already difficult knife. The final production version of the Mark 3 Mod 0 did not include the wirecutter. As produced by the Ontario Knife Company, the Mark 3 Mod 0 knife has a black oxide coated stainless steel blade with a fine-tooth saw edge back intended for rapidly cutting rope or cable.

EXPLORER SWISS ARMY KNIFE

One particularly interesting issue knife at SEAL Team Two during the early 1980's was more of a pocket tool box than a knife. Obtained for issue to team members was a quantity of the Victorinox Explorer model Swiss Army knife. The Swiss Army knife, long noted for its versatility, was found to be a highly useful tool by many of the SEALs who carried one. Purchased as an off-the-shelf item directly by SEAL Team Two, the Explorer was basically the standard commercial model with a few requested additions. Specifically, the trademark red side covers were replaced with black covers and a small jewelers-type screwdriver inserted into the corkscrew.

SWISSCHAMP SWISS ARMY KNIFE

SEAL Team Six issued another Swiss Army knife later in the 1980's. The knife was the SwissChamp model and it was issued in roughly the 1987-1990 time period. As Team Two had earlier, the knife was purchased as an off-the-shelf item with black side plates instead of the trademark red ones. The SwissChamp is almost too big to qualify as a pocketknife and can be more accurately described as a belt-pouch tool kit.

LEATHERMAN

At least one other folding knife has been issued as a regular item by SEAL Team Six. Though it does contain a knife blade, the Leatherman tool is most obviously a pair of folding pliers. Carried in a belt pouch, the Leatherman tool unfolds into a very serviceable pair of needle-nosed pliers with a serrated nut driver section and efficient wire-cutters. Issued at about the same time as the SwissChamp, the Leatherman actually became more popular with the men of Team Six than the SwissChamp. The versatility of the tool is such that several SEALs in the other Teams have bought them out of their own funds rather than wait for a possible issue.

During the 1980's, a number of knife designs were examined by the SEAL Teams for use as an issue knife. Because of the flexibility allowed SEAL operators in purchasing and carrying any worthwhile blade they prefer, a number of commercial knives have been used. One result of this is the quantity of commercial and custom blades on the market that are advertised as "SEAL issue." Individual qualities aside, only a very few knives have been examined and evaluated by the Teams in numbers large enough for them to be considered "issue" items.

SEAL BUCKMASTER

One of these few blade designs was developed in about the mid-1980's by Phrobis International Ltd. to fit requirements put forward by SPECWAR Command.

A SEAL insertion during a training exercise. The SEAL on the right is carrying a Buckmaster knife that has had its shiny metal handle covered in camouflage tape and a M-4 carbine with a 100 round drum. The SEAL on the left has a M60E3 lightweight machine gun suspended upside down on a sling.
PHOTO CREDIT: US NAVY

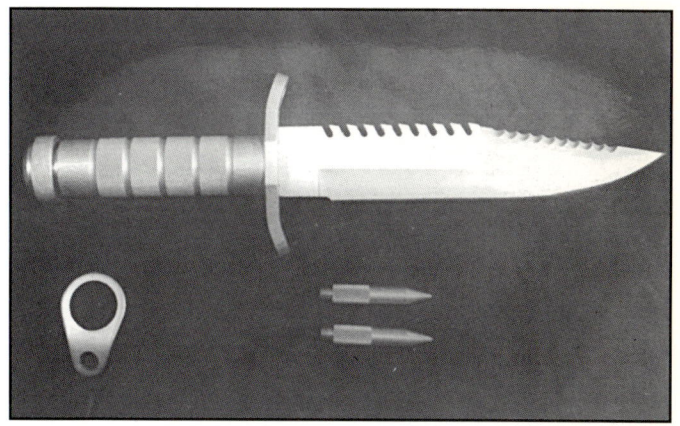

The left side of the Model 184 Buckmaster knife as made for the SEALs. The white, matt finish of the stainless steel knife shows up well against the dark background in this photograph. The anchoring pins and lug plate are shown beneath the knife. When these are installed, the Buckmaster may be used as a securing device (anchor) for a rubber boat or other such small craft.
PHOTO CREDIT: KEVIN DOCKERY

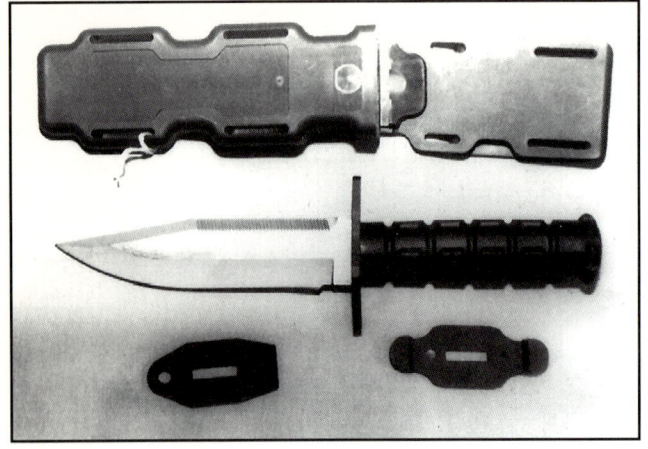

The commercial version of the Phrobis CUK knife. The flat extension above the mouth of the scabbard is the locking piece that snaps over the guard of the knife, securing it in place. The multiple slots in the scabbard allow the CUK to be carried in a number of positions according to the tastes of the individual SEAL. Two alternative guards supplied with the commercial CUK are shown below the knife. By unscrewing the pommel and removing the handle, the guards can be easily changed.
PHOTO CREDIT: KEVIN DOCKERY

"For all of the CUK's innovations, the knife was not accepted beyond the initial evaluation quantities. About 200 blades were sent to the west coast and SEAL Team Three in 1989. As few as a dozen CUK's were sent to the East coast for evaluation at roughly the same time."

TECHNICAL DATA—Phrobis Combat Utility Knife (CUK)
KNIFE PATTERN— Short-blade modified bowie
BLADE TYPE—Single edge w/forward rake saw back, deep fuller
EDGE TYPE—Concave grind w/double bevel edge
POINT TYPE—Spear point
TANG TYPE—Threaded partial tang w/separate threaded rod through grip and flat knurled pommel
BLADE MATERIAL—Modified 420 Stainless w/5% molybdenum
BLADE FINISH—Black oxide
HANDLE MATERIAL—Zytel plastic w/five deep grooves with knurling between grooves
SHEATH MATERIAL—Zytel plastic w/clip-type blade keeper and rotating Zytel hanger, multiple belt loops on hanger and sheath body
DIMENSIONS
KNIFE—10.06 (25.6 cm)
BLADE—5.44 in (13.8 cm)
CUTTING EDGE (PRIMARY)—5 in (12.7 cm)
CUTTING EDGE (SECONDARY)—2.5 in (6.4 cm) saw back
BLADE THICKNESS (MAXIMUM)—0.197 in (5 mm)
BLADE WIDTH (MAXIMUM)
SHEATH—10.38 in (26.4 cm)

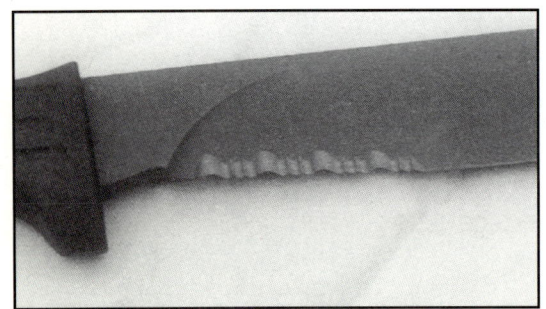

The serrated section of the MPK blade, ground on the right side only. The different sized serrations aid in the rapid cutting of rope and other fibrous materials.
PHOTO CREDIT: KEVIN DOCKERY

The initial design was modified for production by Buck Knives who manufactured the blade as the Model 184 BuckMaster.

The BuckMaster was purchased in some quantity by the Navy and supplied to the SEALs. The knife itself is an all-metal design, constructed of stainless steel to minimize corrosion. The BuckMaster has several unique features, the most prominent of which are the removable guard horns.

The guard horns are two, pointed steel rod sections with threads on one end. Screwed into the sockets at either end of the guard, the horns stick out from the base of the guard, spreading away from the grip. At the base of the grip, held in place by the threaded pommel, is a removable metal lug. By securing a line through the hole in the lug, the entire knife can be used as a grappling hook. Or, according to some of the people who have carried the BuckMaster, the knife can be used as a small boat anchor.

The scabbard of the BuckMaster also has some special features. On the back of the scabbard, covered by a nylon web strap, is a sharpening stone sufficient to touch-up the blade when in the field. Particularly handy is the belt loop design. Holding the belt loop closed is a plastic squeeze-type buckle. By unlatching the buckle, the scabbard assembly can be removed from a combat harness or belt without requiring the operator to remove his gear.

The deeply knurled grip of the Buckmaster is hollow. By unscrewing the pommel, waterproofed with a rubber O-ring, a storage space is exposed where a small supply of emergency gear can be stowed.

Though interesting, the BuckMaster was not well received by the operators intended to use it. For all of its possible utility, the Buckmaster was simply too heavy and complex for acceptance. Most of the BuckMasters that did arrive at the SEAL Teams remained on the supply room shelves.

Knives continued to be evaluated and tested in the Teams. While the Mark 3 Mod 0 remained the standard issue Team knife, a replacement multi-purpose blade was strongly desired by the SEALs. Modifying an in-house design called the MPK (Modular Utility Knife) according to SEAL Team suggestions, Phrobis International developed a new knife for evaluation by the SPECWAR community.

Phrobis Combat Utility Knife (CUK)

Called the CUK for Combat Utility Knife, the Phrobis design had a forged blade manufactured in Spain from modified 420 stainless steel. An addition of 5% molybdenum to the stainless steel alloy increased its toughness. Using forging as part of the manufacturing process adds to an overall increase in the strength of a knife. A deep fuller on the CUK blade also added to the blade's strength as well as reducing some of the overall weight of the knife.

The idea behind the CUK was for a knife that would be primarily a tool rather than a weapon. The short blade of the CUK, very close to the same length as the old Mark 1, has a fine-toothed saw back to aid in cutting rope or thin sheet alloy such as the skin of an aircraft. A modular approach was used in the overall construction of the CUK. Six individual parts make up the knife with the components being held together by a threaded tang rod.

The CUK blade has a short threaded section, heat treated to be softer than the cutting edge for increased toughness. The blade's stub tang threads into the tang rod which in turn has a three-inch long Allen bolt screwed into it. The Allen bolt holds the pommel cap in place, retaining the grip and guard in position on the knife. The grip of the CUK is made of Dupont Zytel plastic with deep rings and knurling cast into it. Outside of the grip and blade, all of the other components of the CUK are made from 410 stainless steel.

The scabbard of the CUK retains the knife in place with a locking plate that bears on the guard of the blade. When the lock has snapped over the guard, the blade is secured in place until the grip is intentionally pulled away from the hangar. A nylon screw on the back of the scabbard allows the tension of the blade retention to be adjusted. The screw also acts as a pivot point between the scabbard and the hanger. With the scabbard strapped in place on an operators leg, the hanger can pivot on the tension screw when the leg is bent such as when the operator is sitting down.

For all of the CUK's innovations, the knife was not accepted beyond the initial evaluation quantities. About 200 blades were sent to the west coast and SEAL Team Three in 1989. As few as a dozen CUK's were sent to the East coast for evaluation at roughly the same time.

After the failure of the CUK to gain acceptance with the SEALs, the Teams remained with the Mark 3 Mod 0 as their issue knife. A modified CUK design did remain with the military as the M9 bayonet, adopted for use with the M16A1/A2 rifle. As the SEALs entered the 1990's, the search for a new issue knife continued.

In August 1991, a number of different knives were examined by the Teams for possible adoption. After an exhaustive testing procedure where 31 different blades were tried, three finalists remained. In April 1992, a final series of examinations was begun and a single blade

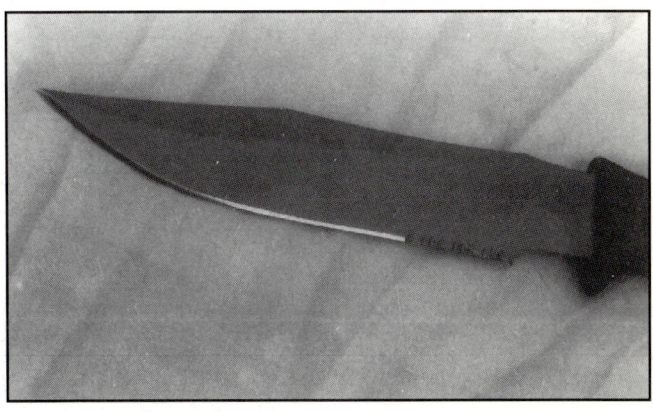

The coated blade of the SK2000 knife. On the rear part of the edge, just in front of the choil, can be seen the serrated cutting section. The smooth, ground cutting edge stands out as a bright line against the dark gray coating on the blade.
PHOTO CREDIT: KEVIN DOCKERY

TECHNICAL DATA—SOG ST2SS
KNIFE PATTERN— Two-step, curved back Bowie
BLADE TYPE—Single edge clip point w/1 large-2 small serrations per 0.44 in (1.1 cm) in front of choil
EDGE TYPE—V-grind, double edge bevel
POINT TYPE—Concave clip point
TANG TYPE—Full, insulated from grip
BLADE MATERIAL—6A Stainless
BLADE FINISH—Kalgard-type gray matt
HANDLE MATERIAL—Glass fiber reinforced Zytel w/ molded checkering and four finger grooves, lanyard hole
SHEATH MATERIAL—Black Cordura-type nylon w/leather stiffener/spacing material, stiffened hanger w/2-snap closures at bottom (sheath), two 2-piece snap button loop keepers, two large grommets at sheath mouth and one grommet on bottom of sheath back for drainage. Plastic tie-down loop on bottom of sheath
WEIGHTS
KNIFE—0.78 lb (0.35 kg)
SHEATH—0.33 lb (0.15 kg)
DIMENSIONS
KNIFE—12.31 in (31.3 cm)
BLADE—7.06 in (17.9 cm)
CUTTING EDGE (PRIMARY)—4.75 in (12.1 cm) w/o serrated portion
CUTTING EDGE (SECONDARY)—1.47 in (3.7 cm) serrations
BLADE THICKNESS (MAXIMUM)—0.238 in (6.05 mm)
BLADE WIDTH (MAXIMUM)—1.40 in (3.6 cm)
SHEATH—13.31 in (33.8 cm)

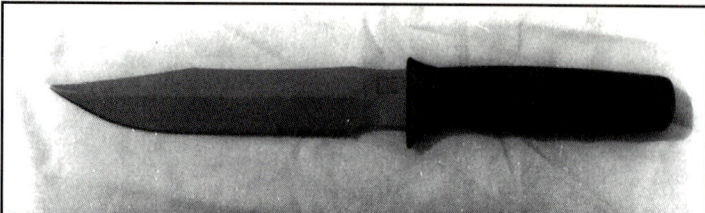

One of the two newest SEAL knives, the SOG SK2000.
PHOTO CREDIT: KEVIN DOCKERY

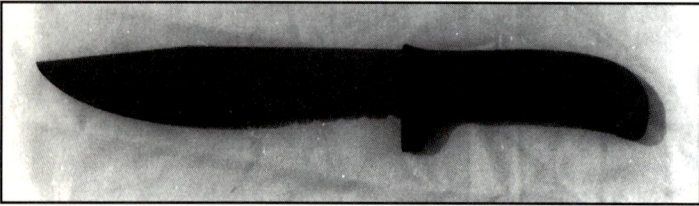

The other of the two newest SEAL knives, the Mission Knives Titanium MPK.
PHOTO CREDIT: KEVIN DOCKERY

"With the addition of the serrations at the base of the cutting edge, the SK2000 can quickly cut through rope, cardboard, and other harder materials."

TECHNICAL DATA—MPK (Multi Purpose Knife)
KNIFE PATTERN— Broad-blade bowie
BLADE TYPE—Single edge clip point w/1 large-3 small serrations per 0.5 in (1.3 cm) in front of choil
EDGE TYPE—V-grind, double edge bevel
POINT TYPE—Flat clip point
TANG TYPE—Full tang insulated from grip, serrated and holed internally for secure attachment of grip
BLADE MATERIAL—Beta titanium alloy
BLADE FINISH—Matt finish heat-treat oxide
HANDLE MATERIAL—Kevlar fiber reinforced Hytrel copolyester elastomer, textured w/multiple grooves on flats, integral guard
SHEATH MATERIAL—Kevlar fiber reinforced Hytrel copolyester elastomer one piece w/integral hanger, one 2-piece snap button loop keeper, rubber slip-over snubber ring, internal and external raised ribs to reduce radar signature, drain hole at base sides of sheath
WEIGHTS
KNIFE—0.56 lb (0.25 kg)
SHEATH—0.38 lb (0.17 kg) w/o snubber ring
DIMENSIONS
KNIFE — 12.00 in (30.5 cm)
BLADE—7.17 in (18.2 cm)
CUTTING EDGE (PRIMARY)—4.72 in (12 cm) w/o serrated portion
CUTTING EDGE (SECONDARY)—2 in (5.1 cm) serrations
BLADE THICKNESS (MAXIMUM)—0.247 in (6.27 mm) prototype models, Production blade 0.255 in
BLADE WIDTH (MAXIMUM)—1.53 in (3.9 cm)
SHEATH—12.6 in (32 cm)

chosen. The final knife was the custom made ATAK (Advanced Tactical Assault Knife) submitted by Kevin McClung of Mad Dog Knives. The knife was a straightforward design with a seven-inch single edge blade, insulated grip, and kydex plastic sheath.

In 1992 the Navy ordered 275 ATAK knifes for issue to the west coast SEAL Teams. Problems in delivery times for the effectively custom-made blades caused the Navy to finally suspend purchase of the ATAK knife after as few as 50 were delivered. The Navy reopened the contract for a new issue SEAL knife and fourteen cutlery companies responded with submissions. The requirements put forward for the new knife were stringent and made a long list.

The blade had to be 6 to 7 inches in length with a choil big enough to be held with a gloved hand. It had to have a tip strong enough to pry with while still being sharp enough for penetration, hard enough to hold a good edge without easily dulling, be corrosion resistant and non-reflective (have a dull finish).

The handle was required to be insulated from the blade and nonconductive, able to fit the hands of at least 95 percent of SEAL operators, resistant to petroleum products (not react after a 10 minute soak in gasoline), heat resistant (survive a 10 second exposure to the flame of an oxyacetylene torch), and not be slippery in a wet hand. In addition, it had to cover the full tang of the blade, have a lanyard hole, have a small crossguard so that the blade could be held "choked-up" in the hand for detail work, and have a pommel capable of driving nails.

Finally, the sheath had to be salt water resistant, quiet when struck against a hard object, and removable from a belt or harness without requiring a removal of the rig.

Both heavy and light lines were cut during the testing as well as crates being pried open, hammered shut, and electrical cables being severed. After the extensive testing and analysis of the personal input of a number of active SEALs, a knife was decided on. The knife chosen was the ST2SS, a modified commercial pattern of the Tech II knife produced by SOG Specialty Knives.

SOG ST2SS (SK2000)

During the Vietnam War, a knife was manufactured specifically for issue to the members of the 5th Special Forces group and occasionally given out to the men who operated with MAC-V SOG. The SEALs were among the personnel who worked as part of MAC-V SOG and operators would occasionally be given one of the blades. As the SOG Specialty Knife company began by making a close duplicate of the rare 5th SF knife, it is easy to see how the general lines of the Vietnam blade are in the slimmer new knife.

The SOG SEAL knife leans much more towards being a fighting knife than a general tool. The shape of the tip and back edge aid in penetration. The back edge of the knife can be easily sharpened according to the tastes of an individual operator but the knife comes as issued with a fully ground but dull back. The sheath material, being a stiffened black nylon, is not as hard and inflexible as a plastic sheath would be but is silent when the knife is drawn and makes no noise when struck. With the

The stiffened nylon sheath of the SOG SK2000 is shown at the top of the photo, just above its knife. At the bottom is the sheath for the MPK titanium knife with its knife just above.
PHOTO CREDIT: KEVIN DOCKERY

addition of the serrations at the base of the cutting edge, the SK2000 can quickly cut through rope, cardboard, and other harder materials.

While the SOG SK2000 was being accepted as the new issue steel SEAL knife, it is important to note the term steel knife. Another knife came forward to the SEALs' attention during the tests which ran from June to October 1993. The knife noted was not of a particularly unusual design but the blade material was very unique. Titanium has long been known for its lightness and strength and a blade made of titanium would be very tough, much more so than an equivalent blade made of steel. But titanium is also very difficult to work with, almost impossible to grind efficiently, and there was no treatment available that could harden a titanium blade sufficiently for it to hold a good working edge. For the 1993 SEAL knife tests, Mission Knives of California submitted their Multi Purpose Knife (MPK) with a titanium blade.

MPK (Multi Purpose Knife)

By using beta titanium alloy, Mission Knives was able to make an effective knife blade for their MPK. Though not as hard as a steel blade could be, the MPK blade is extremely tough and has several other valuable characteristics. Titanium will not corrode easily. Salt water, humid air, moisture, chemical fumes, even many acids, will not readily effect the MPK's blade. During some jungle tests, an MPK became covered in tree sap and other sticky juices. To clean the blade, the testers washed it off with hydrochloric acid followed by soap

Knives

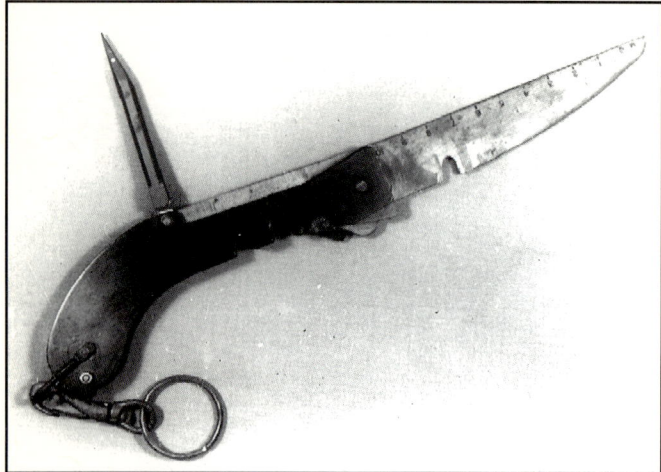

The rare folding demolition knife. Attached to the shackle at the end of the knife is a snap ring placed there by the last user. The blade of the knife is extended and locked into place showing the centimeter scale engraved on the right side of the blade as well as the deep notch used as part of the cap crimper. Unfolded and extending above the knife is the nonsparking punch or awl used to make blasting cap sized holes in explosive materials.
PHOTO CREDIT: KEVIN DOCKERY

TECHNICAL DATA—Folding Demolition Knife
KNIFE PATTERN— Multiblade non-sparking folding tool
NUMBER OF BLADES/TOOLS—1 blade, 6 tools
CUTTING BLADE TYPE—Locking single edge, straight back w/crimping cut
EDGE TYPE—flat grind to edge
OTHER BLADES/TOOLS—Awl/piercer (demolition cap setter), locking 1/4 in flat screwdriver, wire stripper notch (in screwdriver), fuse/primacord cutter, cutthroat cap crimper, inch/cm scale on cutting blade, locking clip on handle, lanyard shackle on handle
MATERIAL—Copper/beryllium alloy, blades and springs
FINISH—Black painted scaled
HANDLE/SCALE MATERIAL—Aluminium
WEIGHTS
KNIFE—0.48 lb (0.22 kg)
DIMENSIONS
OVERALL FOLDED/OPEN—5.5/9.38 in (14/23.8 cm)
CUTTING BLADE—4.44 in (11.3 cm)
WIDTH — 0.88 in (2.2 cm) blade
1.81 in (4.6 cm) folded knife

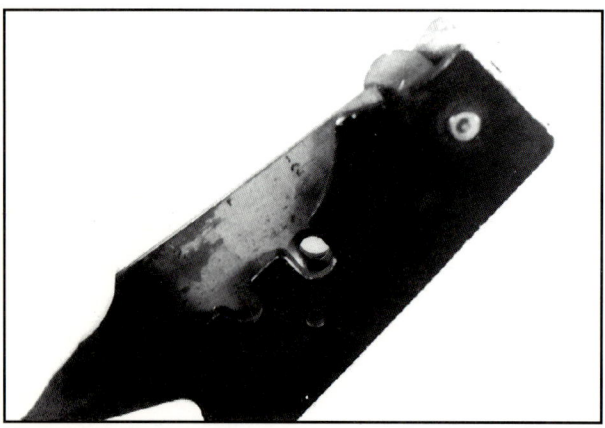

The blade of the demolition knife in the folded position. The open cap crimper notch can be seen in the position that it would be in if a blasting cap was being crimped to a fuse or other firing line. The notch closed off by the blade is the fuse cutter. On this (left) side of the blade can be seen a portion of the engraved inch scale.
PHOTO CREDIT: KEVIN DOCKERY

and water and then a coating of baby oil. There were not only no signs of corrosion or other damage to the blade, the baby oil reacted chemically with the titanium, making a dark black coating. The MPK came out of the jungle testing actually looking better than it did before going in.

Another characteristic of titanium is its lack of a magnetic signature. By careful choice of materials for the handle, sheath, and fittings, the MPK package was completely nonmagnetic. The knife has since been adopted as a replacement for the earlier Imperial nonmagnetic knife. Along with the corrosion resistance and nonmagnetic aspects of the MPK, it has an additional feature, the strength of titanium when it comes to resisting abrasion and breakage.

One tester took his MPK and wedged the point of the blade some distance underneath a safe's door. Stomping on the handle finally managed to stress-crack the tip of the knife and it broke off. But this was after the handle had been stomped on several times a day, each working day, for many weeks. Under such punishment, any steel knife would break almost immediately. The blade of the MPK is soft when compared to a steel blade but it cannot be sharpened with a normal oilstone. The abrasion resistance of titanium causes the blade of the MPK to just slide across the surface of a honing stone. To sharpen the titanium blade, an EZE-Lap Model M diamond coated sharpener is issued with each knife.

Though the MPK is hard to sharpen with anything but a diamond abrasive, the blade will still dull quickly when it is used to cut anything harder than itself. But it is rare to use a knife to cut anything harder than 44 on the Rockwell C scale. The MPK's blade, though it will not take as sharp an edge as hardened steel, it will hold the edge it takes longer. The MPK will out cut a steel knife when used against rope, cardboard, wood, or nylon. Even when used for digging in the sand, the MPK will not quickly dull. Along with all these features, the MPK is an amazingly light knife. With a blade larger than a Mark 2, the heaviest part of an MPK is still the handle.

Well liked by all of the SEALs who tested it, the MPK is being purchased in quantity by the Teams. Instead of just being a special-issue nonmagnetic knife, the MPK is becoming a popular underwater knife with the SEALs. The blade of the MPK cannot rust and the knife can be used for cutting, prying, and pounding without damage to the blade or handle.

Special Weapons

For all of the quality knives available for issue by the SEALs, there is still a strong desire by individual operators to carry privately purchased blades more specific to their tastes. Some men prefer a smaller, lighter blade while others like a bigger, heavier knife. During one operation a SEAL demonstrated a further advantage of a good knife.

While wearing a Randall bowie-style knife on his combat harness, a SEAL became involved in a fire fight along with his unit. During the course of the action, something smashed into the SEAL's chest, knocking him back from his position. What had struck the man was a 7.62mm bullet fired from an AK-47. Getting back up and ignoring his sore chest, the SEAL continued with his mission without being a casualty. But there had been at least one loss on the SEALs' side during the fight. What had stopped the bullet from severely injuring the SEAL was the blade of his Randall knife. The force of the projectile had been absorbed when it struck and deformed the blade of his knife where it was strapped to his rig, Though the SEAL was all right, his Randall needed replacement after the operation.

Folding Demolition Knife

In 1969, during what was the high point of the SEALs' involvement in the Vietnam War, a unique "pocket knife" was received by SEAL Team Two. Besides being made of exotic materials, the knife also had an unusual job to perform, that of replacing a number of basic demolition tools. The folding demolition knife could measure, cut demolition materials, and crimp blasting caps.

The design for the demolition knife came out of the Navy Research and Development Unit, Vietnam office in Saigon. Manufacture of the knife probably took place in the United States but relatively few were made. As the demolition knife had no markings and records of its development are scarce, the manufacturer is unknown.

According to one report from the US Army Limited Warfare Laboratory, dated 30 June, 1968, the demolition knife was requested by the US Army Special Forces school at Fort Bragg on 15 March, 1967. It may be that the Army extended their request to a design already in progress for the Navy for the Teams. This is reinforced by a single excerpt from the SEAL Team Two Command and Control History for 1969. On page 14, the history states:

> "A demolition knife which can fulfill the job of three other basic demolition tools was also introduced during 1969. This knife is so designed that it permits the user to measure, cut, and crimp demolition materials. It was developed by the Navy Research and Development Unit, Vietnam."

All other official references to the demolition knife are still in classified files and further information has yet to become available. Issue of the blades was very limited and the design did not catch on. As it was, of the 200 demolition knives reported to have been produced, 150 went to the SEAL Teams and the remaining 50 went to the Army Special Forces.

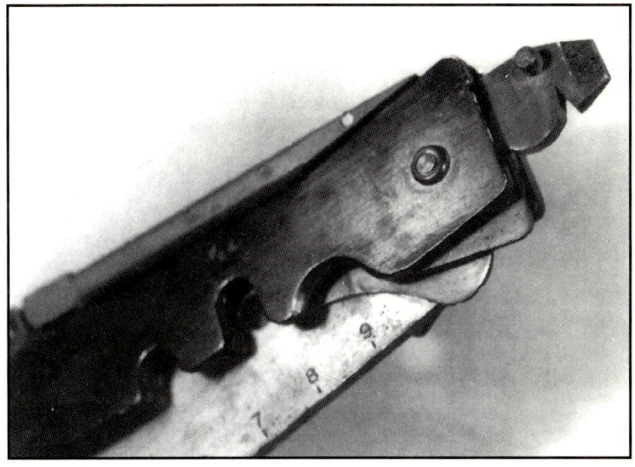

The combined screwdriver/wire stripper blade of the demolition knife extended and locked into place for use. The deep v-notch in the blade has a bevel on one side, sharpening the edge for cutting away wire insulation. The ends of the two locking springs, one for the main blade and one for the screwdriver, can be seen between the handle scales. The small stud on the side of the screwdriver blade is for unfolding the blade against the strong pressure of the spring that holds it closed.
PHOTO CREDIT: KEVIN DOCKERY

Probably the most interesting features of the demolition knife center on the main blade. As are most of the working parts of the demolition knife, the main blade is made of a non-sparking alloy. Non-sparking alloys, usually based on copper, are the normal materials of use when making tools for working with explosives. The blade has a cutting edge and, though the material is soft when compared to steel, does maintain an edge sharp enough for cutting and working explosive charges.

On the handle underneath the blade are two notches. One notch, underneath the cutting edge, is intended for cutting primacord or time fuse. By placing the primacord in the notch and squeezing the blade closed, a clean, square cut can be made.

The second notch in the handle, closer to the hinge point of the knife, has a corresponding notch in the main blade. These two notches make up a particularly unique feature on the knife. With the two notches acting together, a crimp can be made on a blasting cap attaching it to a line or firing device. By inserting the material to be secured into the cap and placing the cap in the handle notch, the blade may be squeezed against the handle and the crimp made.

Also on the demolition knife's blade are deeply stamped graduations with a metric scale on one side and an inch scale on the other. A flat screwdriver blade with an integral wire stripper are next to the main blade, both of which lock into place when opened. On the back of the knife is a non-sparking metal awl, called a demolition cap setter in the one known illustration of the knife. The awl is dimensioned so that it can form a blasting-cap sized hole in an explosive charge.

Pistols

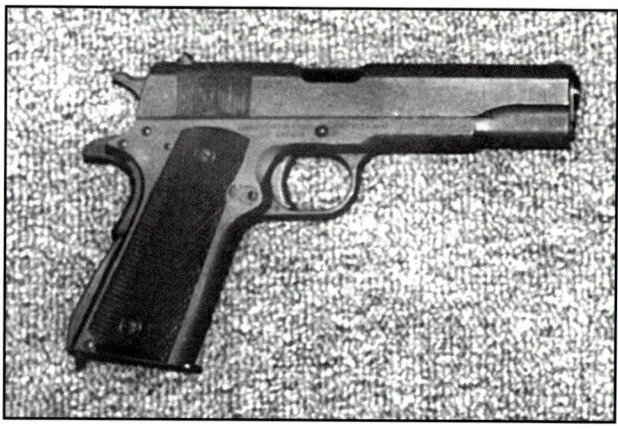

TECHNICAL DATA Colt M1911A1 Government Model FSN 6U1005-726-5655, NSN 1005-00-726-5655
CARTRIDGE—.45 ACP (11.43x23mm)
OPERATION—Short recoil
TYPE OF FIRE—Semiautomatic
RATE OF FIRE—35 rpm
MUZZLE VELOCITY—830 fps (252 m/s)
MUZZLE ENERGY—370 ft/lbs (502 J)
SIGHTS Open, V-notch/blade, fixed, adjustable for windage only
FEED—7 round removable box magazine
WEIGHTS
WEAPON (EMPTY)—2.31 lbs (1.05 kg)
WEAPON (LOADED)—2.80 lbs (1.27 kg)
MAGAZINE (EMPTY)—0.16 lbs (0.07 kg)
MAGAZINE (LOADED)—0.49 lbs (0.22 kg)
SERVICE CARTRIDGE—M1911 Ball 331 gr (21.5 g)
PROJECTILE—230 grains (15 g)
DIMENSIONS
WEAPON OVERALL—8.63 in. (21.9 cm)
BARREL—5 in. (12.8 cm)
SIGHT RADIUS—6.5 in. (16.5 cm)
EFFECTIVE RANGE—50 yds. (45.7 m)

A right side view of the .45 ACP caliber M1911A1 pistol that was the standard sidearm of the armed forces until replaced by the Beretta.
PHOTO CREDIT: KEVIN DOCKERY

"The large, slow moving, jacketed .45 caliber projectile struck hard and tended to put a target down quickly."

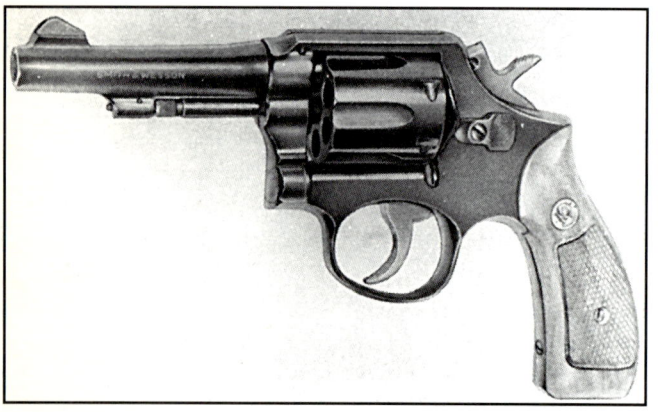

A right-side view of a Smith and Wesson Model 10, .38 Special revolver. This model was produced in large numbers during World War II as the S&W Victory model. Maintaining its position as a very plain, workhorse revolver, this 6-inch barreled weapon has a fixed, blade front sight and the rear sight is a nonadjustable notch at the rear of the receiver, just above and in front of the hammer.
PHOTO CREDIT: US ARMY

TECHNICAL DATA—S&W Military & Police revolver FSN 1005-214-0934 w/hip holster
CARTRIDGE—.38 Special (9x29mmR)
OPERATION—Manual, double-action revolver
TYPE OF FIRE—Repeater
RATE OF FIRE—18 rpm
MUZZLE VELOCITY—760 fps (232 m/s)
MUZZLE ENERGY—203 ft/lbs (275 J)
SIGHTS—Open, U-notch/blade, Fixed
FEED—6 round cylinder
WEIGHTS
WEAPON (EMPTY)—1.75 lbs (0.79 kg)
WEAPON (LOADED)—1.95 lbs (0.88 kg)
MAGAZINE (LOADED)—6 rounds 0.20 lbs (0.09 kg)
SERVICE CARTRIDGE—Steel-jacketed ball 231 gr (15 g)
PROJECTILE—158 gr (10.2 g)
DIMENSIONS
WEAPON OVERALL—9.13 in (23.2 cm)
BARREL—4 in (10.2 cm)
SIGHT RADIUS—5.94 in (15.1 cm)
EFFECTIVE RANGE—30 yds (27 m)
MAXIMUM RANGE—1085 yds (992 m)

Special Weapons

In the Navy, as in many other services, handguns, or side arms as they are officially called, are limited in their issue. Not being considered a primary combat weapon, side arms are usually issued to officers for self protection with other direct-combat forces using standard shoulder weapons. Personnel whose jobs prevent them from easily carrying a shoulder arm, such as radio operators or signalmen, are also often be issued a handgun. When the NCDUs were first formed, their makeup of a single officer leading five enlisted men meant that the officer carried a sidearm and the others were equipped with shoulder arms, usually carbines.

Being that the primary mission of the NCDUs and UDTs did not involve direct, face-to-face combat with the enemy, small arms were rarely carried on regular missions. The limited issue of side arms didn't result in a great hardship for the men of the Teams since in combat, those who really want a handgun usually end up with one eventually. Theorists tend to agree that the handgun has no real use among modern combat forces. That same idea was put forward during World War Two and is still argued today. But for a man facing the enemy, the comfort of a readily available weapon that can be carried on a hip or even stuck in a pocket is no theoretical idea but a solid fact.

Colt M1911A1 Government Model

In 1911, along with the U.S. Army, the Navy accepted the M1911 .45 ACP pistol as the new standard issue sidearm. Now, for the first time, a semiautomatic pistol would be the issue handgun for all the US military. The Navy sent in their initial request for 7,000 of the new pistols in July, 1911 and began issuing them soon after. After extensive use of the M1911 by US forces during World War One, modifications were added to the weapon's design resulting in the M1911A1 being designated in 1922. By the 1940's and the involvement of the US in World War Two, the ".45" as it was commonly called, was a favorite with all the US military.

No small part of the popularity of the M1911 was due to the heavy bullet it fired so dependably. The large, slow moving, jacketed .45 caliber projectile struck hard and tended to put a target down quickly. Complaints were heard about the relative inaccuracy of the M1911 pistol but those problems that arose can be traced to limited wartime training with a handgun. The M1911 is a difficult weapon to master without consistent practice, time for which is in very short supply during a war.

In fact, the M1911 was usually considerably more accurate than the average military shooter was able to take advantage. That the .45 has become a popular target weapon for various type of competitive shooting demonstrates the soundness of the design. And what really made the .45 stand out as a military semiautomatic pistol was its reliability. Covered in mud, sand, or snow, the M1911 and M1911A1 would continue to function.

But with the acceptance of the M1911A1 came also the problem of limited production. World War One production of the M1911 had never matched the demand for the weapon and additional revolvers chambered for the .45 ACP round were produced to fill in the shortage. During the first years of World War Two, the same situation existed. Even with the American industrial complex geared up for wartime production, available M1911A1s could not meet the demand.

Smith & Wesson Military & Police revolver

In the Navy, side arms were issued in limited numbers aboard ships and available M1911A1s were reserved for direct-combat troops and shore police. Commercial revolvers were available in quantity and the Navy began purchasing a number of these, beginning in late 1942. Though several types of revolvers were used in the Navy during World War Two, the most common was the Smith and Wesson .38 Special caliber Victory model. The

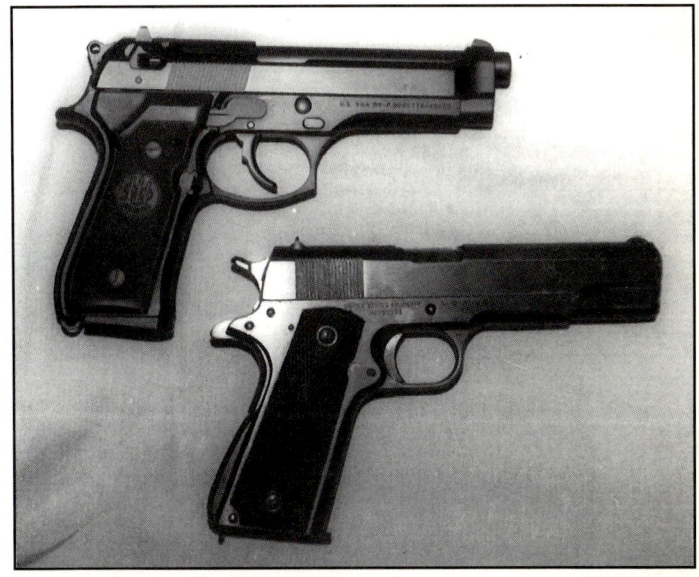

A right side view of the 9mm Beretta M9 (top) and the .45 ACP caliber M1911A1 pistol that it replaced.
PHOTO CREDIT: KEVIN DOCKERY

Pistols

TECHNICAL DATA—Smith & Wesson K38 Combat Masterpiece Model 15
FSN 6U1005-054-7452, NSN 1005-00-052-7452
CARTRIDGE—.38 Special (9x29mmR)
OPERATION—Manual, double-action revolver
TYPE OF FIRE—Repeater
RATE OF FIRE—24 rpm
MUZZLE VELOCITY—758 fps (231 m/s)
MUZZLE ENERGY—202 ft/lbs (274 J)
SIGHTS—Open, Square notch/blade, adjustable
FEED—6 round cylinder
WEIGHTS
WEAPON (EMPTY)—2.0 lbs. (0.91 kg)
WEAPON (LOADED)—2.2 lbs (1.00 kg)
MAGAZINE (LOADED)—6 rounds 0.20 lbs (0.09 kg)
SERVICE CARTRIDGE—Steel jacketed ball 231 gr (15 g)
PROJECTILE—158 gr (10.2 g)
DIMENSIONS
WEAPON OVERALL—9.13 in. (23.2 cm)
BARREL—4 in. (10.2 cm)
SIGHT RADIUS—5.88 in. (14.9 cm)
EFFECTIVE RANGE—40 yds. (36.6 m)

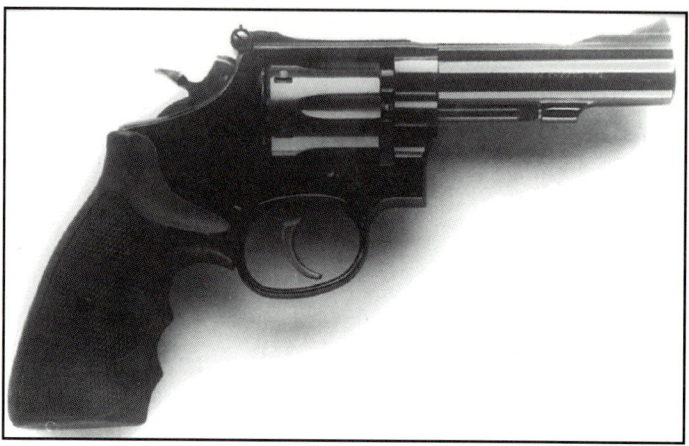

Right-side view of a four-inch barreled Smith & Wesson Model 15 Combat Masterpiece. The grip on this specimen is a recent production item and was not part of the weapons used by either the SEALs or UDTs.
PHOTO CREDIT: SMITH & WESSON

A left side view of a Colt Detective Special .38 caliber revolver.
PHOTO CREDIT: KEVIN DOCKERY

"The Model 19 enjoyed a high reputation with police forces throughout the United States and this was what brought the weapon to the notice of the new SEALs."

TECHNICAL DATA—Colt Detective Special
FSN 1005-699-1678 w/shoulder holster
CARTRIDGE—.38 Special (9x29mmR)
OPERATION—Manual, double-action revolver
TYPE OF FIRE—Repeating
RATE OF FIRE—18 rpm
MUZZLE VELOCITY—686 fps (209 m/s)
MUZZLE ENERGY—165 ft/lbs (224 J)
SIGHTS—Open, U-notch/blade, Fixed
FEED—6 round cylinder
WEIGHTS
WEAPON (EMPTY)—1.31 lbs (0.59 kg)
WEAPON (LOADED)—1.51 lbs (0.68 kg)
MAGAZINE (LOADED)—6 rounds 0.20 lbs (0.09 kg)
SERVICE CARTRIDGE—Steel jacketed ball 231 gr (15 g)
PROJECTILE—158 gr (10.2 g)
DIMENSIONS
WEAPON OVERALL—6.75 in (17.1 cm)
BARREL—2 in (5.1 cm)
SIGHT RADIUS—3.5 in (8.9 cm)
EFFECTIVE RANGE—20 yds (18 m)
MAXIMUM RANGE—950 yd (869 m)

Special Weapons

Victory was a variation of Smith and Wesson's Military and Police revolver but with a gray parkerized finish and less hand fitting than the prewar weapon. A popular firearm, 900,000 of the nearly 1,000,000 revolvers produced by Smith and Wesson during World War Two were Victory models

The NCDUs and UDTs were issued M1911A1s, especially later in the war as the number of available weapons increased. But the .38 Special revolver was the standard issue sidearm to the Teams through much of World War Two. There were few complaints about the stopping power of the .38 Special cartridge and those men who felt the .38 bullet a little too anemic for their tastes would eventually find a .45.

But several factors were in the favor of the revolver for use by the Teams. For instance, in a revolver, a rotating cylinder is mechanically turned to line up a fresh cartridge with the barrel and the firing pin. In the case of a misfired round, such as one that had been water-soaked too long, just pulling the trigger again would line up a new round to be fired. In a semiautomatic pistol such as the M1911A1, a misfired round has to be cleared from the chamber by pulling back on the slide, normally a two-handed operation. Military ammunition is much more waterproof than its civilian counterpart, but in the very wet environment of the UDTs, dud ammunition due to water was a distinct possibility.

Another advantage of the revolver over the semiautomatic pistol was particularly useful to the UDTs and has been noted by the SEALs today. Because the cylinder of a revolver has to be free to rotate, there is a small gap between the cylinder and the rear of the barrel. Because of this cylinder gap, water will drain from a revolver's barrel more quickly than water from a semiautomatic's barrel.

The safe and effective use of a revolver is generally found to be simpler to teach to recruits in the military and the NCDUs and UDTs proved no exception. Some individuals proved very competent pistol shots.

After receiving the worst individual losses of any UDT during World War Two (due to an enemy bomb striking their ship), UDT 15 was given a month's recreation at Saipan after leaving Iwo Jima. After relaxing at the Officer's Club, one officer of UDT 15 returned to his quarters to get some rest. When he was awakened by an air raid signal, the officer noticed several lights were still shining in the company street. Picking up his revolver, the officer calmly shot out the offending lights. The duty officer placed the man on report, with the official write-up of the incident stating: "… and this officer, at 50 yards, did draw his revolver and fire at three light bulbs, hitting same (good shooting!)."

Because of limitations prescribed in the Hague Convention, standard commercial .38 Special ammunition with plain lead bullets could not be used in a combat zone. During the early part of 1943 Remington Arms began producing a copper-plated, steel jacketed .38 Special round for the Navy. The round proved satisfactory enough that the other services, who also had numbers of .38 Special revolvers, adopted the round and the steel jacketed

This close-up of the early Seal Team Two airborne platoon shows the S&W M15 Combat Masterpiece revolvers in their commercial holsters on the equipment belt of each Seal. Also unique to Seal Team Two during the period of this photo are the twelve-round loop-type leather cartridge holder each is carrying. Each Seal was issued two of the holders, giving each thirty rounds. Worn to the individual's taste, many secured them to the shoulder straps of their M1945 suspenders.
PHOTO CREDIT: KEVIN DOCKERY

load became the most common .38 Special round produced during World War Two.

S&W K38 COMBAT MASTERPIECE MODEL 15

After World War Two ended, the M1911A1 pistol remained the standard issue sidearm throughout the U.S. forces. The UDTs retained a number of revolvers as they found the weapon had advantages for some of their operations. During the Korean War, the UDTs who operated on land found themselves equipped almost exclusively with the M1911A1. Several years after World War Two, Smith and Wesson developed a new handgun based largely on their earlier .38 caliber M&P revolver. The new weapon was a target-quality revolver, the K-38 Masterpiece. When later fitted with a four-inch barrel, after numerous police requests, the weapon became known as the Model 15 Combat Masterpiece. By 1960, both the K-38 and the Combat Masterpiece had been purchased by the Navy and a number of the weapons were in the UDT inventories.

When the SEALs were commissioned in 1962, one of the weapons they asked for was a revolver, but a considerably more powerful one than that which the Navy had available. The .357 Magnum cartridge is a slightly longer version of the .38 Special round and is loaded to much higher pressures than the .38. The higher pressures of the .357 Magnum round give the bullet a higher velocity and commensurately greater energy and stopping power. During the mid-1950's Smith and Wesson had developed the .357 Magnum Model 19 Combat Magnum revolver. The Model 19 enjoyed a high reputation

TECHNICAL DATA—S&W Model 36 Chief's Special
NSN 1005-00-166-2765
— Smith & Wesson Model 38 Airweight Bodyguard
NSN 1005-00-005-2312
CARTRIDGE—.38 Special
OPERATION—Manual, Double-action revolver
TYPE OF FIRE—Repeating
RATE OF FIRE—15 rpm
MUZZLE VELOCITY—691 fps (211 m/s)
MUZZLE ENERGY—167 ft/lbs (226 J)
SIGHTS—Open, Square-notch/blade, Fixed
FEED—5 - round cylinder
WEIGHTS
WEAPON (EMPTY)—Model 36 1.22 lbs (0.55 kg)
Model 38 0.88 lbs (0.40 kg)
WEAPON (LOADED)—Model 36 1.39 lbs (0.63 kg)
Model 38 1.05 lbs (0.48 kg)
MAGAZINE (LOADED)—5 rounds 0.165 lbs (0.075 kg)
SERVICE CARTRIDGE—Lead ball 231 gr (15 g)
PROJECTILE—158 gr (10.2 g)
DIMENSIONS
WEAPON OVERALL—6.31 in (16 cm)
BARREL—2 in (5.1 cm)
SIGHT RADIUS—3.25 in (8.3 cm)
EFFECTIVE RANGE—15 yds (14 m)
MAXIMUM RANGE—950 yds (869 m)

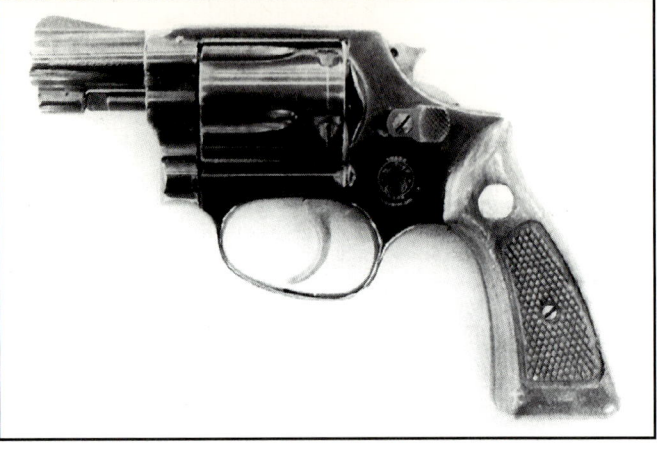

A left side view of a Smith and Wesson Model 36, .38 caliber Chief's Special revolver. This example has the Square-butt type of grip bottom.
PHOTO CREDIT: KEVIN DOCKERY

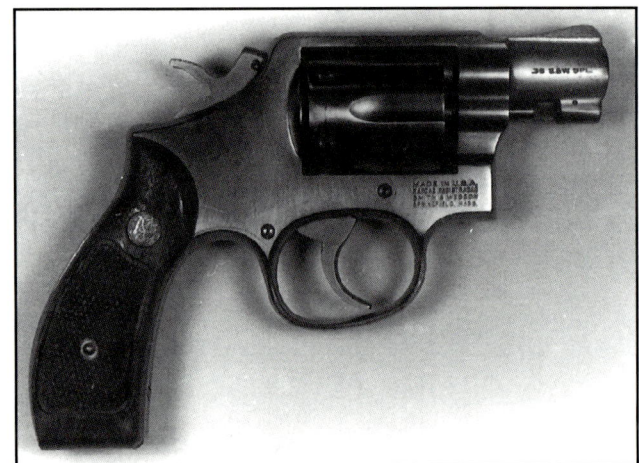

A right side view of a Smith and Wesson Model 60 revolver. Identical to the S&W Model 36 Chief's Special except for its construction of corrosion resistant stainless steel. This example has the round-butt type of grip bottom for maximum concealability.
PHOTO CREDIT: KEVIN DOCKERY

TECHNICAL DATA—Smith & Wesson Model 39
FSN 6U1005-087-0111, NSN 6D1005-00-087-0111
CARTRIDGE—9mm Parabellum, (9x19mm)
OPERATION—Short recoil, double-action
TYPE OF FIRE—Semiautomatic
RATE OF FIRE—24 rpm
MUZZLE VELOCITY—1,250 fps (381 m/s)
MUZZLE ENERGY—399 ft/lbs (510 J)
SIGHTS—Open, square notch/blade, adjustable
FEED—8 round removable box magazine
WEIGHTS
WEAPON (EMPTY)—1.66 lbs (0.75 kg)
WEAPON (LOADED)—2.03 lbs (0.92 kg)
MAGAZINE (EMPTY)—0.16 lbs (0.07 kg)
MAGAZINE (LOADED)—0.37 lbs (0.17 kg)
SERVICE CARTRIDGE—M1 Ball 180 gr (11.7 g)
PROJECTILE—115 grains (7.45 g)
DIMENSIONS
WEAPON OVERALL—7.63 in. (19.4 cm)
BARREL—4 in. (10.2 cm)
SIGHT RADIUS—5.56 in. (14.1 cm)
EFFECTIVE RANGE—50 yds (45.7 m)

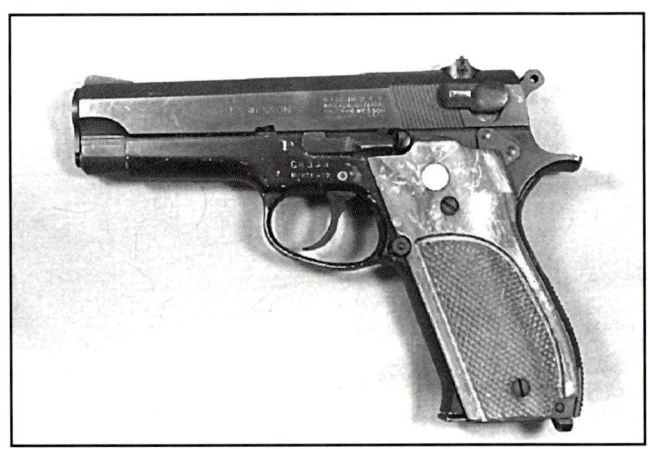

A left-side view of the Smith & Wesson Model 39 automatic as used by the SEALs during the 1960's. This specimen has the light-colored checkered walnut grips common on the commercial Model 39 pistol. The safety switch, above the rear of the grip panel and mounted on the slide, is in the forward, off, position. This specimen does not have a magazine loaded into it.
PHOTO CREDIT: KEVIN DOCKERY

Special Weapons

with police forces throughout the United States and this was what brought the weapon to the notice of the new SEALs. But obtaining the new weapons was not an easy process.

"We asked for Smith & Wesson Model 19 Combat Magnums, a .357 magnum revolver …What we finally received were Smith & Wesson Model 15 Combat Masterpieces, a .38 Special revolver. The .357 is a much more powerful cartridge than the .38 Special and there is no mistaking the difference between the two calibers, or at least so we thought…"

"There was a Navy Commander supply officer somewhere in DC who had changed the order from the .357s to the less expensive .38s. As it turned out, this officer had been at a pistol range firing a .357 magnum revolver but the range officials had issued him .38 Special ammunition to use… This officer was convinced that he could save the government money by issuing us the regulation .38 Special Combat Masterpiece. When questioned on the subject, the Commander stated that he, 'Had fired the .38 in a .357 and he could see no difference in the weapon.' "

COLT DETECTIVE SPECIAL

The final result of this was that the SEALs never did receive the Model 19 Combat Magnums they had asked for. Due to the "undercover" nature of many of the SEALs' guerrilla-warfare activities, a more concealable weapon than the Combat Masterpiece was called for. To fill this need, a number of short-barreled Colt Detective Specials were supplied to the SEALs by 1963-64. The Detective Special was available through regular supply channels as the weapon was used by the Office of Naval Intelligence. Individual SEALs who desired an even more concealable revolver purchased weapons on their own.

SMITH & WESSON MODEL 36 CHIEF'S SPECIAL

Two weapons that were popular among the SEALs were the Smith and Wesson .38 Special Model 38 Airweight Bodyguard and Model 36 Chief's Special. Both of these weapons were very compact revolvers, the Chief's Special having a steel frame, and the Airweight Bodyguard being almost identical except for an alloy frame and shrouded hammer. The shroud on the frame of the Bodyguard covered most of the hammer and prevented it from snagging on clothing when drawn. The size of both revolvers makes them very concealable but at the same time difficult to use by a large-handed individual.

COLT .380 AUTOMATIC

Other handguns were occasionally issued to the SEALs on a trial basis. The idea of a counter-guerrilla force was still very new in the early 1960's and exactly what was needed, or even useful, in the way of weapons was still being worked out by higher command. Some weapons, such as the Colt Detective Special were reasonably well received. Other weapons, offered because they were already in the supply system, were not nearly as accepted

TECHNICAL DATA—Colt .380 Automatic
FSN 1005-317-2468
CARTRIDGE—.380 ACP (9x17mm)
OPERATION—Blowback
TYPE OF FIRE—Semiautomatic
RATE OF FIRE—21 rpm
MUZZLE VELOCITY—970 fps (296 m)
MUZZLE ENERGY—198 ft/lbs (268 J)
SIGHTS—Open, U-notch/blade, Fixed, adjustable for windage only
FEED—7 round removable box magazine
WEIGHTS
WEAPON (EMPTY)—1.44 lbs (0.65 kg)
WEAPON (LOADED)—1.65 lbs (0.75 kg)
MAGAZINE (EMPTY)—0.06 lbs (0.03 kg)
MAGAZINE (LOADED)—0.21 lbs (0.10 kg)
SERVICE CARTRIDGE—Ball 146 gr (9.5 g)
PROJECTILE—95 gr (6.2 g)
DIMENSIONS
WEAPON OVERALL—6.75 in (17.1 cm)
BARREL—3.75 in (9.5 cm)
SIGHT RADIUS—5.13 in (13 cm)
EFFECTIVE RANGE—25 yds (23 m)
MAXIMUM RANGE—1089 yds (996 m)

The Colt Model M .380 pocket automatic pistol. This particular specimen has the early rubber grips while most military models had checkered walnut grips with the Colt medallion inlet into their upper half. This very compact automatic was only used on an experimental basis by the SEALs Teams during their early, pre-Vietnam years. The small lever above the grip and just below the slide is the safety catch. When pushed up into the on position, the safety catch locks into the slide and prevents it from moving. The safety catch is also used to lock the slide to the rear for cleaning or disassembly.
PHOTO CREDIT: KEVIN DOCKERY/NRA MUSEUM

by the Teams. While conducting combined exercises with other forces on Vieques Island in the Caribbean in latter half of 1962, a group of SEALs were issued Colt Pocket Automatic pistols left over from World War Two.

"We had been issued pistols for this operation, .380 automatics [Colt Pocket Automatics]. No ammunition, instructions or anything had come with the little mothers. How we ended up with these miserable weapons nobody would say or at least nobody ever owned up to it."

Pistols

TECHNICAL DATA—Tokarev TT-33 (PRC Type 51)
CARTRIDGE—7.62mm Short (7.62x25 mm)
OPERATION—Short recoil
TYPE OF FIRE—Semiautomatic
RATE OF FIRE—32 rpm
MUZZLE VELOCITY—1378 fps (420 m/s)
MUZZLE ENERGY—367 ft/lbs (498 J)
SIGHTS—Open, Square-notch/blade, fixed, adjustable for windage only
FEED—8 round removable box magazine
WEIGHTS
WEAPON (EMPTY)—1.69 lbs (0.77 kg)
WEAPON (LOADED)—2.07 lbs (0.94 kg)
MAGAZINE (EMPTY)—0.19 lbs (0.09 kg)
MAGAZINE (LOADED)—0.38 lbs (0.17 kg)
SERVICE CARTRIDGE—Type P Ball (PRC Type 50) 167 gr (10.8 g)
PROJECTILE—87 grains (5.64 g)
DIMENSIONS
WEAPON OVERALL—7.8 in. (19.8 cm)
BARREL—4.6 in. (11.7 cm)
SIGHT RADIUS—6.1 in. (15.5 cm)

Another automatic pistol offered to the SEALs later in the 1960's was much better received. During the early 1950's, several new pistols were developed to answer complaints about the use of the M1911A1 in the Services. The primary complaint about the M1911A1 was that the heavy recoil of the .45 ACP round made the weapon difficult to handle and extended the training time needed to master the weapon. To answer this problem, Smith and Wesson submitted their new Model 39 pistol for government testing in 1954.

SMITH & WESSON MODEL 39

The Model 39 was a lightweight, alloy-framed automatic pistol chambered for the 9mm parabellum round. Among other features, the Model 39 had a double-action trigger mechanism. The pistol could be carried safely with a round in the chamber and the hammer down on the firing pin. The weapon would remain safe until the trigger was intentionally pulled, raising and dropping the hammer. After the first shot, the hammer would remain cocked in the single-action position until lowered. An advantage to the double-action system is that if a round misfired, the trigger could be pulled again in another attempt to fire the round.

The Model 39 was also a very accurate handgun as it came from the factory. A number of successful competition match pistols were brought out by Smith and Wesson based on the Model 39. The Navy examined the Model 39 in the mid-1960's as a possible issue weapon to its naval aviators. The Model 39 was considerably lighter than the issue M1911A1 and held more rounds of ammunition than a revolver. It was through this venue that the pistol was brought to the attention of the SEALs.

The SEALs liked the weapon for its mechanical

The Soviet TT-33 Tokarev pistol. The hammer at the rear of the slide is in the cocked position, ready to fire. This specimen can be identified as Soviet manufacture by the letters CCCP surrounding the star on the black plastic grips.
PHOTO CREDIT: KEVIN DOCKERY

Another view of the same Tokarev TT-33 pistol. The hammer of this weapon is in the uncocked position and is visible as the serrated knob just behind the rear sight.
PHOTO CREDIT: KEVIN DOCKERY

features and the fact it was chambered in 9mm parabellum. The U.S. was the only major military force in NATO to use the .45 ACP round. The most common pistol ammunition in the world was, and still is, the 9mm parabellum, called the 9x19mm in NATO terminology. With the Model 39 as a handgun, the SEALs could be certain of a supply of ammunition almost anywhere they might operate.

SEAL Team Two began receiving the new pistol in 1966, just prior to their first direct action platoons being sent over to Vietnam. After being allowed to try out the Model 39, the SEALs being deployed were allowed to chose which handgun they would prefer to carry, the Combat Masterpiece or the Model 39. A number of SEALs chose the Model 39, beginning a long involvement of the SEALs and 9mm handguns.

Though most of the SEALs liked the Model 39, there was one part of the design that few of them cared for. The Model 39 had a magazine safety as part of the design. In the system, if a magazine was not locked in place in the grip, the hammer would not drop if the trigger was pulled. This was considered a safety feature to prevent the accidental discharge of a supposedly "empty" weapon when the operator had only removed the magazine and not cleared the chamber. When possible, individual SEALs liked having the magazine safety removed from their Model 39s, though this practice was officially discouraged.

Though the ratio of side arms to men in the SEALS was much greater than it had been in the UDT, not every operator who went to Vietnam was able to have a Team issued handgun. Model 39s and Combat Masterpieces tended to end up in the hands of the officers and senior NCOs who wanted them. M1911A1s were also available for issue and a number of these were carried by SEALs in Vietnam. An example of what could be accomplished by a competent pistol shot armed with the M1911A1 was clearly demonstrated on 29 March 1969 by RM2 Robert J. Thomas, as recalled by a SEAL who had earlier operated with him.

> "Later on, Thomas was to receive the Navy Cross for holding off an NVA platoon from his downed chopper. Thomas was the only person not [badly] injured in the crash and all he had for weapons were two .45 automatics. Thomas kept his cool and acted like he was back on the pistol range where he was a champion-quality pistol shot. Every time an NVA raised his head, Thomas would shoot it off, at fifty to sixty yards range! Finally extracted, Thomas had saved all the men on his bird single-handedly".

It is the easy of carry that makes a handgun so popular with the SEALs. When going into town on official business or liberty, SEALs would almost always have a sidearm with them, either in a holster on their hip or slipped into a trouser belt and concealed under a uniform shirt. It was in the confined spaces of a bunker or tunnel that the compact size of a pistol was considered a definite asset. A handgun can be effectively used with one hand while the other hand might be otherwise engaged.

> "For hootch searches I would carry the CAR-15 and a Chicom pistol. Both weapons were light and handy and the pistol was especially nice for those closed-in spaces like bunkers."

In the Viet Cong and North Vietnamese Army, such as in many of the worlds armies, a sidearm is not as freely issued as in the US military. Considered something of a mark of rank, pistols were only carried by officers and senior enlisted men in the VC and NVA. As these people soon became the primary target of the SEALs, enemy handguns became available in reasonable numbers.

The VC used almost any weapon they could obtain, and those they couldn't get, they tried to make. As the war progressed and supply became a little more regular, small arms became a little more standard with the VC. The most common handgun found with the VC and NVA forces was the Chicom (Chinese Communist) Type 51 and 54 pistols as well as the Soviet TT33 Tokarev. The Type 51 and 54 pistols were Chinese copies of the Soviet Tokarev differing only slightly from each other.

TOKAREV TT-33 (PRC TYPE 51)

The Tokarev fires the 7.62x25mm round (7.62mm Short in SEAL parlance), a round not at all common outside of the Communist forces. Ammunition, though not available through regular supply channels, was usually found in sufficient amounts in captured ammunition caches to supply any needs the SEALs might have. Though firing a light .30 caliber bullet, until the advent of the .357 magnum round in the mid-1930's, the 7.62x25mm round was the highest velocity production pistol round in the world. Few SEALs who carried the Tokarev and its copies in Vietnam found reason to complain about the weapon.

The Central Intelligence Agency ran a number of intelligence gathering operations throughout Southeast Asia during the Vietnam War. Noteworthy among these was the Phoenix program with its goal being the elimination of the Viet Cong Infrastructure and command net in South Vietnam. The action arm of the Phoenix program was the Provincial Reconnaissance Units or PRUs. Each province had a least one PRU made up of local citizens, Hmong, Vietnamese, and ex-VC as a paramilitary force. The CIA outfitted and supplied these units and they were led by American advisors, often SEALs.

BROWNING HP-35

The CIA equipped many PRUs with non-US made weapons and the advisors were also able to draw weapons from the same source. One of the most prized of these weapons was the Browning High Power pistol, not available through any other military channels. The Browning High Power is every bit as reliable as its "older brother" the M1911A1, but is chambered for the 9mm parabellum round. The big advantage of the High Power was that its magazine held thirteen rounds of ammunition and a fourteenth round could be carried in the chamber. This was the highest magazine capacity of any free world military handgun in the world at that time. Another

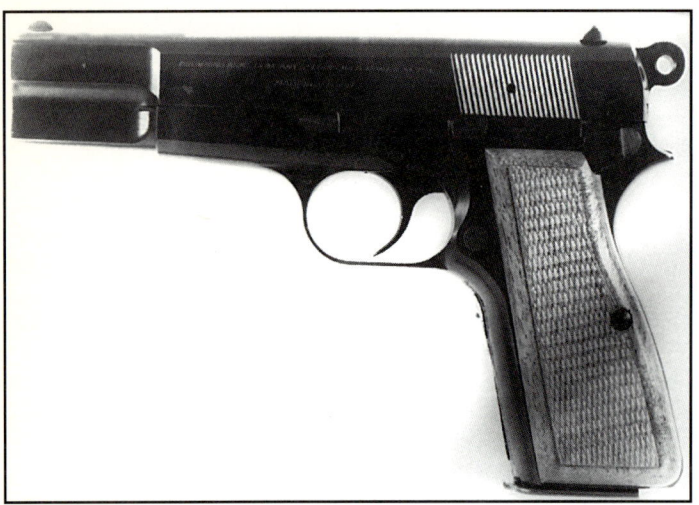

A commercial example of the Browning High Power. This particular specimen has markings on its slide that indicate it was imported into the United States.
PHOTO CREDIT: SMITHSONIAN INSTITUTION

TECHNICAL DATA—Browning HP-35
CARTRIDGE—9mm Parabellum (9x19mm)
OPERATION—Short recoil
TYPE OF FIRE—Semiautomatic
RATE OF FIRE—40 rpm
MUZZLE VELOCITY—1148 fps (350 m/s)
MUZZLE ENERGY—369 ft/lbs (500 J)
SIGHTS—Open, V-notch/blade, fixed, adjustable for windage only
FEED—13 round removable box magazine
WEIGHTS
WEAPON (EMPTY)—1.79 lbs (0.81 kg)
WEAPON (LOADED)—2.28 lbs (1.03 kg)
MAGAZINE (EMPTY)—0.16 lbs (0.07 kg)
MAGAZINE (LOADED)—0.49 lbs (0.22 kg)
SERVICE CARTRIDGE—M1 Ball 180 gr (11.7 g)
PROJECTILE—115 grains (7.45 g)
DIMENSIONS
WEAPON OVERALL—7.87 in. (20 cm)
BARREL—4.65 in. (11.8 cm)
SIGHT RADIUS—6.26 in. (15.9 cm)

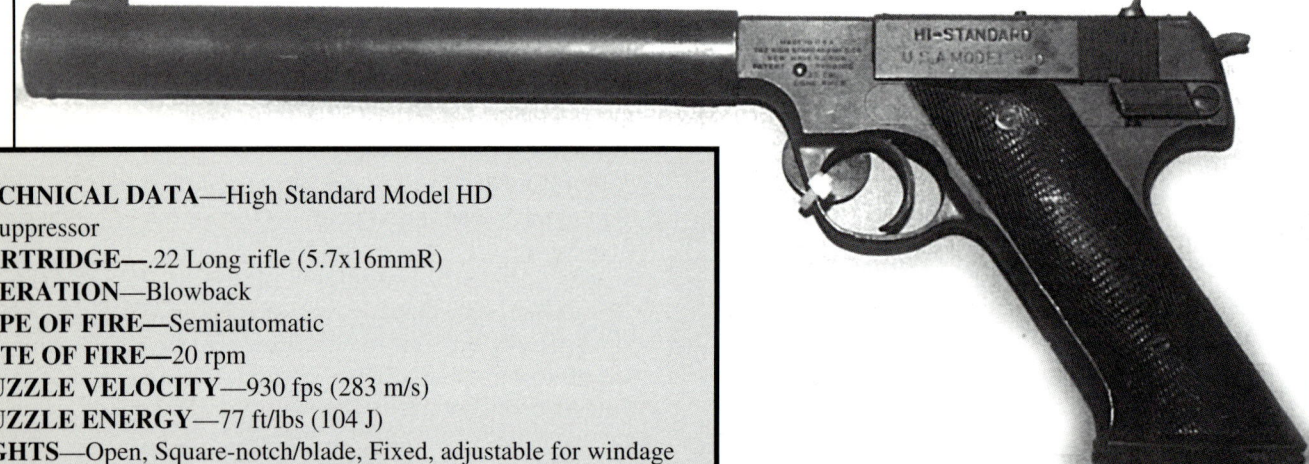

TECHNICAL DATA—High Standard Model HD w/suppressor
CARTRIDGE—.22 Long rifle (5.7x16mmR)
OPERATION—Blowback
TYPE OF FIRE—Semiautomatic
RATE OF FIRE—20 rpm
MUZZLE VELOCITY—930 fps (283 m/s)
MUZZLE ENERGY—77 ft/lbs (104 J)
SIGHTS—Open, Square-notch/blade, Fixed, adjustable for windage
FEED—10 round removable box magazine
WEIGHTS
WEAPON (EMPTY)—2.37 lbs (1.08 kg)
WEAPON (LOADED)—2.58 lbs (1.17 kg)
MAGAZINE (EMPTY)—0.13 lbs (0.06 kg)
MAGAZINE (LOADED)—0.21 lbs (0.10 kg)
SERVICE CARTRIDGE—M24 jacketed ball 54 gr (3.5 g)
PROJECTILE—40 gr (2.6 g)
DIMENSIONS
WEAPON OVERALL—14.0 in (35.6 cm)
BARREL—6.69 in (17 cm)
Suppressor 9.19 in (23.3 cm)
SIGHT RADIUS—11.13 in (28.3 cm)
EFFECTIVE RANGE—20 yds (18 m)
Peak sound pressure for an unsuppressed HD is 136 db with the suppressor 113 db

The High-Standard Military model H-D .22 pistol with the OSS suppressor. These pistols were produced during World War II and continued in use until well after the Vietnam War. The exposed external hammer, distinctive of the H-D model, can be seen in the uncocked position to the right behind the slide. The full-barrel suppressor completely covers the original barrel and extends past where the barrel muzzle ends.
KEVIN DOCKERY/BATF REFERENCE COLLECTION

factor that made an Agency issue Browning popular with SEALs and other advisors was that the weapon didn't always have to be turned in after an individuals tour was over.

> "The Agency [CIA] issued 9mm Browning High-Power automatics to their men and I wanted one. In the Team, you couldn't get a Browning unless you bought your own and now this [Agency] man was willing to issue me one. Nice pistol, holds thirteen shots, it lets you be obnoxious longer between re-loadings.
> The average guy would only count up to eight shots from a pistol. Then he would think you had to reload. Surprise, with a Browning, you had five more shots ready, something I like in a pistol."

As in the case of the Model 39, the Browning High Power had a magazine safety as part of its design. Without a magazine in place, the weapon could not be fired. Most SEALs disliked the magazine safety feature on what they otherwise considered an excellent firearm. Whenever possible, the magazine safety mechanism, only a few minor parts, was removed and the Browning continued operating dependably.

Other organizations operating in Vietnam occasionally made use of the SEALs. The Military Assistance Command, Vietnam - Special Operations Group, later renamed the Studies and Observation Group ran a number of intelligence gathering operations in Vietnam including long range reconnaissance patrols deep behind enemy lines and cross-border prisoner snatch operations. Occasionally SEALs would find themselves attached to MACV-SOG on TDY (Temporary additional Duty) when their particular skills were needed for an op.

Working closely with the intelligence community gave MACV-SOG access to some unusual hardware that the Teams had a hard time getting early in the war. For the kind of operations that the Teams, and MACV-SOG, did in Vietnam, surprise was a major weapon on the operator's side. Suppressed weapons would increase that surprise in some situations, but very few weapons of that type were available during the early years of the war up to late 1967. MACV-SOG did have some of the World War Two vintage OSS weapons available and the SEALs were able to make occasional use of them.

One SEAL operator from SEAL Team Two who operated with MACV-SOG specifically remembered being issued a suppressed .22 pistol for his SOG missions. The pistol was the High Standard Model D Military that had been fitted with an integral barrel suppressor. The normal barrel of the pistol had been turned down slightly in diameter and four rows of eleven 1/8 inch diameter holes drilled into the bore. Encasing the barrel was a 1 inch steel tube that extended 2.5 inches past the muzzle of the barrel. Between the barrel and the tube was wrapped brass wire mesh with an additional stack of brass mesh washers between the muzzle of the barrel and the end of the suppressor tube. The end of the tube was capped with a metal disk and a front sight blade was soldered onto the tube.

HIGH STANDARD MODEL HD W/SUPPRESSOR

The suppressed High Standard Model D military pistol was manufactured during World War Two for the OSS. Mr. Warren P. Mason of the Bell Telephone Laboratories, New York did the design work on the two-stage wire mesh suppressor found on the Model D beginning in January 1943. By November, 1943, production began on the suppressed High Standard and by the wars end, several thousand had been made. It is no small complement to Mr. Mason's design that the suppressed High Standard was still in use during the Vietnam war and was even being functionally copied by other countries, including Communist China and North Vietnam.

The High Standard pistol is a semiautomatic design with an exposed hammer. The design of the suppressor is such that, even when fired with high-speed ammunition, the bullet is slowed to below the speed of sound, eliminating any sonic "crack". Though the .22 caliber rimfire round is not considered much of a military cartridge, and the slowed .22 Long Rifle round has about the same power as a .22 Short, the suppressed .22 pistol was very effective and could be fired in close proximity to troops without anyone hearing the sound and recognizing it as a gunshot.

The value to the SEALs of suppressed weapons had been noted prior to the Teams deploying for combat operations in Vietnam. Beginning in Fiscal Year 1966, the project to develop a suppressed pistol suitable for the SEALs' special needs was begun at the Naval Surface Ordnance Center in White Oak, Maryland.

To satisfy the SEALs' desire for inter-operability with NATO, the envisioned suppressed handgun was to be chambered for the 9mm round. The general tendency of the military to "buy American" leaned the project towards a pistol that was already headed toward the Teams, the Smith and Wesson Model 39.

A good deal of work had already been conducted in 9mm suppressor design under the direction of the CIA. As early as 1958, the CIA had a "silenced pistol kit" available for issue to their field agents under the official name of "Sound Moderator, Pistol, Walther P-38". The kit consisted of a gray, hard-sided case similar to a camera case containing the suppressor, a threaded P-38 barrel, a box of subsonic 9mm ammunition, a bottle of oil, and a cleaning rod.

The Walther had been chosen because of its general availability throughout the world and its lack of connection to the United States. Mechanically, there was also an advantage to the P-38 design in that the barrel slid straight back under recoil with a separate locking block that was disengaged by a pin striking the frame of the weapon. This system allowed a suppressor to be more easily mounted on the exposed barrel of the P-38 while still allowing effective semiautomatic operation.

The suppressor was of the "wipe" type, that is a number of flexible plates were spaced inside of the suppressor body and the bullet penetrated the plates as it left the muzzle of the gun. By slowing down the passage of the propellant gases pushing the bullet, the

The Mk 3 Noise Suppressor
(Wipe Type)

TECHNICAL DATA—9mm Pistol Accessory Kit Mk 26 Mod 0
NSN 1305-00-166-6386
CONTENTS—
1 - 9mm Noise suppressor Mk 3 insert (10001-2504718)
Length 2.56 in (6.5 cm)
Diameter 1.125 in
Weight 0.112 lbs (0.051 kg)
24 rounds - Cartridges 9mm Mk 144 Mod 0
1 - O-ring (MS-29513-24)
1 - Back cap plug assembly
6 - Muzzle plugs
4 - Chamber plugs
1 Barrel cap
TOTAL WEIGHT—1.03 lbs (0.48 kg)
SIZE—4.75 x 3.25 x 1.38 in (12.1 x 8.3 x 3.5 cm)
PACKING—28 kits per wooden box
Suppressor insert is a sealed aluminium can containing four equally spaced 0.25 inch (6.4 mm) thick soft plastic discs. The suppressor insert is to be replaced after every 24 rounds of Mk 144 Mod 0 fired.

A disassembled view of the Mark 3 noise suppressor. The silver-colored aluminum back end cap is still attached to the body of the suppressor in this photograph. Its knurled edge can be seen at the right end of the suppressor body. The spring retainer is located above the suppressor body in the same orientation it would have when the Mark 3 is assembled. The lugged end of the retainer spring holds the suppressor insert securely forward against the front end cap of the suppressor.
PHOTO CREDIT: KEVIN DOCKERY

The rear of an unused Mark 3 suppressor insert. The unperforated soft plastic baffle disc can be seen in the center of the half-inch hole in the end of the suppressor insert. The x-cut weakening the center of the disc can be faintly seen in this photo. The body of the insert, exposed just around the opening, is made of aluminum covered with a black corrosion resistant coating. A white marking and arrow on the opposite (unseen) side of the suppressor insert indicates which end of it to point towards the muzzle of the suppressor.
PHOTO CREDIT: KEVIN DOCKERY

plates helped seal off the muzzle blast of the weapon, suppressing the major sound of the gunshot. The wipe design had been developed in Austria prior to World War Two and had proven satisfactory in a number of wartime suppressed weapons.

By loading the ammunition for the suppressor with a heavy bullet, 158 grains as compared to the normal 115 or 124 grains, a subsonic cartridge could be made that had very close to the same recoil characteristics as a standard 9mm round. Because the fired bullet never broke the speed of sound, the sonic crack of the projectile passing through the air was eliminated. For more complete suppression of the noise of firing, the mechanical sound of the weapon functioning needed to be eliminated as much as possible. The easiest way this could be done was to make the firing weapon a single-shot.

The advantage of the early CIA issue kit was that the suppressor could be mounted on any available P-38 by simply replacing the barrel of the pistol with the one supplied in the kit. The intent was for the operator to use the weapon for a mission and then get rid of the suppressor. This helped eliminate a problem with the wipe style suppressor in that the wipes wore away quickly under the stress of firing. This situation was reasonably satisfactory for the CIA, but the SEALs had a need for a much more permanent kind of suppressed weapon.

In the early 1960's, a new kind of P-38 suppressor was tried out and brought to the attention of the Navy designers at White Oak. Instead of having the wipes sealed inside the suppressor, a series of flexible plastic baffles were placed inside a cylindrical cartridge. The cartridge would be inserted into the body of the suppressor and held against the exit end of the suppressor by a spring. This gave the suppressor an expansion

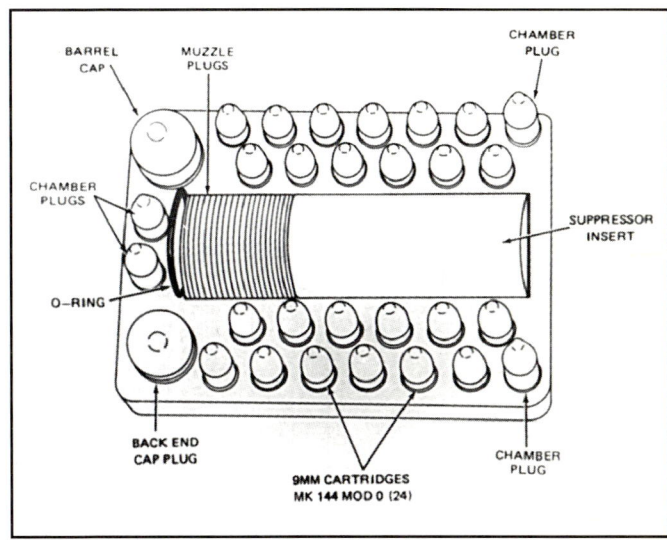

A drawing of the Mark 26 9mm Pistol Accessory Kit with the top styrofoam piece removed showing the contents of the kit. Sufficient ammunition in the form of Mark 144 Mod 0 subsonic cartridges are issued in the kit for the Mark 3 sound suppressor to maintain a good level of suppression while using the suppressor insert also in the Mark 26 kit.
PHOTO CREDIT: US NAVY

A developmental Smith & Wesson Model 39 pistol with suppressor. The suppressor on this specimen is attached to the receiver of the pistol by an extension that is secured to the slide stop by a bolt. The extension is visible just below the front portion of the slide in this photo. The body of the suppressor is off-center with the barrel of the pistol, the majority of the suppressor being below the line of flight of the projectile. This eccentric mounting allows the standard sights of the pistol not to be blocked by the body of the suppressor. By attaching the suppressor to the receiver of the weapon, excess weight is kept off the barrel allowing for more dependable semiautomatic fire. This design was not kept in the final model of the Mark 23 Hush Puppy suppressed pistol. Note that the grips on this example are standard commercial wooden models. These were replaced with plastic ones on the production Mark 23 weapon.
PHOTO CREDIT: US NAVY HISTORICAL CENTER

Pistols

An early illustration of the developmental Mark 22 suppressed pistol (Hush puppy). This illustration shows the attachment points on the rear grip strap for the removable shoulder stock. Only a few of the skeleton metal stocks were produced as the design was found unnecessary for the SEALs. Note the waterproofing muzzle cap over the muzzle of the weapon.
PHOTO CREDIT: US NAVY

"By 1968, each deploying platoon was issued at least one Mark 22..."

TECHNICAL DATA—Pistol, 9mm MK 23 Mod 0 w/Noise suppressor Mk 3
FSN 6U1005-L99-2167 NSN 6D1005-00-021-5137
CARTRIDGE—9mm Parabellum (9x19mm)
OPERATION—Manual or short recoil, double-action
TYPE OF FIRE—Manual repeater or semiautomatic
RATE OF FIRE—12 rpm
MUZZLE VELOCITY—925 fps (294 m/s) w/o suppressor 900 fps (274 m/s) w/suppressor
MUZZLE ENERGY—300 ft/lbs (407 J) w/o Suppressor 284 ft/lbs (385 J) w/ Suppressor
SIGHTS—Open, square notch/blade, adjustable
FEED—8 round removable magazine
WEIGHTS
WEAPON (EMPTY)—1.63 lbs (0.74 kg) w/o suppressor 2.13 lbs (0.97 kg) w/suppressor
WEAPON (LOADED)—2.04 lbs (0.93 kg) w/o suppressor 2.54 lbs (1.15 kg) w/suppressor
SUPPRESSOR—0.5 lbs (0.23 kg)
MAGAZINE (EMPTY)—0.16 lbs (0.07 kg)
MAGAZINE (LOADED)—0.41 lbs (0.19 kg)
SERVICE CARTRIDGE—9mm Mk 144 Mod 0 ball, 223 gr (14.5 g)
PROJECTILE—158 grains (10.2 g)
DIMENSIONS
WEAPON OVERALL—8.5 in (21.6 cm) w/o suppressor 12.75 in (32.4 cm) w/suppressor
SUPPRESSOR LENGTH—5 in (12.7 cm)
SUPPRESSOR DIAMETER—1.57 in (4 cm)
BARREL—5 in (12.7 cm)
0.5 in end length threaded 1/2x20 tpi
SIGHT RADIUS—5.75 in (14.6 cm)
EFFECTIVE RANGE—40 yds (36.6 m)
9mm Pistol and Suppressor Kit Mk 23 Mod 0 consists of the 9mm pistol Mk 22 Mod 0, two magazines, 9mm Pistol Noise Suppressor Mk 3 Mod 0, a belt holster w/integral pouch for the spare magazine, and a package of replacement parts for the pistol. The replacement parts are the ejector depressor plunger and spring (S&S #6013, 6014), a standard slide stop lever (S&W #6125), and a sear release lever (S&W #6103)

The right side view of a Mark 22 pistol with the Mark 3 noise suppressor attached. Just below and in front of the ejection port can be seen the notch in the slide and the corresponding slide lock lever below it. The slide lock is in the unlocked position, allowing the slide to be pulled back for reloading. The black plastic grips seen on the Mark 22 pistol replaced the wooden grips of the parent weapon, the S&W Model 39. The plastic grip panels were considered more water resistant than the original walnut grips of the Model 39.
PHOTO CREDIT: KEVIN DOCKERY

chamber just in front of the muzzle of the weapon and a set of wipes that could be easily replaced when worn.

To eliminate the mechanical noise of the weapon, a slide lock was installed on the P-38. The slide lock was a lever on the left side of the weapon, just above the trigger, that could be moved by the firer's thumb. With the slide lock pressed up, it engaged a notch in the slide of the weapon. When the gun was fired, the lock prevented the slide and barrel from moving to the rear, eliminating the noise of the action opening and closing. To reload, the firer had to pull the slide lock down with his thumb and manually pull the slide to the rear. This made for a very quiet weapon overall. If there was a need for semiautomatic fire, the slide lock could be disengaged and the weapon fired normally, but with an increase in the sound level of firing.

The general design of the suppressor was proven and the idea of a locked, single shot repeater shown to be sound. The next step in the process was to modify the Smith and Wesson Model 39 to fit the general pattern of the locked P-38. The barrel of the Model 39 was simply lengthened by one inch and the final one half inch length threaded 1/2"-32 tpi. The Model 39 uses the same locking system as the Browning High Power. When the pistol is fired, the barrel is locked to the slide by a lug in the upper surface of the barrel engaging a matching slot on the slide. As the barrel and slide recoil when fired, a slot in the underside of the barrel engages a camming pin in the frame of the pistol. By recoiling backward some distance, the barrel and slide are locked firmly together a sufficient time to allow the bullet to leave the barrel and the gas pressure to have dropped to safe levels. At this time, the slot in the barrel cams the rear of the barrel down, disengaging the locking surfaces of the barrel and slide. Recoil continues to push the slide rearward until it is stopped by the frame. The mainspring then drives the slide forward, stripping a fresh round from the magazine and chambering it.

The moving barrel of this system (it not only must move backwards a short distance but also angle downward when unlocking), complicates attaching a muzzle suppressor. The suppressor has to be light enough so as not to interfere with the operating cycle of the weapon. For the Model 39, the suppressor was made of aluminum to help keep the weight on the barrel down. The wipe cartridge was also made of aluminum, sealed to contain the four 1/4 inch thick soft plastic wipes. The wipe cartridge, called the suppressor insert, was held against the muzzle end of the suppressor body by a wide steel spring. The threaded end cap of the suppressor body was securely sealed by the addition of a neoprene O-ring. When accepted for issue, the suppressor, developed as the WOX-1A gun silencer, was type-classified as the 9 millimeter noise suppressor Mark 3 Mod 0.

The locking lever used to hold the slide closed on the P-38 was carried over to the Model 39 design with some modifications. Instead of being pushed up and engaging the slide behind the barrel on just the left side, as on the P-38, the locking lever on the Model 39 was pushed down at the rear, raising the front of the lever which engaged cutouts on both sides of the slide, forward of the breech and locking lug area. The locking lever was at a greater mechanical advantage in holding the slide shut in its new configuration than in the earlier P-38 system.

To clear the wide suppressor body, higher sights had to be installed. The higher, micrometer adjustable sights of the Smith and Wesson Model 52 match pistol were installed on the production weapon, the rear sight being protected by raised wings on either side of the sight. The final mechanical change in the Model 39 pistol was the removal of the magazine safety parts and the sear release lever. In the model 39, putting the thumb safety on while the hammer is cocked back, locks the firing pin in place and drops the hammer. Removing the sear release lever allows the thumb safety to be put on while still retaining the hammer in the cocked position.

While the pistol and suppressor were being made ready, ammunition also had to be developed. Experiments were conducted with heavy tungsten inserts placed in the back of standard 9mm bullets. That took the weight of the bullet up to about 150 grains and made the round subsonic. The tungsten cored rounds functioned the suppressed pistol about ninety percent of the time, but being that the intent was for the weapon to be fired single-shot, ten percent failures to reload semi-automatically were considered acceptable.

Remington Arms assisted in adopting a fully-jacketed 158 grain .38 Special bullet to a subsonic 9 millimeter round. Though they helped supply the initial lot of projectiles, Remington was not further interested in producing the ammunition for the new pistol. Final development resulted in a full jacketed 9mm round with a nominal muzzle velocity of 965 feet per second and a recoil impulse equal to that of the 9mm M1 round. The new round was suitable for use in pistols and sub-machine guns chambered for the 9mm round but was reserved for use in the suppressed pistol. Identified with a green bullet tip, the cartridge was given the nomenclature; Cartridge, Mark 144 Mod 0, and produced by the Super Vel Cartridge Corporation of Shelbyville, Indiana as well as Industries Valcartier Inc., Valcartier, Quebec, Canada.

Additional material was designed for the weapon system to waterproof it for a marine environment. A plastic muzzle plug in the form of a flat disk could be pushed over the front of the suppressor. A back end cap plug could be inserted into the suppressor when it was not mounted on the pistol. A barrel cap fitted tightly over the threaded section of the barrel, sealing it. And a chamber plug in the shape of a plastic cartridge sealed the barrel of the pistol with a rubber O-ring. With the waterproofing seals in place, the pistol and suppressor could be transported at a depth of 200 feet safely, either with the pistol and suppressor separate or with the suppressor mounted on the barrel. With the pistol and suppressor together, an operator could ready the weapon for firing by simply drawing back the slide, ejecting the chamber plug, and chambering a live round. The muzzle disk was designed so that it could be safely shot off of the

This is a left side view of the Mark 22 pistol with the Mark 3 noise suppressor removed. The threaded end of the pistol barrel can be plainly seen and most of the exposed portion of the barrel would be covered when the suppressor is attached. In this photo, the Mark 3 noise suppressor is reversed above the pistol with the muzzle end of the suppressor pointing towards the rear of the weapon. The safety of the Mark 22 is mounted on the slide, just in front of the hammer, and is in the safe position in this example.
PHOTO CREDIT: KEVIN DOCKERY

"The slide lock did cause its own problems with the weapon. Holding the slide closed during firing placed a severe strain on the slide of the Mk 22, concentrating in the notches on the slide itself. Slides would be battered or cracked at the notches, requiring replacement."

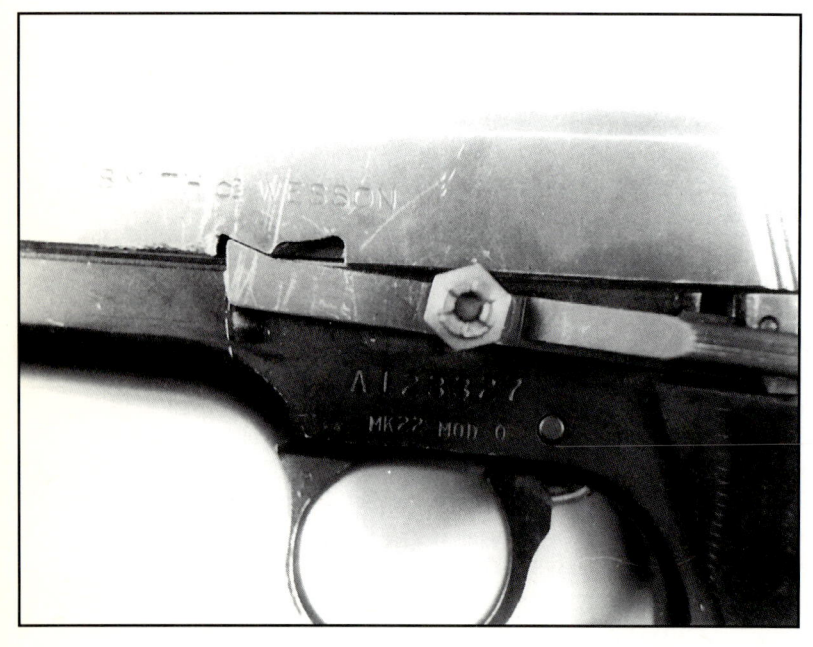

A left side closeup of the Mark 22 pistol showing detail of the slide lock system. The rear of the slide lock lever has been depressed, raising the front portion of the lever into the corresponding notch in the slide of the weapon. In this position, the slide cannot move when the weapon is fired. The gap in the front of the tip of the slide lock is indicative of the weak point in the slide lock system. As the Mark 22 is fired with the slide locked, the notch is gradually battered forward, opening the gap that can be seen in this photo.
PHOTO CREDIT: KEVIN DOCKERY

weapon without damage to the gun or firer.

MK 23 MOD 0 W/NOISE SUPPRESSOR MK 3

Developed as the WOX-13A 9mm pistol, the new suppressed pistol received the nomenclature 9mm Pistol Mark 22 Mod 0. When fired with the special subsonic ammunition designed for it, the sound of the shot was unnoticeable at 50 yards. Since the wipe system of the suppressor only lasts for about twenty-four rounds of Mk 144, and about six rounds of standard velocity 9mm, additional suppressor inserts, ammunition, and materials are issued in the form of an accessory kit. The initial accessory kit contained a single suppressor insert, suppressor body O-ring, and twenty-two rounds of Mk 144 Mod 0 ammunition. When the waterproofing materials became available, a new kit was issued including these items. The new kit was given the nomenclature Accessory Kit Mark 26 Mod 0. Finally, a special holster was issued with the Mark 22 capable of holding the pistol with the suppressor installed and with an outside pocket to secure an additional ammunition magazine.

Finally available to the Teams, the Mark 22 Mod 0 began being issued late in 1967. Almost immediately, controversy began about the new weapon;

"When we originally asked for a suppressed pistol, the powers that be did not want it called a silencer, we were asked what we wanted it for. Since the idea of killing men with a suppressed handgun was somehow "unsportsmanlike" we told them the weapon was wanted to shoot dogs. Every VN village had some dogs hanging around that would sometimes bark as we approached. Since the weapon was intended to silence dogs, and any other vermin who happened to get in front of it, the pistol was named the 'Hush Puppy'."

An immediate success with the Teams, there never seemed to be enough of the new weapons to go around. By 1968, each deploying platoon was issued at least one Mark 22 though the weapon was far more commonly called the Hush Puppy;

"The "silent pistol shot to the head" a favorite story of the anti-Phoenix people did take place. But the target of the shot was usually a noisy village dog that could alert people that we were there. On different ops, we would carry a Hush Puppy (suppressed pistol) in the squad. Often, the point man would carry the weapon as he would be the first to make contact where a silent shot might be needed. Not many of the weapons were available so what we had would be rotated around the squads...

There would have been times that having a Hush Puppy for each man on an op would have been great. You can't call 911 when in the bush and the element of surprise was everything sometimes. Silent rounds snapping out in an ambush could eliminate a following enemy group, without drawing attention from a larger force nearby."

The Mark 22 did suffer from some problems in the field, at least one of these was noted in the official Command history for SEAL Team Two in 1969. Mention was made in the record of an improvement in the ammunition for the Mark 22 Mod 0 pistol under the heading of Research and Development Projects;

"A special 9mm downloaded 158 grain round has been made for the Smith & Wesson 9mm pistol with silencer. The original 158 grain round lacked the essential penetration power needed for the pistol to be effective. The new round is now in-country for test and evaluation."

Production of the Mk 22 pistol and the Mk 3 noise suppressor was undertaken by Smith and Wesson at their factory in Springfield, Massachusetts. Production continued for a number of years beginning in 1967 and ending sometime in the early 1970's. Further mention of the Mark 22 was made in the 1970 Command History of SEAL Team Two which indicated that the overall design of the weapon was considered quite acceptable to the Teams;

"SEAL Team TWO acquired forty-five new silent 9mm Smith and Wesson Pistols (Hush Puppy's). These weapons should increase the Teams current operating capability."

Depending on how an operation was going to be conducted, a Hush Puppy may or may not be carried along. In a situation where a "sneak and peek" of deep penetration was going to be done in enemy territory, a Hush Puppy was a definite asset. Many SEALs developed a taste for the unique weapon and carried it in their own way;

"The Hush Puppy was a suppressed Smith & Wesson Model 39 with a special slide lock. Though a holster was available for the weapon, I usually carried it hanging from my neck on a lanyard. From the lanyard, I could put the Hush Puppy into action faster than by pulling it from a holster and speed could be important. Others may have had different experiences but my Hush Puppy was used mostly for the very reason it had been given its name, silencing yapping village dogs. Very seldom did I used the Hush Puppy against a person, dogs and ducks raising an alarm were a much more common target. And even hitting the dog didn't always silence it right away, a few yelps would get out. But the pistol was quiet, especially with its slide held shut during firing by the slide lock. I always used the weapon as a single-shot anyway as the subsonic ammunition we had then wouldn't work the slide reliably for semiautomatic fire".

The slide lock did cause its own problems with the weapon. Holding the slide closed during firing placed a severe strain on the slide of the Mk 22, concentrating in

Pistols

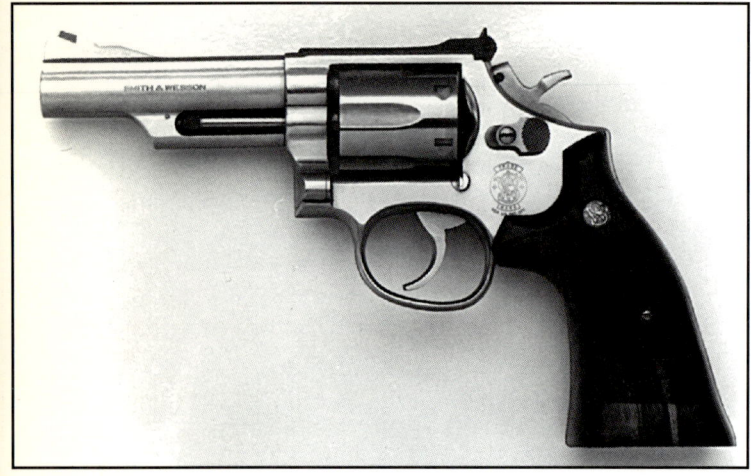

This is a left-side view of the present-production S&W Model 66 revolver. This specimen has a four-inch barrel and the new style Magna-grips with the cutout on the upper left grip for the used of a speed-loader. The entire weapon is made from stainless steel giving the pistol a bright, silver finish. The rear sight is a standard model made of blued steel for visibility.
PHOTO CREDIT: SMITH & WESSON

TECHNICAL DATA—Smith & Wesson Model 66
NSN 1005-01-088-1107
CARTRIDGE—.357 Magnum (9x33mmR)
OPERATION—Manual, double-action revolver
TYPE OF FIRE—Repeating
RATE OF FIRE—24 rpm
MUZZLE VELOCITY—1206 fps (368 m/s)
MUZZLE ENERGY—404 ft/lbs (548 J)
SIGHTS—Open, white outline Square-notch/blade, Adjustable
FEED—6 round cylinder
WEIGHTS
WEAPON (EMPTY)—2.25 lbs (1.02 kg)
WEAPON (LOADED)—2.44 lbs (1.11 kg)
MAGAZINE (LOADED)—6 rounds 0.19 lbs ((0.09 kg)
SERVICE CARTRIDGE—.357 Magnum JHP 219 gr (14.2 g)
PROJECTILE—125 gr (8.1 g)
DIMENSIONS
WEAPON OVERALL—9.56 in (24.3 cm)
BARREL—4 in (10.2 cm)
SIGHT RADIUS—5.87 in (14.9 cm)
EFFECTIVE RANGE—40 yds (37 m)

The Heckler and Koch P9S pistol with an extended, threaded barrel and an H&K manufactured Qual-La-Tech design suppressor. Visible on the slide of the pistol are the raised adjustable sights taken from the P9S Sports Competition model. The slide mounted safety lever, just below the rear sight, is in the off position with a red dot showing, thus indicating the pistol is ready to fire.
PHOTO CREDIT: KEVIN DOCKERY

TECHNICAL DATA—Heckler & Koch P9S w/Qualatech suppressor
NSN OA1005-01-145-6424
CARTRIDGE—9mm Parabellum (9x19mm)
OPERATION—Delayed blowback, double-action
TYPE OF FIRE—Semiautomatic
RATE OF FIRE—27 rpm
MUZZLE VELOCITY—965 fps (294 m/s)
MUZZLE ENERGY—327 ft/lbs (443 J)
SIGHTS—Open, square notch/blade, adjustable
FEED—9 round removable box magazine
WEIGHTS
WEAPON (EMPTY)—1.94 lbs (0.88 kg) w/o suppressor
3.24 lbs (1.47 kg) w/suppressor
WEAPON (LOADED)—2.39 lbs (1.08 kg) w/o suppressor
3.69 lbs (1.67 kg) w/suppressor
SUPPRESSOR—1.31 lbs (0.59 kg)
MAGAZINE (EMPTY)—0.16 lbs (0.07 kg)
MAGAZINE (LOADED)—0.45 lbs (0.20 kg)
SERVICE CARTRIDGE—9mm MK 144 Mod O Ball 223 gr (14.5 g)
PROJECTILE—158 grain (10.2 g)
DIMENSIONS
WEAPON OVERALL—8.19 in (20.8 cm) w/o suppressor
15.38 in (39.1 cm) w/suppressor
SUPPRESSOR LENGTH—7.75 in (19.7 cm)
SUPPRESSOR DIAMETER—1.382 in. (3.5 cm)
BARREL—4.63 in (11.7 cm)
SIGHT RADIUS—6.06 in (15.4 cm)
EFFECTIVE RANGE—30 yds. (27.4 m)

the notches on the slide itself. Slides would be battered or cracked at the notches, requiring replacement. Consistent semiautomatic fire was also not available in the Mk 22 given the operating system of the pistol and the weight of the suppressor, though the lack of semiautomatic fire was not considered a major drawback by the SEALs who used the Hush Puppy in Vietnam. In fact, the weapon was so successful, the name Hush Puppy was given to any suppressed pistol used by the US and its Allies during the Vietnam War and for some time afterwards.

When tested with and without the slide lock in operation, very little increase in noise was noticed when the Hush Puppy operated semiautomatically. It was when the slide only went part way back and then returned to battery that there was a great deal of mechanical noise with the system. Experiments were conducted to examine other ways of mounting the suppressor on the Model 39 that would increase the reliability of semiautomatic suppressed fire. The Naval Weapons Center at China Lake, California tried a very unusual experiment where the suppressor was mounted on the frame of a Model 39 pistol. In the experimental weapon, the suppressor was mounted off-center on the barrel so that the majority of the suppressors body was below the line of the barrel. A long extension was on the bottom rear of the suppressor reaching back on either side of the pistols frame to just above the trigger. By attaching the suppressor to the slide to lever pin of the pistol, the majority of the weight of the suppressor would not be bearing on the barrel. It is not known how well the design operated but apparently only a single experimental weapon was produced. By 1969, the Hush Puppy was being issued as part of the Swimmer Weapons System as the 9mm Pistol and Suppressor Kit Mark 23 Mod 0. In the Mark 23 kit, two styrofoam supports hold the Mark 22 Mod 0 pistol complete with a barrel cap, chamber plug, and magazine. Along with the pistol, inside the kit was a Mark 3 Noise Suppressor complete with a muzzle plug and back end cap plug. A polyurethane plastic holster is in the kit along with a small container of grease and a humidity desiccant package and indicator. The two styrofoam supports cradle the contents of the kit and are inserted into an M19A1 ammunition box for storage.

During the development of the Mk 22 pistol, some thought was given to making a high-capacity version that would hold more ammunition. The Browning High Power was highly thought of because of its magazine capacity, so the Naval Ordnance Laboratory and Smith and Wesson examined making a conversion of the Model 39 that would accept a modified Browning magazine. In 1964, Smith and Wesson had built two fourteen-shot 9mm automatics and these were examined by the Navy. In addition, a Model 39 frame was cut and modified to accept a Browning magazine, establishing the mechanical parameters of the proposed pistol. The weapons desired by the Navy were to be made of stainless steel to minimize corrosion. With input from a steel manufacturer on which alloys would be suitable, Smith and Wesson accepted a contract from the Navy to produce ten fifteen-shot, stainless steel suppressed 9mm handguns for a contact price of 33,000 dollars.

Because of the manner in which their production lines were set up, Smith and Wesson took eighteen months to produce twelve of the new pistols. Delivery to the Navy of the ten requested guns took place in early 1970. In addition to having the slide lock, extended barrel, sights, and suppressors of the Mark 22 pistol, the fifteen-shot pistols also were fitted with removable shoulder stocks. The stocks slid into a groove on the back strap of the experimental pistols and locked in place with a thumbscrew. By installing special inserts under the handgrips of the Model 39 and Mark 22 pistols, they too would accept the shoulder stock. Even though the new experimental weapons had all the improvements Smith and Wesson had developed for the Model 39 over the course of several years, the weapons were not accepted for production by the Navy. Within a few years, Smith and Wesson issued alloy-frame versions of the Navy weapon, minus the Mark 22 modifications, for commercial sale as their Model 59 pistol

Terrorism developed on a global scale during the 1970's and became a force to be reckoned with by the US military. As part of the US response to international terrorism, the Navy commissioned SEAL Team Six and tasked it with combatting terrorism in the marine environment. While outfitting the new Team, thought was given to which handgun the operators would carry as their standard sidearm. There was a much greater need for powerful terminal effects on the target as a wounded terrorist was still very much a threat, more so than the average soldier. Given their penchant for attacking unarmed and vulnerable civilian targets, a terrorist would be easily able to turn his weapon on hostages if not immediately neutralized.

Experienced SEAL operators who made up the new SEAL Team had witnessed the mechanical reliability of the revolver for operating in a wet environment. Simply put, without any special waterproofing, a revolver could be pulled up out of the water and fired faster than any other handgun available. Terminal effects could be enhanced by using a more powerful caliber than a .38 Special. Smith and Wesson had developed a line of revolvers made of stainless steel and designed after their very successful K-frame weapons. The original sidearm requested by the SEAL when they were first commissioned in 1962 had been the Model 19 Combat Magnum, a K-frame .357 magnum. For the new SEAL Team, they requested, and received the S&W Model 66, a stainless steel version of the Combat Magnum.

SMITH & WESSON MODEL 66

As terrorism was considered a nonmilitary threat, the restrictions of the Hague convention were not considered applicable by the US government. This meant that the restrictions on the military use of deforming ammunition was not in effect when terrorists were the target. Deforming ammunition has a much greater level of terminal effects than does the normal full-jacketed military round. Using soft-nose or hollow-point ammunition made a handgun a much more effective weapon in terms of immediately incapacitating a target.

Pistols

A right side view of the 9mm Beretta M9 (top) and the .45 ACP caliber M1911A1 pistol that it replaced.
PHOTO CREDIT: KEVIN DOCKERY

TECHNICAL DATA—Beretta M92S-1
CARTRIDGE—9mm Parabellum (9x19mm)
OPERATION—Short recoil, double-action
TYPE OF FIRE—Semiautomatic
RATE OF FIRE—45 rpm
MUZZLE VELOCITY—1280 fps (390 m/s)
MUZZLE ENERGY—447 ft/lbs (606 J)
SIGHTS—Open, square notch/blade, fixed
FEED—15 round removable box magazine
WEIGHTS
WEAPON (EMPTY)—1.91 lbs (0.87 kg)
WEAPON (LOADED)—2.57 lbs (1.17 kg)
MAGAZINE (EMPTY)—0.25 lbs (0.11 kg)
MAGAZINE (LOADED)—0.66 lbs (0.3 kg)
SERVICE CARTRIDGE—9mm Ball M882 190 gr (12 g)
PROJECTILE—124 grains (8 g)
DIMENSIONS
WEAPON OVERALL—8.54 in (21.7 cm)
BARREL—4.94 in (12.5 cm)
SIGHT RADIUS—6.34 in (16.1 cm)

"The Berettas stood up to the variety of ammunition the SEALs put through them as well as passing what was in effect an endurance course considering the thousands of rounds fired by each Team Six member in the course of normal training."

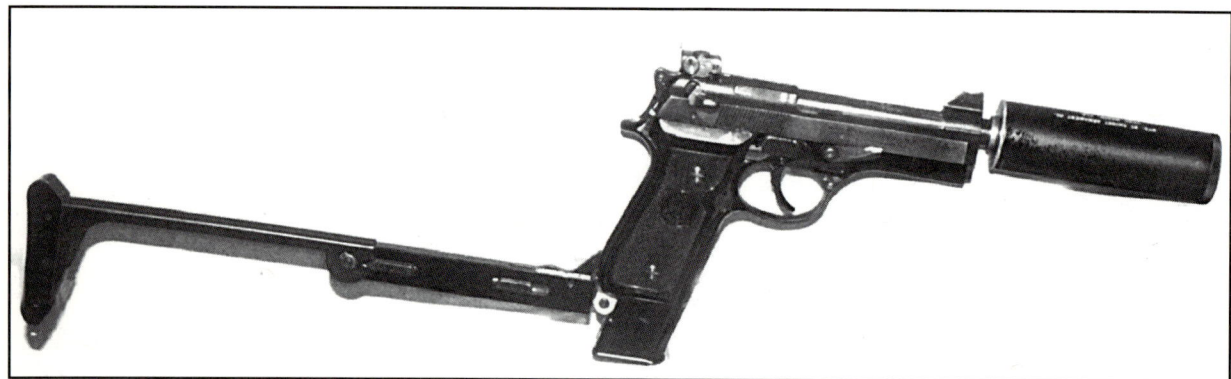

A special-purpose suppressed pistol intended for limited SEAL use. The basic weapon is a Beretta Model 92F with an extended barrel for the attachment of the Mark 3 noise suppressor shown in the photograph. The front sight of the pistol has been built up so that the line of sight can clear the large diameter of the suppressor body. To match the front sight, the fully adjustable rear sight is a much taller than normal model. Just above the front of the trigger guard can be seen the right-side component of the slide-lock system. This weapon is loaded with an extended 20-round magazine and has been modified to accept the removable shoulder stock from the Beretta 93R machine pistol.
PHOTO CREDIT: KEVIN DOCKERY/KNIGHT ARMAMENT COMPANY

Ammunition initially used by SEAL Team Six in their Model 66s was high-performance 158 grain jacketed hollow-point magnum loads. As more effective ammunition became available, it was evaluated for possible use.

A new suppressed handgun was desired by the SEALs in general by the late 1970's. The Vietnam era Mark 22s were becoming worn and needed replacement. A German design, the Heckler and Koch P9S pistol held a great deal of promise as a possible basis for a new suppressed pistol.

HECKLER & KOCH P9S

The H&K P9S is a double-action, semiautomatic pistol with a unique operating system common in H&K weapons. By utilizing a roller-locked breech system, the P9S could fire high-pressure 9mm rounds in complete safety without requiring a moving barrel. In the roller-locked system, two rollers hold the bolt locked to the barrel when the round is first fired. A strong mechanical disadvantage keeps the rollers from moving inward and releasing the bolt until after the bullet had left the barrel and pressures have dropped to a safe level. During the entire firing cycle of the P9S, the barrel remains stationary.

H&K P9S w/QUALATECH SUPPRESSOR

Using an extension barrel, the P9S was fitted with a stainless steel, wipe-less, QualaTech suppressor. Designed by Mickey Finn on the West Coast, the QualaTech suppressor requires only periodic cleaning and minimum maintenance without needing any rebuild parts as in the case of the Mark 3 noise suppressor. Almost twice the size of the earlier Mark 3 suppressor, the QualaTech device maintained the same level of sound suppression without an increase in noise levels over time as would happen in the earlier suppressor as the wipes wore away.

The slide locking feature was done away with on the suppressed P9S as the noise level was not considered a problem. Also the mechanism of the P9S made the weapon function semiautomatically much more reliably than the earlier Mark 22. Higher sights were installed on the suppressed P9S to raise the sight plane enough to clear the suppressor, otherwise the weapon was very much as issued. The P9S became the standard 9mm suppressed pistol of the SEALs during the 1980's with the Mark 22 systems being held in reserve.

Beginning in 1979, the Joint Service Small Arms Program (JSSAP) began what was to be a very long series of evaluations and tests to determine a new sidearm for all of the US services. The new weapon was to be a double-action, ambidextrous control pistol chambered for the NATO standard 9mm parabellum cartridge and having a minimum magazine capacity of thirteen rounds. After three years of testing in which ten different pistols were examined, including the M1911A1 as a control weapon, a clear winner stood out and was recommended for adoption. That pistol was the Beretta M92S-1.

BERETTA M92S-1

The Beretta M92S-1 was a modified version of their M92S pistol which had been on the market for several

In an M12 kevlar Universal Military Holster on his equipment belt, a SEAL has secured his M9 Beretta pistol to his rig with an issue lanyard. Beneath the butt of the pistol can be seen the grip of a Mark 3 Combat Knife. The belted ammunition at the upper right is 7.62mm linked, 4 M80 ball to 1 M62 tracer, for use in the M60 series of light machine guns.
PHOTO CREDIT: US NAVY

TECHNICAL DATA—Heckler & Koch P9S
LSN 1005-LL-HDK-N483
CARTRIDGE—9mm Parabellum (9x19mm)
OPERATION—Delayed blowback, double-action
TYPE OF FIRE—Semiautomatic
RATE OF FIRE—27 rpm
MUZZLE VELOCITY—1148 fps (350 m/s)
MUZZLE ENERGY—361 ft/lbs (490 J)
SIGHTS—Open, square notch/blade, fixed
FEED—9 round removable box magazine
WEIGHTS
WEAPON (EMPTY)—1.87 lbs (0.85 kg)
WEAPON (LOADED)—2.27 lbs (1.03 kg)
MAGAZINE (EMPTY)—0.16 lbs (0.07 kg)
MAGAZINE (LOADED)—0.40 lbs (0.18 kg)
SERVICE CARTRIDGE—9mm Ball M882, 190 gr (12 g)
PROJECTILE—124 grains (8 g)
DIMENSIONS
WEAPON OVERALL—7.56 in (19.2 cm)
BARREL—4 in (10.2 cm)
SIGHT RADIUS—5.78 in (14.7 cm)
EFFECTIVE RANGE—50 yds. (45.7 m)
Most often issued w/suppressor

TECHNICAL DATA—Ruger Mark II w/suppressor
CARTRIDGE—.22 Long rifle (5.7x16mmR)
OPERATION—Blowback
TYPE OF FIRE—Semiautomatic
RATE OF FIRE—20 rpm
MUZZLE VELOCITY—984 fps (300 m/s)
MUZZLE ENERGY—86 ft/lb (117 J)
SIGHTS—Open, Square-notch/blade, adjustable
FEED—10 round removable box magazine
WEIGHTS
WEAPON (EMPTY)—2.54 lbs (1.15 kg)
WEAPON (LOADED)—2.91 lbs (1.32 kg)
MAGAZINE (EMPTY)—0.29 lbs (0.13 kg)
MAGAZINE (LOADED)—0.37 lbs (0.17 kg)
SERVICE CARTRIDGE—Lead ball 54 gr (3.5 g)
PROJECTILE—40 gr (2.6 g)
DIMENSIONS
WEAPON OVERALL—11.61 in (29.5 cm)
BARREL—6.18 in (15.7 cm)
SIGHT RADIUS—9.72 in (24.7 cm)
EFFECTIVE RANGE—20 yds (18 m)

> "The Ruger proved itself a very quiet weapon of excellent accuracy, the integral suppressor surrounding the barrel giving the weapon the appearance of a heavy-barrel target gun"

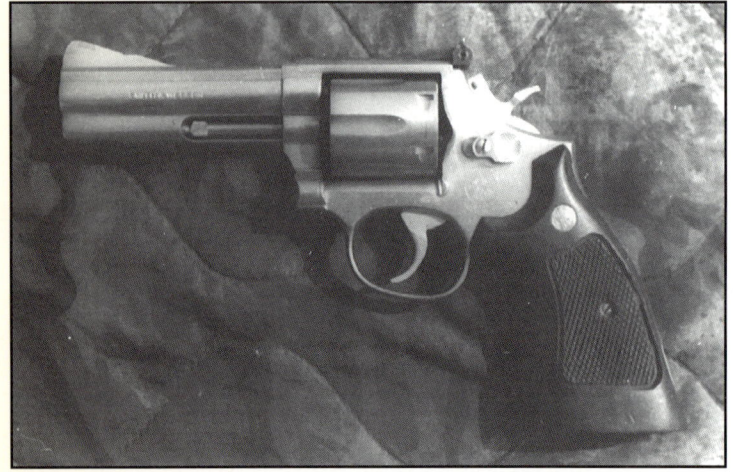

The .357 Magnum caliber Smith and Wesson Model 686 revolver. This example has the large magna type grips attached that are cut away at the top of the left grip to facilitate reloading the weapon using a speed-loader.
PHOTO CREDIT: KEVIN DOCKERY

TECHNICAL DATA—Smith & Wesson Model 686
NSN OA1005-LL-L99-5196
CARTRIDGE—.357 Magnum (9x33mmR)
OPERATION—Manual, double-action revolver
TYPE OF FIRE—Repeater
RATE OF FIRE—24 rpm
MUZZLE VELOCITY—1206 fps (368 m/s)
MUZZLE ENERGY—404 ft/lbs (548 J)
SIGHTS—Open, White outline Square-notch/blade w/red insert, adjustable
FEED—6 - round cylinder
WEIGHTS
WEAPON (EMPTY)—2.63 lbs (1.19 kg)
WEAPON (LOADED)—2.82 lbs (1.28 kg)
MAGAZINE (LOADED)—6 rounds 0.19 lbs (0.09 kg)
SERVICE CARTRIDGE—.357 Magnum JHP 219 gr (14.2 g)
PROJECTILE—125 gr (8.1 g)
DIMENSIONS
WEAPON OVERALL—9.75 in (24.8 cm)
BARREL—4 in (10.2 cm)
SIGHT RADIUS—5.88 in (14.9 cm)
EFFECTIVE RANGE—50 yds (45.7 m)

Special Weapons

years before the JSSAP tests began. Among the modifications for JSSAP was moving the magazine release from the bottom rear of the right grip to just below the trigger guard as well as making the mechanism reversible for use by left-handed firers. The original safety lever was made longer and duplicated on both sides of the slide for use by either hand. The safety mechanism also locks the firing pin in place and drops the hammer when engaged, something specifically required for the JSSAP trials.

SEAL Team Six was quick to pick up the new pistol and had Berettas available for issue in 1982. For several years the Team used their Berettas extensively, resulting in a much longer and more extensive trial than the weapon had originally received from JSSAP. The Berettas stood up to the variety of ammunition the SEALs put through them as well as passing what was in effect an endurance course considering the thousands of rounds fired by each Team Six member in the course of normal training.

Second place in the original set of JSSAP trials was held by the Smith and Wesson Model 459. Because of the showing of the Smith and Wesson pistol, the adoption of the Beretta was suspended and an additional series of trials were conducted by JSSAP. The second set of trials were due in no small part to a lawsuit brought by Smith and Wesson against the government, declaring unfairness in the terms of the original tests. The second set of tests included a number of new pistols being submitted for evaluation including the Saco-Maremont (Sig-Sauer) P226. Beretta changed their Model 92S-1 slightly, incorporating a trigger-operated firing pin block as part of the safety mechanism. With the block in place, the firing pin was not released until the trigger was intentionally pulled. The new Beretta was designated the Model 92SB.

The results of the second test were much the same as the first set. The Beretta M92SB was declared the winner with second place now being held by the P226. In January, 1985 the Beretta Model 92SB-F, a modified version of the test gun, was declared the new M9 service sidearm. Now the rest of the SEAL Teams would receive the Beretta.

During the JSSAP testing period, the SEALs underwent a major change in their organization. On May 1, 1983, the last UDTs were decommissioned. UDTs 11 and 20 became, respectively, SEAL Teams Five and Four. UDTs 12 and 22 became SDV Teams One and Two, respectively. With the changes in the Teams came also an increase in manpower and greater needs for new equipment and ordnance.

Ruger Mark II w/suppressor

In an action familiar to some of the SEALs who carried suppressed High Standards in Vietnam, a new .22 caliber suppressed pistol was adopted into the Teams during the 1980's. The new pistol was the Ruger Mark II .22 Long Rifle semiautomatic pistol fitted with an integral suppressor. The Ruger proved itself a very quiet weapon of excellent accuracy, the integral suppressor surrounding the barrel giving the weapon the appearance of a heavy-barrel target gun. The .22 caliber Long Rifle round has sufficient penetrating power and makes up for its lack of terminal energy with accuracy and slight recoil. Over-penetration with the .22 round is also not the problem it can be with other suppressed weapons, especially those in the 9mm class.

The Smith and Wesson Model 66 revolvers used by SEAL Team Six had been proving themselves a worthwhile weapon for the Teams. The Model 66, built on the stainless steel K-frame, had first become available when .357 magnum rounds were available in only a fairly limited number of loads. With the increasing interest in handgun ammunition, and the strides taken in the 1970's in bullet performance, modern high-performance loads were increasing the amount of wear and strain on the Model 66 frame. To counter this problem, Smith and Wesson came out with a new intermediate frame size in 1981.

The largest and most powerful of the Smith and Wesson revolvers are the heavy .357, .41, and .44 magnums built on the large N-frame. The K-frame was developed near the turn of the century as the basis for the first of the extremely popular line of Smith and Wesson .38 Special weapons. Long known to the SEALs and UDTs, the Victory Model and Model 15 Smith and Wesson pistols are both K-frame designs. Smallest in the frame sizes offered by Smith and Wesson are the diminutive J-frames used by the SEALs in the Model 36 Chief's Special.

Smith & Wesson Model 686

The new frame size brought out by Smith and Wesson was the L-frame, maintaining the popular grip and trigger guard size of the K-frame but having a beefed up frame very close to the size of the N-frame. In addition to having a greater cylinder diameter, giving much more metal around the individual chambers, the barrel on the new L-frame weapons was much heavier than anything offered in the K-frame size.

The heavy barrel of the L-frame guns also had an integral under-barrel lug that extended the full length of the barrel. The result of the lug was to place extra weight forward on the gun where it would help minimize muzzle flip and hold the barrel down for a fast second shot. The first L-frame guns offered by Smith and Wesson were the blued steel Model 586 and the stainless steel Model 686. SEAL Team Six quickly picked up on the Model 686 as the weapon was proved out by a number of competition shooters throughout the United States. By January 1984, the changeover was complete and the Model 686 was the primary revolver for SEAL Team Six.

The only other revolver of note used by the Teams was the small Model 36 Chief's Special. The Model 36 had been issued during the 1970's and well into the 1980's. as a personal-defense weapon for operators assigned to countries in Central America and elsewhere as the situation warranted. In several Central American countries, SEALs operated as advisors and trainers, often in plain clothes. To arm these men as unobtrusively as possible, the Model 36 was the best combination of firepower and small size available. The international availability of the Smith and Wesson line also helped the

Pistols

TECHNICAL DATA—M9 pistol (Beretta M92SB-F)	
NSN 1005-01-118-2640	
CARTRIDGE—9mm Parabellum (9x19mm)	
OPERATION—Short recoil, double-action	
TYPE OF FIRE—Semiautomatic	
RATE OF FIRE—45 rpm	
MUZZLE VELOCITY—1280 fps (390 m/s)	
MUZZLE ENERGY—447 ft/lbs (606 J)	
SIGHTS—Open, square notch/blade, fixed	
FEED—15 round removable box magazine	
WEIGHTS	
WEAPON (EMPTY)—1.89 lbs (0.86 kg)	
WEAPON (LOADED)—2.53 lbs (1.15 kg)	
MAGAZINE (EMPTY)—0.23 lbs (0.11 kg)	
MAGAZINE (LOADED)—0.64 lbs (0.29 kg)	
SERVICE CARTRIDGE—9mm Ball M882 190 gr (12 g)	
PROJECTILE—124 grains (8 g)	
DIMENSIONS	
WEAPON OVERALL—8.56 in (21.7 cm)	
BARREL—4.94 in (12.5 cm)	
SIGHT RADIUS—6.09 in (15.5 cm)	
EFFECTIVE RANGE—50 yds (45.7 m)	

In the mid 1980's, this group of SEALs are range firing Beretta M9 pistols. The SEAL in the foreground has a 3-cell submachine gun magazine pouch on his belt at his left hip. A strap is wrapped around the lower half of the pouch, effectively shortening the individual cells to allow a 15-round Beretta magazine to be held securely without slipping too deeply into the pouch to be easily withdrawn. The Beretta M9 in the photo has the hammer cocked to the single-action position.
PHOTO CREDIT: US NAVY

A Beretta M9 pistol (top) and a current issue Sig P226.
PHOTO CREDIT: KEVIN DOCKERY

..."you're not a Navy SEAL until you've tasted Italian steel," has been repeated more than once...

SEALs maintain a low profile with their not carrying an immediately recognizable American weapon.

The small revolver could be easily carried in several convenient ways, belt holsters, ankle holsters, even slipped into a pocket. Intended for self-defense only, the Model 36 was issued as an almost throwaway weapon, the five rounds it carried being too few for any kind of protracted combat.

In spite of a number of their advantages, revolvers have too small an ammunition capacity to remain a primary weapon for modern combat. The Model 686 is used in all the Teams but is primarily a teaching aid for basic pistol marksmanship. In SEAL Team Six, the Model 686 did not go into the field but was used for a specialized form of training. The expression, "you can only shoot paper so much," centered around Close Quarters Battle (CQB) and its need for quick reactions as well as accuracy. After marksmanship had been developed and honed on the range, a reactive target was needed to further develop skill. The very best reactive target for training is another shooter trying to get you first but this can quickly lead to an unacceptable loss in personnel. "Wax shooting" proved an effective answer to the training problem.

Since a revolver fires mechanically and does not depend on the reaction of firing in any way for its operation, the weapon will operate with any kind of projectile. By pressing a primed cartridge case, mouth first, into a slab of properly formulated wax, a cylindrical "bullet" is cut from the slab and lodged inside the case. With all participants wearing proper protective gear, primarily for the face, training can be performed where the target actually shoots back. Wax shooting was conducted by the SEALs in order to polish their skills in CQB. Training could be conducted in actual target environments, such as inside a building, ship, or aircraft, with little or no damage to the area. Wax bullets impacting on the SEALs would graphically show a mistake without costing the Team a highly trained operator.

M9 PISTOL (BERETTA M92SB-F)

In 1985, the Navy began receiving the Beretta Model 92F as the new M9 service pistol. Changes from the earlier Model 92SB were slight and included squaring the front of the trigger guard to facilitate a two-handed grip, a differently shaped front butt strap, a heavier magazine floor plate, chrome plating the barrel bore and chamber, and a matt exterior finish made of "Bruniton", a Teflon-type of corrosion resistant coating.

The testing procedure had been changed for the second set of JSSAP tests and the 5000 round limit before an allowable part breakage had been removed from the test as well as other factors being changed. The new Beretta 92F was considered an improvement over the earlier 92SB and was initially well received by the Teams. SEAL Team Six also received the new M9 pistol and immediately began training with the new weapon.

It was in 1986 that a serious weakness in the Beretta was discovered by the SEALs of Team Six. The main incident took place during a firing demonstration for a visiting political dignitary. After stating the Teams' like of the new M9 pistol, a SEAL operator began firing the weapon on the range. While firing, the Beretta had a catastrophic failure of the slide. The rear portion of the slide broke away from the pistol and, driven by the pressure of the fired round, struck the SEAL in the face.

The demonstration was immediately halted and first aid given to the injured SEAL. The injuries being relatively slight, the visiting dignitary wondered if the whole incident hadn't been staged for his benefit. What had been uncovered was a design flaw in the slide of the Beretta.

SEAL Team Six trained with their side arms to a much greater extent than any of the other services or Teams. Since this firing also involved a great deal of high-performance ammunition, the Team Six Berettas received a correspondingly higher level of stress and wear. The fault in the Berettas design was not able to be quickly corrected to the SEALs' satisfaction. Beretta did address the problem seriously and has since satisfactorily corrected the fault. Though the M9 has remained the standard sidearm throughout the rest of the services, SEAL Team Six replaced theirs within a short time of the original range incident. Though only a very few weapons showed signs of slide cracking, the Teams wanted a replacement. In usual SEAL humor, a joke was made to cover the SEALs' feelings towards the incident with the Beretta. The line "you're not a Navy SEAL until you've tasted Italian steel," has been repeated more than once, much to the embarrassment of the Beretta company.

In 1987, the Austrian Glock pistol was tested as a possible alternative to using the Beretta M9 pistol, especially in the highly corrosive marine environment. The Glock pistol, which is substantially made of plastic parts, performed better than the M9 in the Salt Fog Test, an extreme example of ocean exposure. Except for the corrosion resistance, the Glock showed itself to be significantly less reliable than the Beretta M9 in other respects. The Teams were still in the position of wanting a replacement pistol for the M9 and Team Six wanted the replacement immediately.

SIG P226

A replacement pistol was chosen by Team Six in early 1987, the Sig-Sauer P226, the runner up in the second JSSAP trials. Not being satisfied by the suggested changes in the Beretta, the remaining SEAL Teams followed the example of Team Six and began the process of replacing their M9s with Sig P226s. The initial request for 800 P226 weapons was put out in October 1988 with further testing and safety certification beginning on 17 November. Testing included environmental tests such as exposure to sand, mud, and salt as well as drop tests and exposure to temperature extremes. In addition to the above, five pistols underwent an endurance test of 30,000 rounds fired through each weapon. Acceptance came quickly and the first weapons were in the SEAL Teams hands on 20 January 1989.

Schweizerische Industrie Gesellschaft (SIG) of Neuhausen/Rheinfalls, Switzerland, has a long record of manufacturing excellent pistols to meet the exacting standards of the Swiss military. Because of their country's export restrictions on firearms, Sig allied with the Sauer

"The slide of the P226 consists of a precision metal stamping with the internal components welded, dovetailed, or pinned in place. This technique allows the Sig design to be made lighter and more easily than the more common milled or forged slide."

TECHNICAL DATA—SIG P226
CARTRIDGE—9mm Parabellum (9x19mm)
OPERATION—Short recoil, double-action
TYPE OF FIRE—Semiautomatic
RATE OF FIRE—40 rpm
MUZZLE VELOCITY—1132 fps (345 m/s)
MUZZLE ENERGY—350 ft/lbs (475 J)
SIGHTS—Open, square notch/blade, fixed
FEED—15 round removable box magazine
WEIGHTS
WEAPON (EMPTY)—1.66 lbs (0.75 kg)
WEAPON (LOADED)—2.28 lbs (1.03 kg)
MAGAZINE (EMPTY)—0.21 lbs (0.10 kg)
MAGAZINE (LOADED)—0.62 lbs (0.28 kg)
SERVICE CARTRIDGE—9mm Ball M882 190 gr (12 g)
PROJECTILE—124 grains (8 g)
DIMENSIONS
WEAPON OVERALL—7.72 in (19.6 cm)
BARREL—4.41 in (11.2 cm)
SIGHT RADIUS—6.30 in (16 cm)
EFFECTIVE RANGE—50 yds. (45.7 m)

A Navy SEAL watches a Thai UDT operator familiarize himself with the SEAL standard issue SIG P226 pistol. PHOTO CREDIT: SPECIAL OPERATIONS COMMAND PAO

Special Weapons

*SEALs familiarize French commandoes with SEAL weapons aboard the **USS JOSHUA HUMPHREYS** while in the Red Sea during Operation Desert Storm. The men are firing both SIG P226 pistols and H&K MP5-N submachine guns. The submachine guns are loaded with double magazines and have flash hiders clipped over the muzzle of their barrels.*
PHOTO CREDIT: US NAVY

company of Germany to produce their line of weapons. Already having their P220 pistol in production as the official sidearm of the Swiss Army, Sig modified the design to meet the parameters of the JSSAP trials. The resulting pistol has since made excellent sales throughout the world as a police and military special forces sidearm. The primary reason for the P226 not surpassing the Beretta in the JSSAP trials was the overall cost per unit of the weapon as compared to the Beretta. The Sig is simply a costly handgun.

All of the SEAL Teams have stated their satisfaction with the P226 as their standard sidearm. The one major drawback with the weapon centers around the manufacturing techniques used to produce the gun. The slide of the P226 consists of a precision metal stamping with the internal components welded, dovetailed, or pinned in place. This technique allows the Sig design to be made lighter and more easily than the more common milled or forged slide. The drawback in this design noticed by the SEALs is a tendency for the P226 to rust through in spots on the slide if the weapon is not carefully rinsed after salt water exposure. Given their penchant for maintenance, the drawback is not considered a serious one by the SEALs but it does open the possibility of

A right side view of the Sig P226 9mm pistol.
PHOTO CREDIT: KEVIN DOCKERY

Pistols

TECHNICAL DATA—USSOCOM Colt Offensive Handgun Weapon System (OHWS) w/suppressor
CARTRIDGE—.45 ACP (11.23x23mm)
OPERATION—Short recoil, double action
TYPE OF FIRE—Semiautomatic
RATE OF FIRE—30 rpm
MUZZLE VELOCITY—804 fps (245 m/s)
Special +P 1043 fps (318 m/s)
MUZZLE ENERGY—336 ft/lbs (456 J)
447 ft/lbs (606 J) w/special +P load
SIGHTS—Open, Square-notch/blade, Adjustable for windage only, May be fitted with white plastic parts or luminous dot inserts, one front two rear. S-tron laser aiming module with flashlight, weight (0.676 kg) w/batteries.
FEED—10 round, single-column removable box magazine
WEIGHTS
WEAPON (EMPTY)—3.34 lbs (1.51 kg)
WEAPON (LOADED)—3.97 lbs (1.80 kg) w/loaded magazine (Ball)
4.85 lbs (2.20 kg) w/loaded magazine, suppressor
6.34 lbs (2.88 kg) w/loaded mag, suppressor, and LAM w/batt
MAGAZINE (EMPTY)—0.16 lbs (0.07 kg)
MAGAZINE (LOADED)—0.63 lbs (0.29 kg)
SERVICE CARTRIDGE—45 Ball M1911 331 g (21.4 g)
Special +P JHP (Olin) 282 gr (18.3 g)
PROJECTILE—234 gr (15.2 g)
Special +P JHP 185 gr (12 g)
LENGTHS
WEAPON OVERALL—9.80 in (24.9 cm) w/o suppressor
16.89 in (42.9 cm) w/suppressor
SUPPRESSOR LENGTH—7.09 in (18 cm)
SUPPRESSOR DIAMETER—1.38 in (3.5 cm)
BARREL—4.77 in (12.1 cm)
SIGHT RADIUS—6.88 in (17.5 cm)
EFFECTIVE RANGE—54.7 yds (50 m)
MAXIMUM RANGE—1467 yds (1341 m)

A right side view of the Colt OHWS candidate. The Knight's Armament Company suppressor is shown underneath the pistol. The relatively long pistol grip is necessary to hold the ten round single column magazine used in the Colt design. The ambidextrous safety is seen just below the hammer of the pistol and is in the down (or off) position.
PHOTO CREDIT: KEVIN DOCKERY

TECHNICAL DATA—August 1991 USSOCOM Offensive Handgun Weapon System (OHWS) specifications (condensed)
CALIBER—.45 ACP
MAGAZINE—10 round minimum
LENGTH OVERALL—9.84 in (25 CM)
LENGTH W/SUPPRESSOR—15.75 in (40 cm)
WEIGHT W/EMPTY MAGAZINE—2.86 lbs (1.30 kg)
WEIGHT W/12 RDS BALL, SUPPRESSOR, LAM—5.5 lbs (2.5 kg)
Double-action trigger w/single action capability, decocking lever, adjustable sights w/colored or tritium (luminous) inserts, dual-mode (infrared and visible) laser sight, flashlight, removable sound suppressor providing 30 db sound reduction and 75 percent flash suppression capable of holding those characteristics after firing 15,000 rounds without maintenance. Fire 30,000 rds without a material failure and fire 10,000 rounds without a failure to function. Specialized round used in the non-suppressed mode is envisioned to be a 200 grain truncated cone bullet loaded to +P levels minimum.

The Colt .45 ACP Offensive Handgun Weapon System (OHWS) candidate with a Knight's Armament Company suppressor. The large dovetail mount in the front of the trigger guard is for the laser module. Note the square end of the slide lock protruding above the trigger and just in front of the slide stop lever.
PHOTO CREDIT: KEVIN DOCKERY

another sidearm coming into the Teams in the possible near future.

In 1991, after a number of meetings in which representatives of the Army, Navy, and Air Force Special Operations Commands discussed a number of special equipment requirements, the US Special Operations Command (USSOCOM) put notification out to the firearms industry that a new handgun was desired. The Offensive Handgun Weapon System (OHWS) would be used for special operations and had to fit a specific set of criteria. Most interesting among these was that the pistol be chambered for the .45 ACP round.

USSOCOM OFFENSIVE HANDGUN WEAPON SYSTEM (OHWS)

Some Special Operations forces continued to use .45 ACP M1911A1 pistols, though in a customized form, well after the 9mm became the service sidearm caliber. Primary desire for the .45 centered around the rounds greater stopping power. Drawbacks of recoil, weight, and size, were not considered significant to the special operations community. Modern developments in materials and firearms technology indicated that a new weapon could be designed that would be superior to the aging M1911A1 design while still chambered for the .45 ACP round.

Additional specifications for the OHWS included a minimum 10 round magazine capacity, that it be capable of double or single-action firing, have a dual infrared and visible laser sight, a target illuminator (flashlight) also selectable for visible or infrared light, and mount a detachable sound suppressor. Other requirements included luminous sights, ambidextrous manual safeties, and a separate decocking lever to allow the hammer to be lowered on a chambered round. On top of all this, the entire package, with ten rounds of M1911 Ball, was not to weigh more than 5.5 pounds (2.5 kilograms).

To aid in the stopping power of the OHWS, the weapon had to be capable of accepting special hot-loaded (+P in modern parlance) ammunition for enhanced stopping power. In addition to all of the above, the OHWS candidates would be subjected to the most extensive testing ever given to a Special Operations Force handgun. Each submitted unit would have to fire 30,000 rounds without a parts breakage and two weapons would be fired to failure and examined for safety problems. The firing until failure was specifically put in to prevent any possibility of the Beretta slide breaking incident to repeat itself.

In spite of the difficult parameters and stringent testing procedures, in August 1991 Phase 1 development contracts were awarded to Colt Manufacturing as well as Heckler and Koch. As part of Phase 1, thirty prototypes of each companies OHWS candidates were submitted to Naval Weapons Support Center at Crane, Indiana. The Navy facility is being used since the Navy Special Operations Command has been tasked with developing the OHWS. The OHWS program was to have three phases with the final procurement figure to be around 8,000 systems.

The Colt OHWS Phase 1 candidate is a short-recoil operated design whose barrel rotates slightly to unlock. Portions of the Colt design trace their parentage to the Colt 2000 pistol, the Double Eagle, and the M1911A1. A major number of the components for the Colt OHWS are made of stainless steel to minimize corrosion and given a matt black chrome finish. One interesting point of the Colt candidate is its use of a single column ten round magazine. The single column design gives the Colt OHWS a comfortable, though very long, grip.

The Colt OHWS uses a muzzle break to reduce recoil and muzzle flip when firing the weapon without the sound suppressor. Both the muzzle break and sound suppressor mount on the frame of the pistol rather than the barrel, allowing the rotating barrel system freedom to move. Attachment to the frame is made with a spring-loaded latch allowing quick changing between the break or suppressor. The cylindrical suppressor, developed by Knight's Armament Company, uses a baffle system that gives the suppressor a long service life with minimal maintenance.

The laser aiming module (LAM), containing both a visible and infrared laser as well as a flashlight, mounts on the frame of the OHWS, underneath the muzzle with a quick release securing system. Lastly, there is a slide lock on the system to allow either unlocked semiautomatic fire with the suppressor or single shot, slide locked fire for maximum sound attenuation.

The Heckler and Koch OHWS candidate uses technology the company developed for its Universal Self-loading Pistol (USP) line including a plastic polymer frame, machined steel slide, and mechanical recoil reduction system. Going with a staggered, double-column magazine gives the H&K OHWS a twelve round magazine capacity in a slightly wider but normal length grip.

Using a modified linkless Browning system, the H&K OHWS operates on short recoil with the barrel camming down from its locked position in the slide. Instead of having separate locking lugs on the barrel matching commensurate grooves in the slide, the square-sectioned breech of the H&K design locks solidly into the ejection port opening much like the Sig-Sauer P226 weapon.

The laser aiming module locks into grooves in the frame forward of the trigger guard. Created by Insight Technology Inc., the LAM contains the lasers and flashlight in an easily removed package with an IR filter for the flashlight stowed under a side cover.

Initially, the H&K OHWS was fitted with an unusual suppressor developed by H&K. The compact suppressor is an asymmetrical rectangular design with a rectangular cross-section. Utilizing normal baffle technology, the H&K suppressor is shorter than a normal cylindrical suppressor while still having sufficient internal volume for effective sound suppression. By using an asymmetrical design with an off-center bullet path, the H&K OHWS does not have to have raised sights as the main portion of the suppressor body is below the sight plain.

The mechanical recoil reduction system in the H&K OHWS lowers the felt recoil of the system to significantly less than the original M1911A1 pistol. Another advantage

Pistols

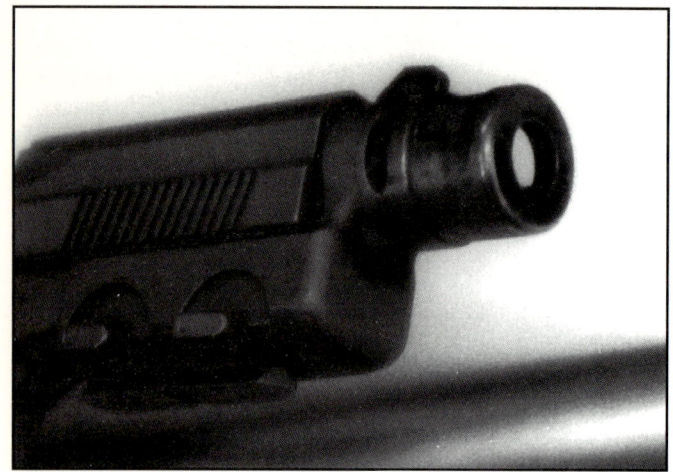

A right side view of the muzzle of the Colt OHWS candidate showing the muzzle break/suppressor mounting. The half-round vertical notch just behind the muzzle break opening is one of the two locking points for the Knight suppressor mounting system. Just above the mounting dovetail for the Laser Aiming Module (underneath the front of the pistol) can be seen the two locking levers for securing the aiming module in place.
PHOTO CREDIT: KEVIN DOCKERY

A left side view of the Phase II H&K OHWS. This particular weapon is fitted with the cylindrical Knight's Armament Company suppressor which has now been adopted for the system. The Laser Aiming Module (LAM) is not fitted to this example, but the mounting rails for the LAM can be seen on the frame of the weapon starting in front of the trigger guard.
PHOTO CREDIT: H&K

TECHNICAL DATA—USSOCOM Heckler & Koch Offensive Handgun Weapon System (OHWS) w/suppressor
CARTRIDGE—.45 ACP (11.43x23mm)
OPERATION—Short recoil
TYPE OF FIRE—Semiautomatic
RATE OF FIRE—26 rpm
MUZZLE VELOCITY—886 fps (270 m/s) Special +P 1142 fps (348 m/s)
MUZZLE ENERGY—408 ft/lbs (553 J) 536 ft/lbs (727 J) w/special +P load
SIGHTS—Open, Square-notch/blade, Adjustable for windage only, May be fitted with white or luminous dot inserts, one front, two rear. Insight Technology LAM (Laser Aiming Module) with infrared and visible light lasers, target illuminator (flashlight), weight 0.46 lbs (0.21 kg) with 2 AA batteries.
FEED—12 round double-column removable box magazine
WEIGHTS
WEAPON (EMPTY)—2.43 lbs (1.21 kg)
WEAPON (LOADED)—3.24 lbs (1.47 kg) w/loaded magazine (Ball)
4.58 lbs (2.08 kg) w/loaded magazine (Ball), suppressor
5.04 lbs (2.29 kg) w/loaded magazine, suppressor, LAM
1.34 lbs (0.61 kg) Suppressor
MAGAZINE (EMPTY)—0.24 lbs (0.11 kg)
MAGAZINE (LOADED)—.81 lbs (0.367 kg) (M1911 Ball)
SERVICE CARTRIDGE—45 Ball M1911 331 g (21.4 g)
Special +P JHP (Olin) 282 gr (18.3 g)
PROJECTILE—234 gr (15.2 g)
Special +P JHP 185 gr (12 g)
DIMENSIONS
WEAPON OVERALL—9.65 in (24.5 cm) w/o suppressor
15.71 in (39.9 cm) w/suppressor
BARREL—5.87 in (14.9 cm)
SUPPRESSOR LENGTH—6.61 in (16.8 cm)
SIGHT RADIUS—7.76 in (19.7 cm)
EFFECTIVE RANGE—54.7 yds (50 m)
MAXIMUM RANGE—1467 yds (1341 m)
Suppressor reduces sound signature from a peak 169 db to 139 db (-30 db).

of reducing felt recoil is a more rapid target re-acquisition after a shot has been fired. Since the H&K weapon has an internal recoil reduction system, felt recoil is even less when the weapon is fired with the suppressor installed, a significant point when the OHWS is fired in its optional slide-locked configuration for maximum sound suppression.

The rectangular sound suppressor was replaced during testing on the H&K OHWS with a unit also manufactured by Knights Armament Corporation. The new suppressor is cylindrical and longer than the H&K design but still remains below the sight plain. Both the Colt and the H&K OHWS candidates met the requirement of a 30 decibel noise reduction and 75 percent flash reduction over the unsuppressed system.

In August 1992, the required 30 prototype weapons were submitted to the Navy for Phase 1 testing. After the testing was completed, the H&K candidate was the one chosen for further development under the second phase of the OHWS program. A number of refined H&K designs were delivered for further testing in November 1994. Requirements on the number of weapons and production schedules were modified by USSOCOM in October 1993. Under the new schedule, Phase 3 production should commence in mid-1995 for 7,500 pistols and 1,950 LAMs and suppressors with deliveries in 1996-97.

Mark 23 Offensive Handgun

This is the production model of the H&K Offensive Handgun Weapon System. Essentially the same pistol described above, there are some differences consisting primarily of the removal of the slide lock system from the weapon and changing to a Knight's Armaments suppressor. The first production Mark 23 pistols were delivered to the U.S. Special Operations Command on 1 May, 1996 for operational deployment with the weapons arriving at the SEAL Teams shortly after that.

In the mid-1960's, the SEALs were conducting research into what would be one of the most unique series of handguns ever issued in the US military. A number of research and development projects were up and running for the SEALs and the UDTs in the field of weapons, tools, and explosive devices. One of these projects, identified as TDP 3801, was a multimillion dollar effort with products beginning to emerge into the Teams in late 1967. Among the systems and equipment being worked on as part of TDP 3801 was the underwater gun system. Identified as the Underwater Gun (WOX-5 Type), Ammunition for U/W gun (WOX-5 Type), and Rocket Projectile for U/W gun (WOX-5 Type), the material being investigated was designed to give an individual combat swimmer a close-in defensive capability in a easy to handle package.

Just a short time prior to 1967, a very new weapon system had been released on the civilian market and brought to the attention of the Special Warfare community. The weapon system was the Gyrojet rocket gun, a handgun that fired solid-fueled, spin-stabilized, miniature rockets instead of normal ammunition. Though the Gyrojet gun itself was not of particular interest to the SEALs or UDTs during the 1960's (at least not in its

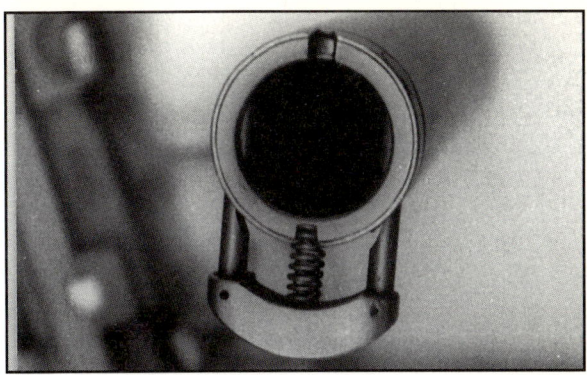

A closeup of the breech end of the Colt/Knight OHWS suppressor showing the quick release mechanism. The square notch at the top end of the breech indexes the suppressor with the front sight of the pistol. Pressing in on the spring-loaded plunger lines up the two semicircular notches in the suppressor locking pins with the bore of the suppressor body. Slipping the suppressor over the muzzle of the Colt OHWS candidate and releasing the plunger securely locks the suppressor in place.
PHOTO CREDIT: KEVIN DOCKERY

available configurations) an underwater version of the weapon, the Lancejet did show promise.

Using the same miniature rocket systems as the Gyrojet handgun, the Lancejet fired a long, spear-like projectile from either a single-shot or repeating weapon. The standard Lancejet projectiles were about one-quarter inch (6.4 mm) in diameter and twelve inches (30.5 cm) long. Weighing in at about two ounces (56.7 g), the Lancejet projectile was powerful enough for most underwater needs, being able to penetrate a 1 inch thick (2.5 cm) sheet of plywood at 25 feet (7.6 m), underwater. Though the loaded repeater weapon was of a manageable size and weight, about eighteen inches (45.7 cm) long and 1.5 pounds (0.68 kg) loaded, the weapon had two bad drawbacks, cost and accuracy.

The Lancejet was able to put half its rockets into a 16 inch (40.6 cm) circle at 25 feet during tests. Accuracy at that level would mean that a diver would miss an average man-sized target with half of his ammunition when underwater, an unacceptable figure. In addition the cost of the ammunition was considerable, and to make it more accurate with the technology available at the time would have made it even more costly. After some examination, the idea of a rocket-powered swimmer weapon was shelved.

By the early 1970's, a piece of ordnance was available to the Teams that would give a swimmer a reasonable weapon

---

TECHNICAL DATA—H&K Mark 23 Mod. 0 .45 ACP Pistol (differences from prototype weapon)
WEIGHTS
WEAPON (EMPTY)—2.42 lbs (1.10 kg)
WEAPON (LOADED)—3.23 lbs (1.47 kg) w/loaded magazine (Ball)
4.23 lbs (1.92 kg) w/loaded magazine (Ball), suppressor
4.69 lbs (2.13 kg) w/loaded magazine, suppressor, LAM
1.00 lbs (0.45 kg) Suppressor
DIMENSIONS
WEAPON OVERALL—16.72 in (42.5 cm) w/suppressor
SUPPRESSOR LENGTH—7.62 in (19.4 cm)
SUPPRESSOR DIAMETER—1.375 in (3.5 cm)

Pistols

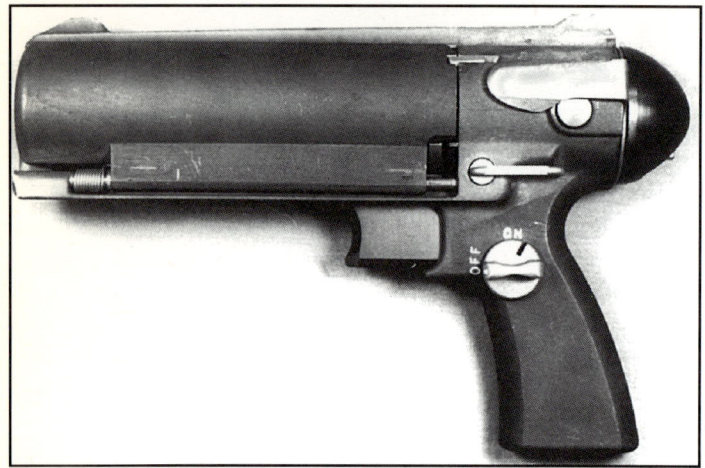

A left-side view of the Mark 1 Underwater Defense Gun ready for firing. The cylindrical control just behind the trigger is the safety switch set in the OFF position. The long vertical control just above the safety switch is the door release lever for the loading door of the weapon that extends along the entire left side of the "Barrel" assembly. Above the release lever, pointing forward from the black, conical rear cap, is the belt clip that secures the weapon to any portion of the swimmer's web gear. The clip can also be rotated to either side of the weapon to suit the operator. This particular example of the Mark 1 is serial number 1.
PHOTO CREDIT: KEVIN DOCKERY

TECHNICAL DATA—Underwater Defense Gun Mark 1 Mod 0 10001-PL2499504
CARTRIDGE—Projectile, Underwater gun Mk 59 Mod 0
OPERATION—Manual, double-action only pepperbox revolver
TYPE OF FIRE—Repeater
RATE OF FIRE—12 rpm
MUZZLE VELOCITY—740 fps (226 m/s)
MUZZLE ENERGY—186 ft/lbs (252 J)
SIGHTS—Open, U-notch/blade, fixed with 3 yellow dots, 2 - notch, 1-blade
FEED—6 round removable cylinder
WEIGHTS
WEAPON (EMPTY)—2.26 lbs (1.02 kg)
WEAPON (LOADED)—4.17 lbs (1.89 kg)
MAGAZINE (EMPTY)—0.56 lbs (0.26 kg)
MAGAZINE (LOADED)—1.91 lbs (0.87 kg)
SERVICE CARTRIDGE—0.225 lbs (0.102 kg)
PROJECTILE—153 grains (9.9 g)
DIMENSIONS
WEAPON OVERALL—9.75 in (24.8 cm)
BARREL—4.25 in (10.8 cm)
MAGAZINE CYLINDER—5.56 in (14.1 cm)
MAGAZINE CYLINDER DIAMETER—1.5 in (3.8 cm)
PROJECTILE—4.25 in
PROJECTILE DIAMETER—0.10 in. (2.54 mm) (1/8 in. [3.18mm] across fins)
SIGHT RADIUS—7.5 in (19.1 cm)
EFFECTIVE RANGE—30 feet @ 60 foot depth (9.1 m @ 18.3 m depth)

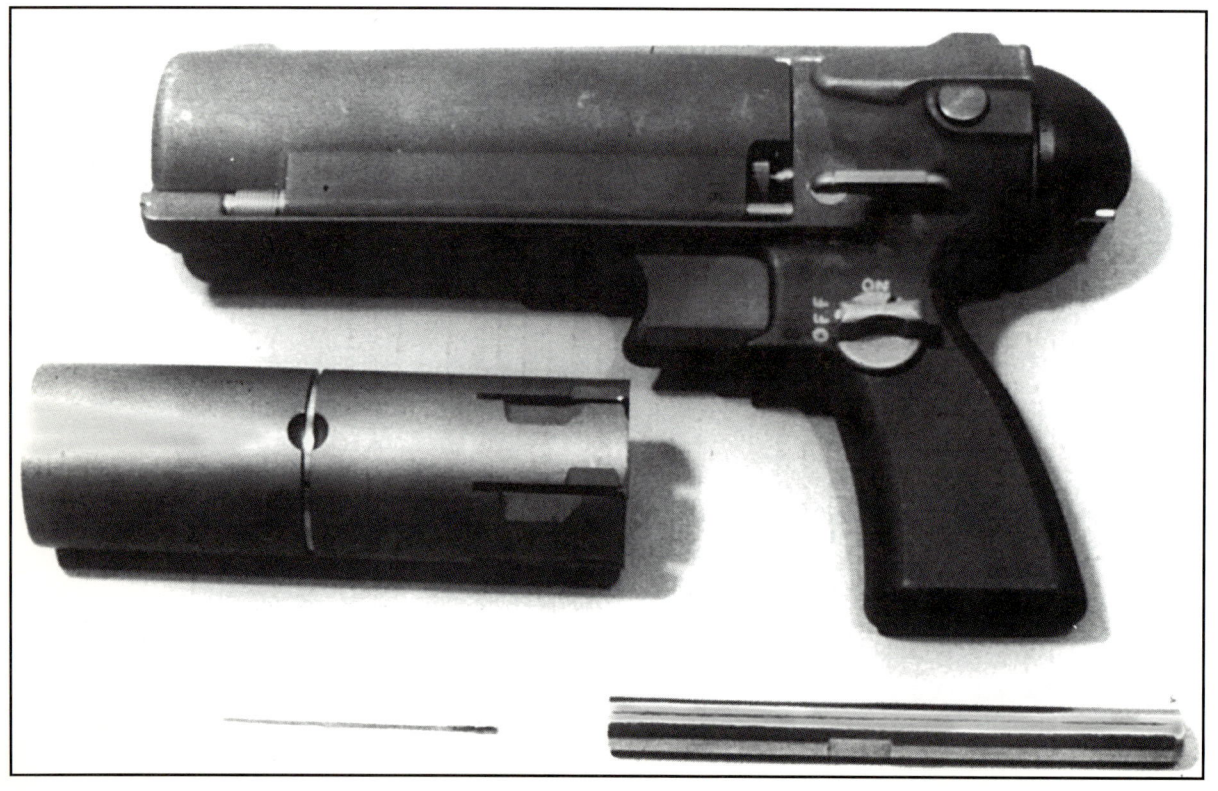

The Mark 1 Underwater Defense gun with its magazine cylinder and a single Mark 59 projectile. The thin line in front of the Mark 59 and below the magazine cylinder is the tungsten dart fired by the weapon.
PHOTO CREDIT: KEVIN DOCKERY

Special Weapons

that he could carry close to hand. Developed as part of the Swimmer Weapons System, the Underwater Defense Gun Mk 1 Mod 0, was a repeating weapon that was effective underwater while not being bigger than a large pistol.

Underwater Defense Gun Mark 1 Mod 0

Developed in part at the Naval Surface Weapons Center White Oak Laboratory in Silver Spring, Maryland, the Underwater Defense Gun uses the very exotic Mk 59 Mod 0 Projectile (cartridge) to launch a long, thin, fin stabilized dart of heavy tungsten metal. As water is almost 900 times denser than air, a projectile has vastly more drag on it than an equivalent round fired in air. The tungsten alloy and extended shape of the projectile give the dart a high sectional density which aid it in penetrating the water, while also helping it maintain a sufficient velocity to give it effective terminal effects. For stabilization in flight, the Mk 59 projectile dart has four fins machined into its rear section. Each fin has a small angle cut into its leading edge allowing the water flow over it to give the projectile a stabilizing spin.

The operating system of the Mark 59 projectile prevents the Mk 1 underwater gun from requiring a normal barrel and allows the weapon to operate either underwater or in the open air. The body of the Mark 59 projectile is a steel cylinder consisting of the barrel, charge plug assembly, shear pin, projectile pusher, and tungsten dart. The charge plug assembly contains a percussion primer and a charge of smokeless powder propellant. Ahead of the charge plug assembly is the projectile pusher, a self-sealing piston that drives against the base of the tungsten dart.

The projectile pusher is secured to the front end of the plug assembly by a metal shear pin. The loaded plug assembly is threaded into the breech end of the barrel with the dart inserted into a socket in the pusher. The front tip of the dart is held centered in the barrel by a light alloy disk. The end of the barrel is left open but is constricted to keep the pusher from leaving the barrel when the cartridge is fired.

The Mark 59 projectile is fired by a normal firing pin crushing the percussion cap and igniting the powder charge. The shear pin holds the pusher in place while the propellant burns until sufficient pressure is built up in the system to force the pusher to shear through the pin, driving the dart down the barrel. As the pusher reaches the constriction at the end of the barrel it begins to slow and collapse in on itself slightly. By this time the dart has reached its maximum velocity and it leaves the muzzle of the weapon. The constriction at the end of the barrel retains the pusher, sealing all of the propellant gases inside of the cartridge body.

Since no gases leave the weapon when it is fired, the Mark 1 Swimmer defense gun is flashless and effectively soundless. This system also allows a normal propellant charge to be used underwater without causing a muzzle blast shock wave that could injure the operator or other swimmers around him.

The underwater defense gun is mechanically rather simple and acts as a double-action only pepperbox

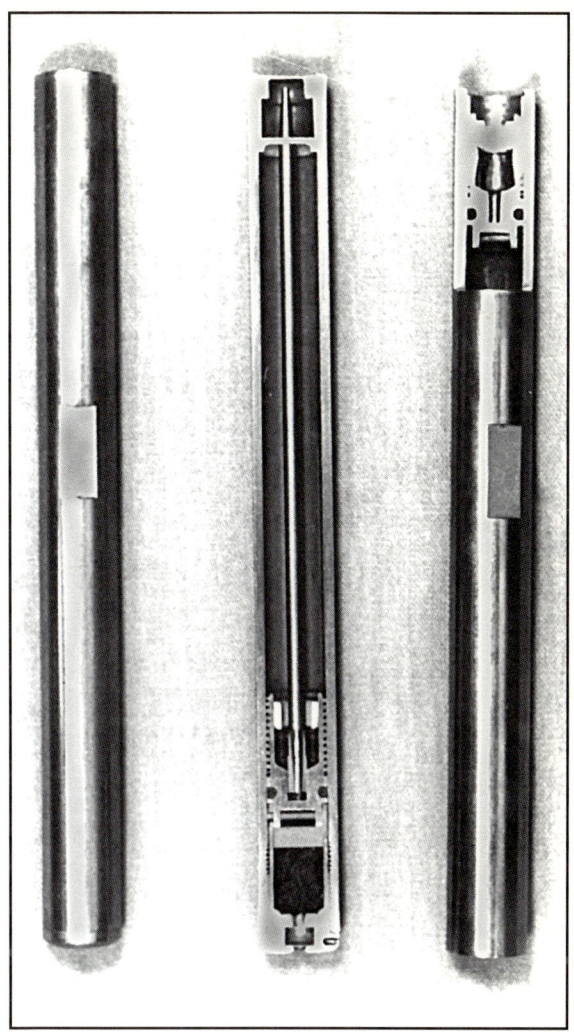

From left to right, a complete, sectioned, unfired, and partially sectioned, fired Mark 59 projectile. The slightly rounded end on the bottom of the left projectile indicates the breech (primer) end of the round. The machined retaining flat is the only other mark on the otherwise cylindrical body. The center round is an unfired Mk 59 showing the tungsten dart that is the actual projectile fired from the round. The breech section of the round is threaded into the stainless steel body, maintaining a gas and water tight seal. When the primer is struck, the powder (shown as the dark mass just inside of the primer end) burns until it has built up enough pressure to break the shear pin, visible as the vertical pin just behind the pusher piston. The pusher piston has the finned end of the dart held securely and is sealed from gas leakage by the O-ring around its base. The ends of the O-ring are visible to the sides of the fins of the dart. At the muzzle (upper) end of the projectile is an aluminum disc that holds the dart centered in the barrel of the Mk 59 body. Beyond the tip of the dart is the sealing disk that keeps the round water tight during transport and is shattered by the dart when the Mk 59 is fired. The right Mk 59 has been fired and the muzzle end sectioned to show the pusher piston at the far end of its travel. The constricted end of the Mk 59 body prevents the pusher from exiting the barrel. With the pusher pistol stopped, all of the firing gases remain in the body of the Mark 59, releasing no bubbles into the water and reducing the sound of firing to a very low level.
PHOTO CREDIT: KEVIN DOCKERY

Pistols

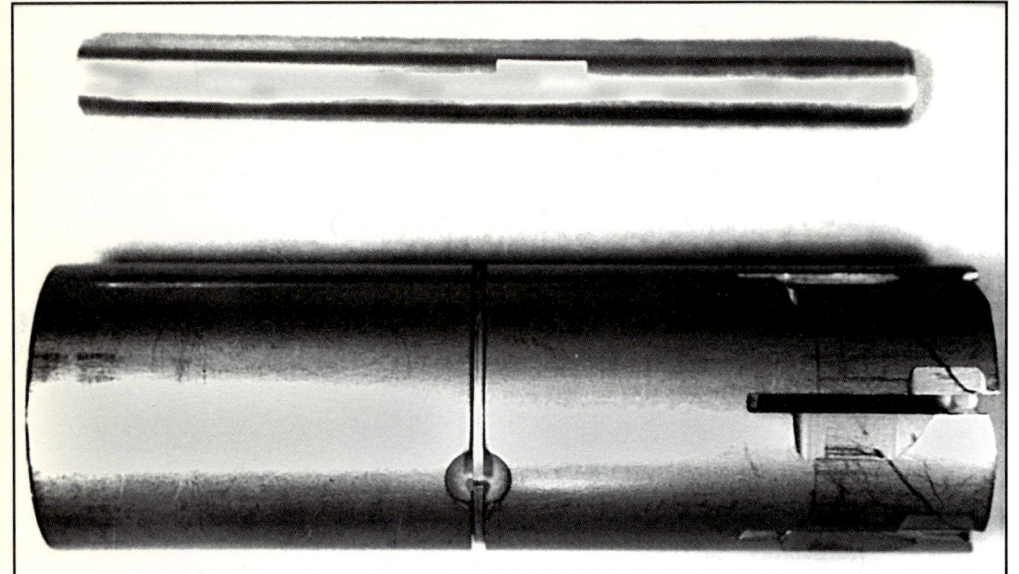

An empty magazine cylinder for the Mark 1 Underwater Defense Gun directly below a Mark 59 Projectile unit for the same weapon. The rear (breech) end of the magazine cylinder is to the right with the machined slots and surfaces that allow the cylinder to be rotated by the mechanism of the weapon plainly visible. The circular retaining ring can be seen at the center of the magazine cylinder that helps to retain the Mk 59 projectile in place. When a Mark 59 projectile is inserted into the magazine cylinder, the retaining ring snaps into the machined flat on the body of the Mk 59 and holds the round in place.
PHOTO CREDIT: KEVIN DOCKERY

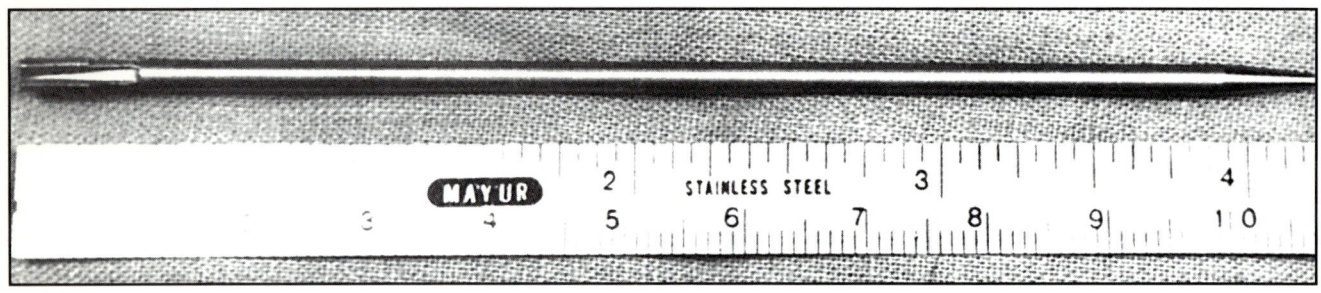

The tungsten-alloy dart launched from the Mark I Underwater Defense Gun. The small rear fins are machined into the body of the dart and it has a flat rather than sharp point.
PHOTO CREDIT: KEVIN DOCKERY

TECHNICAL DATA— Heckler & Koch P11 ZUB Underwater weapon
OPERATION—Electrically fired
TYPE OF FIRE—Repeater
RATE OF FIRE—10 rpm
MUZZLE VELOCITY—352 fps (107 m/s)
MUZZLE ENERGY—158 ft/lbs (214 J)
SIGHTS—Open, square-notch/blade, fixed w/luminous tritium dot inserts
FEED—5 round removable, disposable cylinder (cassette)
WEIGHTS
WEAPON (LOADED)—2.65 lbs (1.20 kg)
PROJECTILE—574 grains (31.2 g)
DIMENSIONS
WEAPON OVERALL—7.87 in (20.0 cm)
PROJECTILE—4 5/8 in. (11.7 cm)
PROJECTILE DIAMETER—0.375 in. (9.5 mm)
SIGHT RADIUS—5.75 in (14.6 cm)
EFFECTIVE RANGE—33 to 49 ft (10 to 15 m) underwater: 98 ft (30 m) in air

A left-side view of the H&K P11 underwater weapon. The large rectangular lever above and in front of the trigger is the locking lever for the ammunition cassette. The ammunition cassette locks into place from the front of the weapon with the raised barrel sides indexing into the formed portion at the upper rear of the receiver. The front and rear sight can be seen at the top of the uppermost barrel on the ammunition cassette. The safety switch is above the trigger and the large trigger guard. The enlarged trigger guard allows the weapon to be used by an operator wearing heavy gloves. Behind the trigger is the rubber boot that waterproofs the electrical firing switch. The large pistol grip contains the batteries that operate the system and they are held in place by the rectangular cap on the butt of the grip.
NO PHOTO CREDIT

revolver. A large cylinder magazine holds six of the Mk 59 projectiles and is carried completely covered by the mechanism of the gun. A large door making up much of the left side of the gun can be opened to allow the magazine cylinder to be inserted or removed.

The outside of the underwater gun has few protruding parts and shows a relatively streamlined appearance. The circular safety switch can be moved to either side of the gun to accommodate a left or right-handed operator. In addition, the large metal clip that holds the underwater gun securely to the swimmers harness can also be moved to either side as the operator desires. No trigger guard covers the trigger of the gun to allow easy operation with a gloved hand.

By pressing a spring catch, the loading door snaps open giving access to the cylinder magazine. The door can be operated underwater allowing a swimmer to insert a fresh magazine and reload the weapon without surfacing. In general, the underwater gun is operated like any other pistol, the luminous sights are aligned and the trigger pulled to fire the gun.

The long trigger pull rotates the cylinder magazine and locks it in place with a fresh cartridge in front of the firing pin. A metal rod protrudes from the back of the gun as the trigger is pulled showing if the firing pin has been released at the end of the trigger pull or not.

Because each dart launches from its own barrel, the underwater gun is considered a pepperbox design rather than a true revolver. In a pepperbox design, each chamber has its own barrel rather than a single barrel and multiple chambers in a rotating cylinder as is found in the true revolver. Each of the precision made Mk 59 projectiles is retained in the cylinder magazine by its snug fit and retaining spring that sets into a small flat machined on the outside of each cartridge.

The precision aspect of the ammunition is shown in the accuracy of the weapon. To be accepted, each lot of ammunition is randomly tested and must place its darts within a 9 inch (22.9 cm) circle at 30 feet (9.1 m) range to be accepted. In addition the standard deviation in velocity of the darts cannot exceed 25 feet per second either way or the lot is rejected. All of the acceptance tests for velocity and accuracy are conducted at a simulated depth of 60 feet of sea water also insuring the operating system of the cartridges.

The underwater defense gun is made of an aluminum frame, cylinder, door assembly, and action, with all other operating parts but the trigger being made of stainless steel. The trigger is made of self-lubricating nylon. Each weapon comes packed in an ammunition can complete with two magazine cylinders, and a plastic bag of small spare parts. The Mark 59 Mod 0 projectiles come packaged in a standard ammunition can, wrapped in cardboard and packed 60 to the can.

In an emergency situation, the Mk 1 gun can be used in the open air as a covert weapon. This is not a normal use of the weapon due to the high cost of its ammunition. But when fired, the loudest sound produced is the mechanical sounds of the action and the slapping noises from the projectile pusher and buffer system. First

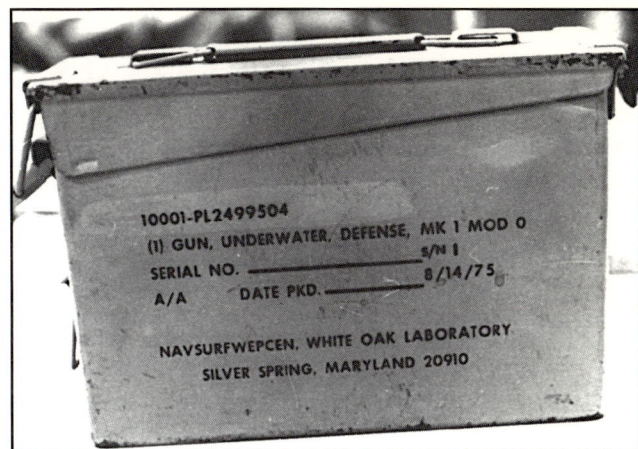

The M1A1 metal ammunition can that holds the Mark 1 Underwater Defense Gun contained in its styrofoam packaging. This specimen is for weapon serial number one, the first production model off the line.
PHOTO CREDIT: KEVIN DOCKERY

available in late 1970, the underwater defense gun has been used by both the SEALs and the UDT throughout the 1970's and into the 1980's As weapons became worn and ammunition stocks ran low, a replacement weapon was sought as the underwater defense gun was a unique and valuable Special Warfare asset.

Heckler and Koch designed an underwater handgun with the same general characteristics as the Mk 1 gun during the 1970's. Entering service in 1976, the H&K P11 underwater handgun is known to be in service with the SEALs but all operational information on the weapon is classified. What information is known has been released by other governments who also employ the P11 pistol.

H&K P11 ZUB Underwater weapon

In general, the P11 operates much the same as the earlier Mk 1 underwater gun. In the P11, five projectiles are held in a reusable, non-rotating barrel unit that has a set of open sights installed on the top barrel. The large projectiles are driven by pusher pistons and the system releases no propelling gas when it is fired. Each barrel is electrically fired, eliminating much of the mechanical noise found in the Mk 1. Batteries for firing are held in the grip section and the barrel unit can be replaced underwater by the operator.

Barrel units must be returned to H&K in Germany for reloading, adding to the maintenance load of the weapon but helping to keep the overall cost down at least slightly. The biggest advantage of the H&K weapon is the range of the system. The large projectile of the P11 can be used accurately in open air against a man-sized target at distances of over 98 feet (30 m). When fired underwater, the P11's range is limited to 32 to 49 feet (10 to 15 m), which is still quite reasonable given the low visibility of underwater operations in general.

Instead of having a belt clip, the P11 has a large, open holster available for it than is normally carried strapped around the swimmer's waist. At the present time, no photographs are available of the P11 in SEAL hands and Heckler and Koch simply denies knowledge of the weapon.

Submachine guns

TECHNICAL DATA—M1928A1 Thompson
FSN 6U1005-726-5641
CARTRIDGE—.45 ACP (11.43x23mm)
OPERATION—Delayed blowback
TYPE OF FIRE—Selective - semiautomatic/full automatic
RATE OF FIRE—Cyclic 600-725 rpm
MUZZLE VELOCITY—920 fps
MUZZLE ENERGY—432 ft/lbs (586 J)
SIGHTS—Open, Lyman leaf w/aperture, notch battle sight/blade or aperture/blade (later models), adjustable
FEED—20 or 30 round removable box magazine, 50 round drum
WEIGHTS
WEAPON (EMPTY)—10.75 lbs (4.88 kg) w/stock
1.73 lbs (0.78 kg) Removable wooden stock
WEAPON (LOADED)—12.67 lbs (5.75 kg) with 30 rounds
MAGAZINE (EMPTY)—20 round - 0.4 lb (0.18 kg), 30 round - 0.5 lb (0.23 kg), 50 round drum 2.6 lb (1.18 kg)
MAGAZINE (LOADED)—20 round - 1.35 lb (0.61 kg), 30 round - 1.92 lb (0.87 kg), 50 round drum - 4.96 lb (2.25 kg)
SERVICE CARTRIDGE—M1911 Ball 331 gr (21.4 g)
PROJECTILE—230 grains (15.2 g)
LENGTHS
WEAPON OVERALL—33.7 in (85.6 cm) w/compensator, stock
25 in (63.5 cm) w/o stock
BARREL—10.5 in (26.7 cm)
SIGHT RADIUS—22.3 in (56.6 cm)

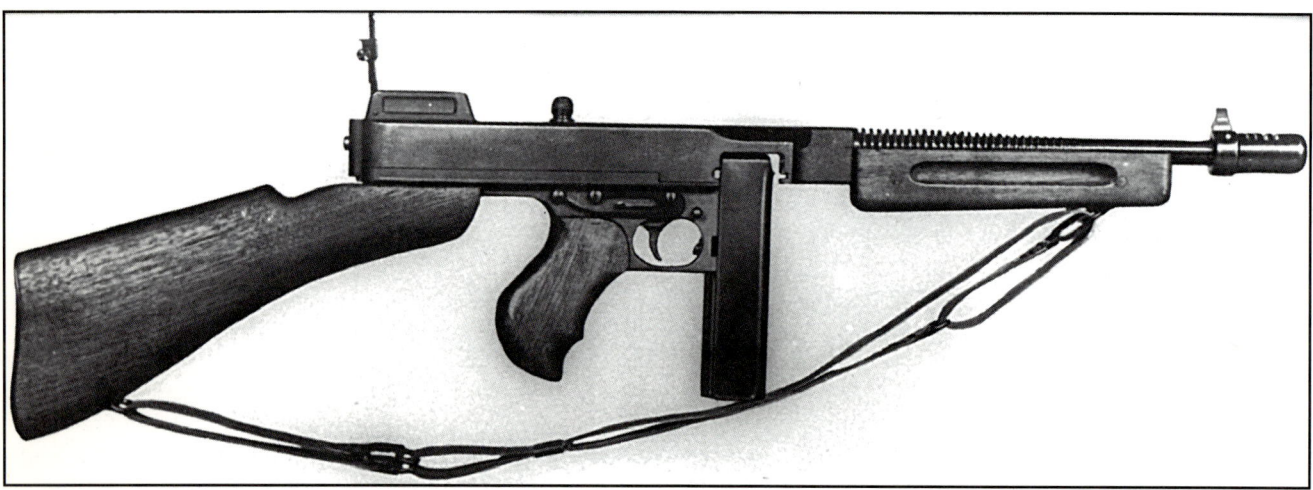

The M1928A1 Thompson submachine gun in full military dress. This weapon is loaded with a 20-round box magazine and has the actuator knob at the top of the receiver in the rearmost, fully- cocked position. The complex adjustable rear sight is in the raised position for precision fire. This type of rear sight was soon found to be unnecessary on a submachine gun-class weapon and was dropped for a much simpler, and less expensive, plain aperture sight.
PHOTO CREDIT: US ARMY

Special Weapons

The submachine gun is one of the few small arms that traces its history only through the Twentieth Century. By the end of World War I, trench warfare had shown a need for a light, easy to handle, fast firing shoulder weapon that had a high volume of fire. To fill this need, the submachine gun was developed.

Under its classic definition, a submachine gun is a shoulder or hand fired weapon capable of full-automatic fire and chambered for a pistol caliber cartridge. Early weapons tended to resemble shortened rifles and were fairly complex machinings. The general operating system for most submachine guns is mechanically simple but was made complicated in the application.

THOMPSON M1928A1

Most submachine guns use the blowback principle as their operating system. In the blowback principle, the gasses of firing make the cartridge case act much like a piston while in the chamber. The propellant gasses push the light bullet down the barrel while at the same time try to push the cartridge case out of the chamber. The heavy bolt used in the blowback system must have its inertia overcome by the pressing cartridge before it starts to move backwards.

The delay time needed for the bolt to start moving backwards allows time for the bullet to leave the barrel and pressures to drop down to safe levels. The backwards momentum of the bolt completes extraction of the fired casing, ejects it, and comes to a stop as its energy has been absorbed by the mainspring.

If the trigger has been released, the bolt remains to the rear, retaining the compressed mainspring. If the trigger is pulled or has been held back, the bolt moves forward under the pressure of the spring, stripping a cartridge from the feed device, chambering, and then firing it. At this time the cycle continues until the ammunition is expended or the trigger released.

The blowback system requires a fairly heavy bolt and strong mainspring to operate safely. The bolt is held to the rear in the open position until the trigger is pulled at which time it moves forward. This is called firing from the "open-bolt" position and is the major drawback of blowback operation. Each time the weapon is fired, the heavy bolt moves forward and slams against the breech face, jarring the weapon and making a precise first shot very difficult, if not impossible.

The firepower of the submachine gun and the fact it is intended to be fired on full automatic minimizes the open-bolt accuracy drawback. A multitude of bullets can be placed on a target in a very short time. Accuracy is achieved by firing short bursts of only a few rounds each which gives the firer a reasonably high hit probability.

The first submachine gun to come to the notice of the US military was the M1921 model Thompson. Though a M1919 model had been completed some time earlier, the hostilities of World War I were over before it could see action in Europe. The Navy purchased a small quantity of M1921 Thompsons for trials with the Marine Corps. The weapons did see some limited combat in Nicaragua in 1927 and '28. The result of the trials and testing was the Navy ordering a quantity of Thompsons modified to their specifications. Among the modifications to the M1921 Thompson were the replacement of the vertical forward grip with a horizontal forearm, inclusion of a smaller recoil spring and pilot as well as a heavier bolt, reducing the cyclic rate of the weapon from 800 rounds

On board his APD transport in the Pacific Ocean during World War II, this UDT operator demonstrates his M1928A1 Thompson submachine gun. This weapon is set up in the classic Thompson style, being loaded with a 50-round Type L drum magazine. The cocking knob on the top of the receiver is in the forward, fired, position indicating that the drum is empty. The operator is aiming through the raised Lyman rear sight that was dropped in later production weapons. This UDT operator is wearing rubber and canvas coral shoes and has a M1911/M1911A1 pistol in a leather M1912 holster. At the side of the holster, between the holster body and the hanger, this UDT man has slipped a Mark 1 Ka Bar knife.
PHOTO CREDIT: UDT-SEAL MUSEUM

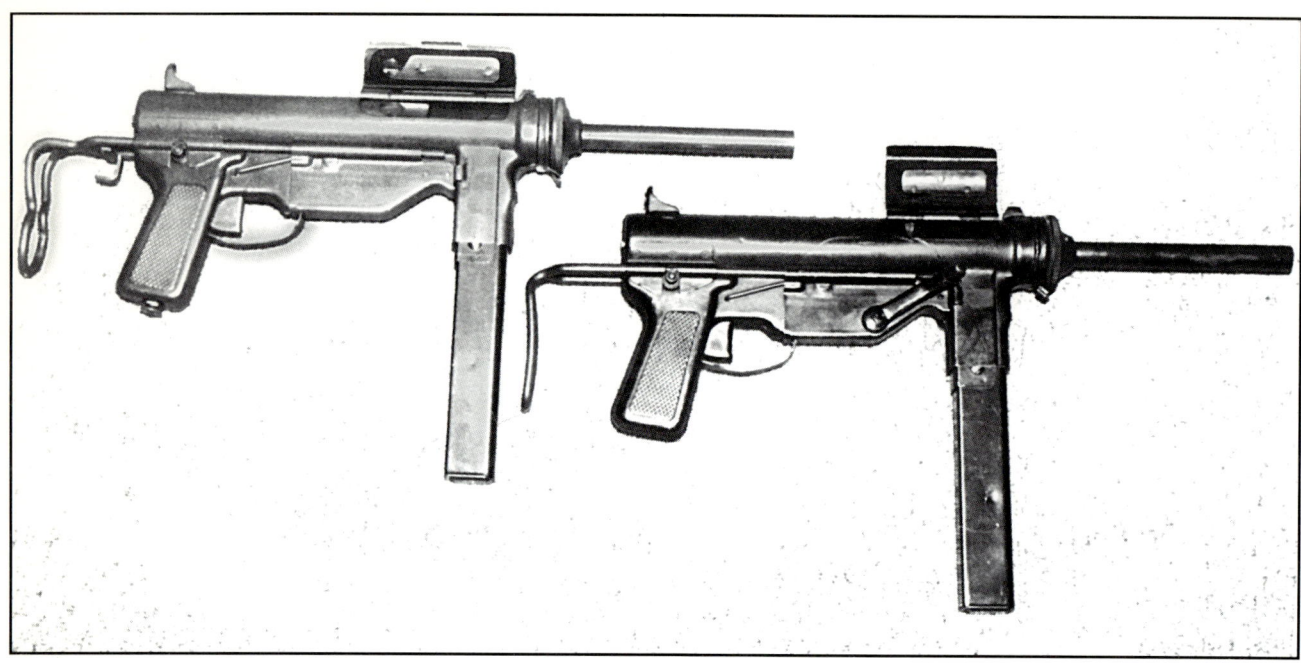

The .45 caliber M3 (right) and M3A1 (left) submachine guns. Both weapons are fully cocked and have their ejection port covers/safeties in the open position ready for firing. The safety catch can be seen as the small attachment riveted to the underneath of both ejection port covers. A protrusion on the riveted part sticks down into the receiver preventing the bolt from moving when the cover is closed. The major difference between the two weapons can been seen in the size of the ejection ports, much larger in the M3A1. The retracting handle assembly is missing in the M3A1, replaced by the simple expedient of pulling the bolt back with the operator's finger.
PHOTO CREDIT: KEVIN DOCKERY/KNIGHT ARMAMENT COMPANY

"Though the UDTs would receive their M3 and M3A1 weapons after World War II, during the war the greasegun saw duty with tank and vehicle crews as well as Airborne, Ranger, and other special-forces type units."

TECHNICAL DATA — Submachinegun M3
FSN 6U1005-672-1767, NSN 1005-00-672-1767
— Submachinegun M3A1
FSN 6U1005-672-1771, NSN 1005-00-672-1771
CARTRIDGE—.45 ACP (11.43x23mm)
OPERATION—Blowback
TYPE OF FIRE—Full automatic
RATE OF FIRE—120 rpm, CYCLIC 450 rpm
MUZZLE VELOCITY—918 fps (280 m/s)
MUZZLE ENERGY—430 ft/llbs (583 J)
SIGHTS—Open, aperture/blade, fixed
FEED—30 round removably box magazine
WEIGHTS
WEAPON (EMPTY)—[M3] 8 lbs (3.63 kg) [M3A1] 7.65 lbs (3.47 kg)
WEAPON (LOADED)—[M3] 10.17 lbs (4.61 kg) [M3A1] 9.82 lbs (4.45 kg)
MAGAZINE (EMPTY)—0.75 lb (0.340 kg)
MAGAZINE (LOADED)—2.17 lb (0.98 kg)
SERVICE CARTRIDGE—M1911 Ball 331 gr (21.4 g)
PROJECTILE—230 grains (15.2 g)
LENGTHS
WEAPON OVERALL—22.81/29.81 in. (57.9/75.7 cm)
BARREL—8 in. (20.3 cm)
SIGHT RADIUS—10.88 in. (27.6 cm)

per minute to about 600 rounds per minute, using a one-piece buffer unit, and making provisions for a sling with sling swivels on the weapon's stocks.

The new weapon was designated the M1928A1 Thompson. In addition to the above changes, most of the M1928A1 Thompsons were fitted with the Cutts Compensator on the muzzle. The Cutts Compensator is a cylindrical device that fits over the muzzle of the Thompson and extends for some distance past it. On the top of the compensator is a series of four different sized slots. Working with the reduced diameter of the compensator muzzle, the slots direct some of the propellant gasses straight up. The force of the gasses help push the muzzle down and keep the weapon on target during a long burst. Though the Thompson had been described as "kicking like a horse," the weapon actually has relatively light recoil, much less than the average rifle. The lack of substantial recoil is due to the high weight of the M1928A1 and the relatively low power of the .45 ACP round it fires. What the Thompson does do is rotate its muzzle upwards (climb) quickly on full automatic fire as well as vibrate heavily from the force of firing.

The M1928A1 Thompson was adopted by the US military just as World War II was beginning. The Navy issued the weapon in some numbers to both the Marine Corps and for use by ship's landing parties. Two feed devices were used on the M1928A1 Thompson, the Type L 50 round drum magazine and the type XX 20 round box magazine. The box magazine made the Thompson a fairly handy weapon but the sustained firepower of the 50 round drum made it quite popular with its Navy users. Drawbacks with the drum, however, were its difficulty in being inserted quickly into the weapon and tendency to rattle when carried.

The Thompson is an example of what is called a first-generation submachine gun. It was an expensive, heavy, complex weapon made up of many milled and machined parts. What stood in the Thompson's favor was its very strong receiver and parts, and good dependability. The weapon was very popular among many of the troops who were issued it, including the UDTs who used a small number of the M1928A1s for guard duty and self-defense on enemy islands. When possible, Thompsons would be begged, borrowed, traded for, or just picked up by individual UDT operators who felt a need for one.

The Thompson continued to see duty with the Navy and the UDTs well through the Korean War. By the 1960's, many M1928A1s were feeling their age, the last one having been made for the Navy in 1945. During World War II, the difficulty and expense in producing the M1928A1 Thompson caused a search to begin for a simpler and easier to produce weapon. Some simplified Thompsons were produced during World War II, specifically the M1 and M1A1 models. But most of these weapons ended up in Marine and Army hands. A new style of submachine gun, the second-generation type, was first developed in the US as the M3, commonly called the "greasegun."

M3 AND M3A1 "GREASEGUN"

Second-generation submachine guns have become the most common type of their class of weapon to be found in the world. This is due in no small part to the vast numbers of this type of weapon that were produced during World War II and throughout the 1950's. A second-generation submachine gun is characterized by being mechanically simple, made up of easily manufactured sheet metal stampings, tubing, and formed parts that are welded and riveted together. A minimum number of machined parts, usually the bolt and barrel, are in the second-generation submachine guns and the weapons are fitted with folding or sliding stocks to reduce bulk.

Because of its close resemblance to a well known garage tool, the M3 and later M3A1 submachine guns were better known as the "Greasegun". The M3 was one of the simplest modern firearms ever produced by the US government. The receiver of the M3 was made from two metal stampings welded together with the barrel being attached to the front of the weapon by a threaded collar. The General Motors Corporation Guide Lamp Division with their long experience in producing stamped car parts was the primary contractor for all of the M3s and M3A1s made during World War II.

Ease of manufacture stood out in the M3; many parts were simple assemblies of stamped parts. The machined bolt with its guide rod assembly and driving springs was slipped into the receiver of the M3 from the front and held in place by the barrel being screwed down over it. The safety of the weapon was a stud on the inside of the ejection port cover. With the cover closed, the stud engaged a hole in the bolt, securing it in place. By just opening the cover, the safety was removed and the weapon was ready to cock or fire. First suggested in 1942, the M3 was in production and being received by troops in mid-1943. Though the UDTs would receive their M3 and M3A1 weapons after World War II, during the war the greasegun saw duty with tank and vehicle crews as well as Airborne, Ranger, and other special-forces type units.

The M3 submachine gun was further simplified and improved by a design study begun in April 1944. The bolt cocking handle assembly was removed and replaced with a finger hole drilled into the bolt. The ejection port was enlarged so that the bolt could be cocked by just putting a finger into the hole and pulling the bolt back. Other improvements were included such as installing a magazine loading tool as part of the sliding metal stock. Even the stock was improved, not only with the loading tool, but one arm of the stock was drilled so that it could be used as a cleaning rod. Officially adopted in December 1944 as the M3A1 submachine gun, the M3 was put on limited standard status. By the end of World War II in Europe, the M3A1 was declared the submachine gun for all US forces and would replace all earlier models in service.

One accessory for the M3 and M3A1 submachine guns was produced during World War II that would be of particular interest to the SEALs later. The long, exposed, and removable barrel of the M3 submachine gun made

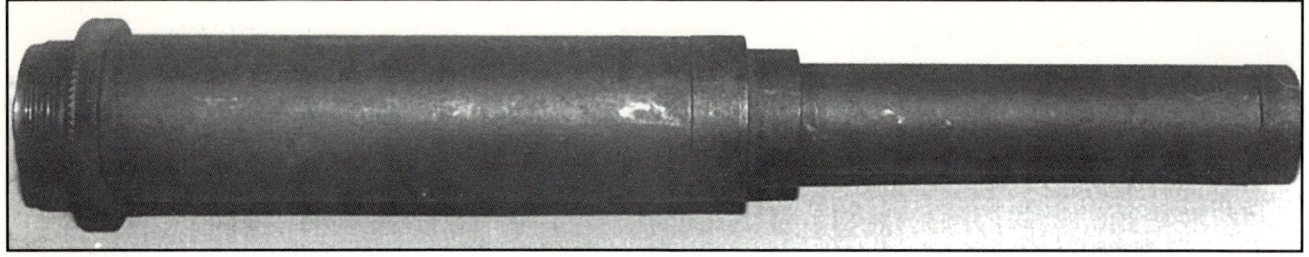

The complete OSS suppressor for the M3 submachine gun. This very rugged unit would be screwed onto an M3 or M3A1 weapon in place of the standard barrel assembly.
PHOTO CREDIT: KEVIN DOCKERY/BATF REFERENCE COLLECTION

"Though the actual sound reduction of the OSS suppressor is not as good as present day weapons, the sound signature is unrecognizable as a firearm at fifty yards."

TECHNICAL DATA—M3 & M3A1 Suppressed barrel
CARTRIDGE—45 ACP (11.43x23mm)
MUZZLE VELOCITY—768 fps (234 m/s)
MUZZLE ENERGY—301 ft/lbs (408 J)
WEIGHTS
SUPPRESSOR—2.63 lbs (1.19 kg)
WEAPON (LOADED)—w/ Suppressor [M3] 11.55 lbs (5.24 kg) [M3A1] 11.2 lbs (5.08 kg)
NORMAL BARREL WEIGHT—1.25 lb (0.57 kg)
LENGTHS
WEAPON OVERALL—29.75/36.75 in. (75.6/93.3 cm)
BARREL—7.88 in (20 cm)
SUPPRESSOR LENGTH OVERALL—14.25 in. (36.2 cm)
SUPPRESSOR DIAMETER—1.630/1.130 in. (4.1/2.9 cm)

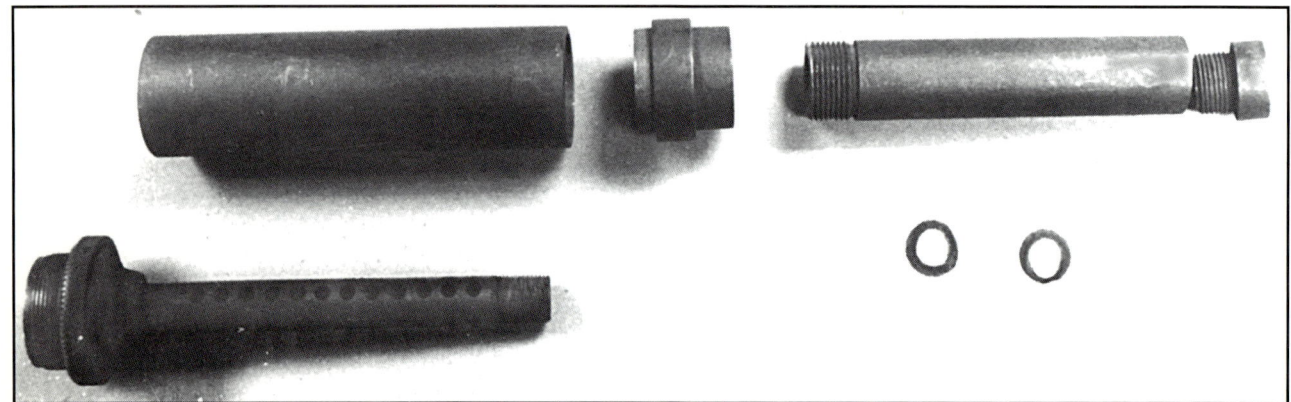

A disassembled view of the Bell laboratories M3 submachine gun suppressor built for the OSS during World War II. The barrel assembly at the lower left shows two of the four rows of 12 gas bleed holes that release propellant gases into the rear expansion chamber. Also visible on the barrel assembly are the machined collar that screws into the front of the receiver of the M3 weapon and the threaded portion of the muzzle that helps hold the entire unit together. The large cylinder above the barrel assembly is the rear expansion chamber that contains a roll of wire mesh screen that surrounds the perforated barrel. At the right end of the expansion chamber is the reduction coupling that threads onto the muzzle of the barrel and clamps the expansion tube in place. The cylinder to the right of the reduction collar is the front suppressor tube. The front suppressor tube is filled with a stack of perforated screen mesh washers to further slow the escaping propellant gases. Below the suppressor tube are two used examples of the of the screen washers showing the large central hole for the passage of the projectile. The final component at the far right is the suppressor cap that closes off the muzzle of the suppressor, holding the screen washer stack in place.
PHOTO CREDIT: KEVIN DOCKERY/BATF REFERENCE COLLECTION

Special Weapons

the weapon particularly adaptable to having an integral suppressor mounted on it. In 1942, Bell Telephone Laboratories in New York had already developed a suppressed .22 pistol for the Office of Strategic Services (OSS) and they were approached to perform the same action with the M3. The M3 suppressor was an adaptation of the Mason suppressor used on the OSS High Standard Model D suppressed pistol (see Pistols). By February 1944, six suppressed M3 submachine guns were supplied by Bell Labs to the OSS and the weapons were tested at Aberdeen Proving Grounds. The design was accepted and by April 1944, the OSS entered into a contract with the High Standard Company for the production of 1,000 suppressed barrels for the M3.

General Motors Guide Lamp supplied 1,000 specially drilled barrels to High Standard for the suppressor order. The barrels were drilled with four rows of 12 one-quarter inch holes drilled into the bore of the barrel. The barrels were threaded at their muzzle end to accept a bushing for the attachment of the two suppressor tubes.

The 7.5 inch long 1.63 inch diameter rear expansion tube was held at the breech end by a cut made into the barrel collar and was secured at the muzzle by a threaded reducing bushing. The expansion tube was filled with a wrapping of 16 mesh brass wire screen for its entire length. The front suppressor tube is 6 inches long and 1.13 inches in diameter. Attached at its rear end to the reducing bushing at the muzzle of the barrel, the front suppressor tube is closed by a metal cap with a 0.5 inch hole through its center. Inside the front suppressor tube is a stack of 30 mesh brass wire screen disks with a 0.5 inch hole in their centers.

The wire mesh screen roll and disks cooled and reduced the speed of the escaping gas when the weapon was fired, eliminating much of the muzzle blast-related noise. The mechanical noise of the M3 was not reduced in any way and the .45 ACP projectile was subsonic, eliminating any sonic crack.

Sound is measured in decibels (db) with the actual measurement of a suppressors efficiency being dependent on several variables. In general, normal conversation can be rated at 65 db. Exposure to sounds over 115-120 db can cause hearing problems, and sounds over 130 db can cause physical pain. An unsuppressed M16 is rated on this scale at 165 db and the unsuppressed M3 at a relatively quiet 130 db. With the OSS suppressed barrel installed, the M3 measures 107 db, a 23 db reduction.

Though the actual sound reduction of the OSS suppressor is not as good as present day weapons, the sound signature is unrecognizable as a firearm at fifty yards. Even when heard and recognized as a firearm, the OSS suppressor makes the firing position of the M3 very

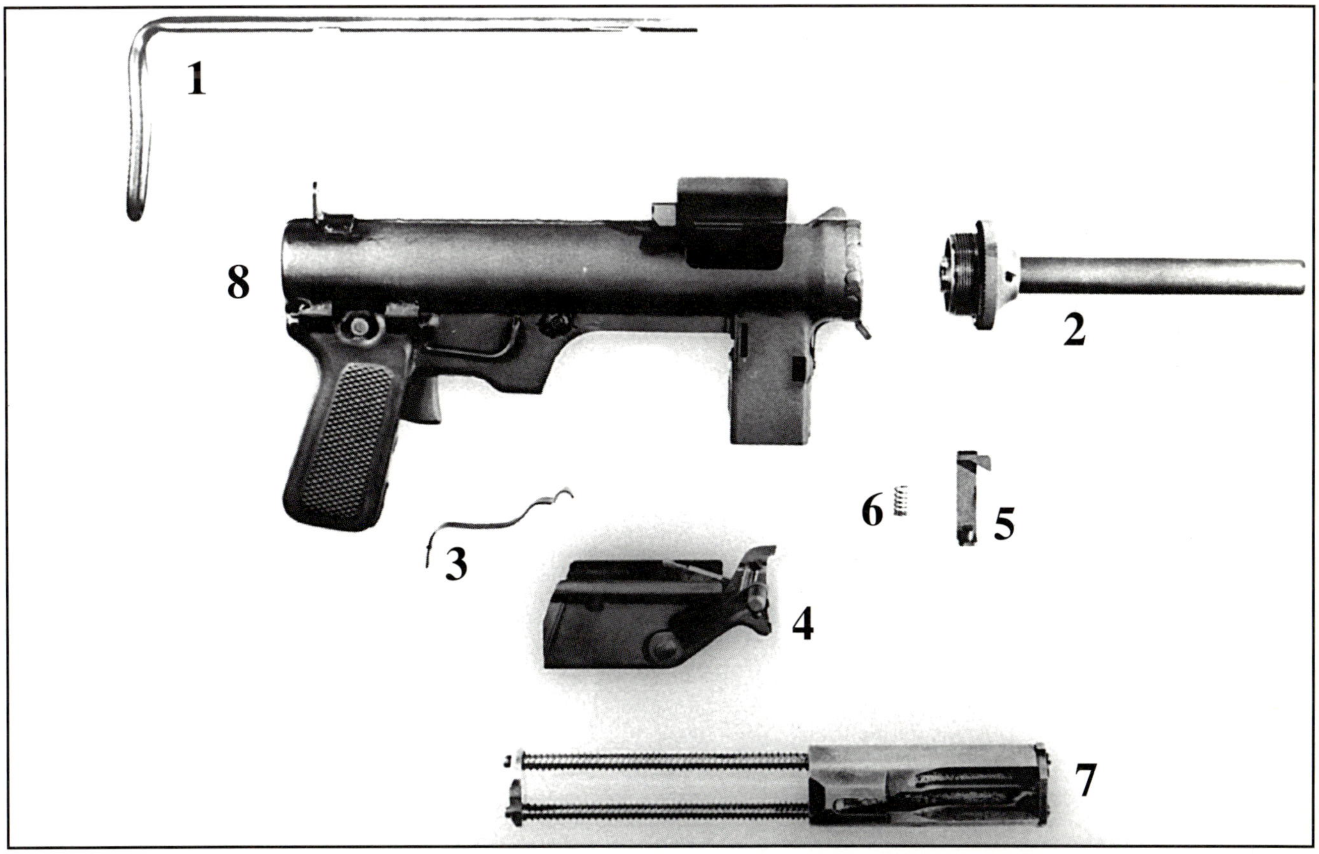

A field stripped M3 submachine gun laid out for display. Part #1 is the sliding wire stock. Part #2 is the barrel assembly. Part #3 is the stamped metal trigger guard. Part #4 is the housing assembly holding the retracting arm mechanism and ejector. Part #5 is the magazine catch. Part #6 is the magazine catch spring. Part #7 is the bolt assembly complete with driving springs, guide rods, and retaining plate. Part #8 is the stamped metal receiver with the ejection port cover/safety open and the trigger/sear assembly still in place.
PHOTO CREDIT: US ARMY

Submachineguns

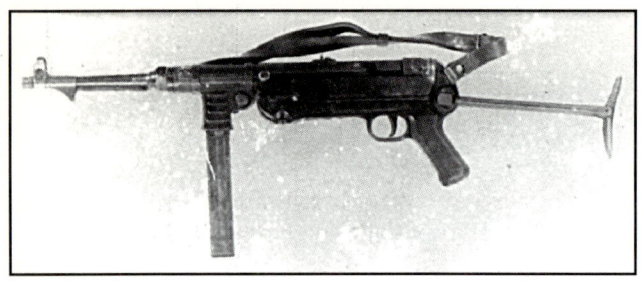

This is a left side view of the German MP-40 submachine gun, often wrongly called a Schmeisser. This weapon is distinguishable from the earlier MP-38 by the ribbed magazine well and button cocking knob among other characteristics. Both the MP-38 and MP-40 are functionally identical. This weapon has the folding stock extended and the bolt in the forward, uncocked, position.
PHOTO CREDIT: US ARMY

TECHNICAL DATA—MP 40
CARTRIDGE—9mm Parabellum (9x19mm)
OPERATION—Blowback
TYPE OF FIRE—Full automatic
RATE OF FIRE—Practical 120 rpm Cyclic 350 to 500 rpm
MUZZLE VELOCITY—1250 fps (381 m/s)
MUZZLE ENERGY—399 ft/lbs (541 J)
SIGHTS—Open, Square-notch/blade, Fixed, flip-up rear blade for 100 and 200 meters
FEED—32 round removable box magazine
WEIGHTS
WEAPON (EMPTY)—8.94 lbs (4.06 kg)
WEAPON (LOADED)—10.32 lbs (4.68 kg)
MAGAZINE (EMPTY)—0.56 lbs (0.25 kg)
MAGAZINE (LOADED)—1.38 lbs (0.63 kg)
SERVICE CARTRIDGE—M1 Ball 180 gr (11.7 g)
PROJECTILE—115 gr (7.5 g)
LENGTHS
WEAPON OVERALL—24.8/32.8 in (63/83.3 cm)
BARREL—9.9 in (25.1 cm)
SIGHT RADIUS—15.38 in (39.1 cm)

A selection of the small arms trained with and used by the Navy SEALs in the early 1960's. This photograph is from a display put on by the SEALs at Saint Thomas island circa 1964. In the front row, from right to left is first a Colt Model 05 AR-15 Carbine loaded with an early, fully curved 30-round magazine. The pistol immediately to the left of the carbine, next to the sling, is the Smith & Wesson Model 15 Combat Masterpiece revolver that was the standard sidearm of the Teams in the 1960's. Next to the Model 15 is a Colt Detective Special, issued as an undercover or backup weapon for non-combat missions. The submachine gun left of the pistols is a Swedish M45b, more commonly called the "Swedish K". The center submachine gun is the Danish Madsen M50. To the left of the Madsen is a World War II vintage German MP40. The long tube with the shoulder strap is an M72 Light Antiarmor Weapon (LAAW), a self-contained 66mm high explosive rocket packed in a disposable launcher. To the far left in the first row is a Mauser "Red 9" Broomhandle automatic pistol attached to its shoulder stock/holster. Just to the left of the stock of the Mauser is the leather harness used to attach the stock/holster to a belt of other carrying gear. Across the back of the table at the left is a Colt Model 01 AR-15 rifle supported by a clip-on XM3 bipod. The AR-15 has the first model two-diameter open-prong flash suppressor and is loaded with an early curved 30-round magazine. On the carrying handle of the AR-15 is the original detachable telescopic sight offered as an option by Colt. This model sight is mounted with the Colt-made first style mount that used separate rings to hold the telescope body itself. At the base of the AR-15, behind the front bipod leg, is a prototype bayonet for the rifle, later adopted by the Army in a slightly modified form as the M7. The three rifle grenades are practice versions of various foreign makes with the only American specimen being the M29 practice Antitank rifle grenade at the right next to the Colt Carbine. At the base of the M29 grenade are a .38 Special, 5.56mm, and 7.62mm NATO cartridge.
PHOTO CREDIT: RICHARD BROZAK COLLECTION

hard to locate.

High Standard manufactured 1,000 of the M3 suppressed barrels for the OSS by the Spring of 1944. The weapons were so well received that an additional 4,000 units were ordered. Barrels were difficult to come by and Army Ordnance was reluctant to release the necessary numbers. By 1945, the barrels became available and High Standard manufactured an additional 4,000 suppressed M3 barrels.

Except for two flats cut into the barrel collar, allowing the wire stock to be used as a disassembly wrench, there is no difference between the barrel assemblies of the M3 and M3A1 submachine guns. The M3A1 weapon was just as easily fitted with the suppressed OSS barrel and this weapon has continued to see duty as a suppressed weapon with the US forces past the Vietnam War.

The M3A1 submachine gun had seen some duty with the UDTs in Korea and was still retained in the Navy armories for use by the Teams when needed. The slow cyclic rate of fire of the M3 and M3A1 weapons allowed single shots to be fired by just releasing the trigger quickly and the weapon was quick and easy to handle. The magazines of both the M3 and M3A1 were identical and both had their difficulties. A slight dent to the feed lips of the M3 magazine could easily cause a malfunction and jam the weapon with a misfed round. In addition to the possible feeding problem, the M3 magazines were considered heavy by the weight conscious UDTs and SEALs. When the SEAL Teams were commissioned in 1962, M3 submachine guns were included in the original allowance lists and were among the first weapons to show up at the new Teams

> "The first weapons that we received were some .45 caliber M3 greasegun submachine guns that the Navy sent us and the AR-15 rifle. The greaseguns we considered just too heavy for our purposes, especially the loaded magazines. Though we kept some around, no one I knew really wanted the greasegun…"

The greasegun remained with the Teams throughout the Vietnam War. Occasionally, an individual operator would like the firepower of the M3 and carry the weapon for a specific mission by preference. Training was continued on the M3 and M3A1 weapons well into the 1970's, but the greasegun was considered an obsolete weapon by 1974. During the early combat tours of SEAL platoons in Vietnam, the M3A1 saw some popularity as the only easily available suppressed weapon. New weapons had been fitted with the old OSS suppressed barrels and worked just as well as when they had left the High Standard plant in World War II. During 1967, when a SEAL mission called for a suppressed weapon, the OSS M3A1 was what was available, and even they were in short supply.

> "During my first tour, the M3A1 greasegun with the World War Two OSS silencer was the only suppressed weapon we had been able to get our hands on. And the operation we had the suppressed greaseguns for was scrubbed…"

Though some firearms training was given to the men of the UDTs during the late 1940's and through the 1950's, it was fairly limited in scope. The primary tool of the UDT operator was explosives and not small arms. When the SEALs were commissioned, this attitude changed greatly. SEALs were trained on all types of weapons, both foreign and domestic. Initial small arms training was conducted by the Teams themselves at Navy or Marine facilities. Training in depth was conducted for the first SEALs at the Army Special Warfare Training Center at Fort Bragg, North Carolina.

The whole of SEAL Team Two went to Fort Bragg in September, 1962. Among the training they received was instruction in small arms. The instruction was comprehensive, detailed, and complete, and the SEALs were an avid audience.

> "The course [at Ft. Bragg] was a two week block of instruction in foreign small arms familiarization, firing, field stripping, unconventional warfare, and kitchen table demolitions (improvised munitions)…The instructors gave us a complete course of instruction in U.S. and foreign weapons. The French MAT-49, British STEN Mark II, German MP40 (Schmeisser) and Swedish K were among the submachine guns taught to us along with the American M3 greasegun and M1928A1 Thompson. Before then we had almost no experience with submachine guns. But once the instructors showed us how to load the weapons and which end the bullets came out of, we had little trouble qualifying as experts on the Army ranges…"

Many of the SEALs developed a lasting fondness for the compact firepower of submachine guns after the Fort Bragg training. Some of the weapons taught at the course were chosen for their likelihood of appearing in guerrilla hands somewhere in the world.

MP40

The MP40, along with its earlier versions the MP38 and MP38/40 are considered among the very first of the second-generation submachine guns. The MP in their designation comes from the European naming of the submachine gun a machine pistol or maschinen pistolen in German. The MP40 family was the standard submachine gun of the German forces in World War II and was first issued in 1938. Made up of plastic castings and stamped metal parts, the MP38 was a far cry from the precision machining found in most German weapons prior to 1938.

Operating efficiently from a simple blowback action, the MP38 field stripped into only five major parts including its magazine. The simplicity and ease of manufacture of the MP38 family was not lost on the Allies. Captured examples of the German weapon were studied in England and the USA. In England, the MP38 led to the development of the STEN series of submachine guns. In the United States, the M3 submachine gun owes some of its development to the MP38 and MP40. Over

Submachineguns

"To field strip the Madsen M1950, the magazine is first removed and then the barrel nut unscrewed. With the barrel removed and the magazine catch held back, the two stamped metal sides of the Madsen unfold like a book, hinged at the rear."

TECHNICAL DATA—Madsen M50
CARTRIDGE—9mm Parabellum (9x19mm)
OPERATION—Blowback
TYPE OF FIRE—Full automatic
RATE OF FIRE—Practical 120 rpm Cyclic 550 rpm
MUZZLE VELOCITY—1250 fps (381 m/s)
MUZZLE ENERGY—399 ft/lbs (541 J)
SIGHTS—Open, Aperture/blade, fixed, zeroed at 100 meters
FEED—32 round removable box magazine
WEIGHTS
WEAPON (EMPTY)—6.95 lbs (3.15 kg)
WEAPON (LOADED)—8.25 lbs (3.74 kg)
MAGAZINE (EMPTY)—0.48 lbs (0.22 kg)
MAGAZINE (LOADED)—1.30 lbs (0.59 kg)
SERVICE CARTRIDGE—M1 Ball 180 gr (11.7 g)
PROJECTILE—115 gr (7.5 g)
LENGTHS
WEAPON OVERALL—20.8/31.25 in (52.8/79.4 cm)
BARREL—7.8 in (19.8 cm)
SIGHT RADIUS—13 in (33 cm)

TECHNICAL DATA—MAT-49
CARTRIDGE—9mm Parabellum (9x19mm)
OPERATION—Blowback
TYPE OF FIRE—Full automatic
RATE OF FIRE—CYCLIC 600 rpm
MUZZLE VELOCITY—1161 fps (354 m/s)
MUZZLE ENERGY—344 ft/lb (466 J)
SIGHTS—Open, Aperture/blade, Adjustable, flip-up rear, 100 and 200 meters
FEED—32 round removable box magazine
WEIGHTS
WEAPON (EMPTY)—8.02 lbs (3.64 kg)
WEAPON (LOADED)—9.41 lbs (4.27 kg)
MAGAZINE (EMPTY)—0.57 lbs (0.26 kg)
MAGAZINE (LOADED)—1.39 lbs (0.63 kg)
SERVICE CARTRIDGE—9mm Ball M1 - 180 gr (11.7 g)
PROJECTILE—115 gr (7.5 g)
LENGTHS
WEAPON OVERALL—16/26 in (40.6/66 cm)
BARREL—9 in (22.7 cm)
SIGHT RADIUS—14.88 in (37.8 cm)

*An unloaded French MAT 49 submachine gun. The unusual MAT 49 folding magazine housing is in the down position, ready for loading. With the magazine missing or partially withdrawn, the magazine housing can be folded forward where it can be secured underneath the barrel. This action will give the MAT 49 a very compact outline. Just ahead of the butt on the sliding wire stock can be seen the grip safety on the back strap of the pistol grip. Unless the grip safety is held forward, the bolt of the MAT 49 cannot move. This action prevents accidental firing if the weapon is dropped or otherwise jarred.
PHOTO CREDIT: KEVIN DOCKERY*

"...the MAT 49 operates as a standard submachine gun with only a few unusual features."

one million of the German MP38, 38/40, and 40 weapons were manufactured in the years between 1938 and 1945. Several postwar armies outfitted their men completely with captured German weapons including the MP40. As time progressed, thousands of the World War II weapons found their way into guerrilla hands including those of the Viet Cong. A number of German MP40s were captured in Vietnam more than 20 years and half a world away from where they had been made.

Madsen Model 50

Two other submachine guns the SEALs trained with at Fort Bragg later turned up in enemy hands in Vietnam. The Danish Madsen Model 1950 was the improved model of the Madsen Model 1946. The Madsen was developed in Denmark after World War II as a possible commercial venture. The Danish Police forces picked up the Model 1950 and it did see some sales in South American and Southeast Asia. Two items in its design cause the Model 1950 to stand out, the forward bolt safety and method of field stripping.

For increased safety, the Model 1950 has a large bolt safety lever just behind the magazine well. The lever must be held in against the magazine well or the bolt will not move, whether it is in the open or closed position. The bolt safety requires the Madsen M1950 be held with both hands in order to be operated (the magazine well acts as a front hand grip) and the safety prevents the weapon from being accidentally discharge if dropped or struck sharply on the butt.

To field strip the Madsen M1950, the magazine is first removed and then the barrel nut unscrewed. With the barrel removed and the magazine catch held back, the two stamped metal sides of the Madsen unfold like a book, hinged at the rear. This unusual system allows the Madsen to be thoroughly cleaned more easily than most other weapons of its class. The fact that the Madsen M1946 and M1950 saw sales in reasonable numbers in Southeast Asia, notably Thailand and Indonesia, allowed the weapon to make its way into VC hands in some numbers.

The French Army needed to be rebuilt after World War II with a need for a concurrent development of French small arms with which to equip it. Though the French military made do with a mix of American and German weapons immediately postwar, new French designs became available within a few years.

MAT-49

By 1949, after several other weapons had been tried, the French Military settled on the M.A.T. (Manufacture Nationale d'Armes de Tulle) Model 1949, commonly called the MAT 49. Composed primarily of metal stampings and having a rectangular cross-section receiver, the MAT 49 operates as a standard submachine gun with only a few unusual features. On the back edge of the rear pistol grip is a grip safety. Unless the grip safety is held in by the firing hand, the sear is blocked and the bolt will not move either forward to fire or backwards to cock.

The forward hand grip of the MAT 49 is the magazine well and has a pivot on its front top edge. By pressing a catch in front of the trigger guard, the magazine well, complete with the magazine, can be pivoted forward and locked in place underneath the barrel jacket. This feature renders the MAT 49 absolutely safe against accidental discharge and also makes the weapon a very compact package.

The MAT 49 remained the standard submachine gun of the French forces up to the present day where it is still seen in both police and military hands. After the French withdrawal from Indochina, thousands of MAT 49s ended up in Viet Cong and North Vietnamese hands. So many MAT 49s were in the hands of the Communist forces in Vietnam that they found it worthwhile to convert a number of the weapons to a communist caliber. The converted MAT 49 has a longer 10.24 inch (26 cm) barrel chambered for the 7.62mm Short (7.62x25mm) round. Other than the longer barrel giving an additional 2.05 inches (5.2 cm) to the overall length of the converted MAT-49, the weapon remains essentially the same as the French model.

Swedish K

One submachine gun that was introduced to the SEALs at Fort Bragg remained in their inventory through the Vietnam War. The Swedish Model 45, also known in Europe as the Carl Gustav, was commonly called by the SEALs the Swedish K. The SEALs had a few Swedish K's in their arms inventory as early as 1964 and the weapon was well liked by a number of SEALs who used them. Though the Swedish K has few outstanding features, it is a simple and robust weapon that showed good reliability in a bad environment.

Sweden, officially neutral during World War II, saw a need for increasing its armed forces to help defend its neutrality and required a simple submachine gun designed for mass-production. Actually put into production after World War II, the Model 45 is a straightforward second-generation submachine gun that was made in a number of slightly different models. The most common variation of the Swedish K seen in the US military was the M45b model. In the M45b, the weapon had a removable magazine well, secured in place by a U-shaped wire clip. By removing the magazine well, the M45b could accept the earlier Suomi 50 round box magazine that had been in Swedish service prior to the M45 being adopted. Later models of the Swedish K have permanently attached magazine wells and only accepted the standard 36 round box magazine. None of the 50 round Suomi magazines were known to be in US service.

The Swedish K had appeal to the SEALs for two reasons, one of which was its being chambered for the 9mm parabellum round. In addition, the Swedish K was found worldwide and had even been produced in Egypt and Indonesia. The US Intelligence community issued the Swedish K as a sterile weapon with no direct ties to the USA. In addition to issuing the standard Swedish K, the CIA had a several different special suppressed versions available. Individual SEAL operators would occasionally use the suppressed Swedish K, especially when operation on intelligence missions with CIA assets.

The exposed barrel attached to the receiver by a

Submachineguns

While in Vietnam, this man poses with one of the more unusual weapons used by the SEALs. He is armed with the suppressed version of the Swedish M45b submachine gun (Swedish K). This specimen is fitted with the "CIA" model suppressor, known to be a particularly heavy design. The bolt of the M45b is forward and the weapon is loaded with a pair of 36-round magazines taped together for a quick reload. The man with the suppressed weapon may be holding it just for the photograph as he is wearing a grenadier's vest with most of it's pockets filed with 40mm grenades.
PHOTO CREDIT: FRANK THORNTON COLLECTION

TECHNICAL DATA—Swedish K, aka Carl Gustav, M45(B)
CARTRIDGE—9mm Parabellum (9x19mm)
OPERATION—Blowback
TYPE OF FIRE—Full automatic
RATE OF FIRE—Cyclic 550-600 rpm
MUZZLE VELOCITY—1,200 fps (365 m/s)
980 fps (298 m/s) w/AMF suppressor
MUZZLE ENERGY—368 ft/lbs (499 J)
262 ft/lbs (355 J) w/AMF suppressor
SIGHTS—Open, U-notch/post, adjustable, flip-up rear for 100, 200, and 300 meters
FEED—36 round detachable box magazine
WEIGHTS
WEAPON (EMPTY)—7.6 lb (3.45 kg)
10.88 lbs (4.94 kg) w/AMF suppressor
WEAPON (LOADED)—9.03 lb (4.10 kg)
12.31 lbs (5.58 kg) w/AMF suppressor
MAGAZINE (EMPTY)—0.50 lb (0.23 kg)
MAGAZINE (LOADED)—1.43 lb (0.65 kg)
SERVICE CARTRIDGE—9mm Ball M1 - 180 gr (11.7 g)
PROJECTILE—115 gr (7.5 g)
LENGTHS
WEAPON OVERALL—21.7/31.8 in (55.1/80.8 cm)
28.4/38.5 in w/AMF suppressor
BARREL—8 in (20.3 cm)
SIGHT RADIUS—14.13 in (35.9 cm)
20.43 in (51.9 cm) w/AMF suppressor
The AMF suppressor reduces the muzzle blast 31 decibels from 155 db to 124 db. The design of the suppressor also reduces standard ammunition to subsonic velocities eliminating the sonic crack.

Two views of the M45b Swedish K submachine gun. The bolt is forward in the uncocked position on the upper weapon. Between the two weapons is one of the 36-round magazines that were standard with this weapon. The M45b model of the Swedish K was commonly used as a sterile (non-US) weapon in the SEAL Teams and other special operations forces in Vietnam especially MAC-V SOG (Military Assistance Command - Vietnam, Studies and Observation Group).
PHOTO CREDIT: US ARMY

This is a right-side view of the early M45 model of the Swedish K submachine gun. In this model, the magazine well could be removed and the 50-round box magazine from an earlier weapon used on the M45. This specimen has had the magazine well removed and is loaded with a 50-round magazine. These weapons and especially the 50-round magazines were very rare and few, if any, were seen in SEAL hands. The later M45b Swedish K had a secured front magazine well and would not accept the larger magazine.
PHOTO CREDIT: KEVIN DOCKERY

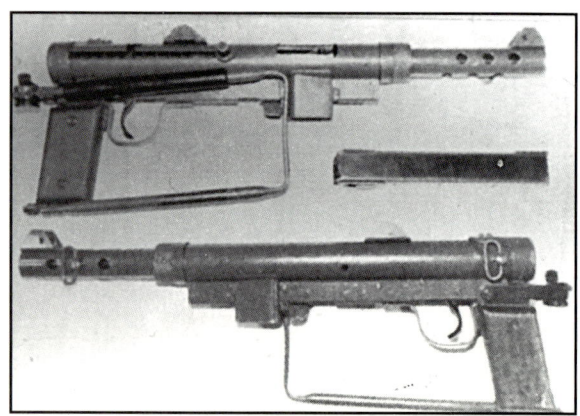

threaded collar gives the same advantages to suppressing the Swedish K as was found on the M3 submachine gun by Bell Labs over twenty years earlier. But the Swedish K fires a supersonic round rather than the subsonic .45 ACP used by the greasegun. To prevent the need for a special ammunition to be issued for maximum noise reduction in the suppressed Swedish K, the muzzle velocity of the weapon while firing standard ammunition was lowered by porting the barrel.

In porting a barrel, sufficient gases are bled off to reduce the velocity of a supersonic round to a subsonic level. One suppressed barrel (the production model) used on the Swedish K had four rows of twelve 0.188 inch holes drilled along its length. Later, another design team found that by placing four 0.125 inch holes just in front of the chamber of the barrel and drilled into the bore at an angle of 10 degrees, the average velocity of a projectile was reduced below that of sound while maintaining maximum accuracy.

The most common suppressor used on the Swedish K greatly resembled the Bell Labs suppressor used on the M3/M3A1 greasegun and was referred to in a study as the production suppressor. The rear expansion tube of the production suppressor surrounded the ported barrel and contained a roll of stainless steel mesh screen. The forward suppressor tube was held to the rear tube by a reduction bushing. The forward tube was filled with stainless steel mesh washers that eliminated much of the muzzle blast.

Several different suppressors were used on the Swedish K by the US forces. Any one of the suppressed Swedish Ks would be used by the SEALs when needed. The preferred model was the one described above, the production suppressor, and is identified by having the suppressor built out of two different diameter tubes. Another model suppressor used on the Swedish K can be identified by its having a group of porting holes just behind the muzzle on the side of the suppressor tube.

Prior to the Teams sending direct action platoons to Vietnam, there was little training given with submachine guns. Though the men were generally trained in how to operate a wide variety of weapons including submachine guns, little emphasis was place on operating in direct combat. With the commitment to Vietnam changing the operations of the SEALs practically overnight, training changed to prepare the men for operations. Small arms training changed from general knowledge and marksmanship to reaction-training against pop-up targets with a variety of weapons.

"For our submachine gun pop-up course B--- set it up so that you not only learned the proper way of shooting a submachine gun, but you also became very familiar with handling a variety of weapons. On the range were a Schmeisser MP40, a Mat-49, a STEN Mark II, and a greasegun. To run the course, you were given a single magazine for each weapon. Starting the course with, say, a Sten gun, you would walk along a trail, shooting at targets as they popped up. When the order was shouted to "Change weapons" there would be another different weapon somewhere at your feet. You would have to quickly load the weapon with the proper magazine. And lord help you if you tried to use the wrong magazine, that sharp-eyed Eagle was just waiting to catch you doing something like that. Very quickly, the whole squad became proficient at using different submachine guns and loading them by feel alone…"

Submachine guns soon became a favorite with a number of SEALs operating in Vietnam. The Swedish K was the most popular weapon used, especially when on "sterile" ops where they did not wish to be identified as Americans by their equipment. A problem arose with the Swedish K that had nothing to do with the functioning or design of the weapon.

The Swedish government, having a law stating that they would not supply weapons to either side in a conflict, refused to sell any more weapons to the United States during the Vietnam War. The Navy had been looking at purchasing a quantity of Swedish K's for the Teams but were stopped by the Swedish law. The number of spare parts for the Swedish Ks in use was limited and the SEALs looked to US companies to supply them with a replacement weapon.

S&W M76

Smith and Wesson saw that a possible market existed for an American-made submachine gun with the US police market as well as the military. By 24 June, 1968, Smith and Wesson had released their Model 76 submachine gun onto the market. Developed in part

During the latter part of the Vietnam War, this SEAL is armed with a production model Smith & Wesson Model 76 submachine gun (Mark 24). The bolt is forward in the uncocked (fired) position and the folding stock of the weapon is extended. At the left shoulder strap of his nylon M1967 Modernized Load Carrying Equipment (MLCE) harness this SEAL has attached an SDU-5/E strobe light in its pouch.
PHOTO CREDIT: T. L. BOSILJEVAC COLLECTION

Submachineguns

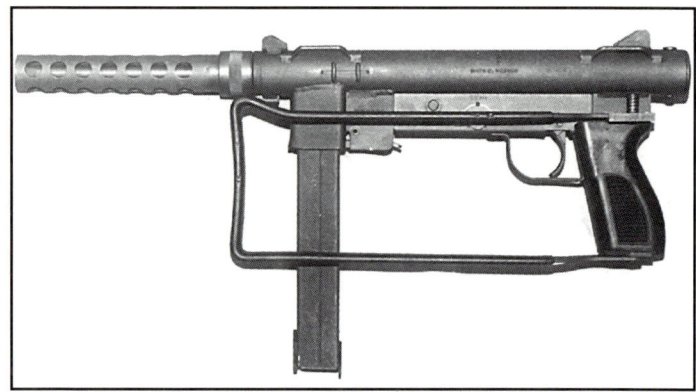

A left-side view of the Smith & Wesson Model 76. The stock is locked in place in the folded position.
PHOTO CREDIT: KEVIN DOCKERY

Patrolling as part of a demonstration in the mid 1970's, this SEAL is armed with a pre-production Smith & Wesson Model 76 submachine gun. The weapon can be specifically identified by the lack of a perforated barrel jacket surrounding the exposed barrel. This SEAL is wearing the Type I Rifleman's Buoyant Ammunition Carrying Coat unique to the Teams during the Vietnam War. On his left hip is a Navy Pilot's Survival Knife in its characteristic sheath with the pocket for a sharpening stone. A cropped version of this photo has been seen in other publications, labeled as SEALs on a patrol deep in enemy territory.
PHOTO CREDIT: US NAVY

TECHNICAL DATA—Submachinegun 9mm Mark 24 Mod 0, Smith & Wesson Model 76

FSN 1005-L99-1124 NSN 1005-01-013-6050
CARTRIDGE—9mm Parabellum (9x19mm)
OPERATION—Blowback
TYPE OF FIRE—Selective - semiautomatic/full automatic fire
RATE OF FIRE—Practical SS - 40 rpm, A - 144 rpm, Cyclic 750 rpm
MUZZLE VELOCITY—1250 fps (381 m/s)
1000 fps (305 m/s) w/suppressor
MUZZLE ENERGY—399 ft/lbs (541 J)
255 ft/lbs (346 J) w/suppressor
SIGHTS—Open, Aperture/blade, Fixed
FEED—36 round removable box magazine
WEIGHTS
WEAPON (EMPTY)—7.25 lbs (3.29 kg) w/standard barrel & jacket
7.93 lbs 3.60 kg) w/suppressor & barrel
0.48 lbs (0.22 kg) standard barrel
0.58 lbs (0.26 kg) perforated barrel jacket
1.44 lbs (0.65 kg) suppressor
0.30 lbs (0.14 kg) suppressor barrel

WEAPON (LOADED)—8.67 lbs (3.93 kg) w/standard barrel & jacket
9.35 lbs (4.24 kg) w/suppressor & barrel
MAGAZINE (EMPTY)—0.49 lbs (0.22 kg)
MAGAZINE (LOADED)—1.42 lbs (0.64 kg)
SERVICE CARTRIDGE—M1 Ball 180 gr (11.7 g)
PROJECTILE—115 gr (7.5 g)
LENGTHS
WEAPON OVERALL—20.25/30.38 in (51.4/77.2 cm)
24.31/34.38 in (61.7/89.9 cm) w/suppressor
BARREL—8 in (20.3 cm)
5.25 in (13.3 cm) suppressor barrel
SUPPRESSOR LENGTH—11.25 in (28.6 cm)
SUPPRESSOR DIAMETER—1.63 in (4.1 cm)
SIGHT RADIUS—11.3 in (28.7 cm)
Issued with 4 magazines

Special Weapons

with the SEALs in mind, the Smith & Wesson Model 76 is a very close duplicate of the proven Swedish K design. The magazines are almost interchangeable between the two weapons and the overall features are very similar.

One significant change in the Smith & Wesson Model 76 over the Swedish K is the S&W weapon incorporates a selector lever. Where the Swedish K fires full-auto only, the Model 76 can be set to semi or full automatic. In the S&W weapon, the selector can also be set on safe while the safety on the Swedish K was a notch up into which the cocking lever could be moved.

The receiver of the Model 76 is made of thick-walled steel tubing with the additional housing parts welded on to it. Early model weapons have a bare barrel sticking forward from the barrel collar. Later production model weapons had a distinctive perforated barrel jacket. The barrel jacket was intended to help protect an operator from the hot barrel while still allowing free circulation of air for cooling. The high cyclic rate of fire of the Model 76 helped make the weapon popular for its fast volume of fire, but also quickly heated up the barrel.

The S&W Model 76 was type classified by the Navy as the Gun, Submachine, 9 millimeter, Mark 24 Mod 0 on 24 March, 1970. In addition to having four magazines issued with the weapon, a suppressor and ported barrel were also included for each SEAL Mark 24. Mounting the suppressor onto the Mark 24 just required the operator to unscrew the barrel collar and jacket from the front of the receiver, remove the barrel, insert the ported barrel, and screw on the suppressor in place of the barrel jacket.

The ported barrel of the Mark 24 has eight 0.093 inch

The SEAL to the right of the picture is resting while operating with a group of Australian SAS troopers in Vietnam. The weapon the SEAL is holding is the seldom seen Australian F1 9mm submachine gun. The magazine of this weapon cannot be seen in this photo due to the F1 feeding from a vertical magazine extending from the top of the receiver. The pad taped to the right side of the buttstock, visible at the bottom center of this photo, is a medium battle dressing. In other publications, this weapon has been mistakenly identified as a British Sterling L2 series submachine gun. It was submachine guns like this that the Ingram series was designed to replace.
PHOTO CREDIT: FRANK THORNTON COLLECTION

holes drilled into the barrel one inch in front of the chamber at a 30 degree angle to the bore and reduced standard 9mm ammunition to subsonic velocities. The suppressor body was sealed and required almost no maintenance by the operator. In addition, the suppressor was made of stainless steel, minimizing problems with corrosion. The sights of the Mark 24 are both mounted on the receiver body and no sighting change was required when the suppressor was installed.

Smith and Wesson only produced about 6,000 Model 76 submachine guns before they suspended production on July 5, 1976. The weapon remained with the Teams throughout the 1970's and into the 1980's. Replacement parts were getting scarce by the early 1980's and SEAL Team One contracted with a manufacturer to produce a number of much-needed parts. By the late 1980's the last of the Mark 24 Mod 0 submachine guns were out of the SEAL inventory.

Submachineguns

TECHNICAL DATA—9mm Ingram M10
NSN 1005-01-061-2477
CARTRIDGE—9mm Parabellum (9x19mm)
OPERATION—Blowback
TYPE OF FIRE—Selective - semiautomatic/full automatic
RATE OF FIRE—Practical SS 40 rpm, A 96 rpm, Cyclic 950 to 1090 rpm
MUZZLE VELOCITY—1206 fps (366 m/s)
MUZZLE ENERGY—371 ft/lbs (503 J)
SIGHTS—Open, Aperture/post, Fixed, zeroed at 100 meters
FEED—32 round removable box magazine
WEIGHTS
WEAPON (EMPTY)—6.25 lbs (2.83 kg)
Suppressor 1.20 lbs (0.54 kg)
WEAPON (LOADED)—7.62 lbs (3.47 kg)
8.82 lbs (4 kg) w/suppressor
MAGAZINE (EMPTY)—0.55 lbs (0.25 kg)
MAGAZINE (LOADED)—1.37 lbs (0.62 kg)
SERVICE CARTRIDGE—M1 Ball 180 gr (11.7 g)
PROJECTILE—115 gr (7.5 g)
LENGTHS
WEAPON OVERALL—11.6/21.57 in (29.5/54.8 cm) w/o suppressor
21.5/31.4 in (54.5/79.8 cm) w/suppressor
BARREL—5.75 in (14.6 cm)
SUPPRESSOR LENGTH—11.44 in 29.1 cm)
SUPPRESSOR DIAMETER—2.13 in (5.4 cm)
SIGHT RADIUS—8.27 in (21 cm)

TECHNICAL DATA—Ingram M10
CARTRIDGE—.45 ACP (11.43x23mm)
OPERATION—Blowback
TYPE OF FIRE—Selective - semiautomatic/full automatic fire
RATE OF FIRE—Practical SS 40 rpm, A 90 rpm, Cyclic 950 to 1145 rpm
MUZZLE VELOCITY—919 fps (280 m/s)
MUZZLE ENERGY—431 ft/lbs (584 J)
SIGHTS—Open, Aperture/post, Fixed zeroed at 100 meters
FEED—30 round removable box magazine (modified US M3 magazine)
WEIGHTS
WEAPON (EMPTY)—6.25 lbs (2.83 kg)
Suppressor 1.2 lbs (0.54 kg)
WEAPON (LOADED)—8.42 lbs (3.82 kg)
9.62 lbs (4.36 kg) w/suppressor
MAGAZINE (EMPTY)—0.75 lb (0.340 kg)
MAGAZINE (LOADED)—2.17 lb (0.98 kg)
SERVICE CARTRIDGE—M1911 Ball 331 gr (21.4 g)
PROJECTILE—230 grains (15.2 g)
LENGTHS
WEAPON OVERALL—11.6/21.57 in (29.5/54.8 cm) w/o suppressor
21.5/31.4 in (54.5/79.8 cm) w/suppressor
BARREL—5.75 in (14.6 cm)
SUPPRESSOR LENGTH—11.44 in 29.1 cm)
SUPPRESSOR DIAMETER—2.13 in (5.4 cm)
SIGHT RADIUS—8.27 in (21 cm)

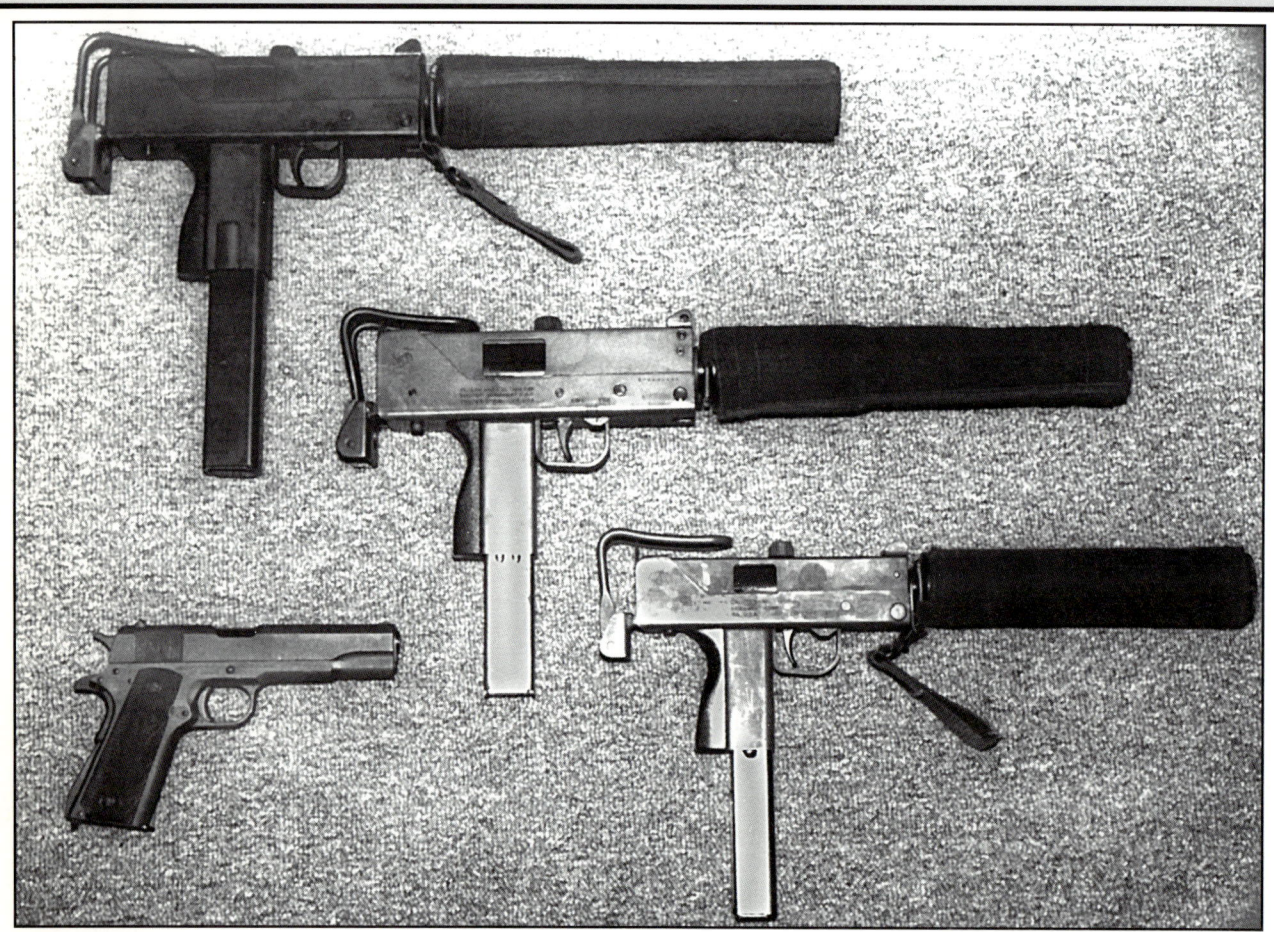

A trio of the best known of the Ingram submachine guns complete with suppressors. The upper right weapon is the Ingram M10 chambered in .45 ACP (11.43x23mm). The center weapon is the M10 chambered for the 9mm parabellum round (9x19mm). The bottom right weapon is the smaller Ingram M11 chambered for the .380 ACP (9x17mm). The pistol at the bottom left is an M1911A1 showing the comparative size of the Ingram family to a standard handgun. All of the weapons have their stocks folded and bolts cocked to the rear, ready to fire.
PHOTO CREDIT: KEVIN DOCKERY/KNIGHT ARMAMENT COMPANY

Special Weapons

In the 1970's, a SEAL tries out a suppressed Ingram submachine gun from the assault position at the range. The weapon is an Ingram M10 chambered for .45 ACP. The SEAL has the sliding stock extended and braced under his right arm. His left hand is holding the Sionics suppressor and he has just completed a short burst, three fired casings being in the air above the weapon.
PHOTO CREDIT: UDT-SEAL MUSEUM

INGRAM M10 9MM AND 45ACP

By the early 1970's, the SEAL Teams were looking for an additional 9mm submachine gun to supplement the Smith and Wesson Model 76's on hand. A very compact submachine gun, almost a machine pistol, had been on the U.S. arms market for a few years and was examined by the SEALs. The weapon was the Ingram Model 10 in 9mm parabellum. The weapon itself was not exactly new to the SEALs as at least two of their number had examined one in mid-1967.

> "Frankford Arsenal gave R— and I the opportunity to fire the first small Ingram submachine gun. 'Nice weapon,' we said, 'But it needs a front strap to give you something to hold on to.'"

The weapon examined was probably M10 9mm gun number 2 which had been purchased by the US Army and was at Frankford Arsenal in Philadelphia for further study. Gordon Ingram, the designer of the M10, later added a web strap to the front of the compact weapon to give it an additional handhold.

Third generation submachine guns are advances on the second generation models with emphasis being placed on reducing overall size and weight. The main identifying feature of a third-generation weapon is its use of a telescoping bolt. In a telescoping bolt, instead of the breech face being on the end of the bolt, it is further back inside of the bolt body. With the bolt face inside of the bolt body, part of the mass of the bolt surrounds and telescopes on the barrel. With the bolt wrapping itself around the barrel, the weight of the bolt can be kept high enough for safe blowback operation while shortening the overall length of the weapon.

The Ingram is a third generation submachine gun and a particularly compact example of the type. The single pistol grip acts as the magazine well, maintaining the center of balance of the weapon just above the grip. The web strap just below the muzzle of the Ingram acts as a forward grip to keep the non-firing hand from straying in front of the barrel. Bracing the M10 against the shoulder is possible, but not very comfortable, by using the short sliding stock attached to the back of the weapon.

The receiver of the M10 is square in cross section and made of stamped, sheet metal parts. The bolt of the Ingram is an investment casting, which helps keep the overall cost of the weapon down. The short bolt travel, relatively light bolt, and small recoil spring of the M10 combine to give the weapon a very high cyclic rate of fire. The 9mm M10 cycles at 1,050 rounds per minute and the .45 ACP version, built on the same receiver, cycles at 1,145 rounds per minute.

The very high cyclic rate of the Ingram makes it a high

Submachineguns

Dressed in first-pattern desert camouflage, this SEAL is shoulder-firing a 9mm Ingram M10 submachine gun. The bolt of the weapon is forward indicating that it is uncocked and not ready to fire. With his right hand holding the pistol grip, this SEAL is pulling down on the muzzle strap of the Ingram with his left hand. Sticking out from where he has it slung across his back can be seen the front portion of the 40mm M79 grenade launcher that this SEAL is also armed with.
PHOTO CREDIT: SPECIAL OPERATIONS COMMAND PAO

A cutaway 9mm Ingram M10. The bolt is drawn back to its cocked position and the main spring, visible through the notches at the top and rear of the weapon, compressed. The small switch above and in front of the trigger is the selector lever, set to semiautomatic on this example.
PHOTO CREDIT: KEVIN DOCKERY/KNIGHT ARMAMENT COMPANY

volume of fire weapon but has a drawback in that the magazine can be emptied in under two seconds. For breaking contact with an enemy, such a high volume of fire has some distinct advantages, and this was one of the reasons the weapon appealed to the SEALs. Another reason was one of the accessories that had already been designed for the weapon.

When Gordon Ingram went to Sionics Inc. in 1969 to complete the design of the submachine gun that would bear his name, the company was already producing a line of suppressors for the US government. Prior to the Ingram submachine gun being ready to go into production in 1970, the company changed its name to the Military Armament Corporation (MAC). When first marketed, the Ingram weapons were offered along with a MAC designed suppressor specifically engineered to the different calibers of Ingrams available. Each Ingram M10 submachine gun had a short length of screw thread at the muzzle of the weapon in order to accept the MAC suppressor.

The internal design of the MAC suppressor was quite complicated. The different parts of the system had been developed and used by Sionics Inc. for a number of years and had been field-tested in Vietnam on the M16 and M14 rifles. As in the Sionic rifle caliber suppressors, the M10 suppressor is a muzzle blast device only and does not effect the velocity of the fired projectile.

The M10 suppressor has two chambers, much as in the earlier Bell Labs M3 OSS suppressor. The rear tube of the suppressor is a large 2 inch diameter by 3.75 inch long expansion chamber with a perforated barrel extension running down its center. The rear portion of the barrel extension is a threaded sleeve that fits over the muzzle of the weapon. At the front of the barrel extension is a perforated reducing bushing that threads onto the extension and clamps the rear tube between itself and the rear sleeve.

Contained within the rear tube and secured by the two end pieces are several hundred "baffles", actually uncrimped lightweight metal eyelets. The eyelets act as a heat diffuser, cooling and slowing the initial blast of propellant gas. After the projectile has gone through the rear diffuser tube, it passes into the front suppressor tube. The hot gases following the projectile are constantly expanding and, after initial passage through the diffuser tube, pass through the reduction bushing. The reduction bushing has a twelve radial 0.188 inch holes drilled around the central tube. The hot gasses are further slowed down as they bleed through the smaller radial holes as well as the large central projectile hole.

In the 7 inch long, 1.5 inch inside diameter suppressor tube is first a conical baffle and then two spiral diffuser assemblies. The baffle is a hollow disk with a conical central protrusion surrounding the projectile hole. The action of the baffle is to further trap and diffuse the propellant gases while also absorbing some of their heat.

The two spiral diffusers in front of the baffle disk are mirror images of each other. Both diffusers are aluminum spiral helixes about 2 inches long, one having a left hand spiral and the other a right hand spiral. A hole goes

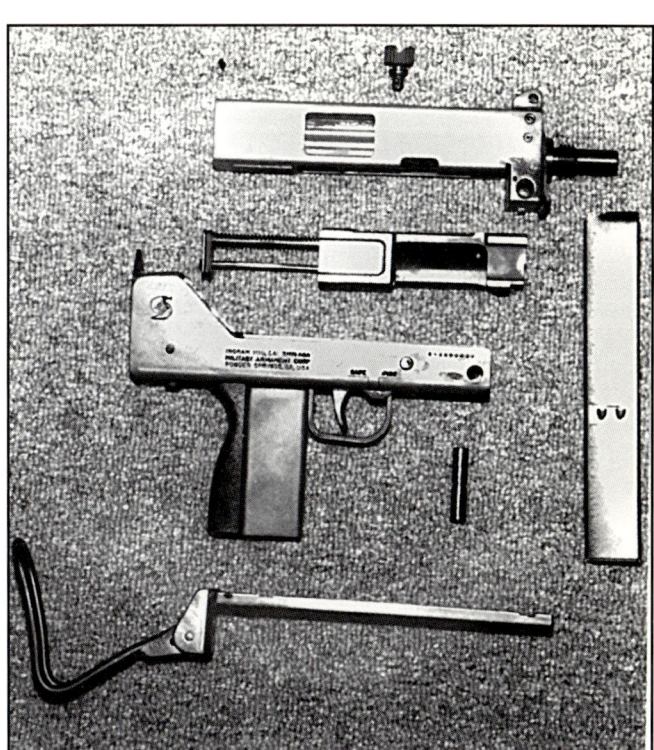

A right-side view of a field-stripped 9mm Ingram Model 10. The small part at the top of the picture is the cocking handle directly above its slot in the barrel and upper receiver group. The center part is the bolt assembly showing the cutout portion of the bolt that clears ejected brass. Visible at the back of the bolt assembly is the small rubber buffer pad and the mainspring around its guide rod. The thin rod below the mainspring is the ejector rod. The short section of rod in front of the magazine housing/pistol grip of the receiver is the receiver pin that fits into the open hole at the front of the receiver and locks the upper receiver group in place. To the right is a standard 32-round box magazine. At the bottom of the picture is the stock assembly with the wire form butt pivoted into the open position.
PHOTO CREDIT: KEVIN DOCKERY/KNIGHT ARMAMENT COMPANY

through the center of each diffuser to allow for the passage of the projectile and 0.125 inch holes are spaced 90 degrees apart between each vane to aid in gas dispersion. The reason behind the spirals is that they present a very large surface area to the propellant gases to help cool and slow them. The two different spirals theoretically cause an additional slight slowing of the propellant gases as they change direction.

Holding the diffusers in place is an "encapsulator" containing a single flexible 1/4 inch thick plastic wipe with a central 1/4 inch hole. Holding the encapsulator in place is the end cap also with two plastic wipes. The end cap wipes are spaced 1/2 inch apart and are of the same material and design as the wipe in the encapsulator.

As the M10 suppressor absorbs a great deal of the heat

These two SEALs, on special duty, are both armed with standard Uzi submachine guns. Given their casual stance and attire, the men are probably checking out the weapons at some form of firing range. Note the Uzi magazine in the gloved left hand of the SEAL to the right.
PHOTO CREDIT: UDT-SEAL MUSEUM

This technician at the Naval Weapons Support Center in Crane, Indiana is range testing a mini-Uzi submachine gun with an attached sound suppressor on the muzzle. Numbers of weapons like this are tested and evaluated at Crane before they go on to the Teams or other Navy units.
PHOTO CREDIT: US NAVY

A right-side view of the mini-Uzi submachine gun. The two angular notches at the muzzle of the weapon act as compensators, helping to hold the muzzle down on full automatic fire. The single-strut folding stock is in the folded position along the side of the weapon. The buttplate of the stock can be used as a forward handgrip in this folded condition. No magazine is in the magazine well underneath the pistol grip but the bolt of the weapon is drawn back, ready for firing. The small rectangular protrusion behind the upper portion of the pistol grip is the grip safety. Unless the grip safety is firmly held in the forward position, the bolt cannot be released and the weapon will not fire. The Uzi and mini-Uzi are not standard issue in the teams, but are sometimes used for special assignments.
PHOTO CREDIT: KEVIN DOCKERY

from the propellant gases, the exterior of the tubes becomes very hot. To protect the operator, the outside of the suppressor is covered with an insulating, heat-resistant Nomex sleeve.

Using the suppressor with the M10 submachine gun cuts down on the sound of firing considerably. At a distance, the weapon is unlikely to be noticed. If the sound of firing the suppressed Ingram is recognized for what it is, the suppressor makes the location of the firer very hard to point out. By using subsonic 9mm ammunition, the weapon is even quieter as the sonic crack of the projectile is eliminated.

Though the Ingram was a very compact and easy to carry weapon, it had the drawback of relatively poor accuracy. Jokingly called the "phone booth gun" by some Special Forces troopers, the general opinion was that you had to be inside of a phone booth, along with your target, to be sure of hitting it with the rapid firing little Ingram. But for a SEAL scout swimmer, the size of the Ingram was what gave it an advantage. And when used with its suppressor, the little M10 could put out a fast hail of bullets, helping a SEAL break contact and withdraw from an unwanted conflict.

For most reconnaissance work, contact with the enemy is something to be avoided if at all possible. But if contact is inevitable, the SEAL philosophy is to put out the greatest volume of fire possible in the shortest time. That philosophy, along with close-in personal defense, is exactly what the Ingram was designed for.

With the end of the 1970's a new mission for the SEALs arose, and with it a need for new hardware. Terrorism on an international scale had been building in intensity during the 1970's and a new force of counter-terrorist units were needed to combat the threat. Most of the Free World's counter-terrorist units were taken from the ranks of elite military services. The SAS in Great Britain, GSG-9 in West Germany, SEAL Team Six and Special Forces Operational Detachment Delta in the United States are all examples of the military response to global terrorism.

One of the most highly visible early actions of a counter-terrorist unit took place in Great Britain in 1980. The Iranian Embassy in London was seized by a number of terrorists and, when the situation was decided to warrant it, the SAS Counter Revolutionary Warfare (CRW) units were ordered in.

Plainly visible in the photographs taken by the press of Operation Nimrod on 5 May 1980 are the members of the SAS Pagoda Teams, their arms and equipment. That the Heckler and Koch MP5A3 was the primary weapon of the CRW troops could be clearly seen in the striking videos and still photographs of the operation. Though not as widely shown, an earlier use of the MP5 weapon had shown its capabilities in a counter-terrorist operation. When the German GSG-9 group attacked the terrorist-held Lufthansa airliner at Mogadishu, Somalia on 17 October 1977, it was not only the first time stun grenades were used against terrorists, but it was the blooding of the MP5 as well.

Submachineguns

> "When the SEALs were looking to equip their new counter-terrorist unit, input from many of the already established units was encouraged and accepted."

TECHNICAL DATA—Heckler & Koch MP5SD3 [MP5SD6]
NSN 1005-01-144-3036 (MP5SD3)
CARTRIDGE—9mm Parabellum (9x19mm)
OPERATION—Roller locked delayed blowback
TYPE OF FIRE—Selective - semiautomatic/full automatic, [w/ three-round controlled burst]
RATE OF FIRE—Practical SS 40 rpm, A 100 rpm, Cyclic 800 rpm
MUZZLE VELOCITY—935 fps (285 m/s)
MUZZLE ENERGY—275 ft/lbs (380 J)
SIGHTS—Open, Aperture/blade, Adjustable
FEED—30 round removable box magazine. Double magazine clip available to hold two magazines together for quick reloading. Wt 0.36 lbs (0.16 kg)
WEIGHTS
WEAPON (EMPTY)—7.50 lbs (3.40 kg)
WEAPON (LOADED)—8.69 lbs (3.94 kg) with 1-30 round magazine
10.24 lbs (4.64 kg) with 2-30 round magazines & clip
MAGAZINE (EMPTY)—30 round .375 lb (0.17 kg)
Two 30 round mags w/clip 1.11 lbs (0.50 kg)
MAGAZINE (LOADED)—30 round 1.19 lb (0.54 kg)
Two 30 round mags w/clip 2.74 lbs (1.24 kg)
SERVICE CARTRIDGE—M882 Ball 190 gr. (12.3 g)
PROJECTILE—124 gr. (8 g)
LENGTHS
WEAPON OVERALL—23.97/30.42 in (61/78 cm)
BARREL—5.73 in (14.6 cm)
SUPPRESSOR LENGTH—12 in (30.5 cm)
SIGHT RADIUS—13.38 in (34 cm)

> "The accuracy and reliability of the H&K MP5 submachine gun are what has made the weapon so popular with the SEALs."

TECHNICAL DATA—Heckler & Koch MP5A3 [MP5A5]
CARTRIDGE—9mm Parabellum (9x19mm)
OPERATION—Roller locked delayed blowback
TYPE OF FIRE—Selective - semiautomatic/full automatic, [w/ three-round controlled burst]
RATE OF FIRE—Practical SS 40 rpm, A 100 rpm, Cyclic 800 rpm
MUZZLE VELOCITY—1312 fps (400 m/s)
MUZZLE ENERGY—474 ft/lbs (643 J)
SIGHTS—Open, Aperture/blade, Adjustable
FEED—30 round removable box magazine. Double magazine clip available to hold two magazines together for quick reloading. Wt 0.36 lbs (0.16 kg)
WEIGHTS
WEAPON (EMPTY)—6.34 lbs (2.88 kg)
WEAPON (LOADED)—7.53 lbs (3.42 kg) with 1-30 round magazine
9.08 lbs (4.12 kg) with 2-30 round magazines & clip
MAGAZINE (EMPTY)—30 round .375 lb (0.17 kg)
Two 30 round mags w/clip 1.11 lbs (0.50 kg)
MAGAZINE (LOADED)—30 round 1.19 lb (0.54 kg)
Two - 30 round mags w/clip 2.74 lbs (1.24 kg)
SERVICE CARTRIDGE—M882 Ball 190 gr. (12.3 g)
PROJECTILE—124 gr. (8 g)
LENGTHS
WEAPON OVERALL—19.29/25.98 in (49/66 cm)
BARREL—8.85 in (22.5 cm)
SIGHT RADIUS—13.38 in (34 cm)

TECHNICAL DATA—Heckler & Koch MP5K [MP5KA4]
NSN 1005-01-259-2895 (MP5KA4)
CARTRIDGE—9mm Parabellum (9x19mm)
OPERATION—Roller locked delayed blowback
TYPE OF FIRE—Selective - semiautomatic/full automatic, [w/ three-round controlled burst]
RATE OF FIRE—Practical SS 40 rpm, A 100 rpm, Cyclic 800 rpm
MUZZLE VELOCITY—1230 fps (375 m/s)
MUZZLE ENERGY—412 ft/lbs (570 J)
SIGHTS—Open, Aperture/blade, Adjustable [Square-notch/blade, Fixed]
FEED—15 or 30 round removable box magazine. Double magazine clip available to hold two magazines together for quick reloading. Wt 0.36 lbs (0.16 kg)
WEIGHTS
WEAPON (EMPTY)—4.41 lbs (2.0 kg)
WEAPON (LOADED)—5.6 lbs (2.54 kg) w/ 1-30 round magazine
MAGAZINE (EMPTY)—30 round - .375 lb (0.17 kg)
15 round - 0.265 lb (0.12 kg)
Two - 30 round mags w/clip 1.11 lbs (0.50 kg)
MAGAZINE (LOADED)—30 round - 1.19 lb (0.54 kg)
15 round - 0.672 lb (0.305 kg)
Two 30 round mags w/clip 2.74 lbs (1.24 kg)
SERVICE CARTRIDGE—M882 Ball 190 gr. (12.3 g)
PROJECTILE—124 gr. (8 g)
LENGTHS
WEAPON OVERALL—12.8 in (32.5 cm)
BARREL—4.5 in (11.5 cm)
SIGHT RADIUS—10.25 in (26 cm) [7.48 in (19 cm)]

H&K MP5A Series

When the SEALs were looking to equip their new counter-terrorist unit, input from many of the already established units was encouraged and accepted. The German GSG-9 group worked closely with the SEALs of Team Six and the German group highly recommended the Heckler and Koch submachine gun family. The MP5A3 was already in the US inventory in small numbers by the late 1970's. A number of the H&K weapons had been purchased by the Department of Defense for Army Special Forces, Rangers, and other special operations units. SEAL Team Six ordered there weapons from the H&K facility in Oberndorf, West Germany. Assistance from the GSG-9 group expedited the delivery of the weapons to Team Six

The Heckler and Koch MP5 submachine gun is part of a family of weapons with a commonality of operating systems. Most of the standard H&K small arms resemble each other in their general operation, controls, and sighting systems. The basic operating system of the H&K small arms family centers around the concept of delayed blowback through roller-locking.

In the closing months of World War II the German military was developing a new assault rifle, the Stg 45(m), with the Mauser developed Gerat 06H being the most likely contender. After the war and the fall of Nazi Germany the designers of the Gerat 06 went to the CETME arms works in Spain where the design was perfected.

The Stg 45(m) utilized much the same Stecke roller locking system of the battle proved MG-42 light machinegun but was chambered for the 7.92x33mm Kurz assault rifle cartridge. The weapon first produced by CETME was chambered for a round of ammunition that was never widely accepted and soon died out. The basic CETME design was modified and perfected for use with the new NATO 7.62x51mm round and was submitted for trials with the new German army.

The rechambering and redesign of the CETME was accomplished in Germany by the new Heckler and Koch company as their first major weapons development. The new rifle passed all tests and was adopted by the German military as the G3.

The roller locking system does not actually lock the bolt to the barrel at the moment of firing. Instead it is a form of delayed blowback that carries with it some substantial problems. Without the camming action of a rotating bolt to help initiate extraction, fired cases tend to stick in the chamber. This problem is solved in the H&K system by the chamber being cut with a series of longitudinal flutes along two thirds of its length. The flutes allow the hot propellant gases to flow along the body of the cartridge along the area of most expansion. This system "floats" the casing on a layer of gas and eases extraction.

The fluted chamber/gas flotation system eliminates much of the sticking case problem but the roller locking system also has a very violent case ejection. Casings ejected from a H&K weapon are often dented and have a series of very distinguishing marks on them indicating the type of weapon from which they were fired. The violent case ejection is not considered a problem among operators who use the H&K weapons, as long as you're not on the right side of someone else who is firing one.

The heart of the roller locking system works is the two movable rollers in the sides of the bolt. The rollers are driven partway into locking recesses in the barrel extension by the forward movement of the wedge shaped locking piece that carries the firing pin. When the locking piece has moved forward enough to allow the firing pin to reach the chambered cartridge, the rollers are pressing securely into their respective recesses, blocking any rearward movement of the bolt.

The rearward pressure of the cartridge being fired presses against the bolt and drives the rollers against the rear of the recesses in the barrel extension. The rear surfaces of the barrel extension recesses are slightly angled and allow the rollers to force themselves inward against the locking piece. The force of the rollers drive the locking piece backwards but at a great mechanical disadvantage to the pressure on the rollers. The disadvantage the rollers have to work against slow the opening of the breech until the bullet has left the barrel and pressures have dropped to safe levels.

Inertia of the bolt carrier continues the rearward travel of the bolt, extracting and ejecting the fired casing. As the bolt carrier continues its rearward movement, it recocks the hammer. When the bolt carrier starts to move forward under the pressure of the recoil spring, the bolt strips a fresh round from the magazine and chambers it. As the bolt carrier closes, it forces the locking piece forward, securing the system. If the trigger has remained pulled, the bolt carrier trips the hammer release as the bolt goes fully into battery.

The roller locking, delayed blowback system has been applied by Heckler and Koch to a large family of weapons including light machineguns, rifles, submachine guns, and pistols. With the roller locking system eliminating the need for the heavy bolt found in most blowback operated submachine guns, the MP5 is lighter than many weapons of its class. But the major advantage is that the MP5 weapons all fire from the closed-bolt position.

Firing from a closed bolt eliminates the sight-jarring slam of a heavy bolt moving forward before the first round is fired as happens in an open-bolt system. This means the MP5 has excellent accuracy for the first round fired in a burst. It is the inherent accuracy in the system that makes the MP5 weapon so popular among the world's counter-terrorist forces. The accuracy and reliability of the H&K MP5 submachine gun are what has made the weapon so popular with the SEALs.

Another point of appeal in the MP5's favor is all of the variations that the basic weapon is offered in. Over a dozen different variations exist, all using the same basic action and operating system. This commonality of operation allows quick familiarity with a different member of the weapons family by anyone trained in one weapon's operation. A partial listing of all of the Heckler and Koch MP5 weapons includes the following;

HK-54 - This was the original designation for the first

Submachineguns

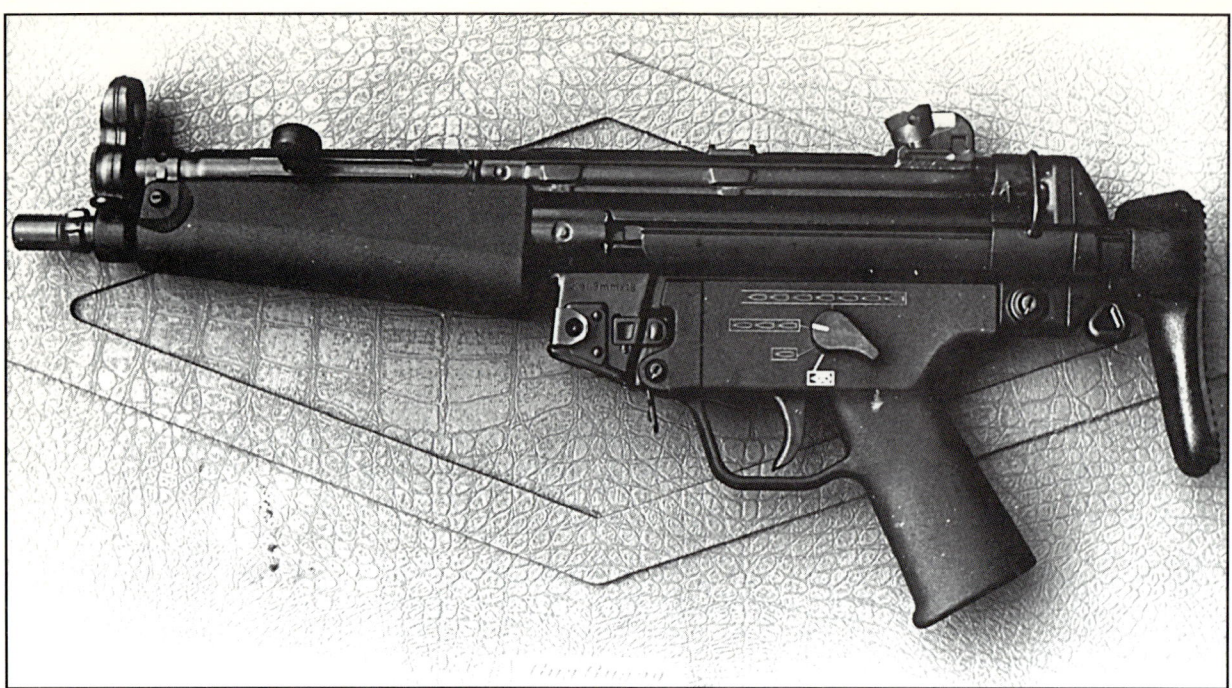

A left-side view of an H&K MP5A6 submachine gun. The designation A6 indicates that this specimen has a sliding stock, collapsed in this picture, and a 3-round controlled burst trigger group. Selector settings on this specimen are shown by pictograph. The white line on the selector lever is pointing to a red box holding the silhouette of three bullets, indicating that a single 3-round burst will be fired for each pull of the trigger.
PHOTO CREDIT: KEVIN DOCKERY

An MP5SD3 fitted with a Navy trigger group, designated an MP5SD-N when assembled with a stainless steel suppressor and tritium-dot front sight. The trigger groups on all of the MP5 submachine guns can be exchanged as desired. The original MP5SD weapons in SEAL hands had the 3-round controlled burst trigger group which was disliked by most of the operators. On this specimen, the selector lever is set to the white box holding a single bullet with an X over it, the pictogram for safe. In addition, this specimen is loaded with a pair of 30-round magazines held together with a dual magazine clamp. A telescopic sight in a removable H&K scope mount is secured on the weapon for additional precision when shooting. This assembly is well-suited for close in sniping as done in the Teams.
PHOTO CREDIT: KEVIN DOCKERY

submachine gun made by H&K and was later modified to the MP5 configuration.

MP5A1 - This model has a receiver cap and no buttstock giving it the shortest overall length of the standard MP5s.

MP5A2 - The standard MP5 with a fixed buttstock.

MP5A3 - The standard model fitted with a retractable sliding metal buttstock.

MP5A4 - The newer model MP5 with a fixed buttstock and a new trigger group among other improvements. The new trigger group allows semiautomatic fire, 3 round controlled bursts, or full automatic fire to be selected.

MP5A5 - The newer model MP5 with a retractable sliding metal buttstock and controlled burst trigger group.

MP5SD1 - The suppressed version of the MP5 with an integral suppressor and receiver cap.

MP5SD2 - The suppressed version with a fixed buttstock.

MP5SD3 - The suppressed version with a retractable metal stock.

MP5SD4 - The suppressed version with a receiver cap and controlled burst trigger group.

MP5SD5 - The suppressed version with a controlled burst trigger group and fixed buttstock.

MP5SD6 - Suppressed version with a controlled burst trigger group and retractable buttstock.

MP5K - The shortest MP5 with no buttstock and a vertical front grip as well as adjustable sights.

MP5KA1 - Shortened MP5 with, low, nonadjustable sights for maximum concealment.

MP5KA4 - Shortened MP5 with adjustable sights and controlled burst trigger group.

MP5KA5 - Shortened MP5 with the small nonadjustable sights and controlled burst trigger group.

In addition to the weapons listed, Heckler and Koch make a very comprehensive line of accessories for the MP5 weapon to which they are continually adding. At the present time the list includes the following: Magazine clips for holding two magazines together parallel to each other, blank firing adaptors, tear gas canister launchers, rifle grenade launchers, removable aiming point projectors, removable telescopic sights, two types of briefcases that can carry an MP5K and fire it while concealed, removable starlight scopes, a subcaliber device firing .22 long rifle ammunition that can be fitted to any standard MP5 and allow it to fire .22s instead of 9x19mm ammunition, an infrared sighting scope, a replacement front grip with a built in flashlight for aiming or illumination, and a miniature laser sight that is built into the weapon for use with night vision goggles.

Only a few of the accessories listed were available when the SEAL first started receiving the MP5 weapons. As their weapons began arriving from Germany, SEAL Team Six became the first SEAL team to use the MP5 as their standard weapon

The first model MP5 to see service with the SEALs of Team Six was the MP5A3. With its sliding stock, the MP5A3 makes a compact package for transportation when size is a consideration. The MP5A3 was first issued with what is called the "SEF" trigger group. In the MP5 system, the trigger group containing the complete trigger

Dressed and equipped for Close Quarters Battle (CQB), this SEAL walks across a beach during a demonstration. He is armed with an unloaded H&K MP5-N submachine gun fitted with a sound suppressor on the muzzle. Also on the MP5-N is an H&K R3/3 multipurpose sling, the square sliding buckle of which can be seen just above the rear sight of the weapon. At his right hip is a SIG-Sauer P226 pistol in a drop-leg assault holster. Directly in front of the holster, attached to the leg strap, is the rectangular pouch of an LM-1 Leatherman Tool. Behind the pistol holster is a day/night signal flare, either a Mark 13 or a Mark 124, attached to the sheath of a knife. His respirator is in a pouch at the small of his back and this SEAL is wearing modular body armor. His face covered by a black balaclava for flash protection. This SEAL is also wearing a PRO-TEC helmet. On top of the helmet is an SDU-5/E strobe light to identify the man to overhead aircraft. Lastly, he is wearing goggles for eye protection and the boom mike for his radio can be seen just in front of his mouth.
PHOTO CREDIT: KEVIN DOCKERY

mechanism, is removable from the weapon for cleaning. As new trigger groups have been developed, they can be added to earlier weapons in order to easily upgrade them.

The name SEF for the most common MP5 trigger group comes from the three letters imprinted on the frame sides, a white S and a red E and F. Since the H&K MP5 is originally a German weapon, the words the letters stand for are German. The S stands for Sicher (safe) with the white color indicating no fire. The E is for Einzelfeuer (single fire) and F indicates **Feuerstäßen** (bursts of fire). Both the E and F are printed in red

Submachineguns

This is a left-side view of the standard MP5K submachine gun loaded with a 30-round magazine. This specimen is fitted with the SEF trigger group which was on the first MP5 weapons examined by the SEALs. In the SEF trigger group the white S indicates safe, the red E semiautomatic fire, and the red F full automatic fire.
PHOTO CREDIT: HECKLER & KOCH USA

Keeping his eyes held low, this combat swimmer is coming ashore after having just left the water during a demonstration. His weapon is an H&K MP5K with its 30-round magazine additionally secured in place with tape for the demonstration. The open ejection port shows that the bolt of this weapon was removed for the public demonstration. Hanging from around his neck, just to the side of his chin, is this SEAL's diving mask. Hanging low on his chest is the hard black casing of a Draeger LAR-V rebreather. The green-painted oxygen tank of the Draeger can be seen underneath the casing of the device with its chromed valve on the right side where it can be easily reached with the operator's hand. This SEAL is wearing a standard set of camouflage BDUs and boonie hat over his neoprene wetsuit and hood.
PHOTO CREDIT: KEVIN DOCKERY

indicating they are live firing positions.

The SEF trigger group also holds the pistol grip. The SEF pistol grip has finger swells on the front strap and a thumb rest of the left upper side for the thumb of the right hand. The fire selector lever is on the left side of the trigger group, just above the trigger itself. The location of the fire selector lever makes it very easy to operate with just the thumb of the firing hand. The butt end of the fire selector shaft has an indicator notch cut into it where it is exposed on the right side of the trigger group. The SEF markings are duplicated on the right side of the trigger group so that the setting of the fire selector lever can be seen at a glance.

The front handguard is a slim, deeply checkered design that inserts into the frame just forward of the magazine well and is held in place by a locking pin just behind and below the front sight. Above the front handguard, on the left side of the weapon, is the cocking lever. Drawing the lever to the rear and releasing it loads the MP5 and cocks the firing mechanism.

When the last shot is fired by the MP5, the bolt does not stay locked to the rear and closes on the empty chamber. By drawing the cocking lever to the rear and pushing it up, the lever can be seated in a notch, locking the bolt open. As the MP5 is fired, the cocking lever does not reciprocate with the bolt and remains in the forward position unless drawn back by hand.

The muzzle of the standard MP5 series has three lugs running concentrically around the barrel. The lugs act as a locking surface for mounting several of the muzzle devices offered by H&K. These devices include a blank firing adaptor, a spigot-type rifle grenade launcher, and a flash hider. The only one of the muzzle devices commonly seen used by the SEALs is the flash hider, used on all the standard MP5's issued in the Teams.

On the left side of the magazine well of the MP5 is a rear-pointing spring metal hook. The hook is only used as part of the H&K multipurpose carry sling. A sliding square buckle clips into the hook on the MP5. With the sling properly adjusted, the MP5 can be carried across the chest in a "port arms" position with the muzzle tilted up and to the left. By just grabbing the weapon by the handguard and pistol grip and pushing the weapon away from the body, the sling loop pops off the clip, releasing the weapon. The MP5 can be easily carried and quickly brought to the shoulder with this method. In addition, if the weapon is dropped after being shouldered, the sling remains attached and holds the MP5 down by the operators side.

The rear sight of the MP5 is adjustable by being loosened with a screwdriver and moved into position. Though the drum-type rear sight has several different sized holes, they all go to the same point of aim with the front sight post. The different sized holes can be changed by the operator to account for different levels of light as well as where the operator places his head on the weapon's stock. In front of the rear sight are two mounting flats on the upper part of the receiver. The two flats allow the standard H&K scope mount to be securely fastened to the weapon. In addition to the scope, other aiming devices such as lights or night vision devices can also be mounted on the MP5.

H&K MP5SD5

The other full-size MP5 first used in the Teams by Team Six was the suppressed MP5SD3. The SD series of MP5s are the standard weapon fitted with an integral barrel suppressor. The designation SD stands for **Schalldämpfer**, the German word for silencer. A very popular weapon for covert operations with the Teams, the MP5SD weapons are considered some of the best suppressed submachine guns in the world.

The MP5SD is intended to be used with NATO standard 9mm ammunition. To eliminate the sound of the sonic crack of the bullet, the SD has a ported barrel to limit the velocity of the projectile to below the speed of sound. A series of thirty 0.118 inch (3mm) holes are drilled into the bore of the barrel a short distance in front of the chamber.

The body of the suppressor is a 12 inch long aluminum tube, threaded at the breech end and covered over at the muzzle with a convex cap. The suppressor fits over the barrel and screws into a threaded seat at the front of the receiver. To insure a gas-tight seal, a rubber O-ring at the base of the threaded section seats itself just into the

During a demonstration at the UDT-SEAL Museum, this SEAL rapidly descends from a flagpole he climbed almost as quickly. He is dressed for close quarters battle in black fatigues and balaclava hood. His weapon is an H&K MP5-N fitted with a model 629 dual-switch tactical lighted forearm and a flash hider. One of the two switches for the flashlight underneath the flash hider is the light-colored band around the pistol grip. The MP5-N is hanging down across this SEAL's back from an H&K R3/3 multipurpose sling. Just visible on his left hip is a 3-cell magazine carrier.
PHOTO CREDIT: UDT-SEAL MUSEUM

Submachineguns

This SEAL gives a thumbs-up during boarding drills aboard the **USS JOSHUA HUMPHREYS** *while in the Red Sea during Operation Desert Storm. He is dressed for Close Quarters Battle (CQB) with a tactical assault vest holding much of his equipment and spare ammunition. He is armed with a Heckler and Koch MP5-N submachine gun fitted with a removable flash hider on the muzzle and slung to be operated left-handed. The MP5-N is loaded with a pair of 30-round magazines held together with a double magazine clamp. The clamp allows two magazines to be securely held together with both magazines facing up for a quick reload. The white plastic loops below the weapon are plastic wire ties held to a carabiner ring. The ties are used a quick "handcuffs" for securing prisoners. The large pouch strapped to this SEAL's right thigh is the carrier for his M17A1 gas mask.*
PHOTO CREDIT: US NAVY

Special Weapons

suppressor base.

The rear section of the suppressor body, the part that surrounds the barrel, is an expansion chamber for the bleed holes on the barrel. From the muzzle forward, the suppressor has an internal baffle assembly made from a section of square metal tubing. In the German patent drawings for the SD suppressor, the square tubing is shown having four baffles made up of two opposite walls of the tube cut free and folded in towards the centerline of the tube. The cut sections form a V-shape with the apex of the V pointing at the chamber. The center of the V baffle has a bullet clearance hole for free passage of the projectile.

Each baffle in the suppressor alternates in orientation, rotating 90 degrees from the one in front and behind it. Surrounding the baffle tube assembly is an open space between the assembly and the suppressor body to allow the gases room to expand. As the propellant gases impinge on the suppressor baffles, they are forced to change direction and cool as they move across the metal.

The rear section of the MP5SD weapons are exactly the same as the regular MP5 weapons. The only internal action change in the SD weapons being a slightly different roller assembly to operate with the reduced gas pressure from the bled-off barrel. The front of the MP5SD receivers are modified to surround and protect the long suppressor tube. The insulated handgrip surrounding the suppressor frame is cylindrical in shape and ribbed for a better grip.

The designations of the MP5SD series follow the same order as the standard MP5's with the 1 suffix indicating no buttstock, only a receiver cap, the 2 being a fixed stock and the 3 being a sliding stock. All three of the weapons utilize the standard SEF trigger group. The MP5SD1 with its receiver cap is a very concealable version of the SD series but required a new method of supporting the weapon in order to be fired accurately.

The Heckler and Koch sling assembly fits on a sling swivel at the back of the receiver cap. By placing the sling around the body and over the shoulders, the MP5SD1 can be carried slung under one arm, muzzle down, and hidden beneath a long coat or jacket. By grabbing the weapon and pushing it forward, a properly adjusted sling will allow the weapon to be pushed out to the extent of the firers arm. Pushing the MP5SD1 hard against the sling, outwards from the body, braces the weapon for firing almost as much as pulling it back against a stock. The added weight of the suppressor stabilizes the weapon and holds the muzzle down on full automatic fire.

The above system of bracing the weapon with a sling has been adopted by some SEAL units as a way of quickly and accurately bringing an MP5SD3 into action from a slung position. The MP5SD3 has the sliding stock assembly which also incorporates a sling mounting point on its receiver housing.

H&K MP5KA5

The third basic type of MP5 used by the SEAL Teams is the MP5K. The MP5K, K for Kurz (short), is the shortest, most concealable member of the MP5 family. First obtained for the SEALs in Team Six, the MP5K was used for VIP protection missions where low-visibility

Standing at attention during a demonstration, this SEAL is dressed for Close Quarters Battle (CQB). His primary weapon is an H&K MP5-N submachine gun, fitted with a muzzle suppressor and R3/3 multipurpose sling. On his left hip is a 3-cell pouch for 30-round MP-5 magazines. He is wearing a black, modular armor vest with attachment sites for different pouches and containers. A black balaclava and goggles cover his face and eyes and his head is protected with a PRO-TEC helmet. This SEAL is wearing a pilot's flight coverall as a uniform and has a pair of black leather glove shells on his hands. PHOTO CREDIT: UDT-SEAL MUSEUM

armament was most needed.

The action of the MP5K is functionally and mechanically the same as the other MP5 weapons. The receiver of the MP5K is shorter than a standard MP5 receiver as there is no provision for the attachment of a shoulder stock. Instead of a stock assembly, the rear of the MP5K is closed off by a flush-fitting flat plate. In the center of the rear plate is a sling swivel loop for the attachment of a sling or other carrying harness. The two longitudinal guide grooves in the sides of the MP5K receiver are used on the full sized weapon as guides for the sliding stock.

Submachineguns

The H&K 54A1 submachine gun with its shoulder stock fully extended. This example is loaded with the special 50-round drum magazine developed as part of the HK54A1 project. This weapon may also use the standard 15 or 30-round magazines from the standard MP5 family. The selector lever is set to the red "3", indicating that the weapon will fire a 3-round burst for each pull of the trigger.
PHOTO CREDIT: KEVIN DOCKERY

TECHNICAL DATA — HK54A1
CARTRIDGE—9mm Parabellum (9x19mm)
OPERATION—Roller locked delayed blowback
TYPE OF FIRE—Selective - semiautomatic/three-round controlled burst/full automatic
RATE OF FIRE—Practical SS 40 rpm, A 100 rpm, Cyclic 800 rpm
MUZZLE VELOCITY—1300 fps (396 m/s) w/vent ports closed
960 fps (293 m/s) w/vent ports open (subsonic)
MUZZLE ENERGY—465 ft/lbs (631 J) standard
254 ft/lbs (344 J) subsonic
SIGHTS—Open, Aperture/blade, Adjustable
FEED—50 round removable spring-loaded drum magazine
WEIGHTS
WEAPON (EMPTY)—6.57 lbs (2.98 kg) w/o suppressor
7.49 lbs (3.4 kg) w/suppressor
Suppressor wt 0.92 lbs (0.42 kg)
WEAPON (LOADED)—9.42 lbs (4.27 kg) w/o suppressor
10.34 lbs (4.69 kg) w/suppressor
MAGAZINE (EMPTY)—1.49 lbs (.68 kg)
MAGAZINE (LOADED)—2.85 lbs (1.29 kg)
SERVICE CARTRIDGE—M882 Ball 190 gr. (12.3 g)
PROJECTILE—124 gr. (8 g)
LENGTHS
WEAPON OVERALL—16.19/24.25 in 41.1/61.6 cm) w/o suppressor
23.5/31.5 in (59.7/80 cm) w/suppressor
BARREL—7.06 in (17.9 cm)
SUPPRESSOR LENGTH—13.13 in (33.4 cm)
SUPPRESSOR DIAMETER—1.854 in (4.7 cm)
SIGHT RADIUS—12.75 in (32.4 cm)

The fully field-stripped HK54A1. The receiver is inverted at the bottom of the illustration with the complicated gas port selection mechanism shown just below the pistol grip of the trigger group.
PHOTO CREDIT: KEVIN DOCKERY

To further insure that a standard stock is not mounted on the MP5K, the rear of the two guide grooves are covered with a welded section of plate.

Since the MP5K has a shortened receiver, the bolt carrier and some other internal parts are modified from those of the standard model to operate in a shorter travel length. If a standard buttstock could be attached to the MP5K, the internal portion of the stock would interfere with the action of the weapon. The trigger group is not modified from the standard and the MP5K is fitted with the SEF group.

For added concealment, the MP5K can be loaded with the optional 15 round box magazine. The shorter length of the 15 round magazine does not protrude from the bottom of the weapon past the pistol grips and give the MP5K a very compact outline.

The main reduction in length on the MP5K is accomplished by shortening the barrel and front portion of the receiver. The very short barrel on the MP5K makes it a very real possibility that the hand of an operator could accidentally move in front of the muzzle while firing. To prevent this, the MP5K is fitted with a special short front handgrip with a vertical grip for the firers non-shooting hand. In addition to the vertical grip, the handguard has a downward protruding lug at the very front of the guard, just below the muzzle of the weapon. The lug helps prevent a hand from slipping up on the handgrip and moving in front of the weapon when the MP5K is recoiling. The muzzle of the MP5K is flush with the front of the weapon and none of the muzzle attachments of the standard MP5 weapons can be mounted on the K model.

As the barrel of the MP5K is shortened from the standard length, the travel of the cocking lever is also shortened. As in the other MP5s, the cocking lever can be pulled to the rear and pushed up into a notch to lock the bolt open. The MP5K uses the same adjustable sights as are found on the MP5 and MP5SD weapons. In addition to the sights, mounting lugs are found on the upper portion of the receiver for the attachment of various H&K aiming devices.

Two unusual accessories are available for the concealed carrying of an MP5K and have been used by Team Six while on escort operations. The two accessories are a hard-sided document case and a soft-sided leather attache case or tool bag. Both cases are designed to hold an MP5K loaded with a 30 round magazine, a spare 30 round magazine, and a cleaning kit. The camouflage cases both allow the weapon to be controllably fired while still secured inside of the case.

The hard-sided document case holds the MP5K in place with a clamp that locks down in the same position as an aiming device at the top of the receiver. A short muzzle guide is part of the case and reaches from the side of the case to around the muzzle of the MP5K. The handle of the case contains a safety catch and trigger. A mechanical linkage connects the handle trigger to the trigger of the MP5K.

With a loaded MP5K inside of the case, with its fire selector set to one of the fire positions, the weapon can be fired with reasonable accuracy by simply bracing the case. A shell deflector inside of the case prevents any ejected brass from jamming the weapon when it is fired. The case itself can be held in any position and fired as long as the safety catch is held back and the trigger on the inside of the handle pulled.

The soft-sided bag works in much the same way as the document case. The same clamp arrangement holds the MP5K in place, securely attached to the top cover of the bag. Instead of a trigger linkage, a slit on the side of the case allows the operator to slip his hand inside of the case and grasp the MP5K directly. A small tube connects the muzzle of the MP5K with the side of the bag, protecting the inside of the bag, and the operators hand, from the muzzle blast.

A spent casing deflector inside of the soft bag protects the operators hand by guiding the ejected brass forwards and down. In addition to the weapon being fired from inside of the bag, releasing the four snap-action connectors on the outside of the bag, two to a side, releases the entire top assembly. The top assembly, with the weapon securely clamped in place, can be pulled free of the carrying bag and held with both hands.

Because of its sophisticated operating system, successful closed-bolt firing, and that it is offered as part of a weapons family, the MP5 is considered a fourth generation submachine gun. Even with all of the points in favor of the MP5 series of weapons, there is considered to be room for improvement. Experimentation was sponsored by the Joint Services Small Arms Program (JSSAP) beginning in the early 1980's in order to identify what was desired in a submachine gun by all the services.

H&K 54A1

The requirements for a new submachine gun specified that the weapon should be able to be carried and used with only one hand. This would leave the operator with a free hand to control a descent rope, climb a shipboard ladder, or even simply open a door. In addition, the new weapon would accept a suppressor, be lighter and smaller than existing weapons, have improved first shot accuracy, full automatic and semiautomatic fire, be very controllable, and have a life expectancy of at least 10,000 rounds.

The Naval Weapons Support center at Crane, Indiana was tasked with guiding the development of what was now the JSSAP 6.2 Exploratory Development submachine gun project. Many of the characteristics of the desired weapon already existed in some form in the MP5 series.

H&K CONCEALMENT CARRIERS

Document case—17.24 x 4.25 x 12.67 inches (43.8 x 10.8 x 32.2 cm)
Weight (empty)—7.72 lbs (3.50 kg)
Weight (with MP5K with 30 rounds, spare 30 round magazine, cleaning kit)—14.88 lbs (6.75 kg)

Attache case (leather bag)—15.74 x 12.20 x 5.62 inches (40 x 31 x 14.3 cm)
Weight (empty)—6.39 lbs (2.90 kg)
Weight (with MP5K with 30 rounds, spare 30 round magazine, cleaning kit)—13.66 lbs (6.20 kg)

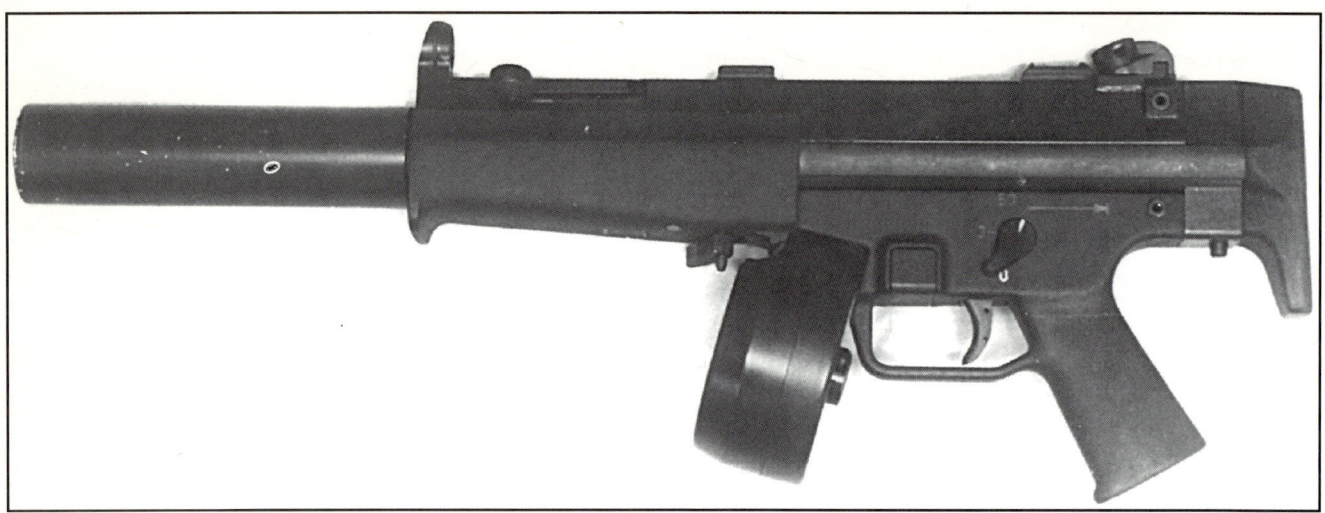

This is one of the rare HK54A1 submachine guns developed for possible use by the SEALs. This specimen is loaded with the 50-round drum magazine unique to the weapon. Behind the drum magazine and above the trigger guard is the square button of the ambidextrous magazine release. The trigger group has four control settings identified by a numeral and a fifth symbolized setting. The white 0 setting at the bottom is safe. Hidden underneath the end of the selector switch is the red number 1 indicating semiautomatic fire. The red number three indicates a mechanically controlled three round burst will be fired for each pull of the trigger. The red 50 is the setting for full automatic fire. The red arrow pointing to the flat line, the selection this specimen is set to, is the special "locked breech" setting. At the locked setting, only one round will be fired for each pull of the trigger and the cocking handle has to be manually drawn back to reload the weapon. This setting is to reduce the mechanical noise of the action when firing the weapon for maximum sound suppression. The small button behind the trigger group is the stock catch, the stock on this specimen being in the fully closed position. The top of the receiver has the standard MP5 cocking knob, sights, and NATO sight mounts. Underneath the foregrip of the weapon, just ahead of the drum magazine, is the port selector switch to set the weapon to fire supersonic or subsonic projectiles. With the selector set in the open position, as it is here, the HK54A1 can fire standard NATO 9mm ammunition and the projectiles will leave the barrel at a subsonic velocity, eliminating the sonic crack of the bullet. The port selector opens or closes a gas port on the barrel that will bleed off sufficient propellant gases from standard ammunition to lower them to subsonic velocity. The removable aluminum suppressor is attached to the muzzle of this example. All of the control settings of this example are for the maximum suppression of the sound of a shot being fired.
PHOTO CREDIT: KEVIN DOCKERY

"For all of its apparent advantages, the HK54A1 did not work out well in combat. In October, 1983 US forces invaded the island of Grenada to assist the official government and rescue American citizens. During the operation, several SEALs used HK54A1s as part of a field trial in combat. The general opinion of the weapons was that they were an expensive answer to a problem that could be better taken care of by other firearms systems already on the market. Reportedly, the HK54A1 also suffered from jams when used under field conditions."

Special Weapons

Because of this, Heckler and Koch received a contract for an advanced development submachine gun in April, 1983. The result was designated the HK54A1.

Several unique features are found in the HK54A1 in an attempt to have a completely all-purpose weapon. Many of these features center around the suppressed use of the weapon.

The suppressor for the HK54A1 is slipped over the barrel and secured by a threaded seat near the breech end of the barrel. The expansion chamber portion of the suppressor surrounds the barrel and is itself covered by the forearm and the extended portion of the receiver. In a reverse of other suppressor designs, the forward suppression portion of the device is larger in diameter than the rear expansion chamber. The large suppression section protrudes from muzzle of the HK54A1 and contains a series of angular baffles. The non-wipe construction of the suppressor eliminates most maintenance problems with there being no parts replacement needed after extended use.

To suppress the sound of the bullet's flight, the HK54A1 has a turn on/turn off porting system. A small lever is located underneath the HK54A1 on the forearm, just in front of the magazine well. By turning the lever so that it points to the open circle (O) symbol, a series of ports are opened in the barrel just on front of the chamber. The ports bleed off the propellant gases into the suppressor, lowering the muzzle velocity of a standard NATO 9mm round to below the speed of sound. By turning the port lever to the solid-colored circle, the gas ports are closed and projectiles travel at their designed velocity.

With the gas ports open, the rear of the suppressor acts as an expansion chamber. With the ports closed, only the front portion of the suppressor functions as a muzzle blast device. This factor is part of the reason the forward portion of the suppressor is so large.

To eliminate much of the mechanical noise of firing, a bolt lock is included in the HK54A1. By turning the safety selector lever to its rearmost position, indicated by an arrow pointing to a solid line, the bolt lock engages. With the bolt lock operating, the HK54A1 will not unlock at all when a round is fired. The weapon has to be manually reloaded by using the bolt cocking knob.

In addition to the bolt locked position, the safety selector has a safe position, indicated by a white 0. The semiautomatic position for the selector is indicated by a red number 1. The three-shot burst position is indicated by the red number 3 and the full automatic position is indicated by the red number 50. The HK54A1 fires from the closed bolt using the HK roller delayed blowback system for operating.

Additional features on the HK54A1 include a last-round bolt hold-open device. When the last round in a magazine is fired, the bolt stays open, locked to the rear, indicating the weapon is empty. By inserting a loaded magazine and pressing the bolt release, the bolt goes forward and loads the weapon. The bolt release is a square button with a forward-pointing arrowhead on it and is located on the left side of the weapon just in front and above the trigger. Though the safety selector is duplicated on both sides of the firearm, the square buttons on either side of the mechanism in front of the selector do different actions.

The button on the left side of the receiver is the bolt hold-open release while the button on the right side of the receiver, engraved with an "M" is the magazine release. The magazine on the HK54A1 is also special in that it is not a box magazine but a large-capacity drum magazine.

Inside of the plastic drum magazine housing is a spiral track cast into the cover and body of the magazine. A spring driven lever follows the spiral track in its three turns around the circumference of the magazine body. At the end of the lever is a short chain of five flexible cylinders. The cylinders drive the ammunition around the spiral track and up through the short, straight section of the magazine that inserts into the weapon.

Further characteristics of the HK54A1 include a forward bolt assist to help silently close the bolt on a chambered round. In addition there is a sliding metal stock on the weapon and integral mounting blocks on the top of the receiver to accept telescopic or electronic sighting devices.

For all of its apparent advantages, the HK54A1 did not work out well in combat. In October, 1983 US forces invaded the island of Grenada to assist the official government and rescue American citizens. During the operation, several SEALs used HK54A1s as part of a field trial in combat. The general opinion of the weapons was that they were an expensive answer to a problem that could be better taken care of by other firearms systems already on the market. Reportedly, the HK54A1 also suffered from jams when used under field conditions.

The further development of the HK54A1 was suspended shortly after the Grenada operations were completed and the JSSAP 6.2 submachine gun project was considered completed. Interest was concentrated on a new submachine gun design that would incorporate some of the lessons learned in the 6.2 project. Funded by JSSAP, development of the new weapon was to be conducted as the 6.3A submachine gun project. The intent of the JSSAP 6.3A project was to stimulate private industry development of a submachine gun based on government supplied characteristics. The end result of the 6.3A project was to complete the engineering package for a submachine gun that could be fielded as a DOD standard weapon service-wide by the mid-1990's.

H&K MP2000

As Heckler and Koch had been the prime contractor on the JSSAP 6.2 project, they continued their work as the contractor for the JSSAP 6.3A project. Though H&K had difficulty in combining all of the required characteristics supplied by JSSAP into a single firearm, they completed the project within a reasonable amount of time. What did stand out was the final program cost for the 6.3A project was below what the original estimates had allowed for. The weapon developed by H&K has been referred to by them as either "SMG I" or by an alternate designation "HK SMG 94054".

The H&K SMG I is a compact, streamlined package with many features taken from earlier H&K designs. The

Submachineguns

TECHNICAL DATA—Heckler & Koch SMG 94054, JSSAP 6.3A SMG project
CARTRIDGE—9mm Parabellum (9x19mm)
OPERATION—Blowback
TYPE OF FIRE—Selective - semiautomatic/full automatic
RATE OF FIRE—Practical SS 40 rpm, A rpm, Cyclic 880 rpm
MUZZLE VELOCITY—NATO Ball 1227 fps (374 m/s)
9mm OSP 1017 fps (310 m/s)
MUZZLE ENERGY—414 ft/lbs (561 J) NATO ball
338 ft/lbs (458 J)
SIGHTS—Open, Aperture/post with 3-dot tritium inserts, Adjustable 0 to 150 meters in 25 meter increments. Rear sight selectable for supersonic or subsonic ammunition, M setting for mask raises rear sight and uses post machined into front sight hood
FEED—30 round removable reinforced-plastic box magazine
WEIGHTS
WEAPON (EMPTY)—6.12 lbs (2.78 kg) w/o suppressor
7.87 lbs (3.57 kg) w/suppressor
Final model stainless steel suppressor 1.8 lbs (0.82 kg)
WEAPON (LOADED)—7.1 lbs (3.22 kg) w/NATO Ball
8.95 lbs (4.06 kg) w/suppressor, 9mm OSP
MAGAZINE (EMPTY)—0.17 lbs (0.08 kg)
MAGAZINE (LOADED)—0.98 lbs (0.44 kg) w/NATO Ball
1.08 lbs (0.49 kg) with 9mm OSP
SERVICE CARTRIDGE—NATO Ball 190 gr. (12.3 g)
9mm OSP 212 gr (13.7 g)
PROJECTILE—124 gr. (8 g)
9mm OSP 147 gr (9.5 g)
LENGTHS
WEAPON OVERALL—14.31/21.38/22.69 in (36.4/54.3/57.6 cm) stock closed/open to first notch/fully open - w/o suppressor
21.63/28.63/29.88 in (54.9/72.7/75.9 cm) stock closed/open to first notch/fully open - w/suppressor
BARREL—5.63 in (14.3 cm)
SUPPRESSOR LENGTH—10.81 in (27.5 cm) overall
7.31 in (18.6 cm) Can length
3.5 in (8.9 cm) Mounting tube
SUPPRESSOR DIAMETER—1.628 in (4.1 cm) Can
1.062 in (2.7 cm) Mounting tube
SUPPRESSOR WALL THICKNESS—0.070 in (1.78 mm)
SIGHT RADIUS—12.5 in (31.8 in)
Forward bolt assist is primarily for "silent loading", by using the system the sound level of chambering a round is only 40 to 45 db. Suppressor reduction on the normal sound signature, 137 db for NATO Ball, was - 29 db to a sound signature of 108 db

The Joint Services Small Arms Program (JSSAP) 6.3A submachine gun project weapon. This is a right-side view of one of the six H&K SMG I supplied to the Naval Weapons Support Center at Crane for testing. The sliding buttstock is in its closed configuration with the later-model enlarged buttplate for larger shooters at the end of the receiver. The complicated rear sight is visible on the top of the receiver, just behind one of the two NATO mounts for additional sighting devices. The ambidextrous cocking knob is in the forward position, just behind the front sight. The long rectangular device extending out behind the ejection port is the forward bolt assist that can be used to close the bolt in poor conditions. The ambidextrous trigger group can be seen at the rear of the receiver with the numerical indicators for the safety setting. In this specimen, the selector is set to the white "0" indicating safe. The bottom of the two square buttons in front of and above the trigger is the magazine release. The upper button, with an different surface texture so that it can be identified by feel, is the bolt release. The plastic 30-round magazine activates the bolt hold open when the last round is fired. This specimen has the original model stainless steel suppressor mounted in place over the barrel.
PHOTO CREDIT: US NAVY

major item not taken from other H&K designs is the basic operating system of the weapon. Instead of using the successful, if complicated roller-delayed blowback system found in the majority of H&K weapons, the SMG I operates using the blowback principle common to many of the world's submachine guns. What makes the SMG I stand out from other blowback operated weapons is that it fires from the closed bolt. Firing from the closed bolt gives the SMG I the same accuracy as the MP5 family of weapons while retaining the relative mechanical simplicity of the blowback system.

To prevent the possibility of an accidental discharge of the SMG I if it was dropped or jarred, a mechanical safety was built into the operating system. The firing pin of the SMG I cannot reach the primer of a chambered round unless the trigger is pulled. When the trigger is pulled, a safety catch releases the firing pin shortly before the hammer itself is released. In addition, the hammer is mechanically blocked from being released unless the bolt is within 2mm of being fully closed.

The HK54A1 locked breech system for holding the bolt closed on a suppressed shot was eliminated in the SMG I though the system was retained as a possible optional offering by the company. In addition, the selective on/off gas porting system for reducing the speed of standard ammunition used in the HK54A1 was also eliminated in the SMG I. Heckler and Koch also offered the selective on/off porting system as an option in their commercial version of the SMG I, the MP 2000.

For suppressed firing, the SMG I has a full-length suppressor available that slips over the barrel and seats on threads near the breech. Originally, a steel suppressor was issued with the SMG I but resulted in an unsatisfactory -20 decibel drop in sound signature when tested. An alternative aluminum suppressor was supplied from the manufacturer which had an acceptable -30 decibel signature drop. The final version of the SMG I suppressor was a stainless steel design incorporating the improvements for in the aluminum version.

Internally, the suppressor acts as a muzzle blast reducer with the rear tube an additional expansion chamber. A series of four angled blast deflectors are welded into an assembly inside of the suppressor body. In addition, at the rear of the baffle assembly, in front of the muzzle of the weapon, is a circular, perforated gas diverter that forces some of the muzzle blast back into the rear expansion chamber. The whole assembly is contained within the steel suppressor tube and retained by a threaded muzzle cap and the front portion of the rear expansion tube.

The overall design of the SMG I suppressor is a particularly rugged, intended for continuous use with little or no cleaning. During testing, the sound pressure of the SMG I decreases from 108.9 db at the beginning of the test to 105.8 db after 3000 rounds had been fired.

Cook-off, the firing of a round from residual chamber heat in a closed-bolt weapon, is considered a possible problem in closed-bolt automatic weapons. Testing was conducted on the SMG I to see just how much ammunition the weapon could fire before cook-off became a problem.

In the initial test, a suppressed SMG I fired 500 rounds in 5 minutes with only 3 stoppages due to feeding. The suppressed weapon cooled to ambient room temperature without firing a round intentionally left in the chamber.

In the second cook-off test, a SMG I fired 900 rounds in 4 minutes 15 seconds, again with 3 stoppages due to feed problems. The heat absorbed by the weapon was tremendous, the rear 2 inches of the suppressor glowing red hot by the end of the test. The heat was enough to soften part of the front grip and melt it off the weapon near the end of the test. Secured in a test cradle, the suppressed weapon cooked-off 5 times while cooling to ambient temperature. After the test, no physical change was noted in the suppressor beyond a heat discoloration of the breech end to a light straw color. In addition, no change in the level of suppression was noted during or after the test.

The SMG I is intended to be used with subsonic ammunition for maximum sound suppression. The rear sight, fully adjustable for windage and elevation, is operator selectable for either sonic or subsonic

The rear sight of the JSSAP H&K SMG I. The complex rear sight can be set for either supersonic or subsonic ammunition and adjusted by the operator by simply switching the indicator bar from one side to the other. The two dot at either side of the rear peep are tritium inserts that glow green for low-light aiming. At the top of the rear sight blade is a wide square notch intended for use when the firer is wearing an M17A1 gas mask. The small button behind the sight is the release catch for the sliding stock that is fully collapsed in this photograph.
PHOTO CREDIT: KEVIN DOCKERY

Submachineguns

This is a left-side view of one of the six H&K SMG I's supplied to the Naval Weapons Support Center at Crane for testing as part of the Joint Services Small Arms Program (JSSAP) 6.3A submachine gun project. The sliding buttstock is in its closed position, minimizing the overall length of the weapon. The large windage adjustment knob of the complicated rear sight is visible on the top of the receiver, just behind one of the two NATO mounts for additional sighting devices. The ambidextrous cocking knob is in the forward position, just behind the front sight. The ambidextrous trigger group can be seen at the rear of the receiver with the numerical indicators for the safety setting. In this specimen, the selector is set to the white "0" indicating safe. The bottom of the two square buttons in front of an above the trigger is the magazine release. The upper button, with an different surface texture so that it can be identified by feel, is the bolt release.
PHOTO CREDIT: US NAVY

A field stripped view of the Joint Services Small Arms Program (JSSAP) 6.3A submachine gun called the H&K SMG I. At the top of the photo is the stainless steel suppressor originally supplied with the weapon. A later aluminum suppressor from H&K was issued for the SMG I during testing and was found to be a superior design. The large rectangular piece below the suppressor is the upper receiver assembly. The long rod and coil spring at the center of the photo is the mainspring. To the right of the mainspring is the bolt assembly. Beneath the mainspring is the rear trigger housing and underneath the bolt is the forward handgrip. The 30-round plastic magazine is between the two handgrips. At the left bottom is the sliding stock. At the right bottom of the photo is the receiver end cap assembly with the bolt buffer being the spring assembly sticking out to the right.
PHOTO CREDIT: KEVIN DOCKERY

ammunition. When adjusted, the sight can be switched from either type of ammunition while retaining the same point of impact. In addition, the rear sight can be set to an extended M setting, raising the rear sight for easy use while the operator is wearing an M17A1 gas mask. The front sight hood has a square post machined into the top of it for use with the rear sight on the M setting.

For use in low-light conditions, both the front and rear sights have luminous inserts. In front of the rear sight, on the top of the receiver, are lugs for the attachment of standard sighting devices. The lugs are a quick-release design that will accept all standard NATO sight bases. Just in front of the lugs on the top of the receiver is the cocking handle, located so that it can be easily reached from either side of the weapon. The cocking handle has a U-shaped cutout to clear the line of sight and does not reciprocate when the weapon is fired.

The last-round bolt hold-open device tested in the HK54A1 was retained in the SMG I in a slightly modified form. On the HK54A1, the bolt release was on the left side of the trigger group, with the magazine release being on the opposite side at the same location. On the SMG I, the square bolt release button is on both sides of the trigger group, above the magazine release button. The magazine release button is also duplicated on both sides of the trigger housing.

To complete the ambidextrous use of the SMG I, the fire selector lever is duplicated on both sides of the weapon. Fire selector setting are indicated by a white 0 for safe, a red 1 for semiautomatic fire, and a red 30 for full automatic fire. Enough room is left in the travel of the fire selector lever to accommodate a third setting for 3 round burst.

Above the fire selector lever on the right side of the SMG I is the forward bolt assist. The forward assist aids in chambering the first round in a very dirty environment since the bolt cannot be forced forward by the operating handle. The forward bolt assist can also be used for "silent loading" a first round. By drawing the bolt back and easing it forward, the forward bolt assist can quietly close the bolt and chamber a round. By using the silent loading system the sound level of chambering a round is only 40 to 45 db, quieter than normal conversation.

The compact sliding stock fits snugly over the rear of the receiver when closed, making a very smooth, compact package. The sliding stock can be extended and locked into place in several different lengths to account for different sized operators or various uniforms or equipment worn while on a mission.

To aid in reducing the overall weight of the SMG I, the 30 round magazines are injection molded of a high-strength synthetic material. The same material is found in the forward and rear pistol grips. The design of the pistol grips follows that of the MP5K series very closely and allow for accurate firing of the SMG I without using the stock.

Overall the SMG I was considered a very acceptable design for use by all the US services. The low-maintenance design was tested and proved durable and effective with the final tests being completed in 1985. A complete specification and engineering package was received and retained by the US government for possible future

This is a left-side view of one of the six H&K SMG I's supplied to the Naval Weapons Support Center at Crane for testing as part of the Joint Services Small Arms Program (JSSAP) 6.3A submachine gun project. The sliding buttstock is in its maximum open position. The large windage adjustment knob of the complicated rear sight is visible on the top of the receiver, just behind one of the two NATO mounts for additional sighting devices. The ambidextrous cocking knob is in the forward position, just behind the front sight. The ambidextrous trigger group can be seen at the rear of the receiver with the numerical indicators for the safety setting. In this specimen, the selector is set to "1" indicating semiautomatic fire only. The bottom of the two square buttons in front of and above the trigger is the magazine release. The upper button, with an different surface texture so that it can be identified by feel, is the bolt release. The plastic 30-round magazine activates the bolt hold open when the last round is fired. This specimen has the original model stainless steel suppressor screwed over the barrel, the model later replaced with a more efficient aluminum suppressor later in the tests.
PHOTO CREDIT: KEVIN DOCKERY

"Overall the SMG I was considered a very acceptable design for use by all the US services. The low-maintenance design was tested and proved durable and effective with the final tests being completed in 1985. A complete specification and engineering package was received and retained by the US government for possible future manufacture."

The Joint Services Small Arms Program (JSSAP) 6.3A submachine gun project weapon. This is a right-side view of one of the six H&K SMG I supplied to the Naval Weapons Support Center at Crane for testing. The sliding buttstock is in its closed configuration with the buttplate fitting neatly over the end of the receiver. The complicated rear sight is visible on the top of the receiver, just behind one of the two NATO mounts for additional sighting devices. The ambidextrous cocking knob is in the forward position, just behind the front sight. The long rectangular device extending out behind the ejection port is the forward bolt assist that can be used to close the bolt in poor conditions. The ambidextrous trigger group can be seen at the rear of the receiver with the numerical indicators for the safety setting. In this specimen, the selector is set to "1" indicating semiautomatic fire only. The bottom of the two square buttons in front of and above the trigger is the magazine release. The upper button, with a different surface texture so that it can be identified by feel, is the bolt release. The plastic 30-round magazine activates the bolt hold open when the last round is fired. This specimen has the original model stainless steel suppressor lying below the weapon. The threaded portion of the barrel used to secure the suppressor is visible through the rear one of the two cooling ports above the front grip. This is the most compact configuration of the JSSAP 6.3 SMG.
PHOTO CREDIT: KEVIN DOCKERY

manufacture. Since the end of the JSSAP 6.3A submachine gun project in 1987, the SMG I design has been offered as a commercial product by Heckler and Koch. The H&K weapon, designated the MP2000 has been produced in only very small numbers but offers a number of options first tested in the HK54A1 and SMG I.

While the JSSAP SMG programs were going on, SEAL Team Six was continuing their use of the MP5 submachine gun family. The other SEAL Teams were continuing their use of the Mk 24 Mod 0 and Ingram submachine guns through the first few years of the 1980's. With the planned expansion of Navy Special Warfare and the SEAL Teams beginning in 1983, the amount and quality of submachine guns available in Navy stores was considered insufficient to meet expected needs. Since a reasonable large number of new weapons would be needed, comparison testing was initiated in order to find the best commercially available "off-the-shelf" submachine gun design. The investigation was titled the Navy Near-Term SMG project and was begun in February 1983.

By July 1984, the Navy Near-Term SMG project had been completed and the MP5 weapons family was chosen to be the new SEAL basic issue submachine gun. Initial weapons purchased for the Teams were the same as those used earlier by SEAL Team Six, the MP5A3, MP5SD3, and MP5K. The first weapons to arrive at SEAL Team 2 at Little Creek were 25 MP5SD3's followed soon by an equal number of MP5A3's.

The SEALs found the new MP5s a great improvement over earlier issue weapons. The closed-bolt action of the MP5 gave the entire line of weapons a much greater first-round accuracy than any of the open-bolt systems the SEALs had been using for years. The MP5s were also generally very compact and were a much handier weapon for using in close areas than even the CAR-15 had been. In addition, there is much less danger of over-penetration and ricochets are slightly less hazardous with the 9mm cartridge than with a .223 or 7.62mm rifle round when boarding and searching ships.

The new SEAL MP5s were slightly different in details from the earlier models. The new issue MP5A3 is fitted with the smooth, wider "tropical" handguard. The original handguard has a round cross section and four lengthwise panels of checkering to give a secure gripping surface. The tropical handguard, originally offered as an optional accessory for the MP5 by H&K, has a textured surface and a triangular cross section. The wide-bottomed shape of the handguard offers a better grip to wet or gloved hands, something the SEALs find themselves using often.

For the most part, the SEALs' MP5s were all fitted with the SEF trigger group. According to an individual Team's mission, the MP5K weapons were also available. Shortly later, the first MP5's arrived at SEAL Team Two, a limited number, 25 each, of MP5A5's and MP5SD6's for field testing and evaluation. Reportedly, SEAL Team Two was the only East coast Team to receive the A5/SD6 configuration weapons.

Several new developments were incorporated into the MP5A5 and MP5SD6 weapon. Foremost among these changes was the addition of a controlled burst mechanism to the trigger group. According to the standard designations put out by Heckler and Koch, the MP5A5 is a standard MP5 fitted with a controlled burst trigger group and sliding buttstock. The MP5SD6 is identified by the company as the suppressed MP5 with the controlled burst trigger group and sliding buttstock. Sometime during the first procurements of the MP5's for the Teams at large, a clerical error was made and all of the MP5's have been listed in Navy documents as the MP5A5, SD5 and KA4. This mis-identification has remained to this day.

Trigger groups among all of the different MP5s can be easily changed one for the other. MP5A3's with the SEF trigger group can accept a controlled burst trigger group and be changed to the MP5A5 model. The only real difference in the weapons is that the controlled burst trigger group has a setting where only three rounds will be fired on full automatic for each pull of the trigger.

The internal mechanism of the controlled burst trigger group remains the same as the earlier SEF group with some additions. The burst control itself is centered on a ratchet device fitted to the trigger mechanism. With the fire selector lever set on burst fire, the ratchet holds the sear back from the hammer when the trigger is pulled. The ratchet mechanically counts the number of times the bolt carrier moves past and releases the sear after the programmed number of rounds have been fired. If the trigger is released before the set number of rounds have been fired, the ratchet resets back to 0.

Because of the arrangement of the burst control ratchet, the number of rounds in a burst can be set by the number of teeth on the ratchet. Settings for two, three, or more rounds are available on the burst control trigger group though the normal setting, and the one supplied on the SEALs' weapons, is for three shot bursts.

Setting indicators for the controlled burst trigger groups are pictographic in style rather than having numbers or letters. The pictographic representations of the different control settings are considerably more graphic than the original SEF letters.

The safety setting is indicated by a single white bullet in a closed rectangular box with an X superimposed over the bullet. For semiautomatic fire, the symbol is a closed red box containing a single red bullet silhouette. Three round burst is indicated by a closed red rectangle holding three red bullet shapes. Automatic fire is at the top setting, moving up from the trigger, and is indicated by an open-ended red rectangle containing seven red bullet shapes. All the bullet silhouettes point forward towards the muzzle of the weapon, an additional indicator of what the fire selector lever settings mean.

The pistol grip shape of the controlled burst trigger groups is of a considerably different shape than that of the SEF group. The finger swells found on the SEF pistol grip are removed on the new grip. The new grip has a smoother, more conical shape with an oval cross-section. A noticeable protrusion is on the bottom of the front strap of the new grip to help keep a hand from slipping

Submachineguns

The Heckler & Koch MP5-N, the present standard-issue submachine gun in the SEAL Teams. As for all of the N model MP5s, this specimen has the ambidextrous trigger group with controls on both sides of the weapon. Control settings are in a "pictogram" style, the selector on this specimen being set to full automatic fire. There are two magazine releases on the N models, the paddle type, visible as the small lever between the trigger guard and the magazine, and a push-button on the right side of the weapon that can be operated with the trigger finger. This specimen has the wide forearm common to all N models that is often found exchanged for a tactical lighted forearm with a built-in flashlight. The small dark cylinder at the muzzle of the weapon is the knurled protective cap over the threaded portion of the barrel. The weapon is loaded with a standard, curved, 30-round magazine with a standard 15-round magazine shown outside of the weapon.
PHOTO CREDIT: KEVIN DOCKERY

TECHNICAL DATA—Heckler & Koch MP5-N (1988)
NSN 1005-01-360-7146
CARTRIDGE—9mm Parabellum (9x19mm)
OPERATION—Roller locked delayed blowback
TYPE OF FIRE—Selective - semiautomatic/full automatic
RATE OF FIRE—CYCLIC 800 rpm
MUZZLE VELOCITY—M882 Ball 1312 fps (400 m/s)
9mm OSP 1092 fps (333 m/s)
MUZZLE ENERGY—470 ft/lbs (637 J) M882 ball
389 ft/lbs (527 J) 9mm OSP
SIGHTS—Open, aperture/post with 3-dot tritium inserts, adjustable
FEED—30 round removable box magazine
WEIGHTS
WEAPON (EMPTY)—6.34 lbs (2.88 kg) w/o suppressor
w/suppressor 7.57 lbs (3.43 kg)
Suppressor wt 1.23 lbs (0.56 kg)
WEAPON (LOADED)—7.53 lbs (3.42 kg) w/o suppressor, w/1 - 30 round magazine M882 Ball
8.82 lbs (4.0 kg) w/suppressor, 1 - 30 round magazine 9mm OSP

MAGAZINE (EMPTY)—30 round .375 lb (0.17 kg)
Two 30 round mags w/clip 1.11 lbs (0.50 kg)
MAGAZINE (LOADED)—30 round - 1.19 lb (0.54 kg) with M882 Ball
30 round - 1.29 lbs (0.59 kg) with 9mm OSP
Two - 30 round mags w/clip 2.74 lbs (1.24 kg) with M882 Ball
Two - 30 round mags w/clip 2.93 lbs (1.33 kg) with 9mm OSP
SERVICE CARTRIDGE—M882 Ball 190 gr. (12.3 g)
9mm OSP 212 gr (13.7 g)
PROJECTILE—124 gr. (8 g)
9mm OSP 147 gr (9.5 g)
LENGTHS
WEAPON OVERALL—19.29/25.98 in (49.0/66.0 cm) w/o suppressor
27.94/33.06 in (71/84 cm) w/suppressor
BARREL—8.85 in (22.5 cm)
SUPPRESSOR LENGTH—7.75 in (19.7 cm)
SUPPRESSOR DIAMETER—1.385 in (3.5 cm)
SIGHT RADIUS—13.39 in (34.0 cm)
Barrel threads for suppressor are covered with a knurled cap (wt. 93 gr (6 g)) when the suppressor is not mounted

off. The thumb rest found on the left side of the SEF grip is not on the new grip making it much more comfortable to use left-handed. In addition to being more ambidextrous in use, the new style pistol grip also gives a more secure grasp to a hand covered in a leather or rubber glove.

On both trigger groups, the pistol grip is an integral part of the plastic casting that makes up the outside housing of the group. Markings, whether the letters SEF or the pictographic symbols, are deep engravings on the outside plastic housing.

In general, the controlled burst system was not accepted by the Teams. The control mechanism itself was somewhat sensitive and extra care had to be given to it during routine maintenance.

For all of the Teams, it was found to be preferable to train in burst control by fast manipulation of the trigger. Experience and training would give an operator the ability to fire three-round bursts by automatically releasing the trigger as soon as the third round had been fired. Using the trigger-control system also had the advantage that full automatic fire was immediately available by just holding the trigger down if the situation arose where a high volume of fire was needed.

MP5-N

The MP5A3s and SD3s that had arrived at the Teams in 1984 acted as an interim measure until weapons modified to SEAL specifications became available. By midyear 1985 the MP5-N and MP5K-N (Navy) became available

*A French Commando shoulder fires a SEAL MP5-N while aboard the **USS JOSHUA HUMPHREYS**. The MP5-N is fitted with a flash hider over it's muzzle and is loaded with doubled 30-round magazines. The double magazine assembly shown here has a spacer between the two magazines that are clamped together with two standard screwclamps. This technique allows the weapon to be quickly reloaded by pulling the magazine assembly out and reinserting it into the weapon.*
PHOTO CREDIT: US NAVY

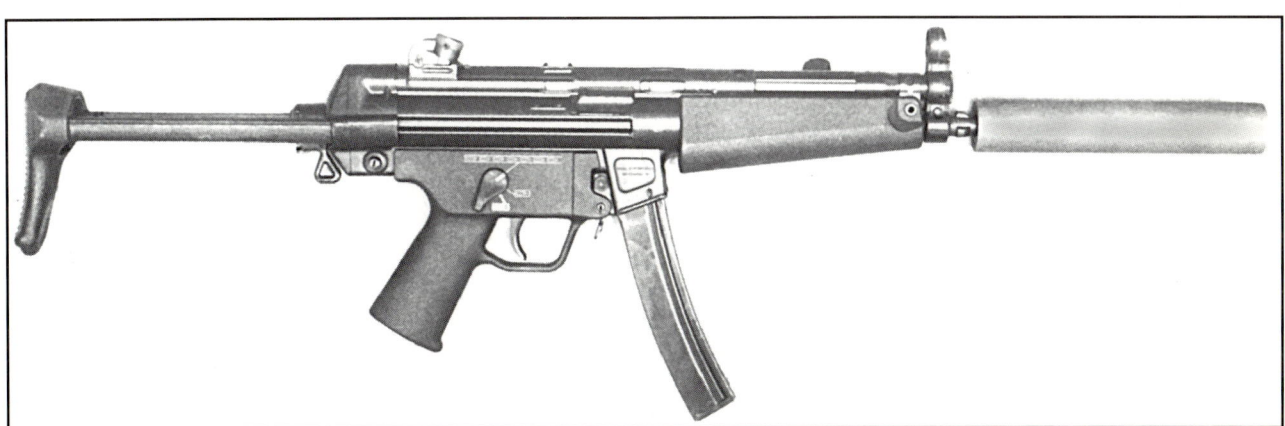

A right-side view of the MP5-N with the stainless steel suppressor mounted on the muzzle and the shoulder stock fully extended. The selector lever is set to the red pictogram of seven bullets pointing forward in an open-ended box. This is the marking indicating full-automatic fire.
PHOTO CREDIT: KEVIN DOCKERY

TECHNICAL DATA—Heckler & Koch MP5K-N (1988)
CARTRIDGE—9mm Parabellum (9x19mm)
OPERATION—Roller locked delayed blowback
TYPE OF FIRE—Selective - semiautomatic/full automatic
RATE OF FIRE—Cyclic 900 rpm
MUZZLE VELOCITY—M882 Ball 1230 fps (375 m/s)
9mm OSP 1010 fps (308 m/s)
MUZZLE ENERGY—M882 Ball 420 ft/lbs (570 J)
9mm OSP 333 ft/lbs (452 J)
SIGHTS—Open, notch/postw/3-dot tritium inserts, adjustable
FEED—15 or 30 round removable box magazine
WEIGHTS
WEAPON (EMPTY)—4.4 lbs (2.00 kg) w/o suppressor
5.63 lbs (2.55 kg) w/suppressor
Suppressor wt 1.23 lbs (0.56 kg)
WEAPON (LOADED)—5.59 lb (2.54 kg) w/o suppressor, w/1 - 30 rd magazine M882 Ball
6.92 lbs (3.14 kg) w/suppressor, 1 - 30 rd magazine 9mm OSP
MAGAZINE (EMPTY)—30 rd - .38 lb (0.17 kg)
15 rd - 0.27 lb (0.12 kg)
Two - 30 rd mags w/clip 1.11 lbs (0.50 kg)
MAGAZINE (LOADED)—30 rd - 1.19 lb (0.54 kg) w/M882 Ball
30 rd - 1.29 lbs (0.59 kg) w/9mm OSP
15 rd - 0.67 lb (0.31 kg) w/M882 Ball
15 rd - 0.72 lb (0.33 kg) w/9mm OSP
Two - 30 rd mags w/clip 2.74 lbs (1.24 kg) w/M882 Ball
Two - 30 rd mags w/clip 2.93 lbs (1.33 kg) w/9mm OSP
SERVICE CARTRIDGE—M882 Ball 190 gr. (12.3 g)
9mm OSP 212 gr (13.7 g)
PROJECTILE—124 gr. (8 g)
9mm OSP 147 gr (9.5 g)
LENGTHS
WEAPON OVERALL—12.8 in (32.5 cm) w/o suppressor
21 in (53.3 cm) w/suppressor
BARREL—4.53 in (11.5 cm)
SUPPRESSOR LENGTH—7.75 in (19.7 cm)
SUPPRESSOR DIAMETER—1.385 in (3.5 cm)
SIGHT RADIUS—10.25 in (26 cm)
Barrel threads for suppressor are covered with a knurled cap (wt 93 gr (6 g)) when the suppressor is not mounted

> "The MP5K-N has the same modifications as the MP5-N consisting of the Navy trigger group with ambidextrous controls, tritium sight insert, and threaded muzzle."

The MP5K-N submachine gun fitted with the stainless steel sound suppressor. This suppressor is the same model used for both the MP5K-N and the standard MP5-N weapons. Special subsonic ammunition, Mark 144 Mod 1, is used by the SEALs in these weapons for maximum sound suppression. At the opposite end of the weapon is the rotating sling swivel centered on the butt cap of the receiver. This particular weapon is loaded with a standard 15 round magazine for concealability.
PHOTO CREDIT: KEVIN DOCKERY

in sufficient numbers to begin issuing them to the Teams. These weapons, which have a detachable suppressor, have remained the primary SEAL submachine gun to this day. MP5SD3s remain available in the armories of the active Teams for use in situations where subsonic ammunition may not be available.

Mechanically, the MP5-N weapons were the same as earlier models of the MP5. Changes requested by the SEALs were primarily centered around handling characteristics. The tropical handguard has been retained on the MP5-N as well as the pistol grip configuration first found on the controlled burst trigger group. The trigger group of the MP5-N weapon has settings for safe, semiautomatic, and full automatic. Heckler and Koch offers an ambidextrous trigger group fitted with a controlled burst mechanism that is virtually identical with the Navy group.

The noticeable difference in the Navy trigger group is that the fire selector lever is duplicated on both sides of the weapon. Either lever can be used to select the fire setting on the MP5-N making the weapon able to be equally well operated from the right or left side. This ambidextrous facility makes the MP5-N even more flexible in a combat situation. Instead of a letter or number system to indicate the control settings, the Navy trigger group utilizes the pictographic system first used by the SEALs on the MP5A5.

The sights of the MP5-N weapon have been fitted with tritium inserts for use in low-light situations. The tritium insert is a small glass tube filled with a low-level radioactive isotope. The inserts glow with a pale green light, easily visible at night or in other low-light situations.

A major modification to the MP5-N is the addition of a threaded portion to the muzzle of the barrel. Normally covered with a knurled cap to protect the threads, the muzzle of the MP5-N is able to accept a suppressor built to Navy specifications. The muzzle-blast suppressor is an all-metal, non-wipe design that significantly reduces the firing signature of the MP5-N. The size of the suppressor is such that it will fit into the same pouch pocket that holds a 30 round MP5 magazine.

The 3-lug locking system is retained on the muzzle of the MP5-N to allow the weapon to use a standard flash hider for normal use. MP5-Ns are issued both with and without the detachable suppressor. In addition to the MP5-N, the MP5K-N is issued to the Teams.

MP5K-N

The MP5K-N has the same modifications as the MP5-N consisting of the Navy trigger group with ambidextrous controls, tritium sight insert, and threaded muzzle. The standard MP5K barrel was increased by 0.47 inches (12 mm) to accept the threaded muzzle. In addition to the threaded muzzle, the MP5K-N also has the 3-lug locking system on its muzzle to accept the H&K flash suppressor.

Several accessories have been put into general use by the SEALs on many of their MP5 weapons. One accessory is the dual magazine clamp offered by H&K. The dual magazine clamp weighs 0.35 pounds (0.16 kg) and securely holds two magazines side-by-side with each other. The two magazines are held mouth up at the same height and parallel to each other, facing forward. The dual magazine clamp holds the magazines spaced far enough apart that one of the two can be loaded into the magazine well. For quick reloading, the dual magazine only has to be pulled from the weapon and quickly reinserted. The popularity, and cost, of the dual magazine system has resulted in a number of SEALs fielding their own version of the system.

In the SEAL dual magazine system, the two magazines are held slightly apart by a spacer and clamped together firmly with a simple pipe clamp. Though quick to reload, the dual magazine has the disadvantage of not fitting in any standard magazine pouch. In addition, the dual magazine makes the MP5 noticeably heavier and changes the handling characteristics of the weapon.

Another accessory seeing use with the Teams is a tactical lighted forearm for the MP5. The lighted forearm replaces the regular handguard of the standard MP5 or MP5-N with no other modification to the weapon. In a swelled portion of the tactical handguard, just below the muzzle of the weapon, is a lithium powered flashlight. The flashlight produces a strong, focused beam of white light usable for searching, target acquisition, and illuminating a low-light situation. A pressure strip switch is located on the side of the forearm where it can be pressed by the operators fingers. The flashlight does not protrude past the muzzle of the weapon to protect the lens from the muzzle blast.

Some difficulties have been noted with the MP5 weapons and the ammunition they use. Though normally extremely reliable, difficulties were noted in using standard subsonic ammunition in the MP5-N. The fluted chamber, necessary to the proper operation of the MP5 roller-locking system, has some difficulty releasing the Mk 144 subsonic ammunition originally developed for the Mk 22 pistol. A program was initiated to develop a product-improved (PIP) Mk 144 round by the Naval Weapons Support Center at Crane, Indiana.

An additional requirement was put forward for a specialized round of ammunition to be developed for the MP5 and Beretta M9 that would be both subsonic and have "enhanced incapacitation" effects. Olin ordnance developed the 9mm OSP round, their commercial designation, to fill the Navy requirement. The OSP (Olin Super Match) round is a subsonic loading of a 147 grain jacketed hollow-point projectile. The specially-designed 147 grain bullet was based on technology developed by Olin for the Winchester Silvertip line of ammunition. The OSP round gives superior terminal effects over the standard NATO 9mm and even the MK 144 round while remaining at subsonic levels.

The use of the hollow-point round, normally banned by the Geneva and other conventions, is allowed only for use in civil or counter-terrorist operations by US forces. The baffle-type suppression system used by the Qual-E-Tech suppressor mounted on the MP5-N and MP5K-N allows the use of hollow-point ammunition which is difficult to use in a wipe-type suppressor such as that found on the Mk 22 pistol.

Shotguns

These SEALs are climbing aboard a Light SEAL Support Craft (LSSC) prior to leaving on a operation in Vietnam. The SEAL on the far left is armed with an Ithaca Featherlight Model 37 shotgun. He is wearing the Type I, Rifleman's version, of the Utility Life Jacket. The utility life jacket was a combination ammunition vest and inflatable life jacket capable of supporting a 250-pound man along with his combat gear when in the water. Manufactured strictly for the Teams, there was also Type II Grenadier and Type III Radioman versions of the jacket. This particular jacket still has the sleeves attached, items that were often removed by SEALs in the field. The baggy condition of the diagonal magazine pouches indicate that this SEAL has filled them with 12-gage shells. The second SEAL from the left, with his back to the camera, is wearing a full set of tiger-stripe camouflage fatigues along with a set of M1956 load bearing equipment, including at least three visible universal ammunition pouches. The standing SEAL, third from the right, with his back to the camera, is carrying an AN/PRC-25 radio on his back. The pillow-shaped object immediately below the radio is an inflated air bladder used by the Teams to add buoyancy to equipment or demolition charges. The radioman's right hand is resting on an M60 light machine gun that has an empty C-ration tin secured on the left side just below the feed opening. The empty can was found to help straighten ammunition belts and improve feed reliability for M60's on helicopters and boat installations where the weapon would be feeding an extra-long belt.
PHOTO CREDIT: US NAVY

TECHNICAL DATA—Ithaca Model 37
NSN 6D1005-00-926-9307
CARTRIDGE—12 Ga 2 3/4 in (18.5x70mmR)
OPERATION—Manual, slide-action
TYPE OF FIRE—Repeating
RATE OF FIRE—15 rpm
MUZZLE VELOCITY—1260 fps (396 m/s)
MUZZLE ENERGY—1903 ft/lbs (2580 J)
  70 ft/lbs (95 J) per pellet (27)
SIGHTS—Front bead
CHOKE—Cylinder bore
FEED—4-round tubular magazine
 WEIGHTS
WEAPON (EMPTY)—6.30 lbs (2.86 kg)
WEAPON (LOADED)—6.83 lbs (3.10 kg) w/4 rds in mag + 1 in chamber
MAGAZINE (LOADED)—5 rds - 0.53 lbs (0.24 kg)
SERVICE CARTRIDGE—M257 #4 Buck 748 gr (48.5 g)
PROJECTILE—540 gr (35 g)
PELLET—20 gr (1.3 g)
 LENGTHS
WEAPON OVERALL—40 in (101.6 cm)
BARREL—20.1 in (51.1 cm)
SHOT SPREAD AT 30 YDS (27 M)—30 in (76.2 cm)

Special Weapons

The modern shotgun is the major surviving example of the earliest smoothbore firearms. Instead of launching a single discrete projectile at a high velocity, the shotgun puts out a swarm of projectiles (shot) at a relatively low velocity. Since the shotgun fires a heavy charge of shot, on the order of an ounce or more, the low velocity keeps the weapons recoil down to manageable levels.

The spreading swarm of shot covers a larger and larger area as its distance increases from the muzzle of the firing weapon. This spreading pattern of shot helps the shotgun make up for errors in sighting and judgements in a moving target's speed. This action is what has helped keep the shotgun popular as a sporting weapon, it increasing the chance of hitting a moving target with at least some of the pellets in its load.

ITHACA MODEL 37

Smoothbore muskets and carbines aside, purpose-made fighting shotguns have used since the early 1600's. The musketoon was short, carbine-like version of the musket noted in Europe around the mid-1600's. With a bore equal in size to today's 12 gage, the musketoon was loaded with large shot and used for close-in fighting. Soon, the musketoon evolved into the blunderbuss, the most common fighting shotgun of the flintlock era. Though the distinctive flared muzzle of the blunderbuss had no effect on the spreading of the shot pattern, it did make the weapon easy to reload while on the move. The blasting spread of shot from the blunderbuss proved it to be very effective on board fighting ships where it was used against crowds of men at very short range. The other well known use of this early fighting shotgun was in protecting moving coaches from armed moving targets (highwaymen).

The US involvement in World War I brought the pump or slide action, repeating shotgun into modern warfare. The short, powerful, 12-gage shotgun was found to be very successful in the sudden, close encounters common in trench warfare. During World War II in the Pacific, trenches were rare, but the Marines found the shotgun worked just as well in the fast face-to-face encounters so common in jungle combat. US Marines would obtain short-barreled (18 to 20 inch) repeating shotguns wherever they could, and the supply was never too many according to the men doing the fighting.

Shotguns were familiar to the men of the World War II UDTs, but primarily as guard weapons or seen in the hands of Marines. Very little direct armed combat between the UDTs and enemy troops ever took place during World War II and shoulder weapons, even light ones like a shotgun, were rarely used by the Teams. The relative long range fighting during the Korean War relegated the fighting shotgun to guard duty, but it still proved its value in the occasional massed charges of communist troops. Against a close-in enemy, there are few weapons as effective as a shotgun.

During the World War II years, over twenty different makes, models, and styles of repeating shotguns were used by the US military. One of these guns, the Winchester Model 97, was the original trench gun used during World War I as the Model 1917. By the 1960's, many of the various World War II shotguns had long been weeded

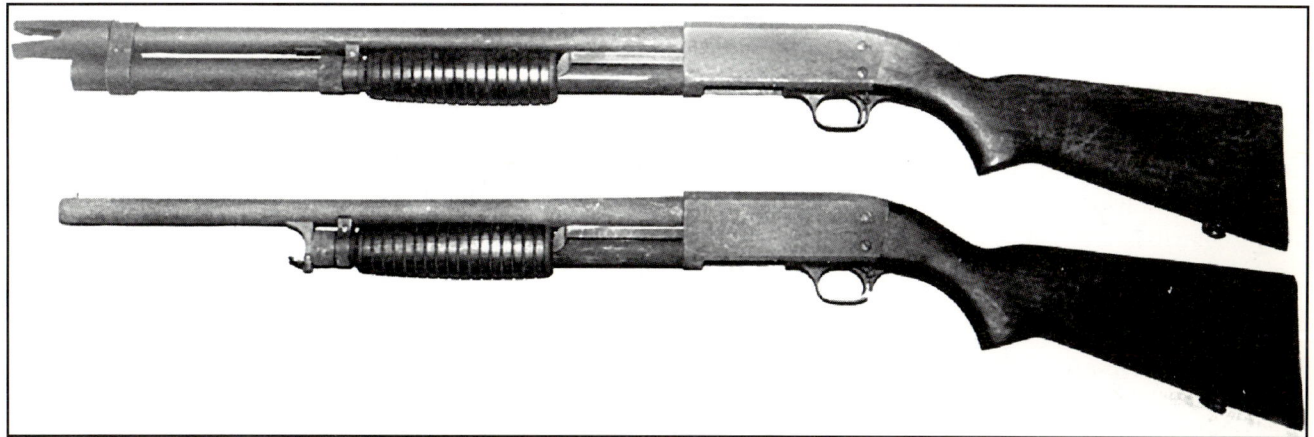

The two most commonly carried SEAL shotguns of the Vietnam war. At the top is the combat conversion of the Ithaca Model 37, consisting of a three-round magazine extension and a horizontal shot spreader attached to the muzzle of the weapon. The lower weapon is the standard-issue Ithaca Model 37 shotgun with a four-round magazine and standard short barrel. The lug underneath the barrel, visible just in front of the magazine cap of the standard weapon, had to be removed for addition of the magazine extension.
PHOTO CREDIT: KEVIN DOCKERY

Shotguns

TECHNICAL DATA—Ithaca Model 37 w/Magazine extension and Duckbill spreader muzzle attachment
CARTRIDGE—12 Ga 2 3/4 in (18.5x70mmR)
OPERATION—Manual, slide-action
TYPE OF FIRE—Repeating
RATE OF FIRE—21 rpm
MUZZLE VELOCITY—1260 fps (396 m/s)
MUZZLE ENERGY—1903 ft/lbs (2580 J) 70 ft/lbs (95 J) per pellet (27)
SIGHTS—Front bead
CHOKE—Special w/horizontal to vertical spread of 4:1
FEED—7 round tubular magazine
WEIGHTS
WEAPON (EMPTY)—6.5 lbs (2.95 kg)
WEAPON (LOADED)—7.35 lbs (3.33 kg) w/7 rds in mag + 1 in chamber
MAGAZINE (LOADED)—8 rounds 0.85 lbs (0.39 kg)
SERVICE CARTRIDGE—M257 #4 Buck 748 gr (48.5 g)
PROJECTILE—540 gr (35 g)
PELLET—20 gr (1.3 g)
LENGTHS
BARREL—20 in (50.8 cm)
SHOT SPREAD AT 30 YDS (27 M)—96 in (243.8 cm) horizontal, 24 in (61 cm) vertical

"**The Model 37 Featherweight was the first true lightweight repeating shotgun with a steel receiver and was produced by the Ithaca Gun Company beginning in 1937.**"

The combat conversion package for the Ithaca Model 37 shotgun as used by the SEALs in Vietnam. This specimen has the early model open duckbill shot spreader on the muzzle of the weapon. Underneath the barrel can be seen the magazine extension that increased the capacity of the weapon from five to eight rounds. A final portion of the conversion was the side mounted sling swivel that was combined with a top-mounted swivel at the rear of the stock.
PHOTO CREDIT: US NAVY

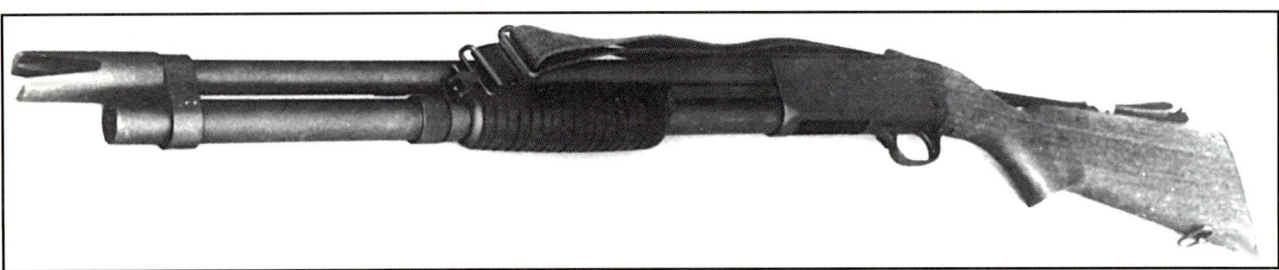

out of the supply system for lack of spare parts or other reasons. When the SEALs were commissioned in 1962, shotguns were among the weapons included in the new Teams allotment lists. The shotgun received by the Teams came from Navy stores and was the Ithaca Model 37 Featherweight.

The Model 37 Featherweight was the first true lightweight repeating shotgun with a steel receiver and was produced by the Ithaca Gun Company beginning in 1937. One reason for the success of the Ithaca Model 37 was its being based largely on the last magazine shotgun design of John Browning before his death in November, 1927.

The first very noticeable feature of the Model 37 is its lack of an ejection port on the side of the weapon. Machined from a solid block of steel, the receiver of the Model 37 is rather short for its caliber with solid, flat sides. The single port in the Model 37 is in the base of the weapon, just in front of the trigger mechanism. The action of the weapon is such that the single port is used to both load the gun and clear ejected cases.

As in almost all other repeating shotguns, the tubular magazine of the Ithaca Model 37 extends underneath the barrel of the weapon. Shells are fed into the magazine nose-first through the bottom port and seated in place with the thumb. The slide handle that operates the action surrounds and lightly guides on the magazine tube. As the slide is pulled back, any fired cartridge case is extracted from the chamber and ejected downwards from the gun.

When the slide handle has reached the end of its rearward stroke, any fired casing has cleared the weapon and a fresh round is released from the magazine. As the slide is pushed forward, a lifter moves the shell into line with the chamber and bolt. With the slide fully forward, the bolt is locked on the chamber and the weapon can be safely fired. With the slide forward, additional shells can be fed into the magazine to help keep it full.

For all the usefulness of the shotgun in combat, the SEALs did not see much practical use for the weapon in the time just after their commissioning. Some of the weapons available to the Teams had the trench gun bayonet adaptors on them. These adaptors consisted of perforated barrel guards to help keep an operator from burning his hands on a hot barrel and heavy muzzle devices than held the barrel guard in place and allowed a long rifle bayonet to be mounted on the weapon.

A bayonet was the last thing that the SEALs would put on a shotgun, but most of the shotguns they had available were the standard, five-shot, 20-inch barreled Ithacas without the added poundage of the adaptor. Few of the Ithacas were used during the first few years of the Teams except for one. Kept in a glass-fronted case on the quarterdeck at SEAL Team Two was a fully-loaded Ithaca Model 37. The weapon was intended for the use of the SEAL on watch and all he had to do was break the glass to be well armed against an intruder.

The opinion of most SEALs about shotguns took a hard turn upwards after the first platoons deployed to Vietnam. Prior to this time, the Teams had trained and exchanged information with some of the British Special Air Service (SAS) men who had combat experience in the jungles of Malaysia. It was during their jungle experience that the SAS troopers had seen first hand the efficiency of the shotgun. Semiautomatic FN-Browning shotguns loaded with 00 buckshot were a favored weapon by the SAS, particularly by their lead scouts (point men), and this was part of the information shared with the SEALs.

The Ithaca Model 37 quickly became a much used weapon among the SEAL point men when they conducted operations in Vietnam. The design of the Ithaca minimized openings into the action and that helped keep mud and jungle debris from jamming the weapon. If a pump shotgun did get jammed up with mud or dirt, it would usually just mean the operator had to jack the slide handle harder to work the weapon. As one SEAL said;

"The fact that I could take my Ithaca and just rinse it off in a muddy stream was one of the reasons I liked it."

Two common rounds of ammunition were available for the SEALs' shotguns, XM162 00 buckshot and XM257 #4 buckshot. 00 or "double-ought" buckshot has long been the favored load for the fighting shotgun and ammunition has been loaded with it since well before the turn of the century. Common paper shotgun shells were noted to swell up in water and quickly become useless. An all-brass 00 shotgun round, the M19, had been developed during World War I just to eliminate the problems with paper shells for combat. Though the M19 round was as waterproof as it could be, and would be used by the SEALs when they could get it, it was just not available in large numbers by the 1960s.

To counter the moisture problem with shotgun ammunition, the plastic cased XM162 and XM257 rounds were developed. Though the 00 buckshot round had been the preferred load, SEALs in Vietnam almost universally used the #4 buckshot round. 00 buckshot is a .33 caliber lead pellet with 9 pellets loaded into a normal (XM162) round. The smaller #4 buckshot, .24 caliber, made room for 27 hardened lead pellets to be loaded into the XM257 round. The triple number of pellets in the XM257 round gave a weapon firing it a very dense shot pattern, making it easier to cause a disabling shot.

The pump-action shotgun, whether loaded with #4 or 00 buckshot, only has an effective combat range of about 75 yards maximum. And at the maximum combat range, it becomes difficult to put enough shot on the target to really be effective. But at the short ranges at which the SEALs tended to operate, the range limitations of the shotgun were more than balanced by the stopping power of the gun when in close. But one limitation of the shotgun could not be as easily ignored. The 12 gage round is very heavy and bulky for a single shot and shotguns are not ammunition efficient. The size and weight of any load of 12 gage shells generally makes them two to four times heavier and larger than an equal number of 7.62mm NATO or 5.56mm rounds. This bulk not only makes shotgun ammunition difficult to carry in quantity, it minimizes the number of rounds carried in a weapon's magazine.

ITHACA MODEL 37 w/EXTENDED MAGAZINE, DUCKBILL

The Ithaca Model 37 carried 4 standard 12 gage rounds in the magazine with a fifth round able to be carried in the chamber. This amount of ammunition can be burned up very quickly in a fire fight. SEALs quickly learned the

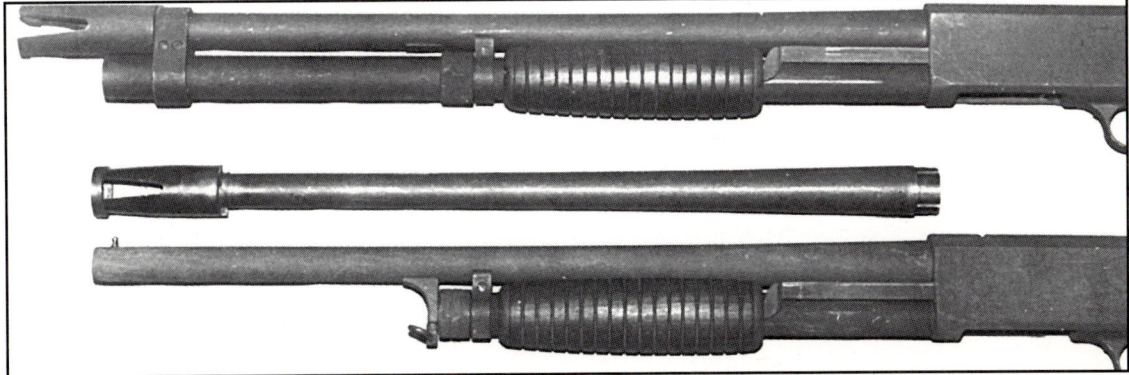

The bottom weapon is the front of a standard Ithaca M37 shotgun with a short barrel and unmodified magazine. The top weapon is a combat conversion of the Ithaca with a three-round magazine extension and 1st model duckbill shot spreader on the muzzle. The barrel at the center of the photograph is an Ithaca barrel with a 2nd model duckbill shot spreader attached to its muzzle. The 2nd model duckbill attachment was a shorter design and had a reinforcing ring around the front of the device. The reinforcing ring prevented the duckbill from opening up with use and kept vegetation from snagging the muzzle of the weapon.
PHOTO CREDIT: KEVIN DOCKERY

Shotguns

"...a full-automatic 12-gage, a machine shotgun, probably the most destructive, close-in fighting weapon ever produced."

A right-side view of the Remington 7188 machine shotgun as used by the SEALs in Vietnam. This version of the 7188 has a perforated guard over the barrel to protect the operator when reloading a hot weapon. The front barrel band assembly includes provisions for mounting a bayonet, something which was not commonly done in the Teams.
PHOTO CREDIT: KEVIN DOCKERY

TECHNICAL DATA—Remington 7188 Mark 1
NSN 1005-LL-L99-5020
—Remington 7180 Mark 1
NSN 1005-LL-L99-5005
CARTRIDGE—12 Ga 2 3\4 in (18.5x70mmR)
OPERATION—Gas
TYPE OF FIRE—Selective - semiautomatic/full automatic
  7180 - Semiautomatic only
RATE OF FIRE—Practical SS 24 rpm, A 35 rpm, Cyclic 420 rpm
MUZZLE VELOCITY—1252 fps (382 m/s)
MUZZLE ENERGY—1817 ft/lbs (2464 J)
  202 ft/lbs (274 J) per pellet
SIGHTS—Open, V-notch/blade, Adjustable
CHOKE—Full

FEED—7 round tubular magazine
 WEIGHTS
WEAPON (EMPTY)—8.50 lbs (3.86 kg)
WEAPON (LOADED)—9.34 lbs (4.24 kg) w/7 rds in mag + 1 in chamber
MAGAZINE (LOADED)—8 rounds 0.84 lbs (0.38 kg)
SERVICE CARTRIDGE—XM162 00 Buck 736 gr (47.7 g)
PROJECTILE—522 gr (33.8 g)
PELLET—58 gr (3.8 g)
 LENGTHS
WEAPON OVERALL—40.94 in (104 cm)
BARREL—20.24 in (51.4 cm)
SIGHT RADIUS—13.11 in (33.3 cm)
SHOT SPREAD AT 30 YDS (27 M)—22.5 in (57.2 cm)

---

trick of constantly reloading or "topping up" their shotgun when ever possible. Some SEALs would carry a few extra rounds of ammunition between the fingers of their operating hand if they were going into a situation where they might need a very fast reload. By simply letting go of the operating slide, two rounds can be quickly thumbed into the magazine with the operating hand without having to draw them from a pocket or pouch.

To help ease the magazine size problem somewhat, a magazine extension was made available for the SEALs' Ithacas by late 1967. Because of the way the front magazine cap is part of the barrel retention system in the Ithaca Model 37, the magazine extension requires some permanent changes to the barrel of the weapon. These changes could be easily done in a field repair shop and the necessary kits were forwarded to Vietnam. With the extension in place, the magazine of the Ithaca could now hold 7 rounds with an 8th round in the chamber.

China Lake had designed the magazine extension first issued for the SEAL's Ithacas. In addition to the magazine extension, China Lake designed an attachment for the barrel of the Model 37 that would spread the pattern of shot in a more effective manner. The shot spreader attachment was initially a four-inch long extension brazed onto the muzzle of the weapon. A horizontal V-slot extending halfway back from the muzzle of the device separated the top and bottom halves of the extension and directed the shot pattern. Because of the shape of the spreader attachment it quickly became known as the "duckbill".

With the duckbill installed on a shotgun, the pattern of the shot changed from a circle to an oval with the long axis in line with the open sides of the duckbill. Instead of having a 44-inch circular pattern with #4 buckshot at 30 yards, the duckbill equipped weapon would have a pattern 96 inches wide and only 24 inches tall at the same distance with the same load. The duckbill equipped Ithaca with the magazine extension became a very well-liked weapon in SEAL units.

"The shotgun with the duckbill was an Ithaca Model 37 and the duckbill was a muzzle attachment that changed the spread of shot from a circle to an oval four times as wide as it was tall. After we started to get some good hits, I picked up the shotgun as a preferred weapon for close-in, especially around hooches. With the duckbill, you didn't have to lead (aim in front of) a moving target as you did a regular shotgun. The spread of the shot made up for any target movement at the short ranges we fought at."

The duckbill attachment was an immediate success with the SEALs even though the design suffered from some drawbacks. Many of the special loads later designed for the SEALs, such as the CS and flare rounds, could not be fired through the duckbill attachment. Slugs could not be used with the duckbill. Even 00 buckshot would not work as efficiently as #4 buckshot when put through the duckbill attachment. Also the open end of the duckbill tended to catch on brush and plants as well as spread apart after extensive use, greatly changing the shot patterns. To eliminate the latter problems a redesigned duckbill with input from Frankford Arsenal was released to the SEALs by late 1968-1969. The new attachment had a ring around the muzzle closing off the front of the side slots and eliminating the spreading apart of the "bills".

An additional combat round was tried out by the SEALs in 1967 but it did not find a great deal of favor with the operators. The flechette round was an attempt to extend the range of the shotgun shell to over 100 yards. Several different rounds were tried out, all with about the same effect. The flechettes, inch-long finned projectiles much like small modified carpenters nails, simply did not have the shocking power found in buckshot loads. Though the flechette rounds did extend the effective range of the 12-gage shotgun to near 150 yards, within 30 yards the rounds were very ineffective.

Because of the aerodynamics of the flechette, the projectiles tended to be unstable when first fired. For the first 20 to 30 yards, the flechette would wobble and yaw badly, having as much chance of hitting a target sideways as point-on. The sideways-striking flechettes has little penetrating power due to their light weight and the flechettes that did hit point first would just penetrate the target, often going straight through. A through-and-through flechette wound would eventually kill a target, but there would be little immediate shock or knockdown power. Though flechette loaded 12 gage rounds did see some combat successes in Vietnam, work still continues to perfect the round.

"The number four hardened buckshot was my preferred load. Double-ought buck was good, but you could hit more with the greater number of pellets in a number four load. Flechette was also good, at least I thought so. You could hit a man at longer range with it than with a regular shot load. But when a man was hit with flechettes, he would keep on running as if he hadn't been shot at all. The targets would bleed to death with a flechette hit rather than get knocked down as with a buckshot load…"

"My favorite shotgun ammunition was the XM257 round with the hardened lead #4 buckshot. The 27 pellets in the shell would knock down any gook I aimed at, which was exactly what I wanted. The flechette shells that were sent to us later would certainly kill a man, at even longer ranges than the XM257. But the sharp pointed little flechettes, they looked like finishing nails with fins, wouldn't stop a man as quickly as a load of #4 buckshot…"

For all the firepower supplied by the pump-action shotgun, even more would be available from a semiautomatic or full automatic weapon using the same ammunition. The British had developed a strong liking for the FN-Browning A-5 semiautomatic weapon during their SAS operations in Malaysia. Though the Browning was strictly a sporting weapon and had a number of drawbacks centering around its somewhat sensitive internal workings, the firepower it produced made up for the special care it needed. Part of the complaints against the Browning came out of the weapon's recoil operated action being sensitive to variations in ammunition. It was problems like these that helped keep the pump-action shotgun the leading favorite in fighting shotguns.

REMINGTON 7188 MARK 1

In early 1967, the Remington Arms Company put the first of a new type of shotgun into the SEALs' hands. The weapon was a full-automatic 12-gage, a machine shotgun, probably the most destructive, close-in fighting weapon ever produced.

Developed with firepower in mind, the Remington 7188 family of weapons certainly delivered. Modified from their gas-operated Remington 1100 product line, the Remington 7188 for the most part resembled a short-barreled sporting shotgun. The Remington 7188 was available in six Marks; the Mark 1 was the primary version issued by the SEALs and had a distinctive perforated barrel shroud, extended seven-round magazine tube, bayonet mounts, and adjustable rifle sights. The Mark 3 also had the rifle sights and extended

A SEAL unit preparing to go out on patrol in Vietnam. The SEAL second from the right is holding a Remington 7188 Mark I in his right hand. The two men in the center of the photo illustrate the two berets often seen in these photos. The SEAL to the left of center, with his left hand resting on his thigh, is wearing the camouflage beret favored by many SEALs. The sailor to the right of center, leaning on the canvas overhead, is wearing the black beret worn by many members of the Brown water Navy. The circular patch on the black beret is that of the River Patrol Force, Task Force 116 of Operation Game Warden.
PHOTO CREDIT: UDT-SEAL MUSEUM

magazine tube but no barrel shroud. The Mark 3 had only the rifle sights with a standard length tubular magazine.

The Remington 7188 Marks 2, 4, and 6 were the same as the odd-numbered marks in that the Mk 2 had the barrel shroud assembly and long magazine, the Mk 4 just the long magazine, and the Mk 6 the standard magazine. But on the even numbered marks the sights were the simple front bead of a sporting shotgun.

What made the Remington 7188 stand out was the small switch put in place of the push button safety behind the trigger guard. With the selector lever, found on the left side of the weapon, turned to the rear, the gun fired semiautomatically, one shot for each pull of the trigger. With the lever pointing down, the weapon was on safe and the trigger would not operate. By putting the lever in the forward pointing position, the 7188 fired full automatic.

Firing on full automatic, the 7188 could spew out its ammunition at a cyclic rate of 420 rounds per minute. Using XM162 OO buckshot ammunition loaded with nine pellets each shell, the 7188 could empty its magazine in just over a second. This rate of fire would put seventy-two .33 caliber "bullets" out of the weapon in under a second and a half. This is heavier and faster firepower than two men firing submachine guns on full automatic in one long burst. By loading the weapon with XM257 #4 buckshot ammunition with its 27 pellets per shell, the 7188 could saturate a target with 216 projectiles in one second.

"I liked the Remington automatic shotgun (the model 7188) a lot as well as the Ithaca. It didn't have a duckbill, and the recoil of that sucker would really put a hum on you, but who cared? During a fire fight, your adrenalin was pumping so hard you didn't even feel the buck and recoil of the weapon much. The only trouble was, Boom, Boom, Boom, Boom…, eight times and whoops, you had to reload. I used the weapon on full auto a lot. It really got everyone's attention, especially the people you were shooting at…"

The magazine capacity and one-round-at-a-time reloading procedure was found to be a drawback in the 7188 design, but that was not what kept the weapon from being a success. The Remington 1100, the parent design of the 7188, is a gas-operated, semi-automatic sporting shotgun. The changes for the 7188 conversion were very minor as far as the internal workings of the weapon were concerned. But these same internal workings were far more sensitive to dirt and fouling than a pump action operating system. The 7188 was just too sensitive to dirt for the muddy conditions in Southeast Asia.

"Other weapons were in the gun shed, including the Remington 7188 full-auto shotgun. When the weapon had first arrived, B— had grabbed on to it as the best thing since sliced bread… I had started carrying a shotgun, a five-shot Ithaca Model 37. B— tried to convince me that the Remington 7188 was the weapon for a point man to carry. But I considered the thing just too heavy to be worth it. Besides, my pump-gun was much more reliable than that complicated full-auto gun.

B— carried the 7188 on about six patrols and finally gave up on it as just being too sensitive to dirt. During one ambush, B— used the 7188 on full auto, and the results were devastating. But the reliability problem finally caused B— to switch to either another Ithaca like mine or the CAR-15 and M16 rifle…"

The gas operating system of the 7188 and 1100 allowed the weapons to operate well with a wide variety of ammunition. The gas piston of the system surrounds the magazine tube and is sealed with the barrel seal. Combat operations were hard on the 7188 weapons and their maintenance did cause some problems. In the weekly situation reports for Fifth Platoon, SEAL Team Two covering the period 24 June to 1 July, 1967 the 7188 shotgun is noted under item 2 (c);

"There is a sixty cent part needed for the automatic shot gun. D— or M— can supply you with information on the part."

The item needed was the barrel seal. Without it, the Remington action does not work dependably. Constant

The author firing a 12 gage Remington 7188 machine shotgun from the hip on full automatic. The bolt of the Remington has locked to the rear as the last shot has been fired from the magazine. Even though the weapon has strong recoil, it can be fired controllably, especially when strongly braced. Two ejected casings can be seen in the air to the right of the weapon, one closer to the camera and appearing to be just above the breech of the weapon, and the other casing is at the lower right of the photo.
PHOTO CREDIT: KEVIN DOCKERY

Data Annex for Combat Shotgun Ammunition

TECHNICAL DATA
CARTRIDGE—12 Gage Guard Paper case
CALIBER—12 Ga 2 3/4 in (18.5x70mmR)
LOAD—00 Buck
NUMBER OF PELLETS—9
NOMINAL MUZZLE VELOCITY—
1325 fps (404 m/s)
NOMINAL MUZZLE ENERGY—
2035 ft/lbs (2759 J)
226 ft/lbs (306 J) Per pellet
TEST BARREL LENGTH—30 in (76.2 cm)
 WEIGHTS
CARTRIDGE—791 gr (51.3 g)
PROJECTILE—522 gr (33.8 g)
PELLET—58 gr (3.8 g)

TECHNICAL DATA
CARTRIDGE—M19 Metal case
CALIBER—12 Ga 2 3/4 in (18.5x70mmR)
LOAD—00 Buck
NUMBER OF PELLETS—9
NOMINAL MUZZLE VELOCITY—
1125 fps (343 m/s)
NOMINAL MUZZLE ENERGY—
1467 ft/lbs (1989 J)
163 ft/lbs (221 J) Per pellet
TEST BARREL LENGTH—30 in (76.2 cm)
 WEIGHTS
CARTRIDGE—930 gr (60.3 g)
PROJECTILE—522 gr (33.8 g)
PELLET—58 gr (3.8 g)
PELLET DIAMETER—0.34 in (8.6 mm)

TECHNICAL DATA
CARTRIDGE—M257 Plastic case
CALIBER—12 Ga 2 3/4 in (18.5x70mmR)
LOAD—#4 Hardened buckshot
NUMBER OF PELLETS—27
NOMINAL MUZZLE VELOCITY—
1335 fps (407 m/s)
NOMINAL MUZZLE ENERGY—
2137 ft/lbs (2898 J)
79 ft/lbs (107 J) Per pellet
TEST BARREL LENGTH—30 in (76.2 cm)
 WEIGHTS
CARTRIDGE—748 gr (48.5 g)
PROJECTILE—540 gr (35 g)
PELLET—20 gr (1.3 g)
PELLET DIAMETER—0.24 in (6.1 mm)

TECHNICAL DATA
CARTRIDGE—Teleshot Silent
Shotgun Shell
CALIBER—12 Ga 2 3/4 in (18.5x70mmR)
LOAD—#4 Hardened buck
NUMBER OF PELLETS—12
NOMINAL MUZZLE VELOCITY—
450 fps (137 m/s)
NOMINAL MUZZLE ENERGY—
108 ft/lbs (146 J)
9 ft/lbs (12 J) Per pellet
 WEIGHTS
CARTRIDGE—
PROJECTILE—240 gr (15.6 g) w/o plastic pusher piston
PELLET—20 gr (1.3 g)
PELLET DIAMETER—0.24 in (6.1 mm)

TECHNICAL DATA
CARTRIDGE—XM162 Plastic case,
NSN 1305-00-92-4254
CALIBER—12 Ga 2 3/4 in (18.5x70mmR)
LOAD—00 Buck
NUMBER OF PELLETS—9
NOMINAL MUZZLE VELOCITY—
1325 fps (404 m/s)
NOMINAL MUZZLE ENERGY—
2035 ft/lbs (2759 J)
226 ft/lbs (306 J) Per pellet
TEST BARREL LENGTH—30 in (76.2 cm)
 WEIGHTS
CARTRIDGE—736 gr (47.7 g)
PROJECTILE—522 gr (33.8 g)
PELLET—58 gr (3.8 g)
PELLET DIAMETER—0.34 in (8.6 mm)

TECHNICAL DATA
CARTRIDGE—Remington Model SP-12F-20
Beehive Flechette
CALIBER—12 Ga 2 3/4 in (18.5x70mmR)
LOAD—Finned steel flechettes
NUMBER OF PELLETS—20
NOMINAL MUZZLE VELOCITY—
2200 fps (671 m/s)
NOMINAL MUZZLE ENERGY—
1620 ft/lbs (2197 J)
81 ft/lbs (110 J) Per flechette
TEST BARREL LENGTH—20 in (50.8 cm)
 WEIGHTS
CARTRIDGE—750 gr (48.6 g)
PROJECTILE—150 gr (9.7 g)
PELLET—7.5 gr (0.49 g)
PELLET DIAMETER—0.087 in (2.21 mm)

TECHNICAL DATA
CARTRIDGE—Penguin Long Range
Tear Gas round
CALIBER—12 Ga 2 3/4 in (18.5x70mmR)
LOAD—Burning-type Tear Gas (CN) canister
NUMBER OF PELLETS—1
FILLER—CN/Bullseye smokeless powder
(Burning mixture)
NOMINAL MUZZLE VELOCITY—
800 fps (244 m/s)
TEST BARREL LENGTH—
20 in (50.8 cm)
FILLER—185 gr (12 g)

TECHNICAL DATA
CARTRIDGE—Flare round
CALIBER—12 ga 2 3/4 in (18.5x70mmR)
LOAD—Red star cluster
NUMBER OF PELLETS—4
BURN TIME—5 to 6 seconds at 5000 Candlepower
EFFECTIVE RANGE—200 ft (61 m) altitude

TECHNICAL DATA
CARTRIDGE—HK CAWS #2 Tungsten
CALIBER—19.5x76mmB
LOAD—#2 Tungsten buck
NUMBER OF PELLETS—8
NOMINAL MUZZLE VELOCITY—
1625 fps (495 m/s)
NOMINAL MUZZLE ENERGY—
2216 ft/lbs (3005 J)
277 ft/lbs (376 J) Per pellet
TEST BARREL LENGTH—26.94 in (68.4 cm)
 WEIGHTS
CARTRIDGE—1073 gr (69.5 g)
PROJECTILE—378 gr (224.5 g)
PELLET—47.25 gr (3.06 g)
PELLET DIAMETER—0.27 in

TECHNICAL DATA
CARTRIDGE—HK CAWS Flechette
CALIBER—19.5x76mmB
LOAD—Finned steel flechettes
NUMBER OF PELLETS—20
NOMINAL MUZZLE VELOCITY—
2953 fps (900 m/s)
NOMINAL MUZZLE ENERGY—
2246 ft/lbs (3046 J)
112 ft/lbs (152 J) Per flechette
TEST BARREL LENGTH—18.11 in (46 cm)
 WEIGHTS
CARTRIDGE—811 gr (52.6 g)
PROJECTILE—116 gr (7.5 g)
PELLET—5.8 gr (0.376 g)

TECHNICAL DATA
CARTRIDGE—AAI CAWS Flechette
CALIBER—18.5x79mm
LOAD—Drag-stabilized flechettes
NUMBER OF PELLETS—8
NOMINAL MUZZLE VELOCITY—
1794 fps (547 m/s)
NOMINAL MUZZLE ENERGY—
1901 ft/lbs (2578 J)
229 ft/lbs (311 J) Per Outer flechette
300 ft/lbs (407 J) Inner flechette
TEST BARREL LENGTH—16 in (40.7 cm)
 WEIGHTS
CARTRIDGE—623 gr (40.4 g)
PROJECTILE—266 gr (17.2 g)
PELLET—32 gr (2.07 g) Outer flechette
42 gr (2.72 g) Inner flechette
27 gr (1.75 g) Steel flechette body
FLECHETTE DIAMETER—0.104 mm (2.65 mm)
Flechette body
FLECHETTE LENGTH—1.62 in (4.1 cm)

TECHNICAL DATA
CARTRIDGE—HK CAWS 000 Buck
CALIBER—19.5x76mmB
LOAD—000 Buck
NUMBER OF PELLETS—8
NOMINAL MUZZLE VELOCITY—
1601 fps (488 m/s)
NOMINAL MUZZLE ENERGY—
3141 ft/lbs (4259 J)
393 ft/lbs (533 J) Per pellet
TEST BARREL LENGTH—18.11 in (46 cm)
 WEIGHTS
CARTRIDGE—1247 gr (80.8 g)
PROJECTILE—552 gr (35.8 g)
PELLET—69 gr (4.5 g)
PELLET DIAMETER—0.36 in (9.1 mm)

Special Weapons

This is one of the few existing photographs of the very rare silent shotgun shell produced for SEAL use during the Vietnam War. The round to the far right is a complete, unfired cartridge showing the steel case with the partial taper to aid in feeding. The center round is a cutaway showing the buckshot charge at the top of the round resting on the pusher piston. The piston is surrounded by the telescoping, folded metal component that is the heart of the "telecartridge" power system. The open chamber at the base of the round would normally hold the powder charge. The casing to the left is a fired round and shows the bulging end of the unfolded telecartridge capsule protruding from the mouth of the case.
PHOTO CREDIT: AAI/THOMAS SWEARENGEN COLLECTION

A cross-sectional drawing of the AAI silent shotgun shell. At the top is an unfired view showing all of the components including the folded telecartridge envelope and the plastic pusher. The lower drawing is of a fired round showing the telecartridge in its fully-extended position, sealing off the release of the propellant gases after having driven the pusher to the maximum velocity given by the round.
PHOTO CREDIT: AAI/THOMAS SWEARENGEN COLLECTION

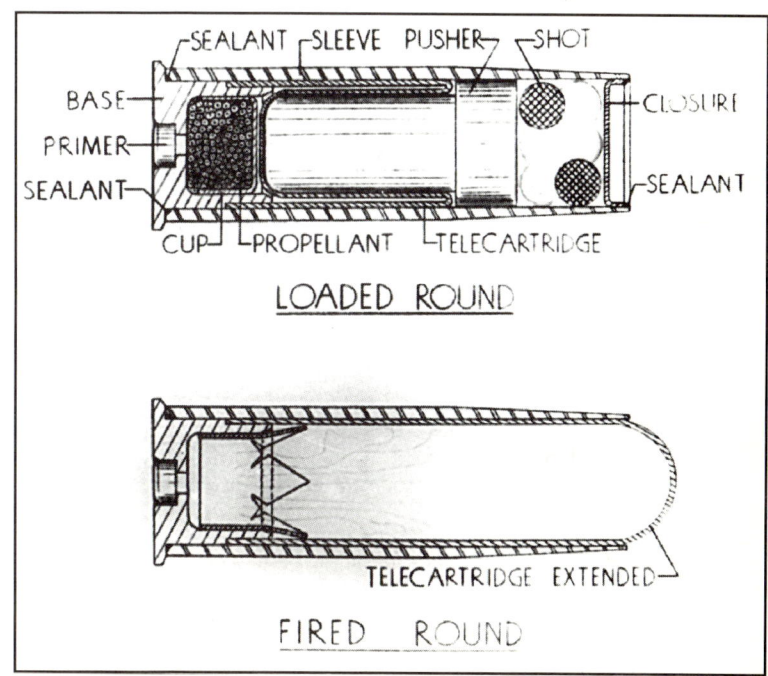

Shotguns

TECHNICAL DATA—Remington 870 Mark 6
NSN 6D1005-00-999-4213 w/20 inch barrel
NSN 6D1005-01-085-1033 w/17 inch barrel
CARTRIDGE—12 Ga 2 3/4 in (18.5x70mmR)
OPERATION—Manual slide-action
TYPE OF FIRE—Repeating
RATE OF FIRE—15 rpm
MUZZLE VELOCITY—20 in bbl - 1250 fps (381 m/s)
   17 in bbl - 1243 fps (379 m/s)
MUZZLE ENERGY—20 in bbl
   17 in bbl - 1791 ft/lbs (2429 J)
   per pellet 20 in bbl
   199 ft/lbs (270 J) per pellet 17 in bbl
SIGHTS—Front bead
CHOKE—Cylinder bore
FEED—4 round tubular magazine

WEIGHTS
WEAPON (EMPTY)—7 lbs (3.18 kg) w/20 in bbl
   6.82 lbs (3.09 kg) w/17 in bbl
WEAPON (LOADED)—
7.53 (3.42 kg) w/20 in bbl, 4 rds in mag + 1 in chamber
7.35 lbs (3.33 kg) w/17 in bbl, 4 rds in mag + 1 in chamber
MAGAZINE (LOADED)—5 rounds - 0.53 lbs (0.24 kg)
SERVICE CARTRIDGE—XM162 00 Buck 736 gr (47.7 g)
PROJECTILE—522 gr (33.8 g)
PELLET—58 gr (3.8 g)
LENGTHS
WEAPON OVERALL—40.5 in (102.9 cm) w/20 in bbl
   37.5 in (95.3 cm) w/17 in bbl
BARREL—20 in (50.1 cm)
   17 in (43.2 cm)
SHOT SPREAD AT 30 YDS (27 M)—30 in (76.2 cm)

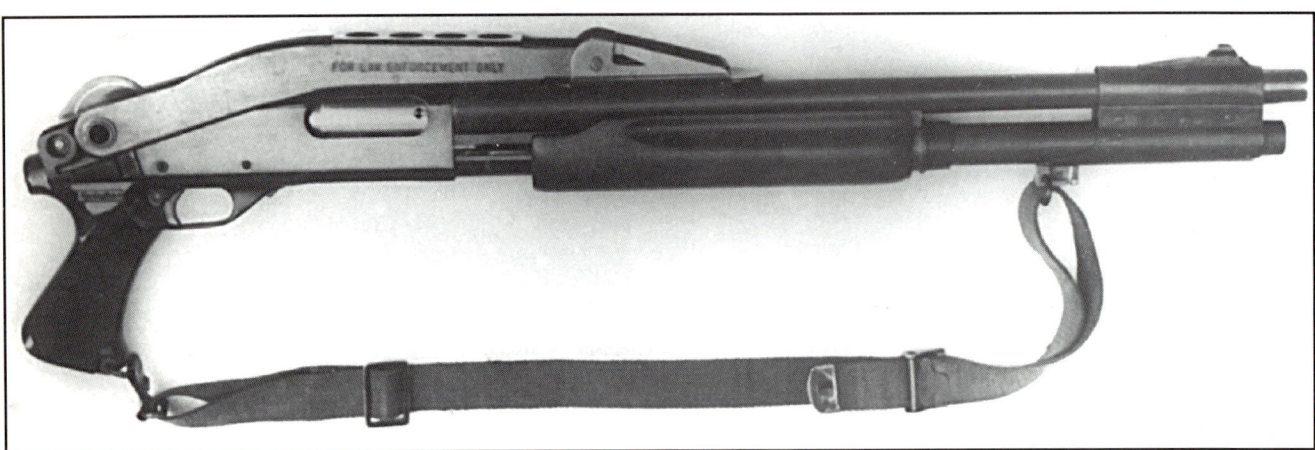

The Remington 870 shotgun with its stock in the folded position on top of the receiver. This specimen is a conversion of the commercial 20 inch barreled 870 with the addition of a magazine extension and police folding stock
PHOTO CREDIT: KEVIN DOCKERY

A SEAL lies quietly in the grass during training. His weapon is a Remington 870 shotgun.
PHOTO CREDIT: US NAVY

"The Mark 1 differs from the normal 870 in that it came equipped from the factory with a two-shot magazine extension giving the Mark 1 an ammunition capacity of eight rounds."

Special Weapons

A group of SEALs preparing for a demonstration as a Vietnam-era patrol. The SEAL to the left has a Remington 870 shotgun slung muzzle-down across his back. His load bearing equipment is nylon ALICE gear (All-purpose Lightweight Individual Carrying Equipment) adopted by the Army in 1974. Two LC-2 canteen carriers are on the back of his pistol belt each holding a 1-quart plastic canteen. The small pocket on the side of the LC-2 carrier is for a bottle of water-purification tablets. Below the canteens, this SEAL has a SIG P226 pistol secured in a low-leg, hard shell, break-front leather holster. The SEAL in the center of the photo is wearing padded fast-roping gloves and is carrying his 30-round M16 magazines in an early-model assault vest. The SEAL to the right of center is wearing a standard BDU (Battle Dress Uniform) blouse over a pair of tiger-stripe trousers. His LC-2 pistol belt is unfastened and he is wearing Nomex flight gloves to protect his hands.
PHOTO CREDIT: KEVIN DOCKERY

maintenance had consumed the supply of parts available in Vietnam.

"B— liked the shotgun [7188], even though it was a bitch to hang on to during full automatic fire…"

In addition to the maintenance difficulties, the Remington 7188 was hard to control when fired on full automatic. The stock design and recoil forces of the 7188 forced the barrel up and back very quickly when the weapon was fired from the shoulder. Training and strength were two items the SEALs had in abundance and both were brought to bear in controlling the 7188. When fired from the hip and properly braced, the 7188 was completely controllable and would put out its swath of fire like a mowing machine. But very quickly the small magazine would be empty and the weapon was just as slow to reload as any other shotgun at the time.

But with its drawbacks, the Remington 7188 Mark 1 remained in SEAL hands through the Vietnam War. Never available in very large numbers, reportedly only a few dozen of all the marks were ever made, the Remingtons that were incountry were coveted for their awesome firepower. After Vietnam had ended, the 7188's were removed from inventory but the full-automatic shotgun question was looked at again in later programs.

"The twelve gage shotgun has been fitted with a specially designed muzzle to give a greater spread to the pellet pattern. Special ammunition has been delivered for shotguns in the form of CS and flare rounds…" From COMMAND AND CONTROL HISTORY - 1968 SEAL TEAM TWO

The 12 gage shotgun had quickly established a place for itself in the SEAL arsenal in Vietnam. To increase the versatility of the weapon, a number of new ammunition types were developed and tried out. The buckshot loads used during the first two World Wars had been made up

Shotguns

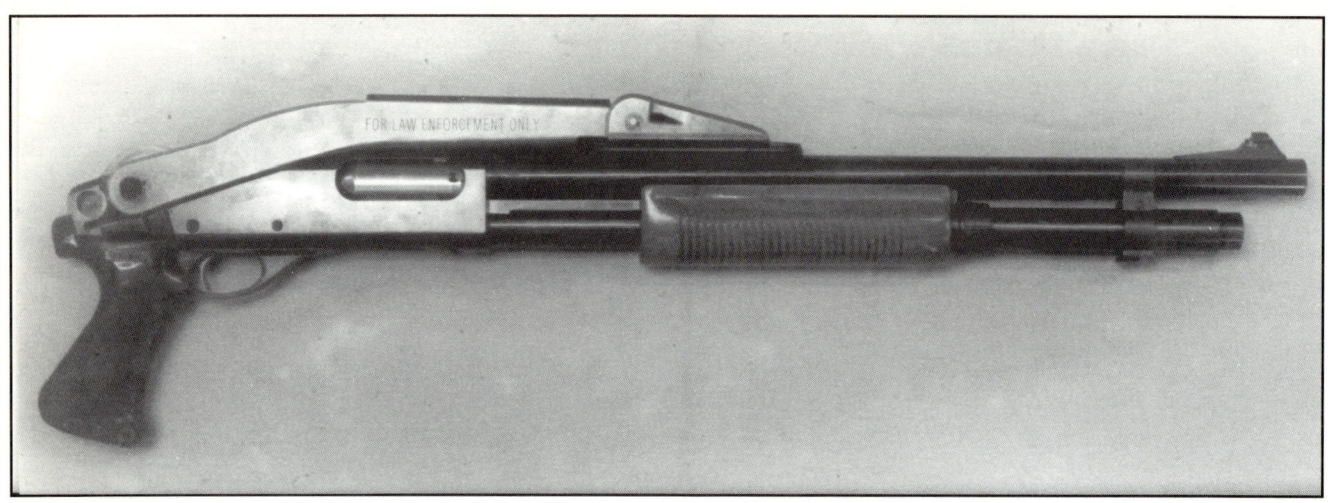

The Remington 870P shotgun with its stock in the folded position on top of the receiver. This specimen has the front barrel band that allows it to accept a standard M7 bayonet.
PHOTO CREDIT: KEVIN DOCKERY

A SEAL assault squad prepares to attack a ship's bridge while undergoing training during Operation Desert Storm. The rear man is armed with a pistol-grip Remington 870 shotgun with a two-round magazine extension. The remaining members of the Team each have MP5-N submachine guns at the ready. The white strap affairs at several of the SEAL's hips are plastic wire ties used as quick handcuffs. The ties are cheap, fast to use, and must be cut off to be removed. The men are all wearing body armor, PRO-TEC helmets, and a variety of nylon load carrying equipment.
PHOTO CREDIT: US NAVY

almost entirely of pure lead pellets. These pellets were found to deform and lose their ballistic shape under the acceleration of being fired. The popular XM257 #4 buckshot load had eliminated this problem in two ways. The 0.24 inch diameter pellets in the XM257 were made up of lead alloy containing 4 percent antimony. The alloy shot were much harder than the commercial lead shot found in the XM162 round. The open space between the #4 buckshot in the XM257 round was filled in with granulated polyethylene with the entire padded shot load enclosed in a sheet polyethylene collar.

The alloy pellets and plastic fillers used in the XM257 round gave it a much more uniform shot pattern when fired and kept the pattern from spreading as quickly as it otherwise would have. When fired from a normal 20-inch cylinder bore barrel, all of the pellets from an XM257 round impact inside of a 40-inch (101.6 cm) circle at 44 yards (40 m). This is what gives the XM257 round and the shotgun such a high hit probability which is increased with the duckbill muzzle attachment. Within 5 yards or less, the pattern of shot opens to be only a few inches wide, effectively hitting as a single, huge projectile.

Several rounds of ammunition used in the SEALs' shotguns in Vietnam were not intended to be direct, casualty-producing rounds. The 12-gage CS tear gas round fired a small metal capsule filled with CS and a burning agent. Acting much like a miniature M7A3 tear gas grenade, the CS round would ignite when fired and could be used to put a small amount of CS into a bunker or hooch. Several CS rounds were usually carried by most SEALs armed with a shotgun, especially when going out on search operations.

The other special pyrotechnic 12-gage round used by the SEALs was an aerial flare cartridge. Much brighter than any small-arms tracer round, the 12-gage flare round launched an aluminum capsule loaded with colored flare composition. Besides being usable for signaling, the flare round could also act as a small incendiary projectile for setting fire to buildings and other flammable structures.

What was probably the most unusual shotgun shell ever produced was manufactured for the SEALs in Vietnam. With the SEALs' strong tastes for shotguns and suppressed weapons, the idea of a suppressed shotgun held a great deal of appeal. But the large caliber and multiple projectile load of a shotgun badly complicates any attempt to put a suppressor on the barrel or muzzle of the weapon. What was attempted was the silencing of the shotgun shell itself.

The requirement put forward by the Navy in 1967 was for a low-signature munition that could be loaded, fired, and ejected from a standard shotgun without modification to the weapon. The round was also to have the high hit probability and lethality of a shotgun shell but could be accepted with a shortened range. The low-signature requirement not only meant the sound of the shot being suppressed but also the elimination of much or all of the flash and smoke of firing. The difficult requirements of the round were met within a year by the AAI Corporation of Baltimore, Maryland.

By using their patented telecartridge device as a base, AAI succeeded in producing what they called the Silent Shotgun Shell by early in 1968. The telecartridge was a method of producing mechanical action through the use of burning propellant. The heart of the telecartridge system was the use of an expanding metal capsule to produce the mechanical motion by retaining the expanding gases of a suitable propellant. A byproduct of the system was the retention of the propellant gases, which eliminated most of the noise of burning as well as all of the smoke and flash. Produced for the aerospace industry, the telecartridge was also able to make an effective silent round of ammunition for the military.

The Silent Shotgun Shell used the expanding metal capsule of the telecartridge system to drive a plastic pusher piston. The piston in turn drove the round's twelve #4 buckshot to a muzzle velocity of 450 feet per second. The expanding metal capsule prevented any gases from escaping the fired round and so the only sound heard when firing the Silent Shotgun Shell was the click of the shotgun's firing pin.

The body of the cartridge was made of steel in the configuration of a 12-gage round. The sides of the body were parallel for about two-thirds of their length and then tapered slightly into the mouth of the casing. The tapering was to help the round feed and extract after firing. The cadmium-plated steel body of the silent shotgun shell was rust-resistant and waterproof. The telecartridge capsule itself was made of 1010 steel and folded into itself to reduce its overall length. An aluminum capsule at the base of the round contained the smokeless-powder propellant charge and acted as a high-pressure chamber to ensure the complete burning of the powder. A standard percussion primer completed the system.

About 200 rounds of silent shotgun shell ammunition was produced overall and supplied to the Naval Ordnance Laboratory for testing. Suggestions put out by the laboratory reduced the muzzle velocity of the original rounds from 550 feet per second to around 450 feet per second. The reduction in velocity removed some of the stopping power of the round but also reduced the chances of the telecartridge capsule rupturing.

Though the silent shotgun shell was not completely silent, it made a weapon firing it very hard to hear and effectively unnoticable. The few rounds made were consumed in testing and none were known to be sent to Vietnam for field testing. The major factor that prevented the silent shotgun shell from being used in quantities by the SEALs in Vietnam was the very high cost of each round. The high cost was not considered balanced by the usefulness of the round as other suppressed weapons were becoming available, and the project was shelved.

REMINGTON 870 MARK 1

By the mid to late 1970's, the shotguns the SEALs had been using in Vietnam were more than seeing their age and a replacement weapon was needed to supplant existing Ithaca stocks. After an exhaustive series of tests in 1966, the Marine Corps had adopted the Remington 870 as their primary issue shotgun.

Shotguns

TECHNICAL DATA — Remington 870 P w/folding stock
NSN 1005-01-282-9104
CARTRIDGE — 12 Ga 2 3/4 in
OPERATION — Manual slide action
TYPE OF FIRE — Repeating
RATE OF FIRE — 15 rpm
MUZZLE VELOCITY — 1243 fps (379 m/s)
MUZZLE ENERGY — 1791 ft/lbs (2429 J)
 199 ft/lbs (270 J) per pellet
SIGHTS — Front bead
CHOKE — Cylinder bore
FEED — 4 round tubular magazine
WEIGHTS
WEAPON (EMPTY) — 6.94 lbs (3.15 kg)
WEAPON (LOADED) — 7.47 lbs (3.39 kg) w/4 rds in mag + 1 in chamber
MAGAZINE (LOADED) — 5 rounds - 0.53 lbs (0.24 kg)
SERVICE CARTRIDGE — XM162 00 Buck 736 gr (47.7 g)
PROJECTILE — 522 gr (33.8 g)
PELLET — 58 gr (3.8 g)
 LENGTHS
WEAPON OVERALL — 27/37 in (68.6/94 cm)
BARREL — 17 in (43.2 cm)
SHOT SPREAD AT 30 YDS (27 M) — 30 in (76.2 cm)

TECHNICAL DATA — Remington 870 Mark 1
NSN 1005-01-065-8989
CARTRIDGE — 12 Ga 2 3/4 in (18.5x70mmR)
OPERATION — Manual slide-action
TYPE OF FIRE — Repeating
RATE OF FIRE — 24 rpm
MUZZLE VELOCITY — 1257 fps (383 m/s)
MUZZLE ENERGY — 1831 ft/lbs (2483 J)
203 ft/lbs (275 J) per pellet
SIGHTS — Open, V-notch/bead, Adjustable
CHOKE — Modified
FEED — 7 round tubular magazine
WEIGHTS
WEAPON (EMPTY) — 8.0 lbs (3.63 kg)
WEAPON (LOADED) — 8.84 lbs 4.01 kg) w/7 rds in mag + 1 in chamber
MAGAZINE (LOADED) — 8 rounds 0.84 lbs (0.38 kg)
SERVICE CARTRIDGE — XM162 00 Buck 736 gr (47.7 g)
PROJECTILE — 522 gr (33.8 g)
PELLET — 58 gr (3.8 g)
 LENGTHS
WEAPON OVERALL — 41.75 in (106 cm)
BARREL — 21 in (53.3 cm)
SHOT SPREAD AT 30 YDS (27 M) — 26 in (66 cm)

A SEAL Breacher member of an assault squad covers a stairway with his shotgun while undergoing ship searching drill during Operation Desert Storm. The weapon is a Remington 870 12-gage shotgun with a police folding stock and two-shot magazine extension. The metal portion of the folding stock has been removed leaving the Remington with just a plastic pistol grip. The SEAL is wearing a PRO-TEC helmet and safety glasses and has a single M1951 glove over his left hand.
PHOTO CREDIT: US NAVY

Special Weapons

The Marine model of the Remington was the 870 Mark 1 designed particularly for military use. The Mark 1 differs from the normal 870 in that it came equipped from the factory with a two-shot magazine extension giving the Mark 1 an ammunition capacity of eight rounds. Distinctive on the Mark 1 is the long double sleeve near the muzzle that acts as a brace between the magazine extension and the barrel. The magazine cap works with a stud on the underside of the brace and allows the Mark 1 to mount the M7 bayonet.

Most Marine 870 Mark 1's have a standard wooden buttstock but some are fitted with the Remington folding stock. The Remington folding stock has a pistol grip and a square-cross section metal stock. The stock can swing over the top of the 870 and lay across the top of the receiver and barrel. Though the rifle-type sights of the Mark 1 are obscured with the Remington stock in the folded position, the pistol grip allows the weapon to be comfortably fired with the stock folded. Some Remington 870 Mark 1's are fitted with a front bead sight in place of the rifle-type sights but the bead is also blocked when the stock is folded.

REMINGTON 870 MK 1 W/SIDEWINDER STOCK

Another very rugged folding stock was acquired by the Marine Corps by the mid 1980's. The Sidewinder stock is a telescoping stock with a swiveling buttpad that can fold over the receiver of the Remington 870 or remain down with the stock collapsed. With the buttpad swiveled up over the receiver, the sights of the 870 are blocked and cannot be used. The advantage of the Sidewinder stock is its high strength and low silhouette when folded. Extended, the Sidewinder stock is strong enough to batter open doors, or batter down an opponent, if necessary.

REMINGTON 870R (20 IN BBL, 17 IN BBL)

The SEALs respected the testing done by the Marines and examined the Remington 870 for their own use. Instead of the Marine 870 Mark 1, the SEALs chose the standard Remington 870 in several different patterns including the 870R and 870P. The Remington 870R is a 20-inch barreled wooden stocked weapon with a five-round ammunition capacity and parkerized military finish. With a bead sight, the 870R is the Mark 6, and with a set of rifle-type sights, it is the Mark 5.

REMINGTON 870P

The Remington 870P is much like the 870R except that the P model has the two-shot magazine extension attached. With the rifle-type sights, the designation is Mark 3 and with a plain bead front sight, it is the Remington Mark 4. The designations get even more blurred when the SEALs start attaching the various accessories and different length barrels they prefer.

In general, the Remington 870 is a very rugged slide action repeating shotgun. Having stood up to severe testing, the 870 is the standard shotgun issued in the Teams since the mid-1980's. The steel receiver of the Remington 870 allows the weapon to accept a great deal of abuse and wear. Individual weapons have fired thousands of rounds without requiring any maintenance beyond cleaning. The Remington folding stock, originally

Dressed in a set of desert-pattern camouflage BDUs, this SEAL is armed with a 12-gage Remington 870 shotgun. The shotgun has been fitted with a Remington police folding stock. At his left thigh, he has his secondary weapon, a SIG P226 pistol, secured in a strapped down Mark III SAS holster.
PHOTO CREDIT: UDT-SEAL MUSEUM

only found on the 870P model intended for police sales, has been used in two different configurations by the SEALs.

The regular Remington 870P with a folding stock is used where size is a major consideration. The ease with which the Remington 870 can be used with the stock folded has led to a number of weapons having the folding metal portion of their stocks removed. The short-barreled, pistol grip 870 is used by the Teams especially as a breachers weapon. The breacher assignment developed from SEALs' involvement in counterterrorism. Learned from their opposite numbers in the British SAS is the SEAL technique for opening locked doors rapidly. Instead of targeting the lock with a shotgun blast and kicking the door open, a breacher uses his shotgun against the hinges of a closed door. With two or three quick blasts of 00 buckshot against their hinges, most doors simply fall open. In the SEALs' case, the door will

Shotguns

A SEAL fire team keeps watch at all points of the compass during a radio contact. The point man at the lower right is armed with a 12-gage Remington 870 shotgun. Direct behind the point man and facing the other way is a sniper wearing his camouflage ghillie suit. The sniper's weapon is held at the ready position, low in the grass in front of him. Above the point man is the automatic weapons man. His M60 machine gun is held in his left hand and is mostly hidden behind the tree trunk. The radioman is carrying an AN/PRC-77 radio with the antenna partially folded down for additional concealment.
PHOTO CREDIT: US NAVY

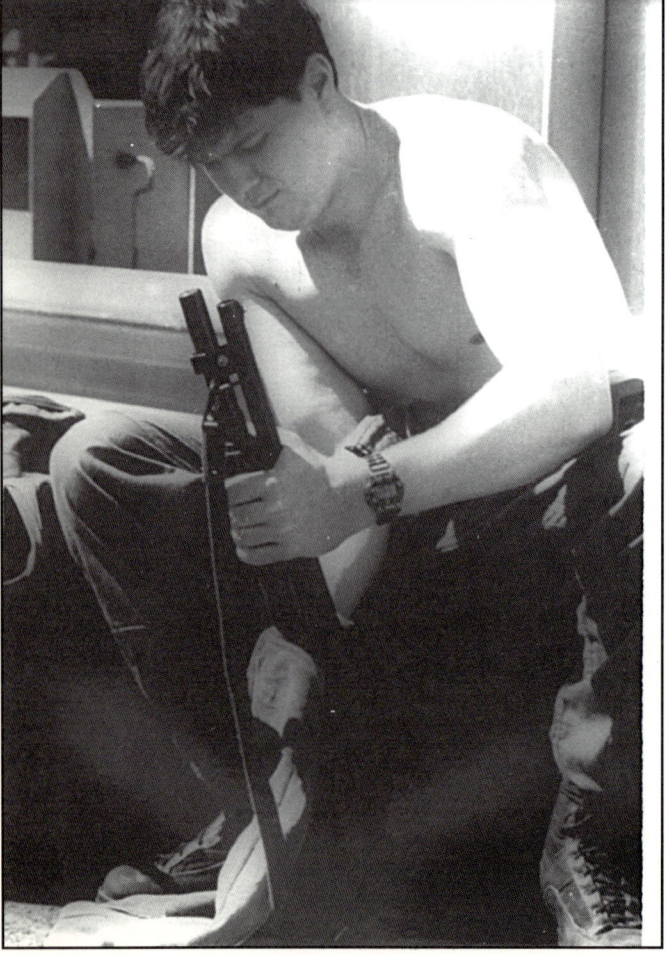

*After a training drill on board the **USS JOSHUA HUMPHREYS** in the Red Sea during Operation Desert Storm, this SEAL wipes down his Remington 870 shotgun. The weapon has been fitted with an extended magazine giving the shotgun an 8 round ammunition capacity. In addition, the metal portion of the Remington police folding stock on this shotgun has been removed, leaving the weapon with a rear pistol grip.*
PHOTO CREDIT: US NAVY

usually fly open and crash to the floor as a close-quarters battle (CQB) trained team of SEALs enters the room.

Special ammunition has been examined in order to open doors with minimum danger to the occupants inside. In a terrorist hostage situation, 00 buckshot can easily overpenetrate a door, becoming a danger to any hostages on the other side. Lock-buster rounds were developed to overcome the penetration problem. Using the Hatton Pattern solid round as an example, the projectile is a flat-ended 1.8 ounce composition cylinder made of pressed plastic and powdered lead. Fired from a standard 12-gage casing, the cylindrical projectile will smash its way through a door lock or hinge easily. Once it has struck the target, the composition projectile breaks up into heavy particles and powder. Since the target has to absorb the tremendous energy of the projectile, it is usually completely destroyed with a single shot. The projectile fragments have very little power and are harmless a short distance beyond the target. The Hatton round was one of the lock-buster ammunition types examined by Navy Ordnance for use by the Teams.

To make their 870's quicker and easier to handle, minimum length barrels would be used by the SEALs when possible. The normal 20-inch barrel is the most generally useful length for a combat shotgun used in the same manner as the Ithaca Model 37 was in Vietnam. For close-in work, a 16 or 17 inch barrel is the best trade-off between handiness and practical ballistics. A shorter barrel loses velocity and becomes very ineffective at range. In addition, the 17-inch barrel can be used on the 870P with the magazine extension with only an inch or so of the magazine protruding past the muzzle.

H&K CAWS

Though the slide-action shotgun is by far the most successful model of combat shotgun used by the SEALs, the lessons learned in Vietnam and the firepower of the full-automatic Remington 7188 were not forgotten. Research was sponsored in the early 1970's by the Defense Advanced Research Projects Agency (DARPA) into developing a 20mm Multi-Purpose Assault Weapon as part of the TRICAP program. Though no adoptable weapon design came out of the TRICAP program, the data it developed proved useful to later projects.

In 1979, the Joint Services Small Arms Program (JSSAP) Management Committee, responsible for new small arms development for the Department of Defense, initiated the sponsorship of a series of new small arms designs. The military shotgun program for JSSAP was initially titled RHINO for Repeating, Handheld, Improved, Non-rotating Ordnance. Within a short time, the project was renamed MIWS for Multipurpose, Individual, Weapons System. For the MIWS project, all the services, Army, Navy, Marine Corps, Air Force, and Coast Guard, submitted their requirements for a military shotgun.

What the project resulted in was the search for a design that would use a whole new family of ammunition. To accomplish the range requirements, lethal over at least 150 meters, a new caliber of high-pressure shotgun ammunition would have to be developed. And to prevent the ammunition from being used in a shotgun not designed for the pressure, it would be a larger size than normal shotgun shells, 3.5 inches long and 12 or 10 gage.

In addition to the range requirements, the new weapons were to be capable of selective fire and loaded with a box magazine. Recoil was not to be excessive and the gun was not to be longer than 39 inches. The magazine would preferably hold 20 rounds of the new ammunition.

JSSAP RHINO (Repeating Hand-held Improved Non-rifled Ordnance) requirements from 1979 evolved into the mid-1980's CAWS (Close Assault Weapon System) project.

The CAWS requirements were as follows:
A semiautomatic weapon with a 10 round box magazine. Length is not to exceed 39 inches and weight is not to exceed 9 pounds unloaded and 11 pounds loaded. The weapon is also required to have a manual safety and a sighting system usable in low-light-level conditions. Reloading time for replacing an empty magazine with a full one is to be less than five seconds. Magazines cannot be capable of being inserted into the weapon backwards and must be refillable in less than 30 seconds

These requirements have changed from the original proposal put forward in 1979. Most notably, the requirement for full-automatic fire capability was dropped.

In 1983, the Navy Weapons Support Center issued two contracts for what was now called the Close Assault Weapon (CAW) system. Contracts went to AAI in Baltimore, Maryland and the Olin Corporation in East

"The short-barreled, pistol grip 870 is used by the Teams especially as a breachers weapon.... Learned from their opposite numbers in the British SAS is the SEAL technique for opening locked doors rapidly. Instead of targeting the lock with a shotgun blast and kicking the door open, a breacher uses his shotgun against the hinges of a closed door. With two or three quick blasts of 00 buckshot against their hinges, most doors simply fall open"

TECHNICAL DATA—
Heckler & Koch CAWS Candidate (Second model - long barrel)
CARTRIDGE—19.5x76mmB
OPERATION—Recoil
TYPE OF FIRE—Selective - semiautomatic/full automatic or semiautomatic only
RATE OF FIRE—Practical SS 30 rpm A 40 rpm Cyclic 240 rpm
MUZZLE VELOCITY—1625 fps (495 m/s) w/long barrel
MUZZLE ENERGY—2216 ft/lbs (3005 J) w/long barrel
 277 ft/lbs (376 J) Per pellet w/long barrel
SIGHTS—Open, Square-notch/post w/luminous tritium dot inserts, Fixed, adjustable for windage
CHOKE—Special extra full
FEED—10 round removable box magazine
WEIGHTS
WEAPON (EMPTY)—8.82 lbs (4.0 kg) w/long barrel
 7.62 lbs (3.46 kg) w/short barrel
WEAPON (LOADED)—10.77 lbs (4.89 kg) w/long barrel
 9.57 lbs (4.34 kg) w/short barrel
MAGAZINE (EMPTY)—0.42 lbs (0.19 kg)
MAGAZINE (LOADED)—1.95 lbs (0.88 kg)
SERVICE CARTRIDGE—#2 Tungsten 1073 gr (69.5 g)
PROJECTILE—378 gr (224.5 g)
PELLET—47.25 gr (3.06 g)
 LENGTHS
WEAPON OVERALL—39 in (99.1 cm) w/long barrel
 30.63 in (77.8 cm) w/short barrel
BARREL—26.94 in (68.4 cm) - long barrel
 18.63 in (47.3 cm) - short barrel
SIGHT RADIUS—10.38 in (26.4 cm)
SHOT SPREAD AT 55 YDS (50 M)—22 in (55.9 cm)

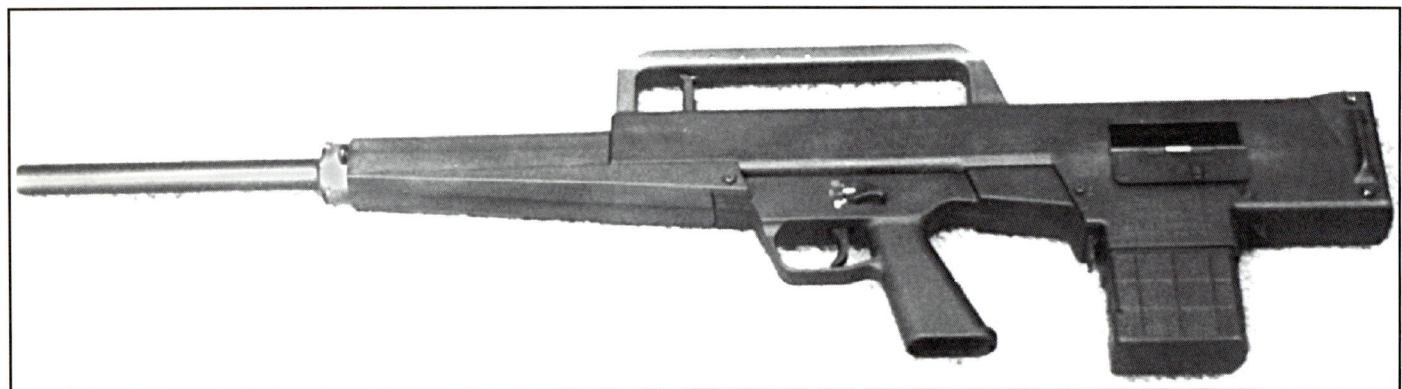

The second-model Olin/H&K Close Assault Weapon System (CAWS) candidate. This specimen has the long barrel added in part to cut down on the excessive muzzle blast suffered by the operator when firing the very powerful special 12-gage ammunition designed for this weapon. The selector switch on this example, located just above the pistol grip, is set to the red 1 indicating semiautomatic fire. The 10 round box magazine is at the rear of this bullpup design and the ejection port is open for left-handed operation.
PHOTO CREDIT: KEVIN DOCKERY

> "Though the slide-action shotgun is by far the most successful model of combat shotgun used by the SEALs, the lessons learned in Vietnam and the firepower of the full-automatic Remington 7188 were not forgotten."

CAWS requirements - A semiautomatic weapon with a 10 round box magazine. Length is not to exceed 39 inches and weight is not to exceed 9 pounds unloaded and 11 pounds loaded. The weapon is also required to have a manual safety and a sighting system usable in low-light-level conditions. Reloading time for replacing an empty magazine with a full one is to be less than five seconds. Magazines cannot be capable of being inserted into the weapon backwards and must be refillable in less than 30 seconds

Alton, Illinois. The Olin Corporation intended to develop the new family of ammunition and subcontracted the weapon development to Heckler and Koch.

The H&K CAWS was a bullpup design, that is the action of the weapon is behind the trigger guard. The bullpup configuration was chosen to give the shortest overall length while allowing for a long barrel. Initially intended for full-automatic fire, the requirements were changed as the project went along and the final H&K CAWS was only a semiautomatic weapon.

The overall design of the H&K CAWS made for a very quick to handle weapon with much greater capabilities than commercially available shotguns. The cocking handle of the H&K CAWS is at the top of the weapon, protected by the raised sight/carrying handle. By moving the sight line up high, the recoil force of the H&K CAWS is kept low, making the weapon more controllable when fired. The low line of recoil force helps keep the muzzle of the weapon down when fired as the force is absorbed directly by the shoulder and does not rotate the barrel upwards.

The box magazine of the H&K CAWS only held 10 rounds but was much faster to insert into the weapon than the traditional single rounds into a tubular magazine. Though the H&K CAWS could use regular 12-gage ammunition for training, the combat ammunition developed by Olin was also found to be very effective.

The Olin ammunition is an all-metal cased round with a raised belt above the rim of the cartridge as found in belted magnum rifle ammunition. The raised rim adds strength to the base of the cartridge as well as preventing it from being chambered in any regular 12-gage weapon. The 12-gage caliber Olin ammunition was loaded with either 000 buckshot, #2 tungsten buckshot, or flechettes. The flechette loading was only considered experimental and development was concentrated on the two buckshot loads.

The 000 buckshot CAWS round holds eight 0.36 caliber hardened lead shot. The round proved itself lethal out to 150 meters but the density of the shot pattern did not raise the hit probability as much as desired. Another round loaded with eight #2 buck (0.27 caliber) made of heavy tungsten alloy was found to hold a tighter pattern and became the primary test round. The hard, dense nature of the tungsten alloy allowed the Olin round to penetrate 0.060 inches of mild steel plate out to 150 meters range, a vast improvement over the XM162 round.

The first H&K CAWS submitted was capable of full-automatic fire and had a 1 power optical sight on the top of the handle. Testing found that the sight could be effectively replaced with a simple open sight arrangement. Ejection of fired cartridges could be user-selected to either side of the weapon. This feature allowed the bullpup design of the H&K CAWS to be used by both right and left-handed firers. It was during the first round of testing that the requirement for full-automatic fire was found to be unreasonable given the ammunition range and power requirements. The full automatic capability was dropped at this time and further development desired on the H&K design.

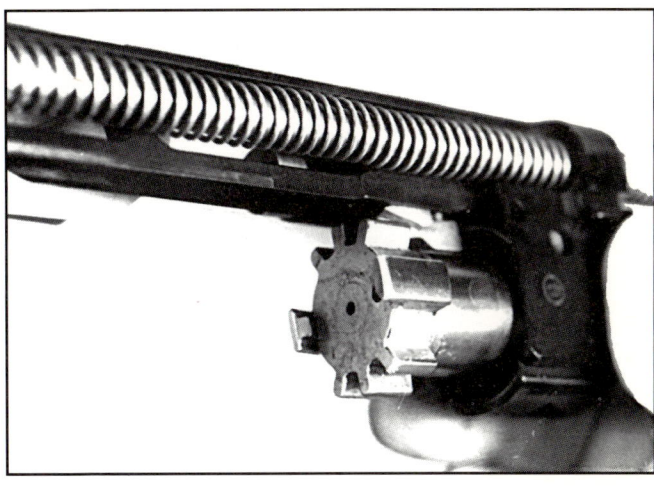

The bolt mechanism of the H&K Close Assault Weapon System (CAWS) candidate. The six locking lugs of the bolt, three top and three bottom, are visible in this photo. The number of lugs were necessary for a good margin of safety to be in the weapon, given that it fires a much higher than normal pressure shotgun shell. The large mainspring above the bolt extends over two-thirds of the length of the H&K CAWS receiver.
PHOTO CREDIT: KEVIN DOCKERY

A right-side view looking into the open ejection port of the H&K Close Assault Weapon System (CAWS) candidate shotgun. The bolt is locked to the rear exposing the ejection port on the opposite side of the weapon. The rectangular button on the left side of the weapon is the latch holding the left side ejection port cover closed. The wide extractor can be seen on the right (outside) side of the bolt face with the blunt pointed ejector being visible on the far side of the bolt.
PHOTO CREDIT: KEVIN DOCKERY

Daewoo USAS-12 Machine Shotgun

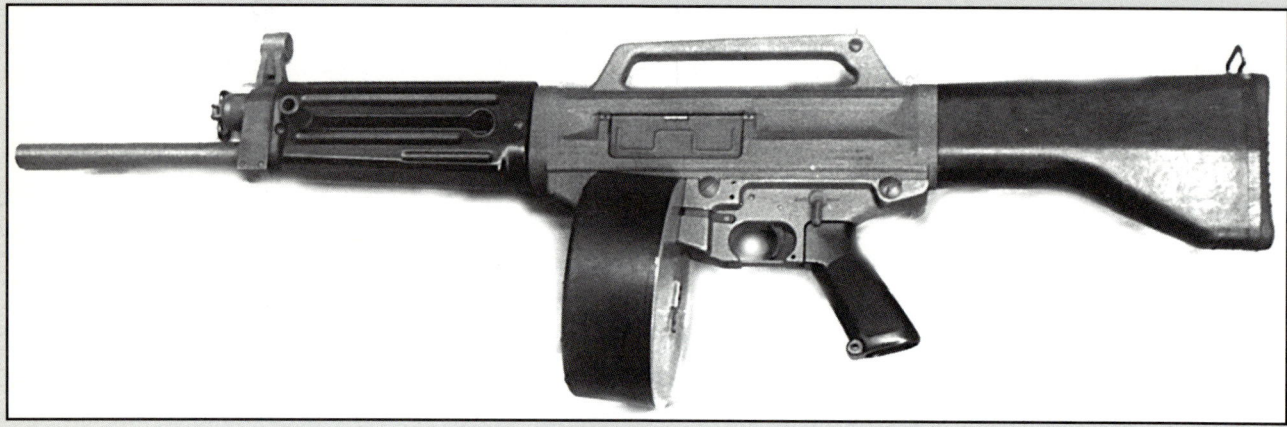

A left-side view of the USAS-12 machine shotgun loaded with the 20 round drum magazine. The protruding rod on the front grip is the cocking handle that can be switched to either side to suit the operator. The ejection port cover, above the drum magazine, is duplicated on the left side of the weapon which can be set to eject to either side.
PHOTO CREDIT: KEVIN DOCKERY

THIS ENTRY INTO THE FULLY AUTOMATIC SHOTGUN ARENA, WHILE NOT GENERAL ISSUE, HAS BEEN EXAMINED BY CRANE. AT PRESENT, IT IS CONSIDERED TOO HEAVY AND BULKY, WITH NO PRESENT MISSION REQUIREMENT FOR THE WEAPON.

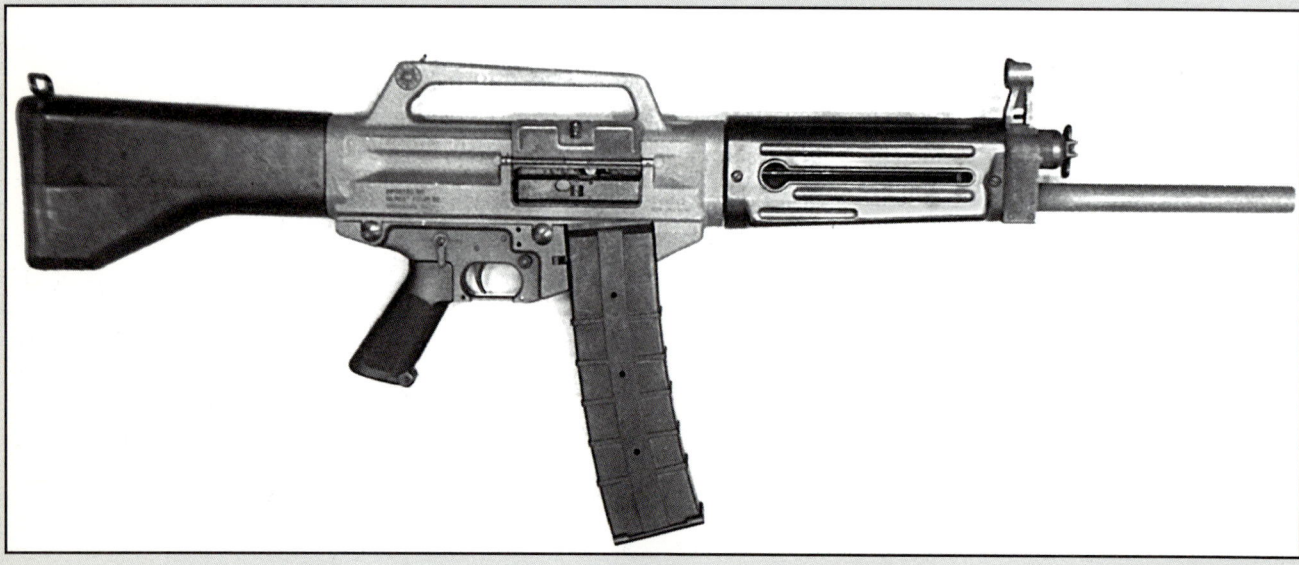

This is the right side of the Daewoo USAS-12 machine shotgun. This specimen is loaded with the in-line 10 round box magazine and has been set up to eject out to the right side of the weapon. The reversible cocking lever is projecting out of the left (down) side of this example otherwise it would be visible at the front of the horizontal keyhole-shaped opening in the handguard, parallel to the barrel.
PHOTO CREDIT: KEVIN DOCKERY

Special Weapons

The final H&K CAWS had open sights in the handle of the weapon with tritium inserts allowing for their use in low-light conditions. A longer barrel was on the last H&K CAWS candidate to try and increase the range and lethality of the weapon while also reducing the very high sound signature. Overall, the Navy testing that ended in 1987 found the H&K CAWS to demonstrate;

"Improved controllability, lighter recoil, reduced flash and faster reloading capabilities than the current military shotgun (Remington 870). The ammunition provides a significant reduction in shot pattern size and gave improved penetration and lethality compared to current military shotgun ammunition."

AAI CAWS

The AAI CAWS candidate followed the lines of a more conventional appearing weapon than the H&K bullpup approach. Using work already done as part of the earlier DARPA 20mm Multi-Purpose Assault Weapon project, the AAI CAWS resembles a large assault rifle. The stock, which is removable, is the same as on an M16A1 rifle which is also where the pistol grip was taken from. The large box magazine holds 12 rounds of ammunition and the weapon can use regular 12-gage ammunition with an adapter.

The heart of the AAI CAWS candidate centered around the ammunition. Using a special plastic, rimless cartridge case, AAI used its past experience with flechette ammunition to have their CAWS launch eight steel flechettes. The flechettes are stabilized with a plastic drag cone to help give them effectiveness from the muzzle out to their maximum range.

Development of the AAI CAWS candidate resulted in some changes to the weapon. The full automatic requirement was dropped as it had been in the H&K weapon and the magazine capacity was reduced by two rounds. The effectiveness of the flechette rounds was proven out in tests. The flechettes could penetrate 3 inches (7.6 cm) of pine boards, 0.125 inch (3.2 mm) of sheet steel, or a flak vest and 11 inches (27.9 cm) of ballistic gelatin, at a range of 150 meters. Plastic sleeves on the flechettes would extend past the base of the projectile after firing. The drag of air on the sleeves would force the flechettes to fly point-first from the muzzle outwards, something that never worked with fin-stabilized flechettes. The stabilization system made the flechette load effective and gave the round its excellent terminal effects at range. But the flechette ammunition for the AAI CAWS could not hold consistent shot patterns. Overall, the AAI CAWS held a great deal of promise as a possible combat shotgun. But no matter how effective the terminal results of the ammunition, it does no good if it cannot hit the target.

Both of the CAWS candidates were shelved after the Navy testing was completed and few weapons spent any time in SEAL hands. The concept was proven out enough to show that a more effective combat shotgun could be produced some time in the future and it would probably be first combat tested in SEAL hands.

TECHNICAL DATA —
AAI CAWS Candidate (Second model)
CARTRIDGE—18.5x79mm
OPERATION—Recoil
TYPE OF FIRE—Semiautomatic,
Selective fire - semiautomatic/full automatic on first model
RATE OF FIRE —
 First model Practical SS 30 rpm, A 40 rpm, Cyclic 450 rpm
MUZZLE VELOCITY—1794 fps (547 m/s)
MUZZLE ENERGY—1901 ft/lbs (2578 J)
 229 ft/lbs (311 J) Per Outer flechette
 300 ft/lbs (407 J) Inner flechette
SIGHTS—Optical 1-power reflex sight w/illuminated reticle, Backup sight Open, Aperture/post, Adjustable
CHOKE—None
FEED—10 round removable box magazine
 WEIGHTS
WEAPON (EMPTY)—8.89 lbs (4.03 kg)
WEAPON (LOADED)—10.23 lbs (4.64 kg)
MAGAZINE (EMPTY)—0.45 lbs (0.20 kg)
MAGAZINE (LOADED)—1.34 lbs (0.61 kg)
SERVICE CARTRIDGE—Flechette 623 gr (40.4 g)
PROJECTILE—266 gr (17.2 g)
PELLET—32 gr (2.07 g) Outer flechette
 42 gr (2.72 g) Inner flechette
 27 gr (1.75 g) Steel flechette body
 LENGTHS
WEAPON OVERALL—39 in (99.1 cm)
BARREL—16 in (40.7 cm)
SIGHT RADIUS—19.69 in (50 cm)
SHOT SPREAD AT 55 YDS (50 M)—42 in (106.7 cm)

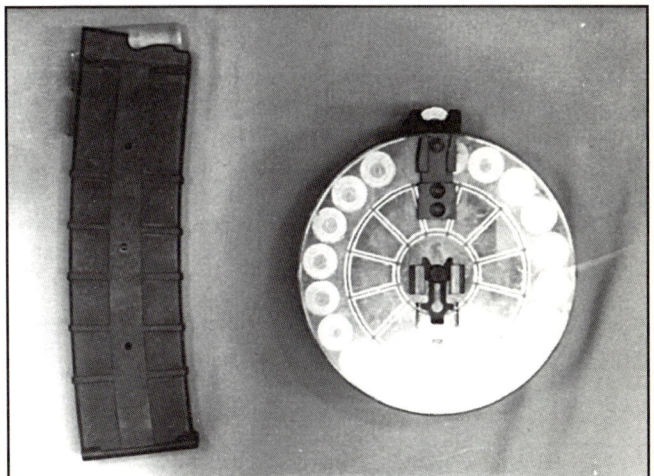

The two magazines to the Daewoo USAS 12 machine shotgun. To the left is the 10 round box magazine with a single dummy 12-gage round loaded in place. The round magazine to the right is the 20-round drum magazine fully loaded with dummy rounds. The transparent plastic back of the drum magazine is visible in this photo and shows the single line of shells along the rim of the drum.
PHOTO CREDIT: KEVIN DOCKERY

Rifles

TECHNICAL DATA—M1 Carbine
NSN 1005-00-670-7672
—M2 Carbine
NSN 1005-00-575-0057
CARTRIDGE—30 Carbine (7.62x33mm)
OPERATION—Gas
TYPE OF FIRE—Semiautomatic
M2 Selective fire - semiautomatic/full automatic
RATE OF FIRE—40 rpm
M2 Practical SS 40 rpm, A 75 rpm, Cyclic 750 to 775 rpm
MUZZLE VELOCITY—1970 fps (600 m/s)
MUZZLE ENERGY—956 ft/lbs (1296 J)
SIGHTS—Open, Ramp-type aperture/blade, Adjustable, graduation marks at 100, 200, 250, and 300 yards
FEED—15 or 30 round removable box magazine
WEIGHTS
WEAPON (EMPTY)—5.31 lbs (2.41 kg)
WEAPON (LOADED)—5.92 lbs (2.69 kg) w/15 rd mag
MAGAZINE (EMPTY)—15 round 0.19 lb (0.09 kg)
30 round 0.22 lbs (0.10 kg)
MAGAZINE (LOADED)—15 round 0.61 lbs (0.28 kg)
30 round 1.06 lbs (0.48 kg)
SERVICE CARTRIDGE—M1 Ball 196 gr (12.7 g)
PROJECTILE—111 gr (7.2 g)
LENGTHS
WEAPON OVERALL—35.58 in. (90.4 cm)
BARREL—18 in (45.7 cm)
SIGHT RADIUS—21.5 in. (54.6 cm) w/rear sight set at 100 yds

A group of UDT swimmers from Underwater Demolition Team 16 prepare to board their boat prior to going in to an island in the Pacific during World War II. The men are wearing standard jungle fatigues and inflatable canvas/rubber life belts along with M1 steel helmets. The man at the center of the picture has an unloaded M1 carbine slung across his back and is wearing an M1910 pistol belt with one-quart canteen and first aid pouch. In addition he has a pair of binoculars slung at his left side in their leather case. The binoculars indicate that the man is probably an officer and the uniforms and equipment suggest that the UDT men are going in to the island after the actual invasion has taken place. At the bottom left of the photograph can be seen the muzzle and front sight of an M1 carbine.
PHOTO CREDIT: UDT-SEAL MUSEUM

Special Weapons

By the middle of World War II (1943) the average Navy sailor was receiving a limited amount of training in small arms while he attended boot camp as a recruit. Small arms were not a priority in the Navy as the force fought from aboard ship with the U.S. Marines being the primary amphibious ground combat unit. In 1943, when the NCDUs began training at Fort Pierce, Florida, the primary shoulder-fired weapon in the Navy was the bolt-action M1903 Springfield rifle. The semiautomatic M1 Garand was not considered a Navy weapon at that time and all production of the M1 was going to the Army and Marines.

For the men of the NCDUs and UDTs, it was not considered a mission priority to have the men offensively armed. Little emphasis was given to small arms training in the NCDU curriculum at Fort Pierce. The men who made up the UDT operating platoons were considered to be skilled demolitionists and not people to augment ground troops. Instruction in armed and unarmed combat was given to the UDTs in order that these highly trained men would be able to effectively defend themselves if necessary.

M1 (M2) CARBINE

The men who made up the Headquarters Platoon of a UDT were given training in small arms to a much greater extent than the men of the operating platoons. Headquarters personnel were expected to supply boat crews, coxswains, radiomen, and other support to the swimmers who would be doing the actual reconnaissance and demolition swims.

It was towards this end that the men of the Headquarters Platoon received hands-on experience with small arms, primarily the pistol and M1 carbine, as well as gunnery instruction for the .30 and .50 caliber machine guns. If, after the normal eight-week training period, there was a delay in sending the NCDU graduates to Maui for their UDT instruction the men would receive the same classes in small arms as the headquarters personnel.

But for all of their training, the men of the NCDUs and UDTs were still in the military. Common military jobs had to be performed such as guard duty. Because of the highly secret nature of their mission, the men of the NCDUs and UDTs were not able to tell anyone what they did to cause all the explosions heard coming from North Hutchison Island near Fort Pierce. The locals could of course hear the blasting, but the island was off limits to almost everyone but the NCDU students.

But the ammunition and explosive magazines on North Hutchison Island had to be guarded, and it was the men of the NCDU school who pulled that duty. The same situation was repeated at the UDT training compound on Maui in the Pacific. When necessary, the NCDU and UDT men were normally armed with the M1 Carbine.

The M1 Carbine was designed early in World War II after a directive for its development was put out by the Army Ordnance Board in June 1940. The intent was to develop a shoulder-fired weapon weighing about five pounds and having an effective range of 300 yards. The weapon was intended as a replacement for the service pistol and submachine gun for officers and noncommissioned officers as well as being a supplementary weapon for mortarmen, machine gunners, radiomen, and other similar duty positions.

The US service rifle cartridge (30-06) was far too powerful for as light a weapon as the carbine was supposed to be, and the service pistol cartridge (45 ACP) was unable to reach the range requirement. A special .30

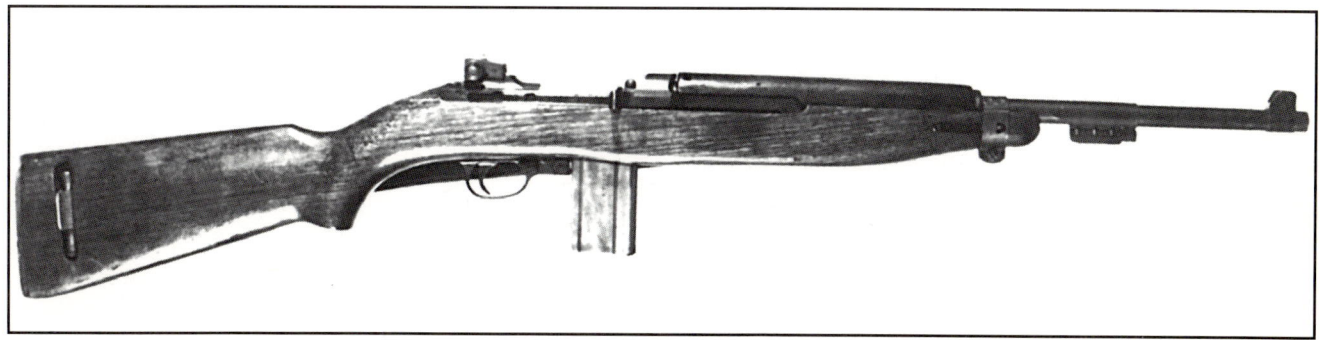

The M2 carbine loaded with a 15 round magazine. The top knob of the small selector lever can be seen at the top of the receiver, above the magazine and just forward of the curved grip of the operating rod.
PHOTO CREDIT: SMITHSONIAN INSTITUTION

Rifles

TECHNICAL DATA—M1918A2 Browning Automatic Rifle
NSN 1005-00-674-1309
CARTRIDGE—30-06 (7.62x63mm)
OPERATION—Gas
TYPE OF FIRE—Full automatic, fast and slow rates
RATE OF FIRE—Practical [slow] 40 to 60 rpm, [fast] 120 to 150 rpm, Cyclic [slow] 350 to 450 rpm, [fast] 550 to 650 rpm
MUZZLE VELOCITY—2800 fps (853 m/s)
MUZZLE ENERGY—2646 ft/lbs (3588 J)
SIGHTS—Open, Leaf-type aperture w/round-notch battle sight/blade, Adjustable, battle sight set at 300 yards, leaf graduated 100 to 1500 yards in 100 yard increments,
FEED—20 round removable box magazine

WEIGHTS
WEAPON (EMPTY)—18.96 lbs (8.60 kg) w/bipod
WEAPON (LOADED)—20.59 lbs (9.34 kg)w/bipod
Bipod 2.44 lbs (1.11 kg)
MAGAZINE (EMPTY)—0.44 lb (0.20 kg)
MAGAZINE (LOADED)—1.63 lb (0.74 kg)
SERVICE CARTRIDGE—M2 Ball 416 gr (27 g)
PROJECTILE—152 gr (9.8 g)
LENGTHS
WEAPON OVERALL—47.8 in. (121.4 cm)
BARREL—24.07 in (61.1 cm)
SIGHT RADIUS—31.13 in. (79.1 cm)

"The Browning Automatic Rifle Model 1918A2, or simply BAR, is a very heavy and powerful rifle."

Men on board a Navy ship stand mine watch. The sailor holding the weapon is armed with an M1918A2 Browning Automatic Rifle (BAR) with the bipod removed. The weapon will be used to shoot and detonate mines as they are detected before they can threaten the ship.
PHOTO CREDIT: US NAVY

Special Weapons

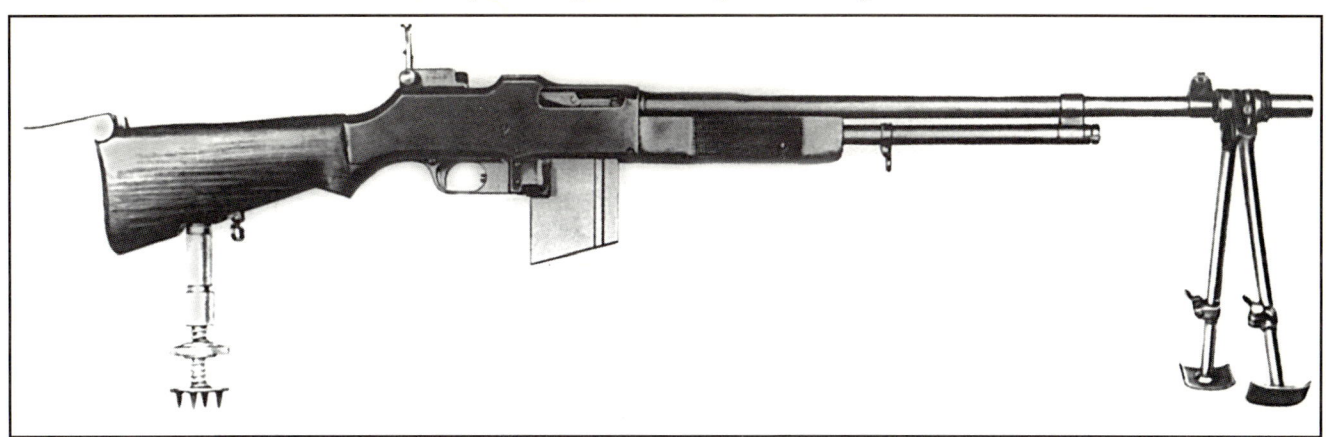

A complete M1818A1 Browning Automatic Rifle (BAR). This example is complete with the rear monopod, an item almost always removed by the user in the field.
PHOTO CREDIT: US ARMY

caliber low-powered round was designed specifically for what was then called the "light rifle" trials in 1941. Several arms manufactures submitted prototype weapons chambered for the new round. By the fall of 1941, only sixteen months after the directive had first been issued, a winner of the light rifle trials had been decided on. The Winchester Light Rifle was adopted as the M1 Carbine in October 1941.

As adopted, the M1 Carbine was a small semiautomatic rifle feeding from a fifteen-round magazine. It was this model carbine that was issued to the men of the UDTs as their duties required. Late in 1944, a selective-fire version of the carbine was developed. Issued as the M2 Carbine, the new weapon had a thirty-round magazine available for it that could also be used in the earlier M1 Carbine. As the M2 Carbine became available, it was issued to the UDTs.

M1918A2 BAR

The only other shoulder weapon trained with and used in any numbers by the UDTs in World War II was at the opposite end of the small arms scale from the M1 Carbine. The Browning Automatic Rifle Model 1918A2, or simply BAR, is a very heavy and powerful rifle. Normally fired from the prone position with the weapon supported by a bipod, the BAR is capable of good accuracy at a long range. The twenty-round magazine of the BAR limits its capacity for sustained fire somewhat as does its lack of a way to change a hot barrel. But the weapon was a great deal more portable that the contemporary belt-fed automatic weapons of the time.

Instead of being selective-fire, that is firing either semiautomatic or full automatic, the M1918A2 BAR instead had two different rates of fire that could be selected by the operator. The fast rate of fire, around 600 rounds per minute cyclic, could put out a rapid volume of fire in order to engage or suppress an enemy position. The slow rate of fire, about 350 rounds per minute cyclic, allowed for single shots to be easily fired by a trained gunner and has more controllable muzzle climb when fired from the standing position.

In the Navy, the BAR would be used for shore or landing party operations. On board ship, the BAR would occasionally be found in use to augment a ship's volume of antiaircraft fire. More important to the men of the UDT, the BAR could be used to give a reasonable amount of firepower to small craft such as a rubber boat. The BAR could be fired from such a boat by a single operator while the light machine gun of the time, the Browning M1919A4 would be very clumsy to use and take up a great deal more room.

Used by the UDT in only limited numbers, the BAR saw little if any combat duty with the Teams during

A technician checks an M1918 Browning Automatic Rifle (BAR) while on board ship in the Pacific during World War II. These early-model BAR's could still be found in Navy arms rooms throughout the war where they were used for ship defense and to arm landing parties. The last weapon on the left is an M1918 BAR with its forearm removed and a pintle adaptor installed. The pintle adaptor would allow the weapon to be placed in any standard machine gun mount on board ship.
PHOTO CREDIT: UDT-SEAL MUSEUM

Rifles

TECHNICAL DATA—AR-15 (Colt Model 601), M-16 (Colt Model 602)
NSN 1005-00-983-6877, (M-16) 1005-00-856-6885
CARTRIDGE—.223 Remington (5.56x45mm)
OPERATION—Gas
TYPE OF FIRE—Selective - semiautomatic/full automatic
RATE OF FIRE—Practical SS 45 to 65 rpm, A 150 to 200 rpm, Cyclic 700 to 950 rpm
MUZZLE VELOCITY—3250 fps (991 m/s)
MUZZLE ENERGY—1313 ft/lbs (1780 J)
SIGHTS—Open, Flip-type aperture/post, Adjustable, battle aperture 0 to 300 meters, long range aperture 300 to 500 meters
FEED—20 or 30 round removable box magazines
WEIGHTS
WEAPON (EMPTY)—6.35 lbs (2.88 kg) w/o sling
WEAPON (LOADED)—7.46 lbs (3.38 kg) w/20 rd mag & sling
Sling 0.40 lbs (0.18 kg)
MAGAZINE (EMPTY)—20 round aluminium 0.19 lb (0.08 kg)
30 round aluminium 0.24 lbs (0.11 kg)
MAGAZINE (LOADED)—20 round 0.71 lb (0.32 kg)
30 round 1.02 lbs (0.46 kg)
SERVICE CARTRIDGE—M193 Ball 182 gr (11.8 g)
PROJECTILE—56 gr (3.6 g)
LENGTHS
WEAPON OVERALL—38.6 in. (98 cm)
BARREL—20 in (50.8 cm)
SIGHT RADIUS—19.72 in. (50.1 cm)

These weapons are among the first of their kind to be used by the Navy. A noticeable characteristic of the early AR-15/M-16 weapons is the shiny appearance of the chromed bolt carrier, visible through the open ejection port, and the green-colored plastic furniture (stocks). Later versions of the weapon had black plastic furniture and the bolt carrier was parkerized a dull grey.

A group of SEAL Team Two operators in the early 1960's. They are wearing uniforms that were part of a large open-purchase of commercially-produced equipment that was made to get the newly commissioned SEAL Teams operational as quickly as possible. The groups weapons are early-model Colt AR-15 rifles. The early style, fully chromed bolt carrier is readily visible through the open ejection port of the weapon held by the SEAL at the left of the picture. The smooth right side of the upper receivers show that these weapons do not have the forward bolt assist required by the Army in the later M16A1 rifle. Additionally, these weapons have the first model, stepped-down, double diameter open-prong flash hiders that were part of the early production units in the series. The SEAL at the lower right in the photo is holding the very rare AR-15 carbine with its flash suppressor mounted just ahead of the front sight.
PHOTO CREDIT: RYAN McCOMBIE COLLECTION

World War II. Photographs of NCDUs at Fort Pierce exist showing at least one man of the six man NCDU armed with a BAR. Training was given on the M1918A2 BAR at Fort Pierce and it is likely that additional training with the weapon was conducted at Maui late in the war. The commander of the UDT school at Maui towards the end of World War II, Commander John T. Koehler, could see the mission of the UDTs expanding inland if the war continued. To account for such a situation, and to expand the capabilities of the UDTs, Commander Koehler added further small arms training and other skills to the UDT training curriculum.

During the Korean War, the land combat application of the UDTs became much more than just a possibility. Guerrilla infiltration and exfiltration, clandestine resupply ops, and behind-the-lines demolition raids all were conducted by the men of the UDT. The M1 and M2 Carbines and BARs again saw duty with the UDTs, only their use was much more serious than simple guard duty. The submachine gun was considered the favorite shoulder weapon, but the carbine, BAR, and even the M1 Garand were seen in UDT hands. Though the UDTs had few small arms of their own, the facilities of a base armory or ship's stores were available to the Teams when necessary.

A watershed event in the weapons of the UDT took place shortly after the commissioning of the SEALs in January 1962. SEAL Team Two on the east coast at Little Creek, Virginia, was faced with the very real possibility of seeing combat operations in Cuba within a short time after its commissioning. Not being satisfied with what was available through Navy supply channels or in the base armory, Lieutenant Roy Boehm, the first officer-in-charge of SEAL Team Two as well as the Team's founder, sought out the best firearms on the market he could then find. Desiring high-firepower, light weight, dependability, and increased lethality over the M1 Carbine, LT. Boehm was highly interested in a very new firearm just available commercially, the AR-15 rifle.

AR-15 MODEL 601

Early in 1962, LT Boehm and some of his new SEALs traveled to Baltimore, Maryland to visit the Cooper-MacDonald offices. The Cooper-MacDonald firm had been representing the AR-15 rifle to the military for several years. The original manufacturers and developers of the AR-15, the Fairchild Stratos Corporation, had sold the license to produce the ArmaLite AR-15 to the Colt Firearms Corporation in 1959. Though the AR-15 had received praise from many of the people who had fired it, the US Military and especially the Army Ordnance Corps were adamantly not interested.

The Army, then responsible for small arms acquisition for the Air Force and Marines as well, had just adopted the M14 as the new service rifle in May, 1957. Difficulties in production and other delays had kept the M14 from being produced in the quantities needed by the military. It was only in 1961 that productions volume had finally started reaching the numbers needed for full issue. In this atmosphere, the Army Ordnance Corps was very much against any new weapon being even remotely

On the range at Little Creek in the early 1960's, these SEALs from SEAL Team Two are firing their 01 model AR-15 rifles. The unloaded weapon visible has the first model, stepped-down, double diameter, open-prong flash suppressor. The fairly light color of the handguards of this AR-15 comes from the very early weapons having light green rather than black stocks. The SEAL holding the weapon is wearing faded Marine camouflage fatigues.
PHOTO CREDIT: RYAN McCOMBIE COLLECTION

considered for adoption. This was particularly true for a weapon that would also add a new caliber of ammunition into the supply system.

The Army had just managed to start coming on line with a new family of weapons, the M14 and the M60 machine gun, that were both chambered for the same 7.62mm NATO round. One of the selling points of the new weapons was that they would eliminate at least one caliber, the .30 Carbine, as well as several weapons, the submachine gun, M1 Carbine, M1 rifle, and BAR. The AR-15 was chambered for the unique .222 Special developed especially for it. In 1959, the new round was renamed the .223 Remington.

The lightweight .223 bullet did not seem at all a proper projectile for a military weapon according to several prominent people in the Army small arms field. These same people set out to disprove any possible advantages the .223 round might have in the military. The most obvious advantage of the new round was its light weight, at the time two loaded 20- round AR-15 magazines weighed less than a single 20 round- M14 magazine.

Rifles

A rare cutaway AR-15 rifle from the Colt Gun Room. This photo shows all of the major internal workings of the AR-15/M16 weapon system. The hammer is forward in the uncocked (fired) position.
PHOTO CREDIT: KEVIN DOCKERY/ KNIGHT ARMAMENT COMPANY

A closeup of a cutaway AR-15 rifle from the Colt Gun Room. The gas tube can be seen inside the bolt carrier key in the slot just below the top of the upper receiver. Gasses from the barrel would be guided through the gas tube, down the bolt carrier key, and into the bolt carrier, behind the bolt itself. The pressure of the gases would drive the bolt carrier to the rear with the bolt itself acting as a piston. The cam pin that locks the bolt to the bolt carrier would be guided through a cam track that would force it to rotate and unlock/lock the bolt depending on the direction of travel. Three thin metal discs on the bolt are the bolt rings and they insure a gas-tight seal between the bolt and bolt carrier.
PHOTO CREDIT: KEVIN DOCKERY/KNIGHT ARMAMENT COMPANY

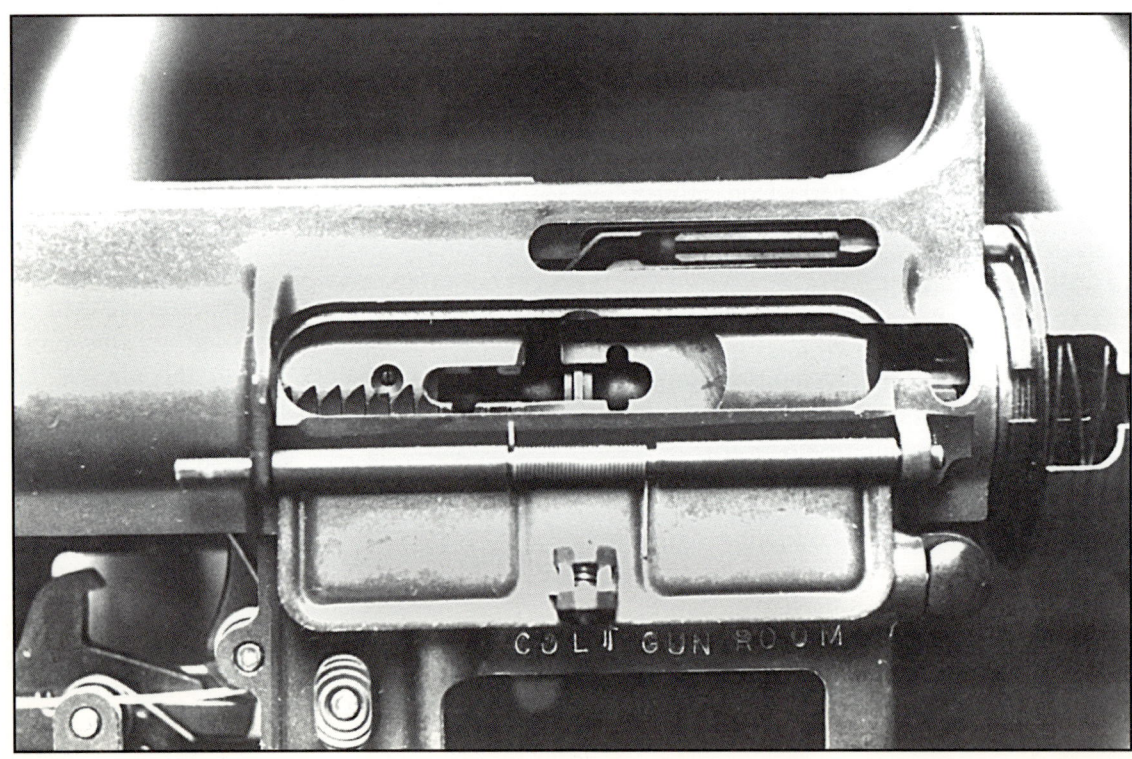

Special Weapons

One problem with the small bore of the AR-15 rifle was strongly pointed out by the Army board examining the weapon. During trials of the AR-15 at the Aberdeen Proving Grounds in 1958, the barrel of one test weapon split while firing during a rain test. Modifications to the barrel were completed by Gene Stoner, the AR-15's designer. But rumors persisted about the danger of the .223 bore retaining water droplets due in part to capillary action.

If the SEALs were to use the new rifle and there was a problem with water retention in the bore, it would be proved useless given the environment of their missions. Not particularly trusting anyone else's tests, Lieutenant Roy Boehm conducted his own examination of the AR-15.

"... Wanting to test the AR-15 himself before making his purchase, Roy took some Team Two men up to Baltimore with him to check out the weapons the dealer had available. Roy and the guys shot the AR and fully tested it. They even tossed the weapon into the surf zone, covering it with sand, silt, and salt water, and it continued operating. With proper care, the AR-15 was able to pass any abuse Roy gave it. Team Two now could issue one of the newest weapons available on the market."

Lt. Boehm found no problem with water retention in the bore of the AR-15. He was in a unique situation where he had to outfit his men and did not have the time to wait for channels. The funds necessary for the equipping of SEAL Team Two were already at Roy Boehm's disposal in the form of open purchases he could make in any market he saw fit. The men of the SEAL Team quickly agreed with "The Boss's" decision.

"The best package of firepower and weight we had were the new AR-15 rifles. This was several years before the Army was to adopt the AR-15 as the M-16, even in limited numbers. But Roy had used his open purchase system and gotten us 66 brand new AR-15's fresh from the Colt factory.

Roy had ordered 136 of the new AR-15 rifles, the selective fire models [Colt Model 601] with green stocks. Half of the weapons were sent to Team One along with instructions, magazines, and spare parts."

Shortly after the new weapon's arrival, the situation in Cuba began heating up. It looked as if the AR-15 would get combat tested on the beaches of that Caribbean island.

"As the men came in, we issued what we had. Watches, pistols, and other gear was given out. Then when Cuba calmed down, the additional men went back to their parent units, and a lot of our gear went with them. One of the items we had before any one else in the Navy were the AR-15 rifles ...Half of the weapons went to the West coast and SEAL Team ONE with the remainder staying with us. Those were the first rifles of their kind in the Navy and were later adopted by the military as the M-16. We had them first because we needed them."

The new weapons were well and enthusiastically received by the SEALs. For the first time, a light weight, highly-lethal, selective fire weapon was available. Though the M2 Carbine had been both light weight and capable of automatic fire, the round it fired was considered underpowered and had proved itself to have less than ideal stopping power. In defense of the Carbine, it must be remembered that the weapon was designed to be a replacement for the pistol as a secondary arm generally for support troops.

Though the M-14 was the intended standard issue shoulder weapon of the early 1960's, it was considered too large and ungainly for use by the SEALs who might easily have to transport the weapon underwater. Another factor in favor of the AR-15 was its intentional design for controlled automatic fire. The M-14 could have a selector switch easily installed, but the weapon is built along traditional lines. The recoil of automatic fire in the M-14 violently pushes the muzzle up and to the right, especially when fired from the shoulder.

A pair of UDT operators set up flags to line up swimmers during a beach survey in Vietnam. The UDT man closest to the camera has a Colt Model 01 AR-15 slung diagonally across his back. His partner closer to the water is apparently unarmed except for the Mark 2 Ka-Bar at his right hip.
PHOTO CREDIT: UDT-SEAL MUSEUM

Rifles

A selection of SEAL shoulder weapons in Vietnam circa late 1967-68. The bottom weapon is a Stoner 63A light machine gun fitted with a left-hand feed mechanism and a 150 round aluminum belt drum. Over the muzzle of the Stoner is a black plastic cap developed at China Lake to help keep the barrels of M16 and Stoner weapons clean and clear of mud. The caps can be easily fired through with no damage to the weapon. Second from the bottom is a Colt Model 07 submachine gun loaded with a 20 round magazine and having the sliding buttstock in the forward (collapsed) position. This specimen has been fitted with a 2nd model flash/noise suppressor on its muzzle. Second from the top is a Colt M16-series rifle with a 2nd type open-prong, conical flash suppressor on the muzzle. The weapon at the top is a M16-series weapon also with a 2nd model flash suppressor and a 40mm XM148 grenade launcher mounted underneath the barrel. The curved cocking lever for the XM148 can be seen just ahead of the magazine in the rifle. This rifle is loaded with two butt-taped 20 round magazines. The bottom magazine is loaded with tracer ammunition (not identifiable in this black-and-white illustration). On the right side of the photo is an unusual set of leather and canvas field gear with three M26 fragmentation grenades attached to it.
PHOTO CREDIT: US NAVY

This SEAL is wearing the so-called black pajama tops that were very popular with some members of the Teams in Vietnam. He is armed with an M16A1 rifle loaded with a 20 round magazine. His web gear is mostly M1956 pattern Load Carrying Equipment with several universal small arms ammunition cases on his belt. A number of M26 fragmentation grenades are secured to the mounting straps on the outside of the ammunition cases. At his left shoulder, this SEAL has secured a Mark 2 Ka-Bar with a painted-over Mark 13 day/night flare taped to the scabbard. Slipped though a loop at his right shoulder is an M18 colored smoke grenade.
PHOTO CREDIT: FRANK THORNTON COLLECTION

The AR-15 has the stock in line with the barrel of the weapon. This causes the AR-15 to have less tendency to climb up and right when fired on automatic, though the weapon still takes a good deal of training to properly control. The training is considered very worthwhile as full automatic fire is very much an advantage for sudden close-in fire fights or the overwhelming fire needed for an ambush. The SEALs liked the fact that the AR-15 could be fired on full automatic with just the flip of a selector switch. Sometimes, the SEALs liked full automatic fire a little too much. The first range practice with the new AR-15s for SEAL Team Two took place at a Marine range since they had the proper firing facilities and the fledgling SEAL Teams did not.

"As we were getting down into the firing position the [Marine] Lieutenant sounded off. "There will be no automatic fire on this range," he said, "Everything will be semiautomatic fire only." That was a bit of a mistake on his part.

"Lock and load one magazine. Ready on the left? Ready on the right? Ready on the firing line! Shooters, you may commence fire!" We all just raised our heads a little bit and looked up and down at each other. At the command "Commence fire" all of us switched over to automatic and let that magazine rip. The Lieutenant immediately confiscated all of the weapons and threw us off the base."

These two SEALs crouch down and watch a helicopter come into their area during a training operation. The SEAL to the left is holding an M16A1 rifle with a plastic mud cap over the flash suppressor. The rifle is loaded with a pair of butt-taped 20 round magazines. He is wearing the early model Type 1 Rifleman's buoyant ammunition carrying vest.
PHOTO CREDIT: UDT-SEAL MUSEUM

One problem that the SEALs did not have was with the lethality of the AR-15. Being the early 601 models, the AR-15s purchased directly by the Teams had barrels rifled with six grooves having a right-hand twist rate of one turn in fourteen inches. This rifling twist rate was the firearms industry standard when Gene Stoner had first designed the AR-15. Since the 55-grain .223 bullet was the same weight as commercial .22 bullets fired in high-velocity center fire rifles, the commercial twist rate was thought to be correct to stabilize the .223 bullet for accuracy.

The problem was that the commercial 55-grain bullets then in use were shorter and blunter than the full jacketed projectile designed for the .223 Remington military round. Standard M193 ball ammunition, when fired from the early AR-15, launched a projectile that was just barely stable in flight. When the bullet struck a target, or entered flesh, it began tumbling wildly, expending its energy rapidly. This rapid energy release resulted in the near-explosive wounds coming out of Vietnam in mid-1962.

Almost 1,000 AR-15 rifles, all early model 601s, and over half a million rounds of ammunition had been purchased by the Defense Department in late December 1961. These weapons and ammunition were part of Project AGILE being conducted by the Advanced Research Projects Agency (ARPA). The project intended, in part, to examine new weapons for use by "the small-stature... Vietnamese soldier and to evaluate the weapon under actual combat conditions."

Project AGILE resulted in the first operational tests of the AR-15 in combat being conducted by selected units of

A cutaway view of the front sight assembly of the M16A1 rifle. The open port that directs the propellant gases from the barrel into the gas tube can be seen just above the sling swivel and in front of the handguard mount. At the upper right portion of the sight assembly can be seen the threaded front sight post and the spring-loaded detent that helps hold it in place. The aluminum reflector that helps keep the handguards cool can be seen riveted to the inside of the left-side handguard.
PHOTO CREDIT: KEVIN DOCKERY/KNIGHT ARMAMENT COMPANY

Rifles

The author firing an M16A1 rifle with a Mark 2 Blast Suppressor mounted on the muzzle. The weapon is firing a short burst on full automatic, two ejected cartridge cases visible as the elongated blurs above the firer's left hand and the weapon's front sight. It is interesting to note the lack of muzzle climb on the weapon, even when fired on full automatic. This lack of rise is a by-product of having the extra weight of the suppressor on the muzzle.
PHOTO CREDIT: KEVIN DOCKERY

TECHNICAL DATA—M16E1 (M16A1) (Colt Model 603)
NSN 1005-00-939-0584 (M16A1) 1005-00-073-9421
CARTRIDGE—.223 Remington (5.56x45mm)
OPERATION—Gas
TYPE OF FIRE—Selective - semiautomatic/full automatic
RATE OF FIRE—Practical SS 45 to 65 rpm, A 150 to 200 rpm, Cyclic 700 to 800 rpm
MUZZLE VELOCITY—3250 fps (991 m/s)
MUZZLE ENERGY—1313 ft/lbs (1780 J)
SIGHTS—Open, Flip-type aperture/post, Adjustable, battle aperture 0 to 300 meters, long range aperture 300 to 500 meters
FEED—20 or 30 round removable box magazines
WEIGHTS
WEAPON (EMPTY)—6.5 lbs (2.95 kg)
WEAPON (LOADED)—7.61 lbs (3.45 kg) w/sling & 20 rd mag
Sling 0.40 lbs (0.18 kg)
MAGAZINE (EMPTY)—20 round aluminium 0.19 lb (0.08 kg)
30 round aluminium 0.24 lbs (0.11 kg)
MAGAZINE (LOADED)—20 round 0.71 lb (0.32 kg)
30 round 1.02 lbs (0.46 kg)
SERVICE CARTRIDGE—M193 Ball 182 gr (11.8 g)
PROJECTILE—56 gr (3.6 g)

LENGTHS
WEAPON OVERALL—39 in. (99.1 cm)
BARREL—20 in (50.8 cm) w/o flash suppressor
21 in (53.3 cm) w/flash suppressor
SIGHT RADIUS—19.75 in. (50.2 cm)
Modifications from the original AR-15 (M-16 rifle for the A1 version included:
Chrome plating the chamber and later the entire bore
Addition of a forward bolt-assist for forcing the bolt closed
A heavier recoil buffer to slow the cyclic firing rate, this buffer was quickly retrofitted to all M16 rifles
A buttstock compartment for holding a set of cleaning gear
A closed "bird-cage" flash suppressor
A wider charging handle
Index lines (windage) on the rear sight
A 30 round magazine was introduced to replace the 20 shot version used in the field. This size magazine had been available since the earliest Colt manufactured weapons but had been available on a very limited basis. Prior to this (about 1968) only the Air Force had been issuing 30 round magazines as a normal item. These larger magazines were a valued "scrounge" item among the SEALs. 20 round magazines remained the norm throughout the Vietnam war.

the South Vietnamese Army supported by American advisors. The tests ran from 1 February to 15 July, 1962. Besides being well-liked by the Vietnamese troops for its size and light recoil, the AR-15 had shown itself to be a very lethal combat weapon. Reports told of almost incredible wounds being caused by single .223 bullets. Amputations of limbs, massive body wounds, and decapitations had all been caused by the very high-velocity AR-15 projectiles.

But there was a drawback that came with the near-instability of the AR-15 bullets being fired in 1-in-14 twist barrels. When the ambient temperature dropped below freezing, the air density changed. In cold air, the AR-15 bullets became unstabilized and accuracy dropped off badly. In independent, unbiased tests run by the National Rifle Association, it was found to be impossible to keep ten rounds on a 3 foot by 4 foot target at 300 meters range with the air temperature below 32 degrees Fahrenheit.

Since SEAL Teams Two did few operations in a cold environment during its first years, the drawback of the AR-15s rifling was not noticed as a problem. By July, 1963, orders had gone out from the Department of Defense that no further AR-15s would be accepted with the old rifling twist rate. The new twist rate, which stabilized bullets in below-freezing temperatures, was 1 turn in 12 inches. All subsequent AR-15s, M-16s, and M16A1s were all made with the 1-in-12 rifling twist rate, including those used by the SEALs.

A SEAL Team Two MTT (Mobile Training Team) 10-62 went to Vietnam to continue training the Beit Hai commandos of the South Vietnamese Navy. The training program had been begun by an MTT primarily from SEAL Team One earlier in the year. Along with "3 to 4 tons" of other equipment, the Team Two MTT took along with them a number of the Team's AR-15s. At the time the AR-15 and its use by the SEAL Teams was still classified. Again, the men of the South Vietnamese military greatly liked the AR-15. In fact the MTT soon ran out of the .223 ammunition they had brought along with them. At the time, the .223 military ball was loaded by Remington Arms and came packaged in a white 20-round cardboard box. As the ammunition was gone, the MTT turned to training the Vietnamese with available weapons including the M1 Garand, M2 Carbine, and BAR. It would be some years later that .223 ammunition would be available in huge numbers in Southeast Asia.

In June, 1963, President John F. Kennedy came to Norfolk and visited SEAL Team Two. While on his tour, President Kennedy saw a number of SEALs who were demonstrating the equipment they used. One man, GMG2 A.D. Clark was holding one of the Team's AR-15 rifles. When President Kennedy approached Clark he asked, "What have you got there, son?"

"This sir," answered Clark, "is the AR-15 rifle, made by ArmaLite."

At that point, one of the officers escorting President Kennedy, an Army Colonel, interrupted, commenting about how the AR-15 was only a limited duty, special-purpose weapon as compared to the issue M-14.

The President cut off the Colonel with a curt, "I am speaking to this gentleman here," and he resumed his conversation with Clark.

That action probably did as much to endear the President with the men of the SEALs as did his signing their commissioning orders only sixteen months before. But A.D. Clark continued with his praise of the AR-15 stating that it was exactly the weapon the SEALs wanted and no other. In a way it is very proper that A.D. Clark is the SEAL who spoke to the President in regard to the AR-15 rifle. Clark had been one of the SEALs who had accompanied Lt. Roy Boehm the year before when he had gone to Cooper-Macdonald in Baltimore to first test the AR-15.

M16 Model 602

By 1965, even the UDTs had at least some AR-15s in their inventory for issue to operating platoons. By this time, the AR-15 had been purchased in some numbers by

Two SEALs during a training exercise. The front SEAL is carrying an M16A1 rifle loaded with a 30-round magazine and with the flash suppressor replaced with a China Lake blank adaptor. He is wearing a later-model SRU-21/P survival vest over his camouflage fatigues. The rear SEAL is armed with one of the XM177 series weapons also loaded with a 30 round magazine. He is carrying an AN/PRC-77 radio on his back with the coiled feed wire of the handset down over his right shoulder. To minimize his silhouette, the radioman has the short antenna to his radio folded down over his left shoulder and secured to his web gear.
PHOTO CREDIT: US NAVY

Rifles

TECHNICAL DATA—CAR-15 Carbine (Colt Model 05)
CARTRIDGE—.223 Remington (5.56x45mm)
OPERATION—Gas
TYPE OF FIRE—Selective - semiautomatic/full automatic
RATE OF FIRE—Practical SS 45 to 65 rpm, A 150 to 200 rpm, Cyclic 700 to 950 rpm
MUZZLE VELOCITY—3050 fps (930 m/s)
MUZZLE ENERGY—1157 ft/lbs (1569 J)
SIGHTS—Open, Flip-type aperture/post, Adjustable, battle aperture 0 to 300 meters,
long range aperture 300 to 500 meters
FEED—20 or 30 round removable box magazines
WEIGHTS
WEAPON (EMPTY)—6.0 lbs (2.72 kg)
WEAPON (LOADED)—6.71 lbs (3.04 kg) w/20 rd mag w/o sling
Sling 0.40 lbs (0.18 kg)
MAGAZINE (EMPTY)—20 round aluminium 0.19 lb (0.08 kg)
30 round aluminium 0.24 lbs (0.11 kg)
MAGAZINE (LOADED)—20 round 0.71 lb (0.32 kg)
30 round 1.02 lbs (0.46 kg)
SERVICE CARTRIDGE—M193 Ball 182 gr (11.8 g)
PROJECTILE—56 gr (3.6 g)
LENGTHS
WEAPON OVERALL—33.6 in. (85.3 cm)
BARREL—15 in (38.1 cm)
SIGHT RADIUS—19.72 in. (50.1 cm)

"The CAR-15, for Colt Automatic Rifle, carbine was the same as the AR-15 rifle except that the barrel had been cut off to just in front of the front sight and the flash suppressor reinstalled."

These SEALs are demonstrating techniques used when landing on a beach with a Combat Rubber Raiding Craft (CRRC). All three of the SEALs are wearing the same type of camouflage uniforms and floppy bush hats. The two visible weapons are M16A1 rifles with the crouching SEAL having loaded his weapon with two butt-taped 30 round magazines. The standing SEAL, with his weapon in his left hand, has his M16A1 loaded with a single 30 round magazine. The bottom of the magazine has been wrapped with tape for additional strength and a small tape tab extends from the bottom of the magazine to assist in drawing it from an ammunition pouch. All of the load bearing gear worn by these SEALs is of the nylon ALICE (All-purpose Lightweight Individual Carrying Equipment) type adopted by the Army in 1974.
PHOTO CREDIT: UDT-SEAL MUSEUM

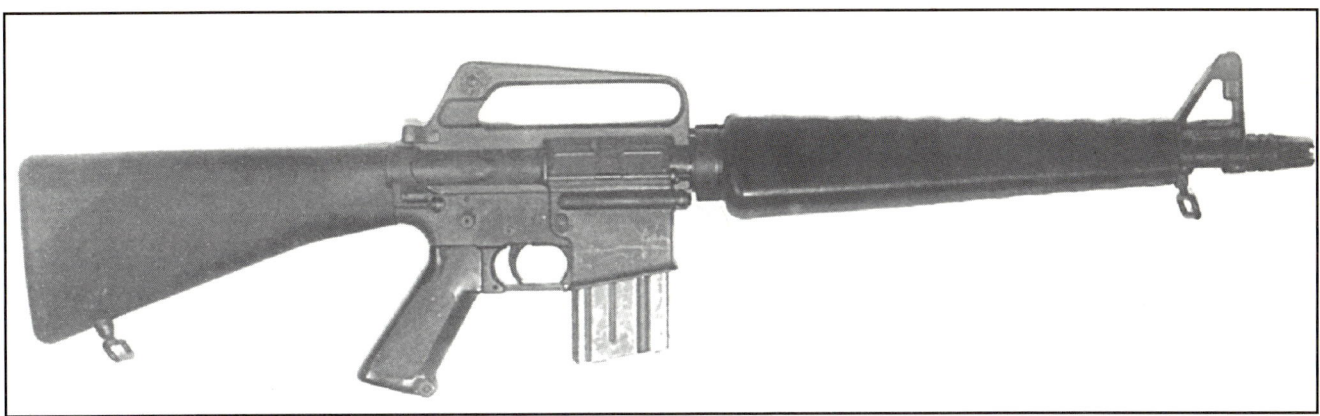

A right-side view of the Colt Model 05 carbine. The weapon is an 01 model AR-15 with its barrel cut back to the front sight assembly. This specimen has the 2nd type conical, open-prong flash suppressor.
PHOTO CREDIT: KEVIN DOCKERY

the Air Force as the M16 rifle. The Navy had purchased an additional 240 M16 rifles, announcing the contract in October, 1964. In the week of 18-22 January 1965, Colt received a priority 04 MIPR from the Navy for an additional 50 M16 rifles. At the time, rifles were shipped with seven 20-round magazines, spare parts and additional materials were shipped separately. The Army was also purchasing thousands of XM16E1s at this time, primarily for use with US Army maneuver battalions in Vietnam.

The AR-15 had been advertised by Colt as an almost self-cleaning weapon needing only "an occasional simple cleaning... [to] keep the weapon functioning indefinitely. Working parts can be cleaned by wiping with a cloth." But in the SEAL Teams and UDTs, maintenance procedures take on an importance close to that of a religion. This attitude stems from the Teams working underwater with Underwater Breathing Apparatus (UBAs). If a diver does not take meticulous care of his UBA, it will fail on him at some point, either killing him outright or causing him to drown. With something like that for a background, it is easy to see how the SEALs and UDTs keep their mania for maintenance.

In the first edition of the UDT Handbook (1965) are listed the cleaning instructions for the AR-15 (M-16) that state; "...all excess carbon [be] simply wiped off the working parts." But with the Team's tradition for complete maintenance, weapons, including the AR-15 were cleaned thoroughly and completely. Because of this situation, the SEALs did not suffer the large numbers of malfunctions experienced by Army personnel when the rifle was fielded in Vietnam.

CAR-15 CARBINE MODEL 605

Several variations of the AR-15 were also obtained by the SEALs in early 1962 in addition to a number of accessories. Very early in 1962, SEAL Team Two had at least one of the rare AR-15 carbines, the Model 605. The CAR-15, for Colt Automatic Rifle, carbine was the same as the AR-15 rifle except that the barrel had been cut off to just in front of the front sight and the flash suppressor reinstalled. It is possible that only one of the CAR-15 carbines was ever procured as the weapon was not very successful and very few were manufactured by Colt. The AR-15 carbine was offered by Colt for situations "where stowage is a problem," which would of course hold appeal to the size-conscious SEALs. Though it shows up in a number of photographs of field exercises conducted by Team Two in 1962 and in a 1964 weapons display, the AR-15 carbine was little used and probably never fielded in Vietnam.

Several accessories for the AR-15 were experimented with by the SEALs prior to the Vietnam War. At least one removable telescopic sight was tried out by SEAL Team Two. The telescopic sight was a Delft Optics 3x25 power telescope (weight 0.875 lbs. [0.397 kg]) adapted from the earlier AR-10 rifle. Though it could be easily mounted and dismounted from the carrying handle of the AR-15, the early scope sight simply would not remained zeroed to the weapon. When mounted on the rifle, hand pressure was enough to push the sight out of alignment with the rifle. Other accessories obtained included AR-15 bayonets, clip-on bipods, and a small number of early model 30-round magazines.

XM16E1 (M16A1) MODEL 603

In 1965, the Army had begun receiving quantities of the XM16E1 rifle and several elite Special Forces and Airborne units were equipped with the new weapon. For Army use a number of modifications had been done to the original Model 601 AR-15. Most of these modifications had also been included in the Air Force issue M16. For the Army XM16E1, the major visible change was the addition of the forward bolt assist, a bolt closure mechanism on the upper receiver of the rifle that allowed the bolt to be pushed forward. To accommodate the new changes, Colt manufactured the M16 and the XM16E1 as their Models 602 and 603 respectively.

In the Spring of 1965, the SEALs were given the opportunity to employ their AR-15s in combat. By April, the rebels in the Dominican Republic had escalated the situation to a crisis point. U.S. Forces were finally called

Rifles

A group of SEALs establish perimeter security while demonstrating a desert mission. The men are all armed with M14 rifles, preferred for the desert due to their longer effective range than the standard M16 series weapons. The SEAL to the left rear in the photo is removing a Compact Laser Designator (CLD) from the pack of the SEAL keeling in front of him. The CLD will be used to illuminate or "paint" a target with laser light for an incoming air strike. These men are all wearing the most recent pattern desert camouflage uniforms.
PHOTO CREDIT: KEVIN DOCKERY

TECHNICAL DATA—M14
NSN 6D1005-00-770-3559
CARTRIDGE—7.62mm Nato (7.61x51mm)
OPERATION—Gas
TYPE OF FIRE—Selective - semiautomatic/full automatic
RATE OF FIRE—Practical SS 20 to 40 rpm, A 40 to 60 rpm, Cyclic 700 to 750 rpm
MUZZLE VELOCITY—2800 fps (853 m/s)
MUZZLE ENERGY—2593 ft/lbs (3516 J)
SIGHTS—Open, Aperture/blade, Adjustable 100 to 1200 meters in 100 meter graduations
FEED—20 round removable box magazine
WEIGHTS
WEAPON (EMPTY)—8.6 lbs (3.90 kg)
WEAPON (LOADED)—11.21 lbs (5.08 kg) w/sling, cleaning kit (in buttstock), & 20 rd mag
Sling 0.31 lbs (0.14 kg)
Cleaning kit/combination tool .67 lbs (0.30 kg)
MAGAZINE (EMPTY)—0.51 lb (0.23 kg)
MAGAZINE (LOADED)—1.63 lb (0.74 kg)
SERVICE CARTRIDGE—M80 Ball 393 gr (25.5 g)
PROJECTILE—149 gr (9.7 g)
LENGTHS
WEAPON OVERALL—44.33 in. (112.6 cm)
BARREL—22 in (55.9 cm)
SIGHT RADIUS—26.69 in. (67.8 cm)

TECHNICAL DATA—M14 w/folding stock
MAGAZINE (EMPTY)—0.51 lb (0.23 kg)
MAGAZINE (LOADED)—1.63 lb (0.74 kg)
SERVICE CARTRIDGE—M80 Ball 393 gr (25.5 g)
PROJECTILE—149 gr (9.7 g)

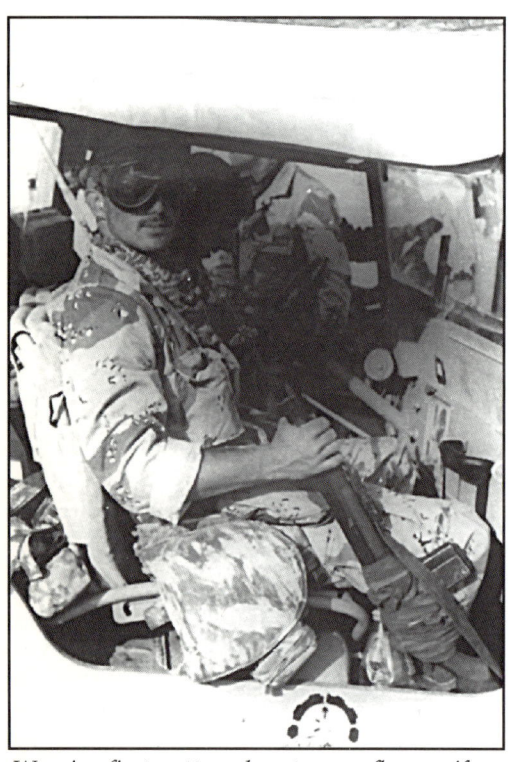

Wearing first-pattern desert camouflage uniforms, these SEALs are patrolling near Kuwait City during Desert Storm. The SEAL in the passenger seat is holding on to his M14 rifle, used in place of the M16 due to its greater range. The action of the M14 has been wrapped in a rag to keep the constant desert dust and sand from the action of the weapon. The large pouch hanging at the SEAL's hip is the M17A1 protective mask carrier with spatters of light paint on the cover in order to help camouflage it.
PHOTO CREDIT: US NAVY

Special Weapons

A SEAL equipped for a rescue in a desert environment. He is carrying an M14 rifle, used for its greater effective range in the open spaces of the desert. The dark goggles he is wearing will protect his eyes from the glare of the sun as well as the sudden flash of a flash-bang (stun) grenade. Taped to the top of his PRO-TEC helmet is a strobe light that can be used to identify the wearer to friendly overhead aircraft. For pickup, the modified parachute harness this SEAL is wearing over his desert-camouflage uniform is an integral part of the Special Purpose Insertion and Extraction (SPIE) rig. For a SPIE extraction, a line lowered down from a helicopter would be attached to the carabiner seen just forward of this SEAL's right shoulder. Just above the trigger finger can be seen the cylindrical selector lock that prevents this particular M14 from firing on full automatic.
PHOTO CREDIT: KEVIN DOCKERY

in to protect US interests and help control the fighting in the streets. Two platoons of SEALs from Team Two arrived in the Dominican Republic complete with their equipment, including the AR-15 rifle. At the same time, components of the US Army's 82nd Airborne Division were also conducting operations on the island. The airborne troops were armed with their new XM16E1s.

One drawback of the AR-15 stood out very quickly for the SEALs after their arrival. As the existence of the SEALs was still considered classified at the time and their presence in the Dominican Republic something the military command wanted to keep secret, the SEALs moved about in civilian clothes for at least part of their duties.

But the SEALs were carrying their AR-15 rifles, a very distinctive appearing weapon to say the least. In this instance, the SEAL's penchant for camouflage didn't quite work out.

Combat employment of the AR-15 against the rebels in the Dominican Republic proved out the AR-15 to a number of SEALs' satisfaction. Incidents of combat for the SEALs was limited during the crisis, but few complaints were voiced against the new rifle.

In addition to the AR-15, the SEALs had at least one additional type of rifle with them during their deployment. Having been issued one of the new AN/PVS-2 starlight scopes for night work, the SEALs mounted the device on an M14 rifle. The power and range of the 7.62mm bullet fired by the M14 proved itself very effective, especially against snipers. Though heavy in comparison to the AR-15, the M14 had a good deal of appeal due to the added range it gave the SEALs. In one instance, the M14 - AN/PVS-2 combination was able to provide security against sniper activity along a beach area at night, something no other weapon system available at the time could have done as well.

M14

The M14 was the last "full-sized" rifle to reach standard-issue status with the US military. An improved version of the M1 Garand, the M14 is chambered for the 7.62mm NATO round. The 7.62mm NATO ammunition, also identified as the 7.62x51mm or .308 Winchester (civilian), came out of the old school of thought as to what constituted an ideal battle rifle. Old-school opinion held that a military rifle must be effective at what we now consider a very long range. One thousand yards would only be considered a medium long range to earlier military planners, even though a soldier who could effectively use his rifle at that range was very rare.

Modifications to the gas system, a provision for full-

Rifles

This SEAL takes a break during a demonstration at the UDT-SEAL Museum in Fort Pierce, Florida. He is wearing the first pattern desert camouflage Battle Dress Uniform (BDUs) as well as a set of nylon web gear (ALICE). He has two LC-2 canteen carriers on his belt on either side of his combat field pack. His weapon is an M14 rifle with the bolt locked in the open position.
PHOTO CREDIT: KEVIN DOCKERY

This SEAL operates as part of a patrol during a demonstration. He is wearing the most recent pattern of desert camouflage BDUs. His nylon web gear is the 1974 pattern All Purpose Lightweight Individual Carrying Equipment (ALICE) with several small arms ammunition cases at the side and front of his belt and an LC-2 canteen cover with its 1-quart plastic canteen at the rear of his left hip. The weapon this SEAL is armed with is the standard M14 rifle, preferred for the desert environment due to its greater range over that of the M16 series. The curved attachment on the muzzle of this M14 is a late production M12 blank firing attachment that allows the weapon to operate with blank ammunition. A low-slung holster on his left hip and the way he is carrying his M14 indicate that this SEAL is left-handed.
PHOTO CREDIT: KEVIN DOCKERY

Special Weapons

A group of SEALs awaiting their turn in a demonstration of SEAL abilities. They are all wearing the latest pattern of desert camouflage Battle Dress Uniforms (BDUs) as well as a mix of different types of load bearing equipment. The SEALs at the center and left of the photograph are both armed with M14 rifles fitted with late-pattern M12 blank firing attachments. The SEAL at the left is wearing a set of chest pouches for 20 round M14 magazines in addition to his regular web gear. The SEAL at the far right is armed with an M60E3 light machine gun, a belt of ammunition for which can be seen just above his left forearm.
PHOTO CREDIT: KEVIN DOCKERY

At a demonstration of SEAL abilities, this operator is walking across a beach equipped for winter warfare. He is wearing a white camouflage shell over his uniform, complete with hood, gloves, and cover for his pack. Strapped to the sides of his pack are aluminum-framed snowshoes. He is also wearing dark goggles to protect his eyes from the cold and glare off the snow and ice. His weapon is a folding-stock M14A1, unique to the SEALs. The stock on this particular weapon has been partially camouflaged with white tape.
PHOTO CREDIT: KEVIN DOCKERY

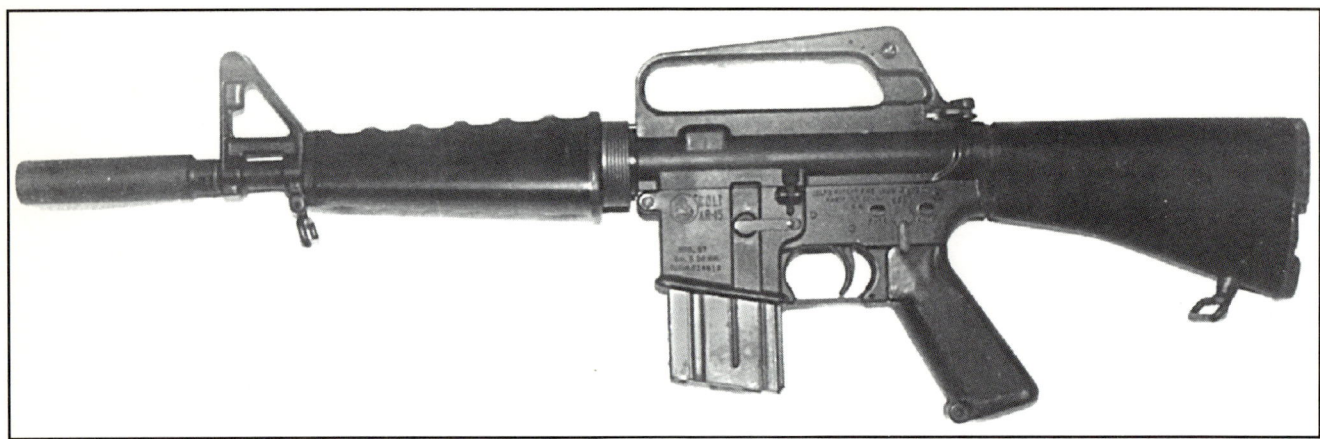

A left-side view of the Colt Model 07 CAR-15 submachine gun. The weapon is loaded with a 20 round magazine and the sliding buttstock is in its fully-forward position. The selector lever, directly above the pistol grip, is set to the semiautomatic fire position. This specimen has the longer, second type noise/flash suppressor.
PHOTO CREDIT: KEVIN DOCKERY

TECHNICAL DATA—CAR-15 Submachinegun (Colt Model 07)
CARTRIDGE—.223 Remington (5.56x45mm)
OPERATION—Gas
TYPE OF FIRE—Selective - semiautomatic/full automatic
RATE OF FIRE—Practical SS 45 to 65 rpm, A 150 to 200 rpm, Cyclic 700 to 950 rpm
MUZZLE VELOCITY—2750 fps (838 m/s)
MUZZLE ENERGY—940 ft/lbs (1275 J)
SIGHTS—Open, Flip-type aperture/post, Adjustable, battle aperture 0 to 300 meters, long range aperture 300 to 500 meters
FEED—20 or 30 round removable box magazines
WEIGHTS
WEAPON (EMPTY)—5.3 lbs (2.40 kg)
WEAPON (LOADED)—6.01 lbs (2.73 kg) w/20 rd mag, w/o sling
Sling 0.40 lbs (0.18 kg)
MAGAZINE (EMPTY)—20 round aluminium 0.19 lb (0.08 kg)
30 round aluminium 0.24 lbs (0.11 kg)
MAGAZINE (LOADED)—20 round 0.71 lb (0.32 kg)
30 round 1.02 lbs (0.46 kg)
SERVICE CARTRIDGE—M193 Ball 182 gr (11.8 g)
PROJECTILE—56 gr (3.6 g)
LENGTHS
WEAPON OVERALL—26/28.7 in. (66/72.9 cm)
BARREL—10 in (25.4 cm)

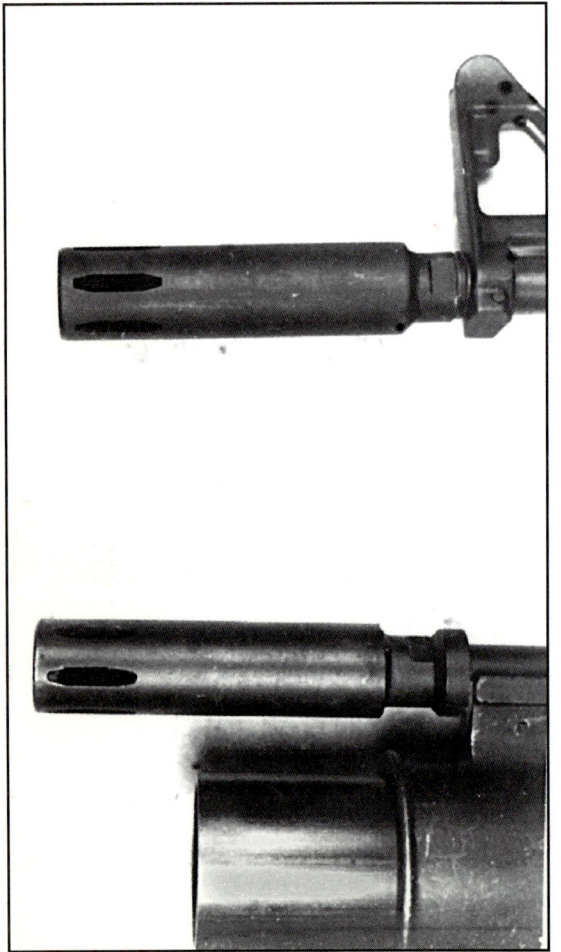

Two examples of the second model noise/flash suppressor. The upper specimen is on a Colt Model 07 submachine gun (CAR-15). The longer body of the second model suppressor and the six elongated ports at the muzzle separate the design from the shorter first model suppressor. The lower specimen is mounted on an XM177E2 with an XM148 40mm grenade launcher mounted underneath the barrel. What appears to be a second part of the suppressor, behind the reduced-diameter section, is actually a shaped metal washer. The large washer acted as a gas check and would allow rifle grenades to be launched from the suppressor if desired. Except for slight manufacturing changes that came over time, the two noise/flash suppressors are the same.
PHOTO CREDIT: KEVIN DOCKERY

Special Weapons

automatic fire, a 20 round box magazine, and other mechanical improvements made the M14 a better overall battle rifle than the earlier M1 Garand. The long range capability and overall dependability of the M14 kept it held in reserve in the military supply system long after it had been supplanted by the M16A1 as the standard-issue US shoulder arm. Hand fitted and tuned to match specifications, the M14 became a highly accurate base for a later family of sniper rifles for the Teams and the Army.

CAR 15 Model 607

An additional AR-15 based weapon was used by the SEALs prior to their major deployment to Vietnam. The CAR-15 submachine gun was a shortened version of the AR-15, offered by Colt as their Model 607 early in 1965. Originally part of the CAR-15 weapons family, which included the Model 605 Carbine, the CAR-15 submachine gun was a very shortened version of the AR-15 rifle. Since the action of the AR-15 requires that the bolt carrier be able to recoil into the stock when the weapon is fired, a folding stock won't work. For the Model 607, a sliding buttstock of generally standard shape was devised.

The sliding buttstock has a switch on the buttplate to lock or unlock the stock system. Using the switch, the buttstock can be slid in or out and locked firmly into either the extended or collapsed position. With the stock in the collapsed position, the CAR-15 can be easily employed for instinctive shooting while held in the underarm position. Since the weapon was so handy when collapsed, many SEALs never bothered extending the stock.

"… For myself, I preferred the CAR-15, the short submachine gun version of the M16. Using the CAR, I would rarely extend the stock as most of our fighting was done close-in with instinctive firing from the hip being the norm."

The barrel of the Model 607 was cut down to only ten inches and the standard flash hider installed. The front sight was also moved back and the gas system modified as needed. The handguards of the Model 607 were of the same triangular style as those on the AR-15, only roughly half as long. Well liked by the SEALs for its short size and fast handling characteristics, the Model 607 CAR-15 was available in very limited numbers. Those weapons that were available were used in Vietnam until they were effectively worn out.

To increase the number of possible military sales of the CAR-15 to the military, especially the Army, Colt made a number of changes to the weapon while it still retained the designation CAR-15 submachine gun. The addition of the XM16E1 model forward bolt assist to the CAR-15 added about 0.2 pounds (0.09 kg) to the overall weight of the weapon. Though the forward bolt assist was not particularly desired by the SEALs, the CAR-15 certainly was. This resulted in a number of slightly different CAR-15 submachine guns being used in the Teams through the Vietnam War.

By late 1966, the Army and the Air Force had shown enough interest in the CAR-15 to have ordered several thousand from Colt. The first weapons examined for the Army were standard model 607s with the forward bolt assist added. During Army testing one serious drawback did stand out immediately when the CAR-15 was fired. The short barrel and standard flash hider gave the weapon a tremendous muzzle blast and loud report accompanied by a large fireball. At night, the muzzle blast from the Model 607 was dazzlingly bright.

To reduce the muzzle blast and report of the CAR-15 submachine gun, Colt developed a combination flash/noise suppressor in September 1966. The first model flash/noise suppressor added only 1.3 inches (3.3 cm) to the overall length of the CAR-15 and about 0.1 pounds (0.045 kg) to its weight. The internal configuration of the combination suppressor eliminated a good deal of the muzzle flash and, when new, reduced the report of firing the CAR-15 to near that of the standard M16 rifle.

Though a number of the first-model flash/noise suppressors were made in the Fall of 1966, the design was not considered completely satisfactory. In order to cut down on the sound and flash of firing, the first model noise/flash suppressor had a tight muzzle hole, only slightly larger than the .223 projectile. Though the design of the suppressor did reduce the muzzle blast of the CAR-15 it also increased the amount of fouling deposited in the barrel of the weapon. The tight exit hole also caused tracer bullets to yaw badly when fired, destroying their accuracy. To limit the barrel fouling and allow tracer bullets to be accurately fired, a new flash/noise suppressor was developed.

The second model flash/noise suppressor had an overall length of 4.25 inches (10.8 cm) and a weight of

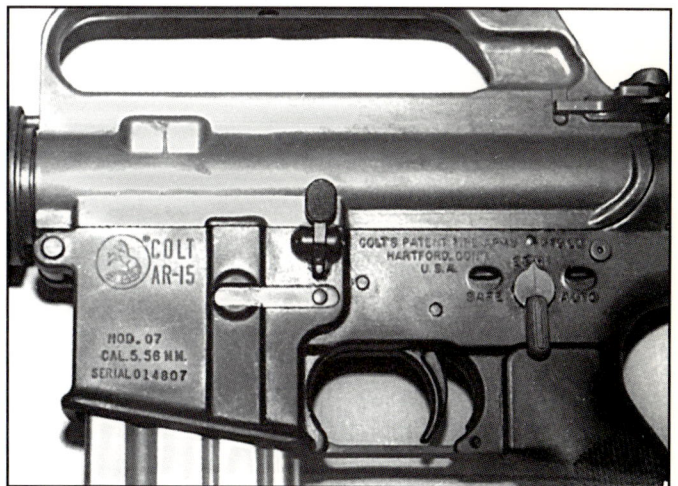

A left-side view of the Colt Model 07 submachine gun (CAR-15). The selector switch can be plainly seen, set at semiautomatic fire, directly above the pistol grip where it can be manipulated by the operator's thumb. The small rectangular part above and in front of the trigger guard is the retaining portion of the magazine catch. Above the rear of the magazine catch is the bolt stop. Pressing in on the serrated portion of the bolt stop releases the bolt allowing it to move forward.
PHOTO CREDIT: KEVIN DOCKERY/KNIGHT ARMAMENT COMPANY

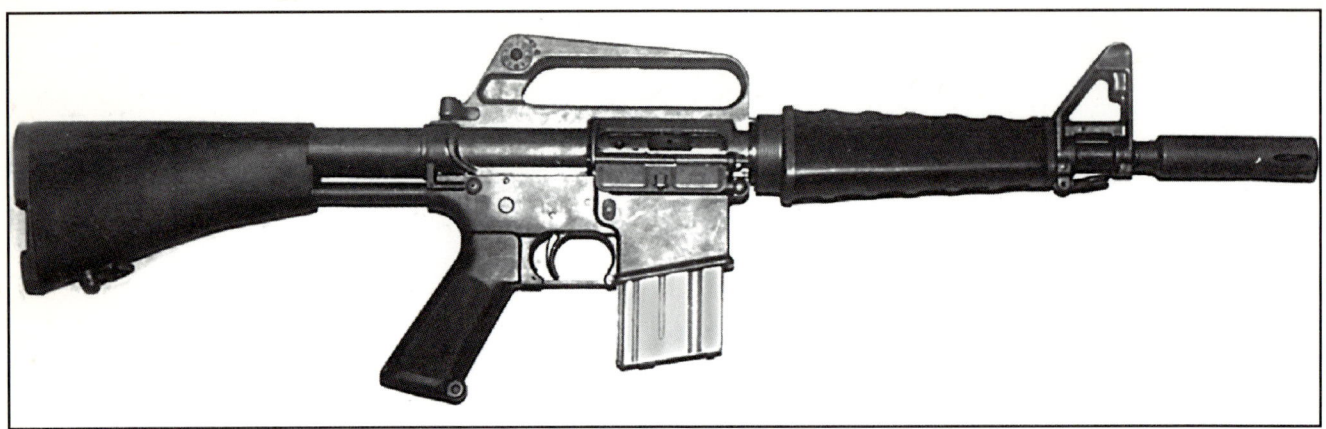

The Colt Model 07 CAR-15 submachine gun. This specimen has the sliding stock fully extended and locked into place. The additional guide rod needed by this design of sliding stock can be seen as the small tube beneath the action spring guide at the rear of the receiver. The noise/flash suppressor on the muzzle of this weapon is the more common second type. This weapon also has an early-type of upper receiver with no allowance for a forward assist mechanism and a lower receiver with no raised guard ridge around the magazine release. The smooth bolt carrier, with no serrations for the forward bolt assist, is visible through the open ejection port.
PHOTO CREDIT: KEVIN DOCKERY

The right side of a Colt Model 07 CAR-15 submachine gun with the spring-operated M3 "clothespin" bipod clamped into place under the front sight. The buttstock is slid back to its open position and the smaller guide rail necessary for this model stock can be seen just below the larger action spring guide. The bolt carrier, visible through the ejection port, is a later model intended for the M16A1 with a bolt closure device. The notches seen on the rear section of the bolt carrier are where the plunger of the closure device would contact the carrier. This specimen has the second-model conical, open-prong flash hider which was mounted on some of the first examples of this model.
PHOTO CREDIT: KEVIN DOCKERY

Special Weapons

TECHNICAL DATA—XM177E1 (Colt Model 609)
NSN 1005-00-930-5595
—XM177E2 (Colt Model 629)
NSN 1005-00-021-2429
CARTRIDGE—.223 Remington (5.56x45mm)
OPERATION—Gas
TYPE OF FIRE—Selective - semiautomatic/full automatic
RATE OF FIRE—Practical SS 45 to 65 rpm, A 150 to 200 rpm, Cyclic 700 to 800 rpm
MUZZLE VELOCITY—2750 fps (838 m/s)
MUZZLE ENERGY—940 ft/lbs (1275 J)
SIGHTS—Open, Flip-type aperture/post, Adjustable, battle aperture 0 to 300 meters,
long range aperture 300 to 500 meters
FEED—20 or 30 round removable box magazines
WEIGHTS
WEAPON (EMPTY)—XM177E1 5.2 lbs (2.36 kg)
XM177E2 5.35 lbs (2.43 kg)
WEAPON (LOADED)—
XM177E1 6.62 lbs (3.0 kg) w/sling & 30 rd mag
XM177E2 6.77 lbs (3.07 kg) w/sling & 30 rd mag
Sling 0.40 lbs (0.18 kg)
MAGAZINE (EMPTY)—20 round aluminium 0.19 lb (0.08 kg)
30 round aluminium 0.24 lbs (0.11 kg)
MAGAZINE (LOADED)—20 round 0.71 lb (0.32 kg)
30 round 1.02 lbs (0.46 kg)
SERVICE CARTRIDGE—M193 Ball 182 gr (11.8 g)
PROJECTILE—56 gr (3.6 g)
LENGTHS
WEAPON OVERALL—XM177E1 28.3/31 in. (71.9/78.7 cm)
XM177E2 29.8/32.5 in (75.7/82.6 cm)
BARREL—XM177E1 - 10 in (25.4 cm)
XM177E2 11.5 in (29.2 cm)
The combination flash/noise suppressor adds about 3.5 inches to the overall barrel length
SIGHT RADIUS—14.72 in. (37.4 cm)

0.14 lbs. (0.6 kg). Threading the suppressor onto the 0.635 inch long threaded portion of the barrel muzzle, including a 0.1 inch thick lock washer, increased the overall length of the weapon by 3.72 inches (9.4 cm). The second model flash/noise suppressor was identified by Colt as part #62370. The inside of the second model noise/flash suppressor had a small expansion chamber surrounding a ported barrel extension much the same as the first model device, but the new suppressor had a longer body that incorporated a six-slotted end piece with a large internal diameter, like a standard flash suppressor.

The second model flash/noise suppressor was fitted onto all subsequent models of the CAR-15 and retrofitted onto older weapons as parts became available. Though at least somewhat effective at cutting down the sound and flash of firing the short-barreled AR-15 variations, the suppressor was still easily clogged with fouling and would quickly lose its effectiveness in a combat environment.

XM177, E1, E2 Models 610, 609, 629

The original sliding buttstock assembly of the Colt model 607 was considered too complex and costly for fielding with the Army. A new type of sliding buttstock was designed and put into production. The new stock was a more skeletal, tubular design while still retaining a full-sized buttplate. To extend or collapse the stock a lever underneath the sliding section was squeezed with the operators fingers, unlocking the rear portion of the assembly. A spring would engage to lock the stock in the extended or collapsed position when the operating lever was released. Lastly, the triangular handguards, which were found to be fragile, were replaced with short, cylindrical handguards with raised reinforcing ribs.

The new weapon, named the "Commando" by Colt, began to be delivered to the military on 7 November 1966 with an initial shipment of 1190 weapons out of a 2815 weapon contract. By January 1967, the Commando had been tentatively type-classified as the XM177 submachine gun (Air Force version) without a forward bolt assist and

This SEAL is holding an XM177E2 with an XM148 40mm grenade launcher mounted underneath the barrel. The XM177E2 is loaded with an early Colt extended magazine for the M16 weapon series. This magazine is three 20 round magazines welded together to feed straight through. This magazine did not work well in the field and only 35 were reported to have been made at the special request of SEAL Team Two. Hanging from around this man's neck is a hand-held AN/PRT-4 transmitter. The companion AN/PRR-9 receiver can be seen as the box with the spiral part at his left shoulder. The small radios were not well received by the Teams as they soon proved to have a very short range, as little as 40 meters, out in the field.
PHOTO CREDIT: FRANK MONCRIEF COLLECTION

Rifles

Two SEALs coming out of the water after a training swim. Both men are armed with XM177E2 submachine guns. The weapon on the left has an early (2nd) model open-prong flash suppressor. The weapon on the right has the standard M16A1 (3rd model) "Birdcage" flash suppressor. Both weapons have their extra-long slings attached to the front sight, allowing them to be carried in a sights-up, muzzle-forward position ready for immediate use. The swimmer on the left has an older pair of UDT "Duck feet" swim fins hanging from his left arm. The swimmer on the right has a newer pair of "rocket" fins developed for the sport-diving industry. Both men are using Mk VI semi-closed circuit breathing rigs.
PHOTO CREDIT: UDT-SEAL MUSEUM

Going out on an operation in Vietnam, this SEAL is armed with an XM177E2. The additional 1.5 inches of barrel on the XM177E2 as compared to the XM177E1 is easily visible in this photo. This weapon has the second model noise/flash suppressor on the muzzle with the additional formed sheet metal washer between the suppressor and the barrel of the weapon. At his left shoulder, this SEAL is carrying a Navy Pilot's Survival knife with the grip covered in tape for additional waterproofing.
PHOTO CREDIT: RYAN McCOMBIE COLLECTION

Special Weapons

the XM177E1 (Army version) with a forward bolt assist. The XM177E1 was sent to Vietnam beginning with the first shipments in November 1966 with the Army's distribution of 2800 weapons being completed by March 1967.

SEALs had been using the model 607 CAR-15 submachine gun from the time of their first combat deployments in Vietnam, circa 1966-1967. As the XM177E1 became available, it was picked up for use with the Teams. Development of the XM177 system continued with the Army, the intention being the future replacement of all M3 and M3A1 submachine guns in service as well as the M1911A1 .45 pistol and M16A1 rifle on a selective basis.

After extensive field testing, the XM177E1 was found to not be completely satisfactory. Problems in accuracy were noted and a number of improvements made. In mid-April 1967, the new Colt model 629 Commando was type-classified as the XM177E2. A contract for 510 XM177E2s was signed with Colt with the weapons to go to the Studies and Observation Group, Vietnam (MAC-V SOG). Delivery of the new weapons was to begin in late September, 1967.

Two noticeable aspects of the XM177E2 stand out in photographs of the weapon. The barrel was extended an additional 1.5 inches (3.8 cm) giving the XM177E2 a barrel length of 11.5 inches (29.2 cm). The additional barrel length was found to help cut down on the muzzle blast and increase the stability, and accuracy, of projectiles. Additionally, the longer barrel allows the XM148 40mm grenade launcher to be more easily attached to the XM177E2. Many elite units, including the SEALs, greatly liked the additional firepower of the XM148 launcher, but adding the weapon to the earlier CAR-15 and XM177E1 was difficult and required modifications to both weapons.

In addition to the longer barrel, the XM177E2 appears to have a third model flash and noise suppressor, one with a noticeable raised boss at the barrel end of the device. The boss is actually a stamped metal washer with an elongated cross section. The washer acts as a forward stop for the XM148 40mm grenade launcher and also allowed rifle grenades to be launched from the XM177E2, something that was rarely, if ever, done.

Since the XM177E1/E2 weapons incorporated all of the up-to-the-minute changes and improvements developed for the XM16E1/M16A1, the Commando was noticeably more reliable than many of the M16-type weapons already in Vietnam. By July 1967, thirty XM177E1 barrels with chrome plated chambers arrived in Vietnam. Later production XM177E2s were all produced with chrome plated chambers to help limit corrosion.

Accuracy of fire with the XM177E2 continued to be a problem throughout the life of the weapon, especially when firing tracer ammunition. In November 1968, Colt estimated that a complete ballistic and kinematic study of the XM177E2 would cost $400,000 and take six months to complete. Recommendations in December 1968 were for the XM177E2 to be reoriented to a $635,000, 29-month long R&D program. Due to the winding down of the US forces in Vietnam after 1970, no action was taken on the XM177E2 program and the weapon went out of production in 1970. Though thousands of the XM177E1/E2 weapons had been built, only a few hundred remained in use by the elite forces who strongly desired them. Cannibalization of damaged XM177s to keep the remaining weapons operational became quite common during the 1970's in the SEAL and UDT Teams.

The strong desire to keep the XM-177E1/E2 weapons operational with the SEALs is clearly shown in the mention of the production model weapons first arrival in the Teams. The excerpt is from SEAL Team Two's Command and Control History for 1969, page 14;

"3. (U) The XM177E1 submachine gun, better known as the CAR 15, appeared at the SEAL Team late in the year [1969]. This weapon is a welcome addition to the Team's family of weapons, because it fills a size gap that had been left open by all our other weapons. Its main characteristic is its relatively short length which makes it perfect for those people in a patrol such as the patrol leader, radio man, and assistant patrol leader, who find the shorter weapon ideal for close-quarter searching and surveillance of prisoners."

On 23 February, 1967 the XM16E1 was adopted by the US Army as the M16A1 rifle. The weapon had received a number of improvements during its testing by the Army, some of which were necessitated by the Army changing the type of powder allowed in loading .223 ammunition. Among other changes the inside of the bolt carrier was chrome plated and the exterior parkerized with a dull finish. The chrome plating minimized corrosion while giving the carrier a non-reflective finish. Earlier bolt carriers had been entirely chromed and could be seen shining through an open ejection port.

A third model flash suppressor was added to the M16A1, this one having a closed muzzle giving it a "bird cage" appearance. The earlier open prong flash suppressors were reported by the Army to hang up on vines, tall grass, and brush, something not noticed by the SEALs. Other changes in the M16A1 included chrome plating the chamber, and later the entire bore, of the weapon. The SEALs simply liked the M16 family completely and used them interchangeably. In a single SEAL platoon in Vietnam could sometimes be seen AR-15s, M16A1s, CAR-15s (model 607s), XM177E1s, and XM177E2s. On the muzzles of the weapons could be found first, second and third model flash hiders, on both long and short barreled weapons, as well as first and second model flash/noise suppressors on the "shorty" weapons.

The SEALs' opinion of the M16E1 shows clearly in the following quote taken from the official Command and Control History for SEAL Team Two, 1967;

"The M16E1 has proven a welcome addition to the SEAL arsenal. The weapon performs very well as long as it is kept reasonably clean.

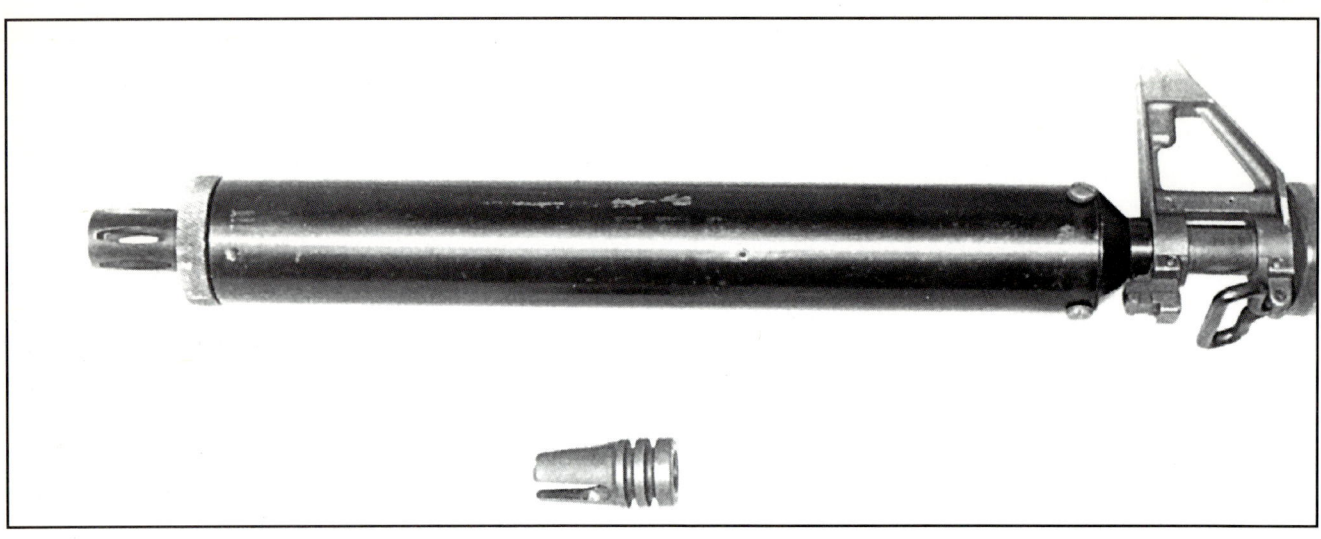

This is the Mark 2 blast suppressor (1st model) mounted on a standard M16A1 rifle. The Mark 2 screws onto the muzzle of the weapon in place of the standard flash suppressor. The conical rear mount of the Mark 2 indexes on the bayonet lug. The suppressor body is turned to line up the screw holes, and the rear mounting screws inserted to lock the device into place. The flash suppressor is the 2nd type, conical, open-prong model. This blast suppressor was based on the earlier design of the Human Engineering Labs (HEL) M4 sound suppressor. Filed for a patent on 12 July, 1968 as a gun blast diffuser, the 1st model Mark 2 did not require the modifications to the weapon that the HEL M4 suppressor did in order to operate. A weapon fitted with the Mark 2 blast suppressor, developed for the Mark 4 rifle, worked equally well with our without the suppressor in place.
PHOTO CREDIT: KEVIN DOCKERY

"The HEL M4 suppressor was mounted as a permanent part of a modified M16A1 and was not intended to be removed.... With the suppressor removed, the modified M16A1 wouldn't operate except as a manually loaded repeater."

A sectioned view of the 1st model Mark 2 blast suppressor. This very simple design has two expansion chambers and a single baffle. The angular piece to the left of center is the threaded cruciform mounting plate that screws onto the barrel of the using weapon. Though outwardly resembling the HEL M4 suppressor, the Mark 2 blast suppressor is greatly more simplified, having only five major parts as compared to the over 16 parts in the HEL M4. The internal design of the Mark 2 blast suppressor allowed water in the system to easily drain out, something that could not be quickly done with the HEL M4.
PHOTO CREDIT: KEVIN DOCKERY

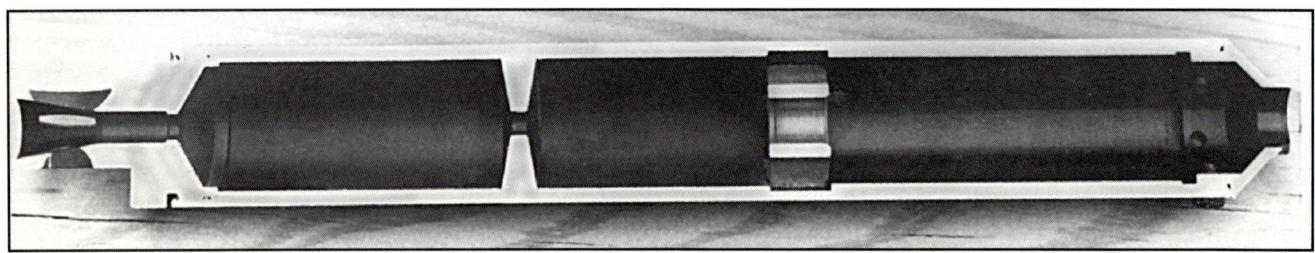

"The chrome [plated] chambers and barrels should substantially lengthen the life of the barrel. It is believed that the bolt assist should be eliminated from the weapon."

For the SEALs' operations in Vietnam surprise was as much of a weapon as any ordnance that could be carried. Specialized weapons could sometimes give an additional edge to an operating group of SEALs deep in the bush. Normally, weapon specialization extended into giving the SEALs as much concentrated firepower, in terms of volume of fire, that they could effectively carry. But other types of weapons could increase the "surprise" factor in the SEALs' favor. And foremost among these weapons are suppressed guns where the sound of firing is eliminated as much as possible.

A suppressor, commonly called a silencer, cuts down on the noise of a weapon's firing, suppressing the sound of the shot. Usually, a suppressor does not effect the velocity of a fired projectile which, if it is moving faster than the speed of sound, causes a sonic "crack" as it passes through the air.

During the first years of the SEALs major deployments to Vietnam, few if any suppressed weapons were available to the Teams. Those that were usually consisted of old World War II weapons that were in very short supply. Back in the States, the US Army's Human Engineering Laboratory (HEL) at Aberdeen Proving Grounds was one of several places developing suppressors for the military. The HEL M4 suppressor became available to the SEALs in the summer of 1967. The HEL M4 suppressor was mounted as a permanent part of a modified M16A1 and was not intended to be removed. For proper operation with the HEL M4 suppressor attached, the bolt carrier of the designated M16A1 had an extra gas bleed-off hole drilled into it, centered and behind the two holes already in place. The extra hole allowed the weapon to function properly, firing in both semi and full automatic modes, but only with the suppressor attached. With the suppressor removed, the modified M16A1 wouldn't operate except as a manually loaded repeater.

A gas deflector shield was attached to the charging handle of the modified M16A1 to protect the firer's face and eyes from any excess propellant gases. The HEL M4 suppressor made the modified M16A1 very difficult to locate by sound when fired. At a distance of 50 meters or so, depending on the surrounding area, the sound of the shot could not be heard.

To increase the efficiency of the suppressor, the SEALs obtained a quantity of special downloaded .223 ammunition. The special ammunition would fire a subsonic projectile that did not break the speed of sound, about 1100 feet per second (335 m/s) at sea level, and yet still operate the action of the modified M16A1. Though very quiet and effective, the subsonic ammunition still would not operate the action as dependably as desired. Neither was the terminal effectiveness of the special ammunition as good as the standard round.

The suppressor-equipped M16A1 was used by the SEALs throughout their operations in Vietnam and was considered a valuable asset. As noted in the SEAL Team Two Command and Control history for 1968, page 8;

"A silencer has been produced which when used with special ammunition, has an indistinguishable noise level. The SEAL Team now has silencers for pistols and rifles."

The weapon was especially valuable on those missions that needed the longer range and accuracy of a suppressed rifle over that of a suppressed pistol or submachine gun. Off-duty SEALs sometimes found additional uses for the suppressed M16A1s they had.

"We shipped out and went on to Song Ong Doc, where we were living on a barge. At night, you'd see groups of rats swimming out from shore in a column maybe twenty feet long, trying to reach the barge and climb up to get into the potatoes that were stacked amidships. When we didn't have operations, the guys would get M-16s with silencers (suppressors) on them and sit out on deck shooting the rats. As long as they used the silencers (suppressors) the officers didn't know what they were doing."

The SEALs were constantly looking for ways to augment the firepower of their small units. This was one of the reasons that the Teams first looked at the AR-15 weapon. One item that was attractive in the AR-15 was that it came outfitted with a twenty-round magazine. Though a thirty-round magazine had been available from Colt since at least 1964, technical difficulties with the large magazines design kept it from being commonly available.

The original Colt thirty-round magazine was a "fully curved" design, that is the magazine had a slight curve, to facilitate feeding rounds, through its entire length. Though the original magazine fed ammunition smoothly, the magazine well of the AR-15 was a straight rectangular hole. Allowances for a curved magazine had not been designed into the weapon. Simply put, not all of the AR-15/M16/XM16E1 weapons made would accept the original thirty-round magazine. If an individual weapon's tolerances were on the large side, it could accept the curved magazine, if not, it could only feed from the standard twenty-round magazine.

The few thirty-round magazines the SEALs had were carefully hoarded and used for combat duty. Though the Teams had at least a small number of the original thirty-round magazines in 1964-65, there were never enough for general issue. The Air Force also had a limited number of the early thirty-round magazines and occasionally individual mags would be "borrowed" by enterprising SEALs.

In January 1966, a requirement was put out for a thirty-round magazine to be delivered from Colt for the M16/XM16E1 program. The late 1966 contract for the XM177E1 Commando specified that the weapon come issued with seven thirty-round magazines. But the thirty-round magazine project was overshadowed at Colt by

"Later production XM177E2s were all produced with chrome plated chambers to help limit corrosion."

A Colt Model 609 XM177E1 "Commando" submachine gun. This specimen has the longer second model noise and flash suppressor mounted on its muzzle. The production model sliding buttstock is in its forward position in this photo. The weapon is loaded with a 20 round magazine and is supported with an M3 bipod clamped in place under the front sight.
PHOTO CREDIT: KEVIN DOCKERY

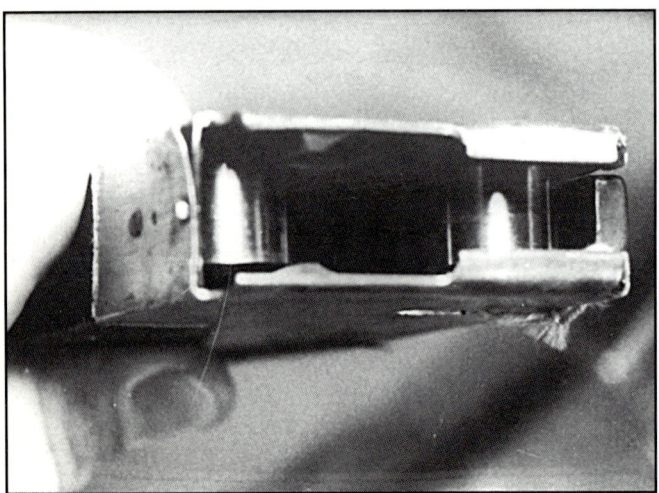

A top view of the Mod 3A 50 round M16 magazine. The cartridge follower has been removed in this photo to show the two constant-force extension springs. The constant-force springs resemble a roll of steel tape. The spring steel coils maintain a smooth pressure on the cartridge follower as the rounds are fed into the weapon with the same pressure driving the first cartridge as the last. Most coil spring designs build up pressure as the spring is compressed making the last rounds to be loaded into a long magazine difficult to insert. The constant-force spring design eliminates the spring-loading problem.
PHOTO CREDIT: KEVIN DOCKERY

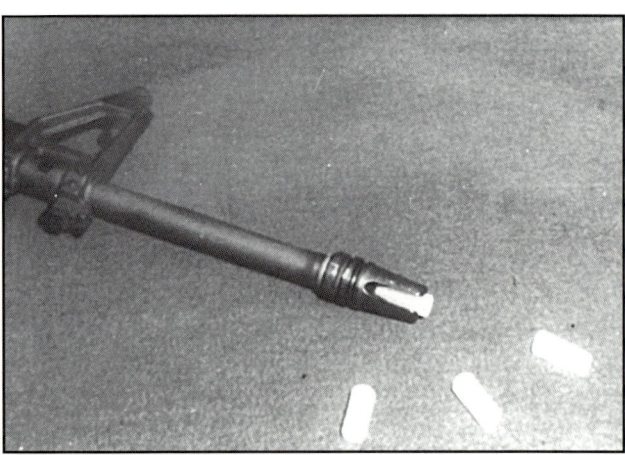

Produced by the Naval Weapons Center at China Lake, these are commercially available polypropylene plugs used to block the muzzle of an M16, AR-15, or Stoner. The soft plastic plugs slip tightly into the bore of the flash suppressor where they seal the end of the barrel from mud or rain. The plugs could be simply removed by hand or even shot-off with no danger to the weapon or firer. One drawback of the internal-style rain/mud plug was that it would not work on the noise/flash suppressor found on the CAR-15 and XM177 series weapons.
PHOTO CREDIT: US NAVY

Special Weapons

other problems and pushed back in priority. XM177E1s were issued with standard twenty-round magazines.

During the initial field testing of the XM177E1 by the US Army in Vietnam, only four early model thirty-round magazines were sent over for testing. This was along with the 2800 XM177E1s being issued. The four magazines ended up with the 5th Special Forces Group. Though the number of magazines available for testing was laughably small, ninety percent of the people asked in the survey that was part of the XM177E1 testing, stated they preferred the thirty-round magazine if available.

By June 1968, Colt had signed a contact with the Army to supply 1,000 new-model thirty-round magazines with delivery expected in 26 weeks. By 1969, the new model thirty-round magazines started to become available in Vietnam with the SEALs being among the first units to receive them. The new magazine has a straight top and bottom portion connected by a curved section and fit all of the AR-15/M16/16A1 weapons produced at the time of its adoption in 1969. The thirty-round magazine was enthusiastically received by the SEALs who accepted all that they could get their hands on.

SEAL Team Two Command and Control History, 1969, page 14:

"8. (U) Another favorite piece of operational gear which is now present on the SEAL TWO inventory is the 30-round magazine for the M16 and CAR 15 weapons. This gives an extra 10 rounds per magazine which is a welcome development to a unit such as the SEAL Team which constantly tries to make up for its lack of numbers with superior firepower."

In 1968, the Naval Research and Development Unit - Vietnam (NRDU/V) sent a representative to Vietnam in order to assess the needs of the Navy units there. During his four-month tour, the NRDU/V representative spent a large portion of his time with the SEALs operating in the Mekong Delta. One of the strong impressions the man came away with was of the SEALs' requirement for sustained firepower with their M16 rifles. This was needed especially to maintain the high volume of fire during the first crucial moments of enemy contact.

There was at least a year's wait before the thirty-round magazine would be available from Colt and the Naval Weapons Laboratory, Dahlgren, decided to address the problem. The first model of a new fifty-round magazine was delivered from Colt in April/May 1969. The Colt magazines were made up from three twenty-round magazines welded together end-to-end. Inside of the magazines were a new follower mechanism designed by the engineers at Dahlgren. Thirty-five of the Colt magazines were made and forwarded to the Navy for testing.

The major engineering problem with such a long magazine is the spring pressure needed to lift the heavy column of cartridges into the rifle. Too heavy a spring and the last rounds loaded will be difficult to insert into the magazine, too light a spring and all of the ammunition will not feed into the weapon. A normal coil spring, such

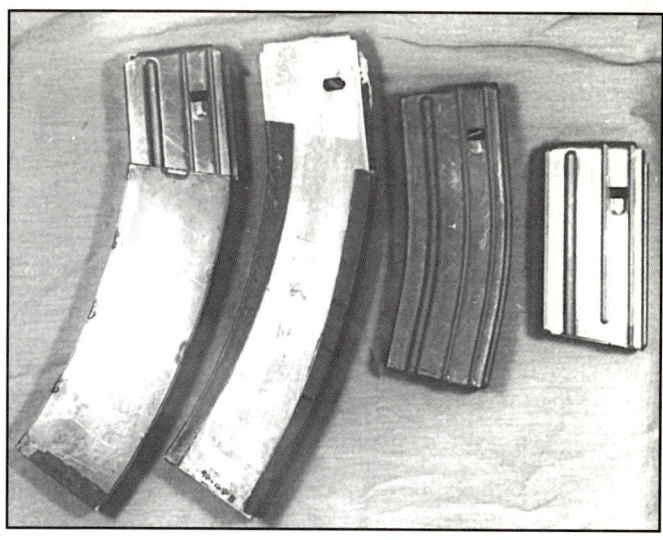

Four of the magazines used by SEALs in Vietnam in the M16-series of weapons. The magazine to the far right is a standard, aluminum 20 round box magazine used in the M16 from its very early days. An earlier steel 20 round magazine was available for the AR-15 but was dropped in favor of the improved aluminum model. Second in from the right is the production-model aluminum 30 round magazine that started becoming available to the SEALs in some numbers in 1969. The production 30 round magazine has two straight sections connected by a curved portion of the body. An earlier 30 round magazine was available in small numbers but had a fully-curved body that did not fit all M16-series weapons due to tolerance differences between magazine wells. The magazine to the far left is the Childers/Monolo Mod 1 50 round magazine produced by the Naval Weapons Laboratory, Dahlgren in 1969. In the Mod 1 design, a curved extension was attached to a standard 20 round magazine body. In addition, a special constant-force extension spring and Teflon follower were part of the design. The Mod 1 design was not successful and only 10 specimens were produced with several being tested in Vietnam. The center magazine is the Mod 3A design, considered the most successful of the series. Ten of the Mod 3A magazines were made and tested by the SEALs in Vietnam and found a valuable addition to the initial volume of fire that could be put out on contact with the enemy. Though the 50 round magazine project was considered a success, the design was shelved in 1970 and no further work was done.
PHOTO CREDIT: KEVIN DOCKERY

as is used in the twenty-round magazine, "loads up", that is increases its spring tension as the magazine is filled. For the proposed fifty-round magazines, the pressure needed to load the final rounds against a coil spring would likely need a loading tool for assistance. In addition, the spring pressure could keep the first rounds in a full magazine from being stripped into the barrels by the weapon's bolt.

To answer this problem, the NRDU/V came up with a new method of pushing the rounds through the long magazine. The follower for the fifty-round magazines, the platform that actually pushes the ammunition itself,

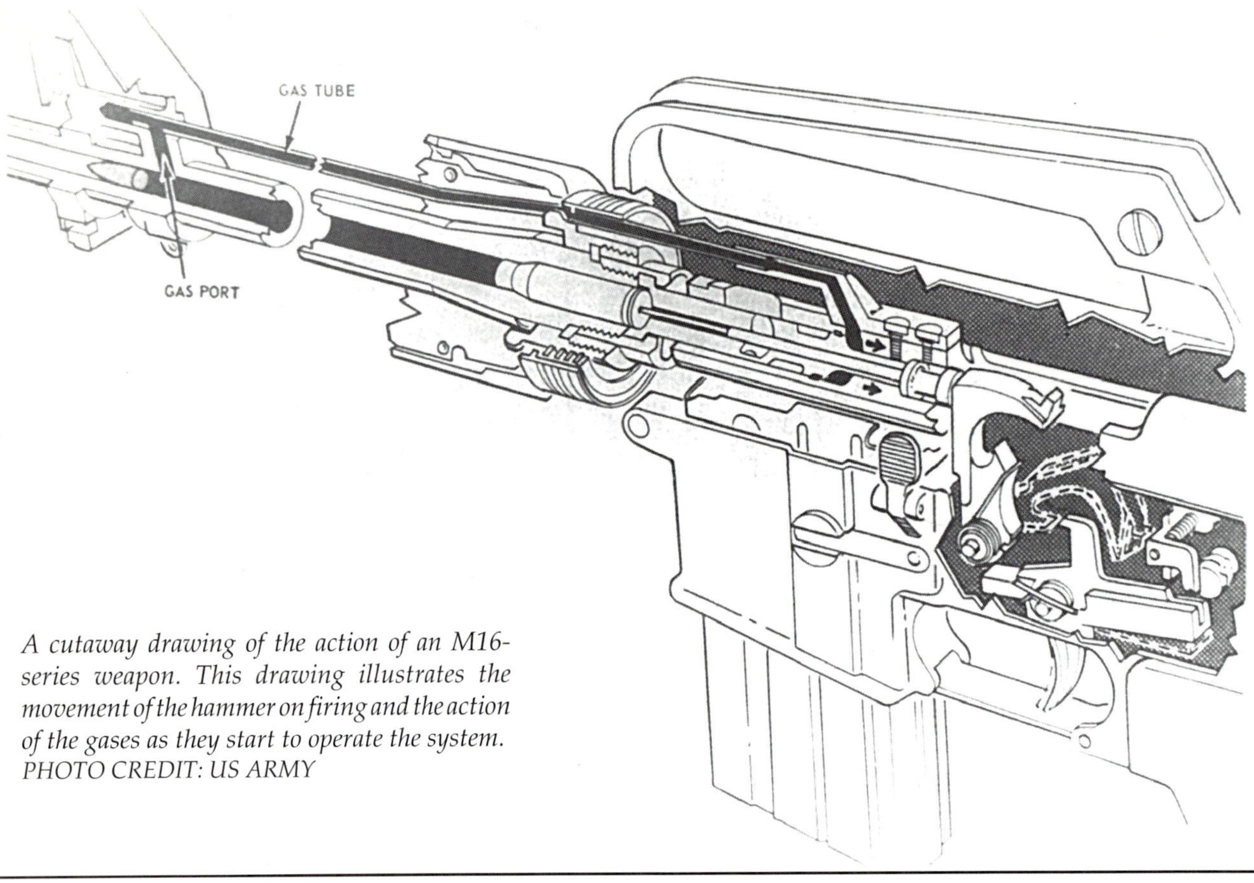

Rifles

A cutaway drawing of the action of an M16-series weapon. This drawing illustrates the movement of the hammer on firing and the action of the gases as they start to operate the system.
PHOTO CREDIT: US ARMY

The rarely seen patch of the NWC Special Projects Division at China Lake, California. This facility produced many specialized pieces of equipment on a quick-reaction basis for use by the SEALs during the Vietnam War and into the 1970's under the sponsorship of the Vietnam Laboratory Assistance Program (VLAP). The figure wearing the cloak and holding a dagger symbolizes the clandestine nature of much of the SEALs' work. The cactus represent the desert where China Lake is located and the background explosion the end effect of much of the material produced for the SEALs.
PHOTO CREDIT: US NAVY

was made of a low-friction plastic. In the base of the follower were placed two constant-force springs, much like the coiled springs in a clock movement. The ends of the springs were attached to the mouth of the magazine rather than pressing against the magazine's bottom. The constant-force springs would unwind as the magazine was loaded, keeping the same pressure on the last rounds loaded as on the first.

The Colt manufactured (first generation) magazines were made at the special request of SEAL Team Two as an interim measure prior to a magazine becoming available from Dahlgren. Results from using the first generation magazines in the field were poor as the magazines were particularly susceptible to mud and damage from the environment. All the first generation magazines were replaced as new designs became available.

The Naval Weapons Laboratory, Dahlgren (NWL) made a Mod 1 magazine consisting of a twenty-round magazine body attached to a curved magazine extension. The Mod 1 magazine used the constant-force springs and follower and operated much better than the Colt magazine. A further nine Mod 1 magazines were made for testing but remained in the United States.

To eliminate some of the problems noted in testing, a Mod 2 magazine was designed. In the Mod 2 magazine, the follower remained much the same as in the Mod 1 but the body of the magazine was made up of two machined halves rather than an extension being attached to an existing magazine. In the Mod 2 design, the curve of the magazine remained the same but the angle where the curved portion met the straight section was increased. The straight section of the magazine had to be retained for easy insertion into the M16 magazine well

The Naval Ordnance Station in Forest Park, Illinois fabricated forty-two Mod 2 magazines according to the NWL design. Testing established the viability of the magazine and the unusual follower design. Ten magazines were found to not operate properly and were removed from the test. Five of the Mod 2 fifty-round magazines were sent to other units in Vietnam and the majority of those remaining, twenty-seven units, were distributed to the members of SEAL Team Two operating in the Mekong Delta.

One difficulty with fifty-round box magazines was noted in particular by 8th Platoon in My Tho. The comment made was that the fifty-round magazine was too bulky and too long. When the platoon was operating from a defensive position, the men would have to expose 50% more of their bodies when firing with the fifty-round magazines from the prone position. It was also pointed out that the magazines operated best when only loaded with forty-five rounds rather than fifty.

All told, the fifty-round magazines were considered an effective and valuable piece of equipment by most of its users. A Mod 3 magazine incorporating several improvements over the Mod 2 design was developed. One improvement on the Mod 3 was the addition of a bolt stop to the follower. Now the weapon's bolt would lock open on an empty magazine when the last shot was fired. Ten of the Mod 3 magazines were made and seven were sent to SEAL Team Two elements in Vietnam.

By February 1971, a final report on the fifty-round magazine project was written as NWL Technical Report TR-2536 by Carroll D. Childers and Joseph C. Monolo. The report listed the recommendation put forward by the SEALs that the fifty-round magazine (Mod 3) be adopted for use and issued one per man as a weapon-ready magazine for deployed platoons. It was suggested that such magazines be serial numbers for positive control and not be considered a consumable item. Cutbacks in the post-Vietnam military kept any funding from being made available for the fifty-round magazine program and the project was shelved.

Other methods were used by the SEALs to extend the firepower of their firearms. The most common technique was to tape together two or more magazine together, upside down to one another. This method allows for a fast reload as the magazine assembly only has to be pulled from the weapon, flipped over, and reinserted. One strong drawback of this technique is that the bottom magazine has its first cartridges exposed to the environment. It is very easy for dirt or mud to enter the exposed magazine and cause a jam when it is used. This problem keeps the technique from being as widely used as it might be.

The problem of dirt and especially mud entering their magazine was one the SEALs discovered very soon after beginning operations in Vietnam. To answer this problem, the Special Operations Branch of the Navy Weapons Center at China Lake, California came up with plastic M16 magazine caps. The caps were simple, black plastic devices, one to fit on the bottom and the other over the top of any size M16 magazine. The caps effectively sealed the magazine against dirt and mud. The top magazine cap had a tab sticking out from one end. The tab could be pulled, with an operator's teeth if necessary, tearing off the cap and clearing the magazine for insertion into a weapon.

In addition to the magazine caps to keep out the mud, China Lake came up with two items to help keep the rain and mud of Vietnam out of the bore of an M16. One device was a simple white plastic plug that could be inserted into the flash suppressor of an M16. The plug was made of a soft plastic and was hollow. The tight fit of the plug into any of the three flash suppressors then in use would effectively seal the bore against rain or mud. But the plugs would not make the weapon waterproof from a full immersion, such as from an underway insertion.

The plugs were just large enough to be pulled from the muzzle with the fingers, or the tip of a knife. The fit was such that the weapon could even be fired with the plug still in place, blowing out the plug with no damage to the weapon.

The other device China Lake found to help keep rain and mud out of the bore of a .223 caliber weapon was a plastic cap. The cap, resembling a plastic film container, could be pressed over any standard-sized flash suppressor on any .223 caliber weapon in the SEALs

Rifles

TECHNICAL DATA —T 223 Rifle (Heckler & Koch HK33)
CARTRIDGE—.223 Remington (5.56x45mm)
OPERATION—Roller locked delayed blowback
TYPE OF FIRE—Selective - semiautomatic/full automatic
RATE OF FIRE—Practical SS 40 rpm, A 160 rpm, Cyclic 650 to 750 rpm
MUZZLE VELOCITY—3150 fps (960 m/s)
MUZZLE ENERGY—1234 ft/lbs (1673 J)
SIGHTS—Open, Drum-type multiple aperture w/V-notch battle sight/blade, Adjustable, Battle sight 100 meters, apertures at 200, 300, and 400 meters
FEED—20 or 40 round removable box magazines

WEIGHTS
WEAPON (EMPTY)—7.65 lbs (3.47 kg)
MAGAZINE (EMPTY—20 round 0.25 lb (0.11 kg)
40 round 0.35 lbs (0.16 kg)
MAGAZINE (LOADED)—20 round 0.77 lb (0.35 kg)
40 round 1.39 lbs (0.63 kg)
SERVICE CARTRIDGE—M193 Ball 182 gr (11.8 g)
PROJECTILE—56 gr (3.6 g)
LENGTHS
WEAPON OVERALL—36.9 in. (93.7 cm)
BARREL—15.7 in (39.9 cm)
SIGHT RADIUS—18.9 in. (48 cm)

Transporting a captured VC, the SEAL in the center of this picture is armed with a Harrington & Richardson 5.56mm T223 rifle. This weapon is the US imported version of the Heckler & Koch HK33. This particular weapon is loaded with a 40 round magazine and has a China Lake plastic muzzle plug over the flash hider. Slung muzzle forward under the right arm of the center SEAL is an M72 Light Antitank Weapon (LAW). At the left of the photo is a SEAL carrying a radio and armed with an early model 07 CAR-15, the stock of which can be just seen behind his left hand, The CAR-15 is loaded with a early-style curved 30-round magazine. Underneath the radioman's left arm is a late-model Chicom Type 56 (AKM-47). The Type 56 is probably the weapon taken from the black pajama-clad prisoner who is wearing a three-pocket chest-type magazine carrier.
PHOTO CREDIT: US NAVY

inventory. The cap fit snugly, even on Stoner machine guns and XM177E1/E2s, sealing out mud, dust, and water. Originally, the caps were made of red plastic but this was soon changed to a black material. As with the muzzle plugs, the weapon could be fired with the cap in place with complete safety to the operator and the weapon. The muzzle cap idea worked so well and had such a universal application that they were adopted by the US Army as the Cap, protective, dust and moisture seal: muzzle, still available today as a standard-issue item.

Other materials produced by China Lake for the SEALs and their M16s predated equivalent Army items. By October 1968, a limited number of M16A1s had been modified by China Lake to have a jungle sling and integral cleaning kit. The jungle sling was simply a side mounted sling that allowed the operator to carry his weapon hanging at his side, muzzle forward, ready for use. To accept the sling, the normal rear sling swivel of the M16A1 was moved from the toe of the buttstock to the rear upper left side. The front sling swivel was moved from below the front sight to a sliding position along a one-piece cleaning rod fitted to the upper left side of the weapons's hand guard, from the front sight to the receiver.

In addition to the sling modifications, a complete cleaning kit was made part of the weapon. A lid was added to the bottom of the hollow pistol grip allowing cleaning materials to be securely stored. In addition, a second storage place was made in the buttstock, covered by a trap door in the buttplate of the weapon. Within a few years, a larger buttstock storage area with a latched cover and a redesigned cleaning kit with a sectioned rod was made part of every M16A1 accepted for US service.

Another accessory was made for the Team's M16s weapons family by China Lake. This item was particularly mundane in nature as it was simply a blank firing attachment. Using standard M200 blanks, the China Lake attachment allowed semi and full automatic functioning on the M16 and all of its variants. The unit screwed onto the weapon's barrel in place of the normal flash suppressor. The attachment would work as well on the XM177E1/E2 as it did on the M16A1. Even ball ammunition could be accidentally fired through the China Lake device without any danger to the firer or the weapon, though the attachment would be destroyed.

The China Lake blank firing attachment was much smaller and lighter than the Army's M15E1 blank firing adaptor. In addition, the China Lake device did not catch on brush and was dark in color as compared to the boxy, bright red M15E1 adaptor.

The Teams were sold on the .223 caliber class of weapons very soon after seeing the round's terminal effects in combat. Along with the M16 family of weapons, the SEALs had a commitment in the .223 round as it was used in their Stoner machine guns. But this commitment did not prevent the SEALs from constantly looking for additional weapons to augment their firepower. But one major requirement was that any new weapons use ammunition available in the US inventory.

 **Special Weapons**

T 233 (HK 33)

Other countries in the NATO alliance could see a strong future for the .223 round after its official adoption by the US military. Several small arms companies developed a number of weapons chambered for the high-velocity round, known as the 5.56x45mm round in NATO terminology. Heckler and Koch of West Germany designed a version of their G3 rifle to use the 5.56mm cartridge. The new weapon, known as the HK33, was imported into the United States by Harrington and Richardson of Worcester, Massachusetts.

Marked as the H&R T 223 rifle, the weapon was submitted to the US Army's Small-Arms Weapon Systems (SAWS) study for evaluation. The SAWS study ran from December 1964 to the submission of the final report in December 1966. During the study, a number of weapons were examined including the T 223, M14, M16E1, AK47, and Stoner weapons system.

One result of the SAWS study was a number of weapons being brought to the attention of the SEALs. Even though the empty H&R T 223 was 0.9 pounds (0.41 kg) heavier than an empty M16E1, the weapon had a forty-round magazine available for it and that made it attractive to the SEALs.

"Choice of weapons were left as much as possible up to the tastes of the individual SEAL ...For myself, I had taken a liking to the Harrington and Richardson T223 rifle... One thing that immediately made the T223 appeal to me was the fact that it came with forty-round magazines."

One SEAL from SEAL Team Two carried the H&R T 223 during his first combat tour in Vietnam, April to October 1968:

"My H&R came with four forty-round magazines which I carried in the leg pockets on my cammies for awhile. The magazines tended to rattle around and make too much noise on patrol but were too long to fit in an American ammunition pouch. I solved my problem by getting one of the chicom AK47 chest-type magazine pouches and carrying my ammo in that..."

One interesting point of the H&R T 223 (HK33) is that it very much resembles a slightly smaller, 3.25 inch (8.3 cm) shorter, version of the 7.62mm NATO G3 rifle. In one much published picture of a number of SEALs in Vietnam, one SEAL is holding a T 223 but the weapon can only be seen from its top side. Since the HK33 and G3 are almost identical when viewed from the top, the weapon was identified as a G3 rifle which the SEALs did not use during the Vietnam war. In an earlier-generation copy of the same picture, the long, curved forty-round magazine can be seen sticking out from the bottom of the weapon.

During the SEALs time in Vietnam, a number of different rifles and carbines were used on an intermittent basis. For the most part, the men of the Teams stuck with the M16 family of weapons as their primary weapon. Unlike the other services, an individual SEAL would be

A group of SEALs preparing to go out on an operation in Vietnam. A number of weapons and equipment are visible in this photograph which has long been misidentified as evidence that the SEALs used the German G3 rifle in Vietnam. The SEAL at the top right corner of the photo is armed with an H&R T223 (HK33) rifle. From this top view, it is almost impossible to see the difference between a G3 rifle and this HK33. In an earlier-generation copy of this photograph examined by the author, the 40 round magazine unique to the HK33 can be made out loaded into this weapon. At the top center of this photo can be seen part of the front handguard and barrel of a Colt Model 07 submachine gun (CAR-15). The SEAL at the right-side center is armed with some form of 40mm grenade launcher as he is wearing an early-model nylon mesh grenade carrier vest.
PHOTO CREDIT: US NAVY

"Even though the empty H&R T 223 was 0.9 pounds (0.41 kg) heavier than an empty M16E1, the weapon had a forty-round magazine available for it and that made it attractive to the SEALs."

The unusual rifle with which this SEAL is armed is the Harrington and Richardson (H&R) 5.56mm T223. H&R was the US importer for the German Heckler and Koch HK33 rifle which H&R designated the T223. The specimen held by the SEAL in this photo is loaded with a 40 round magazine. The large capacity magazines that were available for the T223 are what made the weapon of interest to the Teams.
PHOTO CREDIT: US NAVY

TECHNICAL DATA—SKS (Chinese Type 56 Carbine)	**WEIGHTS**
CARTRIDGE—7.62 Intermediate (7.62x39mm)	**WEAPON (EMPTY)**—8.5 lbs (3.86 kg)
OPERATION—Gas	**WEAPON (LOADED)**—8.86 lbs (4.02 kg)
TYPE OF FIRE—Semiautomatic	**MAGAZINE (LOADED)**—10 rds 0.36 lb (0.16 kg)
RATE OF FIRE—30 to 35 rpm	10 rds w/stripper clip 0.39 lbs (0.18 kg)
MUZZLE VELOCITY—2410 fps (735 m/s)	**SERVICE CARTRIDGE**—M43 Ball 253 gr (16.4 g)
MUZZLE ENERGY—1573 ft/lbs (2133 J)	**PROJECTILE**—122 gr (7.9 g)
SIGHTS—Open, Tangent round-notch/post, Adjustable 0 to 800 meters in 100 meter graduations	**LENGTHS**
	WEAPON OVERALL—40.2 in. (102.1 cm)
FEED—10 round integral magazine	**BARREL**—20.5 in (52.1 cm)

assigned his weapon while still in the States, carry it with him during his deployment, and return with the same weapon after his tour was over. Other services simply issued a man a weapon when he arrived incountry and he turned it back in for reissue when he left Vietnam. The SEAL system allowed a man to care for his own weapon in such a way as to instill maximum confidence and skill with it. It was when a platoon formed-up for deployment and began pre-deployment training that a man was assigned his weapon and began working with it:

"At [Camp] Pickett the platoon worked on ambushes, popup target courses, weapons familiarization, and zeroing in your own weapon. Each man would take his own M16 and zero the sights on the 1,000 inch range.

Carefully sandbagging his weapon, the firer would adjust his sights until he held a good three-shot group exactly 1 inch below his point of aim at 1,000 inches. For an M16, that would put the bullet's point of impact on the point of aim at 250 yards. After a man had zeroed his weapon's sights, that weapon would be assigned to him by serial number for his tour incountry…"

SKS

There were times when the SEALs carried foreign weapons in order to help confuse any enemy observers. In one instance in 1968, two SEALs on patrol deep in enemy territory were reported as a pair of Russian advisors due in part to the materials they carried. Some SEALs developed a taste for the AK47 and its variants and carried that weapon as a matter of preference. Sometimes, it was the mission parameters that determined the choice of weapons. This proved particularly true during the waning years of the SEALs combat deployments to Vietnam. The following was stated by a SEAL officer who was part of the last SEAL Team Two deployment to Vietnam:

"The kind of operations we went on, it would be rare for someone to detect us, let alone fire directly at us. As rare as it would be for us to be shot at, it would be even more rare for us to return fire. With no support, we just didn't let ourselves be seen. With the few men we had, we just didn't have the firepower to take on an enemy unit. This situation greatly affected our choice of weapons. The AK47 and SKS had the same sound signature, muzzle flash and tracer color as the enemy's own weapons. An M-16, M-60, and especially a Stoner, would stand out to the VC and NVA, telling them where and possibly who we were…"

A Soviet-bloc produced AKMS-47 rifle with its folding stock extended. The long selector lever, above the trigger, is set to the mid-position for full-automatic fire. This specimen has the standard laminated wood forend and a plastic pistol grip.
PHOTO CREDIT: KEVIN DOCKERY

TECHNICAL DATA—AKM-47 (AKMS-47)
CARTRIDGE—7.62 Intermediate (7.62x39mm)
OPERATION—Gas
TYPE OF FIRE—Selective - Full automatic/semiautomatic
RATE OF FIRE—Practical SS 40 rpm, A 90 to 100 rpm, Cyclic 600 to 800 rpm
MUZZLE VELOCITY—2329 fps (710 m/s)
MUZZLE ENERGY—1469 ft/lbs (1992 J)
SIGHTS—Open, Tangent round-notch/post, Adjustable 0 to 1000 meters in 100 meter graduations
FEED—30 round removable box magazine
WEIGHTS
WEAPON (EMPTY)—AKM-47 6.46 lbs (2.93 kg)
AKMS-47 6.90 lbs (3.13 kg)
WEAPON (LOADED)—AKM-47 8.27 lbs (3.75 kg) late steel mag
AKMS-47 8.71 lbs (3.95 kg) w/late steel mag
MAGAZINE (EMPTY)—Early steel magazine 0.95 lbs (0.43 kg)
Late steel magazine 0.73 lbs (0.33 kg)
Aluminium magazine 0.37 lbs (0.17 kg)
MAGAZINE (LOADED)—Early steel magazine 2.03 lbs (0.92 kg)
Late steel magazine 1.81 lbs (0.82 kg)
Aluminium magazine 1.45 lbs (0.66 kg)
SERVICE CARTRIDGE—M43 Ball 253 gr (16.4 g)
PROJECTILE—122 gr (7.9 g)
LENGTHS
WEAPON OVERALL—AKM-47 34.5 in. (87.6 cm)
AKMS-47 25.20/35.04 in (64/89 cm)
BARREL—16.3 in (41.4 cm)
SIGHT RADIUS—14.8 in. (37.6 cm)

A right-side view of a late-model Chinese Type 56 rifle with a folding, spike bayonet. This is the Chicom version of the Soviet AK-47 and was the most common weapon of its type encountered by the SEALs in Vietnam.
PHOTO CREDIT: KEVIN DOCKERY

TECHNICAL DATA—AK-47 (AKS-47)
CARTRIDGE—7.62 Intermediate (7.62x39mm)
OPERATION—Gas
TYPE OF FIRE—Selective - Full automatic/semiautomatic
RATE OF FIRE—Practical SS 40 rpm, A 90 to 100 rpm, Cyclic 600 to 800 rpm
MUZZLE VELOCITY—2329 fps (710 m/s)
MUZZLE ENERGY—1469 ft/lbs (1992 J)
SIGHTS—Open, Tangent round-notch/post, Adjustable 0 to 800 meters in 100 meter graduations
FEED—30 round removable box magazine
WEIGHTS
WEAPON (EMPTY)—AK-47 8.53 lbs (3.87 kg)
AKS-47 7.65 lbs (3.47 kg)
WEAPON (LOADED)—AK-47 10.56 lbs (4.79 kg) early steel mag
AKS-74 9.68 lbs (4.39 kg) w/early steel mag
MAGAZINE (EMPTY)—Early steel magazine 0.95 lbs (0.43 kg)
Late steel magazine 0.73 lbs (0.33 kg)
Aluminium magazine 0.37 lbs (0.17 kg)
MAGAZINE (LOADED)—Early steel magazine 2.03 lbs (0.92 kg)
Late steel magazine 1.81 lbs (0.82 kg)
Aluminium magazine 1.45 lbs (0.66 kg)
SERVICE CARTRIDGE—M43 Ball 253 gr (16.4 g)
PROJECTILE—122 gr (7.9 g)
LENGTHS
WEAPON OVERALL—AK-47 34.25 in. (87 cm)
AKS-47 27.52/34.21 in (69.9/86.9 cm)
BARREL—16.30 in (41.4 cm)
SIGHT RADIUS—14.8 in. (37.6 cm)

Special Weapons

A left-side view of a Soviet AKMS-47 with its stock folded. The pattern seen just above the buttplate on the wooden foregrip is distinctive of the laminated wood used in many Soviet Block-produced AK-47 series weapons.
PHOTO CREDIT: KEVIN DOCKERY

The AK47 and its variations was the primary shoulder weapon of communist forces throughout the world from 1948 until the 1980's. The SKS which preceded the AK47, is a light semiautomatic carbine that was the first production weapon chambered for the 7.62x39mm round or 7.62mm Intermediate as it was called by Vietnam-era SEALs.

The SKS, for Samozaridnya Karabina Simonova, is a relatively simple carbine with a ten-round internal magazine. The magazine can be filled with loose rounds or quickly loaded from a ten-round stripper clip. The physical characteristics of the SKS made it a very good weapon for the small-stature Asian soldier. Manufactured in several variations in at least five countries, the most common model of the SKS captured in Vietnam was the Peoples Republic of China (PRC) Type 56 Carbine with an integral, folding, spike bayonet.

The 7.62x39mm round was proved out in the SKS carbine and has become arguably the most common military cartridge in the world. When fired in the SKS or AK-47, the 7.62x39mm round has a very unique sound signature, distinctly different from US weapons. In addition, the tracer loading of the 7.62x39mm round emits a green trace when fired as compared to the US, and NATO's, red trace.

AK-47, AKS-47

By far the most popular weapon chambered for the 7.62x39mm round is the AK47. The original AK47, for Avtomat Kalashnikov, is a very robust, compact, and powerful weapon well suited for the Southeast Asian environment as well as the guerrilla tactics of the Viet Cong. The AK47 will continue to function with little or no maintenance given to it over extended periods. Though not particularly accurate, especially after years in the jungle, the AK47 is capable of putting out a high volume of effective fire when used on full automatic.

AKM-47, AKMS-47

The receiver of the AK47 was manufactured as a complex machining from a solid block of metal. The later, and more common, AKM47 has its receiver made up of sheet metal stampings. Several improvements are incorporated into the AKM47 and it is somewhat lighter, but every bit as rugged, as the original AK47. The AKM47, for Avtomat Kalashnikova Modernizirovanniyi, is also found in a folding-stock version, the AKMS47. The earlier AK47 also had a folding stock version, the AKS47. In both versions, the folding stock swings underneath the weapon and can be locked in the open or closed position. With the stock folded, the AK makes a compact, if heavy, package of firepower.

Literally millions of AK47s have been produced in over ten countries. As found in the SKS, the most common AK47 variant found in Vietnam was the wooden stocked PRC Type 56 assault rifle, found both with and without a folding spike bayonet.

Initially, the AK47 was available in only small numbers to the Viet Cong fighting in South Vietnam. This resulted in the AK47 being something of a prestige weapon among the VC prior to 1968 and the Tet offensive. The SEALs were very quick to notice the importance of finding AK47 armed VC:

"The AK-47 was in very short supply among the VC in 1967. Only the highest ranking VCI [Viet Cong Infrastructure], number one ichi ban, and their number one bodyguards were seen with the weapon..."

Very soon after deployments began in Vietnam, AK47s were kept in stock in the armories of both SEAL Teams. The weapons acted as both training aids and as a possible source of sterile (non-US) weapons if needed. AK47s and SKSs came from captures in Vietnam and elsewhere. Ammunition was also made available from supply caches

Rifles

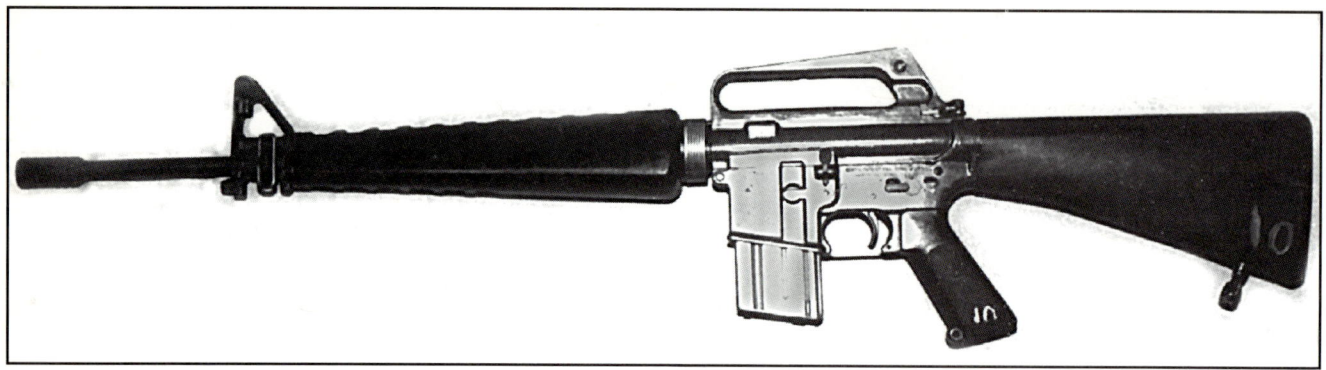

This is the Navy's Mark 4 version of the M16A1 rifle. The dark appearance of the metal parts is due to the special anticorrosion coating that is part of the Mk 4 conversion. A side-mounting sling swivel can be seen projecting just under the front sight assembly.
PHOTO CREDIT: KEVIN DOCKERY

"One of the last specialized weapons received by the UDTs and SEALs while they were still involved in Vietnam was a modified M16A1."

TECHNICAL DATA—Mark 4 Mod 0 w/Mk 2 Mod 0 Blast suppressor
NSN 1005-00-102-8649
CARTRIDGE—.223 Remington (5.56x45mm)
OPERATION—Gas
TYPE OF FIRE—Selective - semiautomatic/full automatic
RATE OF FIRE—Practical SS 45 to 65 rpm, A 150 to 200 rpm, Cyclic 700 to 800 rpm
MUZZLE VELOCITY—3250 fps (991 m/s)
MUZZLE ENERGY—1313 ft/lbs (1780 J)
SIGHTS—Open, Flip-type aperture/post, Adjustable, battle aperture 0 to 300 meters, long range aperture 300 to 500 meters
FEED—20 or 30 round removable box magazines
WEIGHTS
WEAPON (EMPTY)—6.37 lbs (2.89 kg) w/o suppressor or flashhider
8.62 lbs (3.91 kg) w/suppressor
Mk 4 Mod 0 Blast suppressor 2.25 lbs (1.02 kg)
WEAPON (LOADED)—7.39 lbs (3.35 kg) w/30 rd mag, w/o suppressor or flashhider
9.64 lbs (4.37 kg) w/suppressor & 30 rd mag
MAGAZINE (EMPTY)—20 round aluminium 0.19 lb (0.08 kg)
30 round aluminium 0.24 lbs (0.11 kg)
MAGAZINE (LOADED)—20 round 0.71 lb (0.32 kg)
30 round 1.02 lbs (0.46 kg)
SERVICE CARTRIDGE—M193 Ball 182 gr (11.8 g)
PROJECTILE—56 gr (3.6 g)
LENGTHS
WEAPON OVERALL—39 in (99.1 cm) w/o suppressor
45.38 in (115.3 cm) w/suppressor
BARREL—20 in
SUPPRESSOR LENGTH—8 in (20.3 cm)
SUPPRESSOR DIAMETER—1.75 (4.4 cm)
SIGHT RADIUS—19.75 in. (50.2 cm)

Suppressor reduction on the normal sound signature of the weapon, was -32 db. The suppressor is designed to be fully self-draining within eight seconds of removal from immersion.
The Mk 4 Mod 0 rifle is a modified M16A1. The changes are to allow the weapon to be carried at a depth of 200 feet without damage. Provisions are made for the rapid drainage of water from the system and additional protection from the corrosive effects of sea water. Modifications include:
Anticorrosion treatment by applying Kalgard coating to many of the functioning components
Drilling a 1/4 inch hole in the lower receiver extension tube and stock
Installing an O-ring on the end of the buffer assembly
Attachment of the Mk 2 Mod 0 Blast suppressor which is considered an integral part of the Mk 4 rifle.
Basic issue with the weapon includes a sling, complete cleaning kit, and six - 30 round magazines.

Special Weapons

This combat swimmer has just left the water with his Mark 4 variation of the M16A1 rifle. Besides the normal protection from the water that is part of the Mark 4 conversion, this weapon also has a plastic muzzle cap over the flash hider to help keep water out of the barrel. The muzzle cap is plastic and can be easily fired through without any damage to the weapon.
PHOTO CREDIT: US NAVY

captured in the field by SEALs. As the war progressed, the US military had sterile (unmarked) 7.62x39mm rounds manufactured at US ammunition facilities. Though the cartridges themselves were unmarked, that was not the case with the cardboard boxes the rounds came packaged in. In plain black letters is printed *20 CARTRIDGES - AK 47 RIFLE AMMO - 7.62 X 39 MM - LOT xxx-xxx-xx*

But for the Teams, the most common source of supply for 7.62x39mm ammunition was from the original people who made it, captured in Vietnam as shown in the following portion of a BARNDANCE card (Barndance cards were short reports filled out on each SEAL field operation conducted by a SEAL platoon while deployed to Vietnam):

BARNDANCE # 6-19   SEAL TEAM TWO; DET ALPHA; 6 PLT
DATE(S): 10 Jan 68
Located four enemy ammunition caches in vicinity of XT 270330. REMARKS (SIGNIFICANT EVENTS, OPEVAL RESULTS, ETC.): Captured the following: 67 - 75mm rockets, 29 - 57mm recoilless rockets, 197 - B40 rockets, 30 - 81mm mortars, 28,120 rounds of AK 47, 24 hand grenades, 1615 1_o2 lb blocks of C-3, 6 ponchos, 1 gas mask. All ammunition except 7400 AK47 turned over to Army. 7400 rounds of AK47 retained for SEAL Team 2.

The AK47 and its variations have remained part of the SEALs training. Both the SKS and AK47 were listed as weapons a SEAL should be familiar with in the 1974 edition of the SEAL Training Handbook. It is interesting to note that one of the first weapons the SEALs faced in Vietnam, the AK47, was also one of the last weapons they carried on combat missions in Southeast Asia.

MARK 4 MOD 0 (M16)

One of the last specialized weapons received by the UDTs and SEALs while they were still involved in Vietnam was a modified M16A1. The modifications done to the M16A1 were to waterproof the weapon and generally make it easier to transport underwater and prepare for immediate use by combat swimmers. Officially identified as the Rifle, 5.56mm Mark 4 Mod 0 at the time of its adoption in April 1970, modifications to the M16A1 included: an anticorrosion treatment consisting of coating many of the working parts of the weapon with Kal Gard gun coating; drilling a 1_o2 inch hole in the lower receiver extension tube and stock; installing an O-ring on the end of the buffer assembly; and, attachment of the Mk 2 Mod 0 Blast suppressor

157

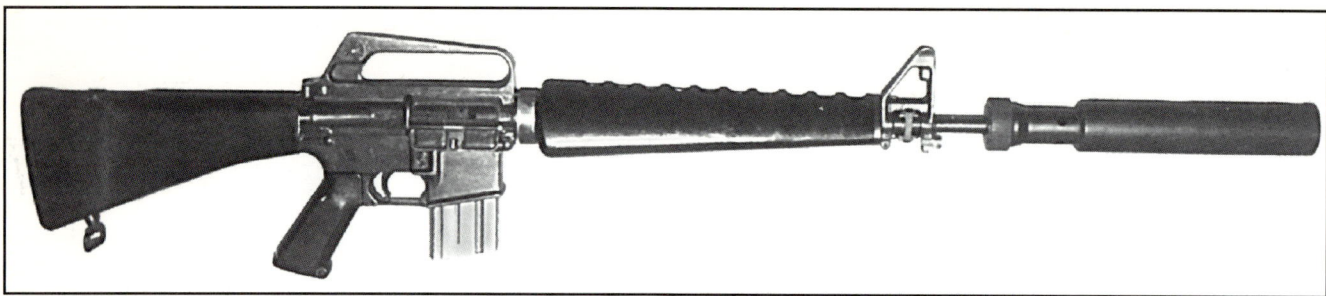

"The KAC suppressor is a stainless steel, baffle type design with a central perforated baffle tube surrounded by an annular expansion space. The suppressor, now identified as the Mk 2 Blast Suppressor, is able to be fully immersed in water and completely self-draining within 8 seconds."

A right-side view of a complete Navy Mark 4 version of the M16A1 rifle with a Mark 2 blast suppressor in place on the muzzle. The Mark 4 package is issued complete with the Mark 2 blast suppressor and five magazines.
PHOTO CREDIT: KEVIN DOCKERY

The Knight Armaments-produced Mark 2 blast suppressor. The top specimen is a standard-production model with the stainless steel body covered with a dark anticorrosion coating. The lower cutaway specimen shows the complex baffle arrangement inside the blast suppressor that slows down the escaping gas of a fired round. The multiple large holes in the reduced-diameter section of the Mark 2 allow a fired cartridge casing to be used to hold the Mark 2 while the collet is tightened or loosened. The collet used to secure the Mark 2 to the barrel of an M16 is adjusted by turning the serrated ring at the breech end of the suppressor.
PHOTO CREDIT: KEVIN DOCKERY/KNIGHT ARMAMENT COMPANY

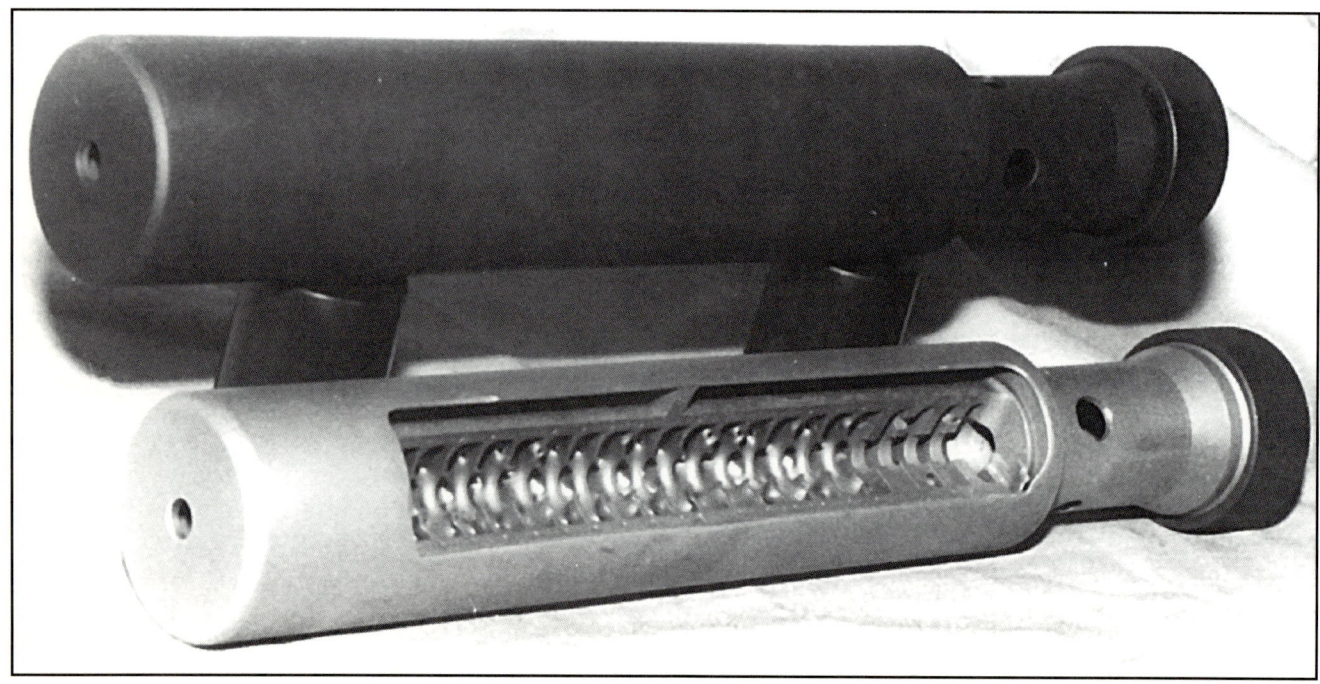

Special Weapons

Two SEALs during a beach insertion demonstration. Both men are holding Colt Model 653 carbines. The weapons are loaded with 30 round magazines and each is fitted with a China Lake blank adaptor on the muzzle. The flat, six-sided cross-section of the blank adaptor can be seen on the weapon at the right. One SEAL is wearing a floppy "boonie" hat while the other is wearing an olive-drab triangular bandage - commonly called a patrol rag - as a bandanna.
PHOTO CREDIT: UDT-SEAL MUSEUM

which is considered an integral part of the Mk 4 rifle.

The changes to the basic M16A1 are to allow the weapon to be carried at a depth of 200 feet without damage. Provisions are made for the rapid drainage of water from the system and additional protection from the corrosive effects of sea water. The basic issue of materials with the weapon includes a sling, complete cleaning kit, and six 30 round magazines.

The original suppressor issued with the Mk 4 was the first model Mk 2 Mod 0 blast suppressor based on the earlier HEL M4. By the late 1970's, the first model blast suppressor was no longer considered adequate for the Mk 4 rifle. Advances in suppressor technology had rendered the earlier design obsolete as a number of new suppressors were on the market with greater sound suppression and durability. After testing a number of available designs, the Navy chose the Knight's Armament Company's (KAC) model

The KAC suppressor is a stainless steel, baffle type design with a central perforated baffle tube surrounded by an annular expansion space. The suppressor, now identified as the Mk 2 Blast Suppressor, is able to be fully immersed in water and completely self-draining within 8 seconds. The advantages of this aspect of the design for the SEALs and UDTs are obvious. The KAC suppressor

Two combat swimmers come ashore in a more obvious manner than is usually done by the SEALs. The swimmers are both armed with Mark 4 versions of the M16A1 rifle. On their chests are Draeger LAR-V rebreathers and they still hold the breathing tubes in their mouths. The green-painted oxygen cylinder underneath the housing of the Draeger is visible on the front SEAL. PHOTO CREDIT: US NAVY

A right-side view of the Colt Model 653 carbine. The buttstock is in the maximum extended position and the weapon is loaded with a production 30 round magazine. The forward bolt assist can be seen on the upper receiver just above the pistol grip. The spring-loaded ejection port is closed in this picture. The weapon is supported by an M3 bipod clamped below the front sight and the muzzle is mounted with the third model "birdcage" flash suppressor.
PHOTO CREDIT: KEVIN DOCKERY

"Since the carbine did not require the longer flash/sound suppressor but had the shorter standard flash hider, the overall length of the model 653 carbine was only slightly longer than the XM177E2. A favorite weapon of the SEALs is produced when the short, handy carbine is mated with the M203 40mm grenade launcher. The powerful combination of automatic rifle and high explosive grenade launcher became a common sight in SEAL hands."

TECHNICAL DATA—Colt Model 653 Carbine
NSN 6D1005-01-029-3866
CARTRIDGE—.223 Remington (5.56x45mm)
OPERATION—Gas
TYPE OF FIRE—Selective - semiautomatic/full automatic
RATE OF FIRE—Practical SS 45 to 65 rpm, A 150 to 200 rpm, Cyclic 700 to 800 rpm
MUZZLE VELOCITY—3020 fps (920 m/s)
MUZZLE ENERGY—1134 ft/lbs (1538 J)
SIGHTS—Open, Flip-type aperture/post, Adjustable, battle aperture 0 to 300 meters, long range aperture 300 to 500 meters
FEED—20 or 30 round removable box magazines
WEIGHTS
WEAPON (EMPTY)—5.6 lbs (2.54 kg)
WEAPON (LOADED)—7.02 lbs (3.18 kg) w/sling & 30 rd mag
Sling 0.4 lbs (0.18 kg)
MAGAZINE (EMPTY)—20 round aluminium 0.19 lb (0.08 kg) 30 round aluminium 0.24 lbs (0.11 kg)
MAGAZINE (LOADED)—20 round 0.71 lb (0.32 kg) 30 round 1.02 lbs (0.46 kg)
SERVICE CARTRIDGE—M193 Ball 182 gr (11.8 g)
PROJECTILE—56 gr (3.6 g)
LENGTHS
WEAPON OVERALL—29.8/33 in. (75.7/83.8 cm)
BARREL—14.5 in (36.8 cm)
SIGHT RADIUS—14.72 in. (37.4 cm)

Special Weapons

This SEAL takes aim with his Colt Model 653 Carbine while undergoing desert training. His radio is an AN/PRC-77 with the handpiece pulled under his left arm while he is seated. His loadbearing equipment is the nylon All Purpose Lightweight Individual Carrying Equipment (ALICE) gear adopted by the Army in 1974. He is also wearing 1st pattern desert camouflage BDUs (Battle Dress Uniform) made familiar to the public in the pictures from Desert Storm.
PHOTO CREDIT: SPECIAL OPERATIONS COMMAND PAO

acts as a muzzle blast device and has a very strong barrel attachment system that is still easily removable. In addition to its being made of noncorroding materials and self-draining design, the KAC Mk 4 suppressor is able to withstand full automatic fire from the M16 at the maximum rate possible without being damaged from the heat or blast.

By the end of their involvement in the Vietnam War, the SEALs and UDTs were already experiencing cutbacks in their numbers and financing. New weapons were relatively few in number and parts difficulties were making repair of some of the Vietnam era weapons difficult.

With the ending of the CAR-15 project by Colt in 1970, spare parts unique to the XM177/E1/E2 family were available in very limited numbers. The short barrels that helped make the CAR-15 weapons so popular were particularly rare. Most units, including the Teams, husbanded their remaining CAR-15s carefully and repaired some weapons by cannibalizing other more worn pieces for parts.

The short barrel of the CAR-15 weapons was never noted for its accuracy and when the barrels became worn, accuracy dropped quickly to unacceptable levels.

When finally no more worthwhile 11.5 inch CAR-15 barrels were available, Colt offered their 14.5 inch carbine barrel. The M16A1 carbine was a new weapon from Colt that shared many features with the CAR-15 weapons. Some XM177E1 and E2 receivers were rebarreled for use with the carbine barrel and became hybrid weapons, appearing to be carbines but marked as XM177E1/E2s.

With the declaration by the ATF (Alcohol, Tobacco, and Firearms) department of the Treasury that the CAR-15 flash/sound suppressor qualified as a silencer under the law, and the State Department's outlawing export silencer sales under the Carter administration, Colt changed the design specifications of the CAR-15 to meet market requirements. Since the flash/sound suppressor of the XM177 weapons was a major sticking point, Colt simply extended the barrel of the new carbine weapon to the point where flash and sound could be held to reasonable levels. In addition, the slightly longer barrel of the carbine made it more accurate than the earlier CAR-15 weapons as the bullets had more time to stabilize for flight.

COLT CARBINE MODEL 653

The Colt Model 653 M16A1 carbine was eventually adopted by the SEALs and UDTs in some small numbers.

Rifles

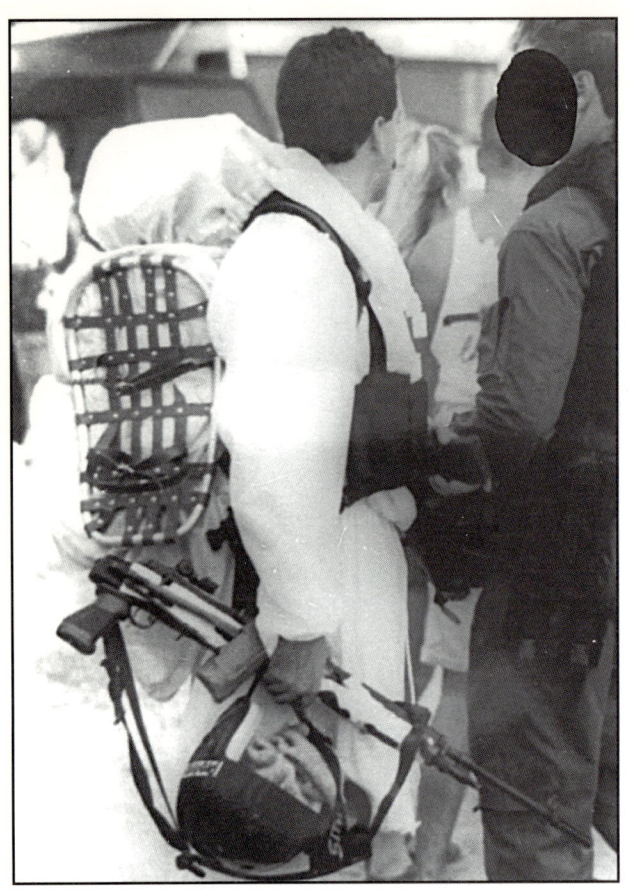

At a demonstration, the SEAL in the center is wearing a full set of winter equipment including a white camouflage cover for his uniform and pack as well as aluminum-frame snowshoes. His weapon is a folding-stock M14A1 only found used by the SEALs. The stock on this specimen is folded forward and the magazine removed; that is in the SEAL's left hand. The buttplate of the folding stock is covered by a pad and is still in the extended (vertical) position. The SEAL to the right in this photo is equipped for Close Quarters Battle. A 3-cell pouch for 30 round MP5 magazine can be seen at his waist. Below the magazine pouch is a special 3-cell pouch for holding Flash-Crash (stun) grenades.
PHOTO CREDIT: KEVIN DOCKERY

Members of SEAL Team Two take part in a military biathlon competition while undergoing cold weather training in Norway. The men are target shooting with their folding-stock M14 rifles after having completed a portion of the cross-country skiing part of the competition. Additional weapons have been thrust into the snow butt-first to indicate additional firing positions on the line. Note the folding stocks on the weapons being fired.
PHOTO CREDIT: RYAN McCOMBIE COLLECTION

Special Weapons

The model 653 shared the same sliding buttstock and short cylindrical handguards as the XM177E2. The most visible difference between the two weapons is the longer barrel of the carbine protruding well beyond the front sight.

The longer carbine barrel is fitted with the Type 3 flash suppressor as found on the standard M16A1s of the era. Since the carbine did not require the longer flash/sound suppressor but had the shorter standard flash hider, the overall length of the model 653 carbine was only slightly longer than the XM177E2. A favorite weapon of the SEALs is produced when the short, handy carbine is mated with the M203 40mm grenade launcher. The powerful combination of automatic rifle and high explosive grenade launcher became a common sight in SEAL hands.

More compact and powerful weapons have long been a priority with the Teams and especially the SEALs. Room is limited at best on many transports and it is at an absolute premium aboard submarines and Swimmer/SEAL delivery vehicles.

M14 with folding stock

Facing much the same problem of space limitations in their armored vehicles, the Army examined fitting the, then standard, M14 rifle with a folding stock during the early 1960's. Four different models of folding stock were developed by the engineers at Springfield Armory. With the winding down of M14 production, the project was abandoned by the Army.

Few of the Army folding M14 stocks were ever made and even fewer still were available for later use by the Teams. A near-duplicate of the M14/M1 Garand was produced by Italy as their BM 59 series of weapons. The Parachutists and Alpine versions of the BM 59 are fitted with folding stocks that proved to be easily adapted to fit the M14 rifle.

The modified M14 stocks with the BM 59 folding buttstock design were obtained by the Teams by the late 1970's. With the stock folded, the M14 is a more compact package, not a great deal larger than an M16A1. The added power and range of the 7.62mm NATO round and the M14 rifle, combined with the compact folding stock gives the Teams the option of fielding the weapon as the tactical situation dictates.

Through the latter half of the 1970's trials were being conducted by the NATO countries to locate a candidate cartridge and possible weapon for NATO standardization. Though the trials did not locate a weapon design that was acceptable to all NATO members, they did focus on a superior cartridge.

What developed out of the NATO trials was not a new cartridge but a better loading for an existing round. The loading chosen was the Belgium SS109 heavy bulleted 5.56mm round. This loading was duplicated in the US counterpart, the XM855 round. The new loading called for a steel-cored, partial armor piercing 61.7 grain (4 g) bullet to be fired from a barrel with a 1 in 7 inch (1 in 30.5 cm) twist. The new projectile held excellent accuracy and terminal effects out to ranges near that of the 7.62mm NATO round.

M16A2

By late 1979, the US Marine Corps was already discussing the possibility of a new issue rifle. The improved range of the XM855 round caught the Marine's attention as a possible answer to their desire for more of a "rifleman's" weapon to arm the Corps. Requirements later formalized for the Marines desired new weapon, a modified M16A1, were as follows: an adjustable sight good to 800 meters; a projectile with good accuracy to 800 meters and able to penetrate all known helmets and military body armor at that range; stronger plastic and metal parts on the weapon to stand up better to the heavier demands placed on it by Marine training doctrine; and, elimination of the full automatic position and its replacement with a controlled 3-round burst setting.

Additional tests conducted by the Navy added more parameters and suggestions to the physical changes in a possible new Marine rifle. Test weapons were ordered from Colt and examined to see if a modified M16A1 would fit the Marines desires. This led to the development of the third-generation M16, the M16A2.

The Joint Services Small Arms Program (JSSAP) approved a joint-services approach to a new and improved M16A1 by ordering 50 Product Improvement Program (PIP) M16A1s from Colt to be delivered in November 1981. Designated the M16A1E1, the new rifles were extensively tested by the Marines during the last weeks of 1981. The results of the testing gave very favorable reports on the accuracy, range, effectiveness, and handling qualities of the M16A1E1. By September 1982, the M16A1E1 was type-classified as the M16A2.

The Marines ordered 76,000 M16A2's as quickly as they were able. The Army did not have as strong a desire for the new rifle to be immediately available, stocks of M16A1s being considered sufficient to cover several years needs. By 1986, the Army contracted for the purchase of 100,176 M16A2 weapons from Colt.

The M16A2 as issued to the US military is identified by Colt as their model 705. The major differences between the M16A1 and the A2 model include:

Modification of the flash hider to a fourth type without bottom slots. The lack of bottom slots on the M16A2 flash hider prevents dust and dirt from flying up when the weapon is fired in the prone position. The flash hider also acts as a muzzle compensator, helping to hold the muzzle down when firing bursts.

A barrel with a heavier contour from the front sight forward. In addition, the new barrel is rifled with a one in 7 inch twist for use with the M855 round.

Different front and rear sights with the rear sight adjustable to 800 meters range with an easily moved elevation drum.

New cylindrical, ribbed handguards. Stronger and more efficient at cooling than the earlier triangular M16A1 handguards, the new handguards are also ambidextrous. Either one will fit on the right or left side of the barrel.

An angled slip ring making it easier to remove the handguards for routine maintenance.

A strengthening of the upper receiver.

Rifles

TECHNICAL DATA—Colt Model 723
NSN OA1005-LL-L99-5287
CARTRIDGE—.223 Remington NATO (5.56x45mm NATO)
OPERATION—Gas
TYPE OF FIRE—Selective - semiautomatic/full automatic
RATE OF FIRE—Practical SS 45 to 65 rpm, A 150 to 200 rpm, Cyclic 700 to 950 rpm
MUZZLE VELOCITY—2900 fps (884 m/s)
MUZZLE ENERGY—1158 ft/lbs (1570 J)
SIGHTS—Open, Flip-type aperture/post, Adjustable, battle aperture 0 to 300 meters, long range aperture 300 to 500 meters
FEED—20 or 30 round removable box magazines

WEIGHTS
WEAPON (EMPTY)—5.9 lbs (2.68 kg)
WEAPON (LOADED)—7.35 lbs (3.33 kg) w/sling & 30 rd mag
Sling 0.4 lbs (0.18 kg)
MAGAZINE (EMPTY)—20 round aluminium 0.19 lb (0.08 kg)
30 round aluminium 0.24 lbs (0.11 kg)
MAGAZINE (LOADED)—20 round 0.73 lb (0.33 kg)
30 round 1.05 lbs (0.48 kg)
SERVICE CARTRIDGE—M855 Ball 190 gr (12.3 g)
PROJECTILE—62 gr (4 g)
LENGTHS
WEAPON OVERALL—29.8/33 in. (75.7/83.8 cm)
BARREL—14.5 in (36.8 cm)
SIGHT RADIUS—14.72 in. (37.4 cm)

A rear-view of the Beta Company 100 round C-Mag without the central magazine or rear cover. The two drums hold over forty round of ammunition in a double column around their circumference when fully loaded. The two pusher bars, braced at the center of the magazine for this photograph, drive the ammunition around the edges of the drum and up through the central magazine assisted by the sprockets at the center of each drum. As the magazine is emptied, the drums feed rounds alternately into the central magazine, maintaining a balance in the system.
PHOTO CREDIT: KEVIN DOCKERY

A Colt Model 723 Carbine with its sliding stock in the fully-extended position. The weapon is loaded with a C-MAG 100 round double-drum magazine. The C-MAG magazine holds 50 rounds on either side of the magazine well of the weapon and feeds rounds alternately from each drum as the weapon is fired. The low-silhouette of the C-MAG design is illustrated in this photograph. The notch around the barrel of the Model 723 carbine is for the mounting of an M203 40mm grenade launcher without further modification to the carbine or launcher.
PHOTO CREDIT: KEVIN DOCKERY

"A short carbine version of the M16A2 has been available to the Teams and is much preferred over the M16A2 rifle."

Special Weapons

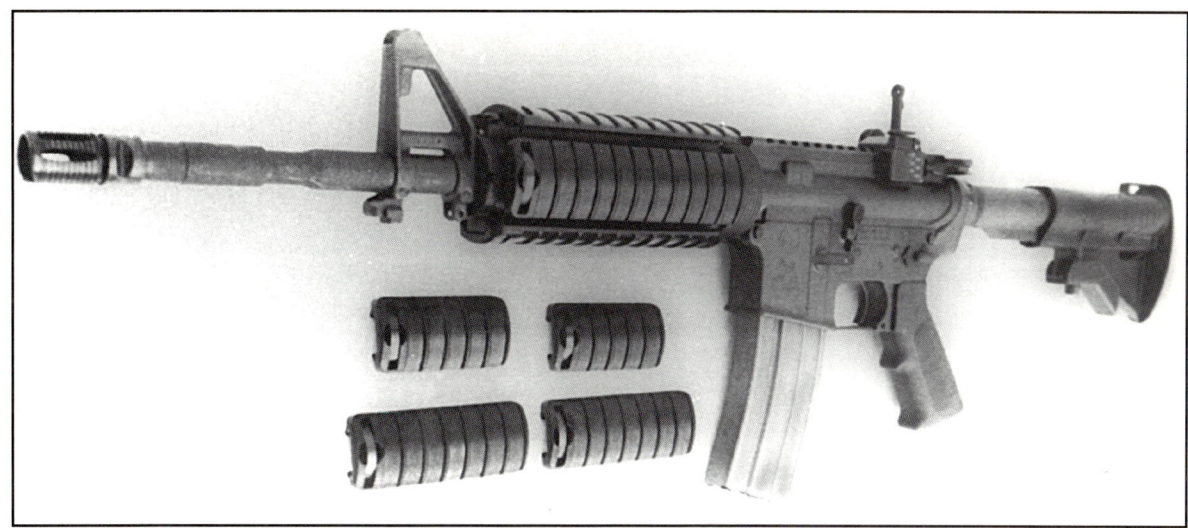

A left-side view of the SOCOM M4A1 carbine with the 800 meter rear sight raised and the forend mounting surfaces covered by grip plates. The different length grip plates below the weapon can be used to cover the forend mounting surfaces when only a portion of the mount is used by a sight or other accessory. On the muzzle of the weapon is the Knight Armament QD muzzle compensator.
PHOTO CREDIT: KNIGHT ARMAMENT COMPANY

A longer buttstock.
A pistol grip that is slightly larger and has a single finger rest.
All plastic parts are now made of a supertough nylon plastic, ten to 12 times stronger than the original M16A1 parts.
A bulge in the upper receiver acts as a brass deflector allowing easier left-handed firing of the weapon.
Replacement of the full auto position with a controlled 3-round burst.

The replacement of the full automatic fire capability in the M16A2 is one of the most discussed arguments against the new weapon. Though having other good characteristics, the lack of full automatic fire limits the appeal of the M16A2 to the Teams. In addition, flaws were quickly noticed by operators who used the 3-round burst position on the M16A2.

If a 3-round burst is attempted to be fired from the M16A2, and the weapon stops or runs out of ammunition, the mechanism does not reset when the trigger is released. If the weapon runs out of ammunition on the second round of a 3-round burst, when the operator reloads and again pulls the trigger, only a single shot will be fired. If the operator releases the trigger when only a single shot of a 3-round burst has been fired, when he pulls the trigger again, 2 rounds will be fired. This fault is part of the design of the M16A2 controlled burst mechanism and cannot be changed.

COLT MODEL 723

As the new standard issue shoulder arm in the US military, the M16A2 is issued to the SEALs as well as all the other branches of the service. A short carbine version of the M16A2 has been available to the Teams and is much preferred over the M16A2 rifle. The M16A2 carbine is identified by Colt as their model 723 weapon. Virtually identical to the earlier model 653 M16A1 carbine, the model 723 weapon has the larger pistol grip of the M16A2, the fourth model flash hider, and the 1 in 7 inch rifling twist. The full automatic capability, sights, and other characteristics of the model 653 carbine, including the thinner contour barrel, remain the same on the new model 723 carbine.

M4 CARBINE (COLT MODEL 720, MODEL 727)

Another version of the M16A2 system is seeing duty with the SEAL teams and is being much more enthusiastically received than the M16A2 rifle. The M4 carbine is a another shortened version of the M16A2 but retains many of the new features found on the full-sized rifle.

The sights on the M4 are the same long range adjustable model as found on the M16A2. The M4 also has the heavier barrel, fourth model flash hider, and brass deflector as on the M16A2. The heavy barrel of the M4 carbine has a slight step in the barrel diameter roughly midway between the muzzle and the front sight. The step is so that the M203 40mm grenade launcher can be mounted on the M4 with no modifications needed on either weapon.

The M4/M203 combination is a very popular one with the Teams. Given the proper circumstances, entire platoons have been armed with the M4/M203 such as during operation JUST CAUSE in Panama. Two different models of the M4 are issued in the military. The Colt model 720 is an M4 carbine with the 3-round controlled burst setting and no other capability for full automatic fire. The Colt model 727 M4 carbine has the capability of full automatic fire and is the preferred model for use by the SEALs.

Rifles

The complete Knight Armaments Company (KAC) Modular Weapon System recently adopted by the Special Operations Command (SOCOM) for issue to their forces including the Navy SEALs as the M4A1 carbine. The basic weapon is the Colt Model R0927 carbine version of the M16A2 rifle with the KAC Rail Interface System (RIS) in place of the standard front handguard. The RIS has four MIL-STD-1913 mounting rails that will accept a wide range of accessories for both aiming or controlling the weapon. Accessories in this photo include (above the weapon from left to right) the KAC low-profile folding 300 meter rear sight, the ITT "pocketscope" night vision device on a KAC mount, and the Aimpoint 5000 also on a KAC mount. Below the weapon from left to right are; the five different lengths of handguard sections that can fit on the RIS forend different lengths filling in for the space remaining from various devices, the KAC basic vertical foregrip, the KAC monopod vertical foregrip assembly with the monopod extended. Directly below the barrel is the Leupold visible laser aiming device with its companion panel switch module. Below the Leupold assembly is the tactical Streamlight poly flashlight package held to the mounting plate with KAC rings. In addition to these devices, a folding bipod assembly is also available to go on the RIS-equipped M4A1 carbine
PHOTO CREDIT: KNIGHT ARMAMENT COMPANY

TECHNICAL DATA—M4 Carbine (Colt Model 720)
CARTRIDGE—.223 Remington NATO (5.56x45mm NATO)
OPERATION—Gas
TYPE OF FIRE—Selective - semiautomatic/full automatic
RATE OF FIRE—Practical SS 45 to 65 rpm, A 150 to 200 rpm, Cyclic 700 to 800 rpm
MUZZLE VELOCITY—2900 fps (884 m/s)
MUZZLE ENERGY—1158 ft/lbs (1570 J)
SIGHTS—Open, Flip-type aperture/post, Adjustable, battle aperture 0 to 200 meters, adjustable long range small aperture 300 to 800 meters in 100 meter graduations
FEED—20 or 30 round removable box magazines

WEIGHTS
WEAPON (EMPTY)—5.65 lbs (2.56 kg)
WEAPON (LOADED)—7.1 lbs (3.22 kg) w/sling & 30 rd mag
Sling 0.4 lbs (0.18 kg)
MAGAZINE (EMPTY)—20 round aluminium 0.19 lb (0.08 kg)
30 round aluminium 0.24 lbs (0.11 kg)
MAGAZINE (LOADED)—20 round 0.73 lb (0.33 kg)
30 round 1.05 lbs (0.48 kg)
SERVICE CARTRIDGE—M855 Ball 190 gr (12.3 g)
PROJECTILE—62 gr (4 g)
LENGTHS
WEAPON OVERALL—29.8/33 in. (75.7/83.8 cm)
BARREL—14.5 in (36.8 cm)
SIGHT RADIUS—14.72 in. (37.4 cm)

The M4A1 carbine with the Knight RIS system. Mounted on the top rail of the RIS forend is an infrared aiming light. On either side of the forend are "11 rib" full length handguard sections. On the bottom of the RIS, held in a firing position by the operator, is the KAC "Masterkey" shotgun, a modified 12 gage Remington 870 pump shotgun used primarily for opening doors by blasting off the hinges/lock.
PHOTO CREDIT: KNIGHT ARMAMENT COMPANY

As of February, 1994, Special Operations Command (SOCOM) awarded a contract to Colt for production of 5,000 to 6,000 M4A1 carbines. The new M4A1, Colt model 927, is intended specifically for Special Operations forces including the SEALs. Firing settings for the M4A1 will be full and semi automatic, with the sights, barrel, and other aspects retained from the standard M4 carbine. The major change will be in the rear sight system.

The M4A1 will be equipped with the "Picatinny Rail" mounting located under the removable carrying handle. The carrying handle will retain the standard M16A2 rear sight but can be removed to allow different sighting devices to be mounted. Mounting on the Picatinny Rail makes for a much lower weapon outline as well as giving a more solid and accurate mounting interface than the handle of the weapon. Other modifications on some M4A1s will allow a laser sight or 12 gauge shotgun to be mounted underneath the barrel for close-quarters combat. Production of the M4A1 was planned to begin in May 1994.

To increase their available volume of fire, the SEALs and Special Forces have obtained a number of special C-MAG 100 round drum magazine for the M16 family of weapons. The C-MAG drum is a large capacity, highly dependable feed device that will fit any magazine well that accepts an M16 magazine.

The C-MAG weighs 2.21 pounds (1.00 kg) empty and will accept and feed a full 100 rounds of ammunition. The use of dual drums feeding from either side of the magazine extension allows the C-MAG to have a very low profile when mounted on the M16 weapon. The drums are spring driven and feed their rounds along a spiral track on the outside diameter of the drum. The rounds feed up into the magazine extension alternating one from each drum.

As the ammunition empties onto the magazine extension, flexible feed chains move from the drums up into the magazine extension. The feed chains insure positive tension is kept on the ammunition until the last round is fed into the weapon. When the last round is fired, the C-MAG activates the bolt lock just as a standard magazine would. The design of the C-MAG is such that the weapon actually has a lower profile with the 100 round drum loaded than it does with a standard 30-round box magazine.

Grenades

TECHNICAL DATA—
Mark II "Pineapple"
TYPE—High explosive fragmentation hand grenade
IDENTIFYING COLOR CODE—Olive drab body or olive drab body w/yellow ring around top of fuze well
BODY—Cast iron w/deep square serrations
FILLER—TNT
FUZE—M204A1 or M204A2 Bouchon-type detonating fuze w/ pyrotechnic delay
FUZE DELAY—4 to 5 seconds
   WEIGHTS
ROUND—1.31 lbs (0.59 kg)
FILLER—0.13 lb (0.06 kg)
   EFFECTS
EFFECT—Blast and fragmentation
AREA OF EFFECT—10 yd (9 m) radius, Individual fragments may be thrown as far as 200 yds
   LENGTHS
LENGTH—4.5 in (11.5 cm)
WIDTH (DIAMETER)—2.25 in (5.7 cm)
AVERAGE RANGE—30 yds (27 m)

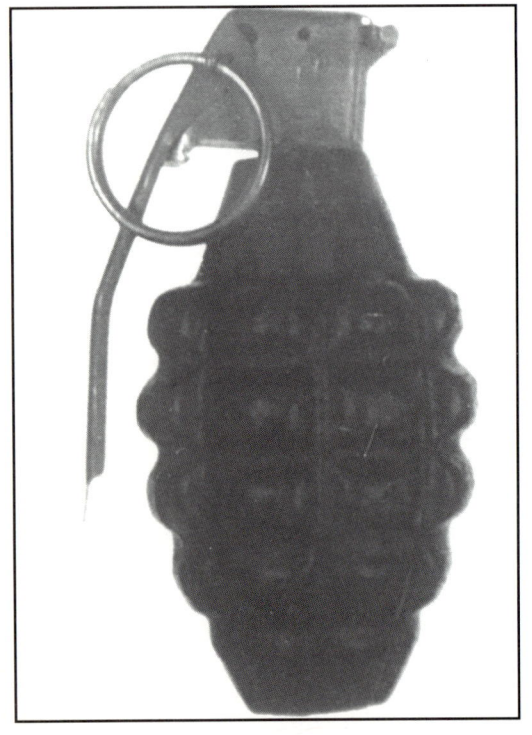

Mk 2 grenades were the most common grenade issued to US forces during World War II ... it is interesting to note just how long the Mk 2 grenade remained in the Navy inventory... In SEAL ammunition manuals dated from the late 1980's, the Mk 2 fragmentation grenade is still listed as being available for issue.

The Mark 2 "Pineapple" fragmentation grenade. The cast iron body of this grenade shows the distinctive square serration pattern that gives the weapon its nickname. This display specimen has been fitted with a used M228 fuze from a practice M69 grenade. For display purposes the internal parts of the grenade fuze have been removed, resulting in the open hole in the grenade body just above the pull ring. The M69 practice grenade is identical to the M67 fragmentation grenade except for not having an explosive charge or detonating fuze.
PHOTO CREDIT: KEVIN DOCKERY

Special Weapons

Hand grenades are sometimes called the pocket artillery of the foot soldier. They are the most common weapon available to the individual fighting man that lets him attack a target that is not in his direct sight. By being able to lob a grenade through a bunker door or over an embankment, a target can be effectively engaged without exposing the thrower to return fire. Hand grenades also effect a reasonably larger area than their immediate point of impact allowing them to make up for the inaccuracy of throwing at an indistinct target.

In general, all hand grenades share three common characteristics. As the weapons are hand thrown, their engagement range is short. The effective casualty radius of the grenade is small, allowing the weapon to effect only its immediate area. And the delay element of the modern grenade allows them to be safely thrown, minimizing the danger to the thrower.

All hand grenades are made up of three major components. The body of the grenade contains the filler, allowing it to be transported and safely handled and employed. In addition, for some grenades the body provides fragmentation. The filler is the chemical or explosive payload of the grenade. The use and characteristics of the grenade are normally determined by what kind of filler it contains. The fuze assembly causes the grenade to function by igniting or detonating the filler. The fuze must be safe to handle, easy to employ, and relatively uncomplicated for economic manufacture.

Mark II Fragmentation

The US employment of hand grenades in numbers only goes back to the last years of World War I. At that time millions of hand grenades of dozens of types were used by all sides of the conflict. It was during World War I that the classic pull-ring grenade fuze was developed that has become so familiar to all of the US services.

In the pull-ring fuze, correctly called the Bouchon fuze, a round metal ring is attached to a cotter pin that extends through the body of the fuze. The cotter pin secures a safety lever, also called a spoon, across the top of the fuze as well as retaining the spring-loaded striker assembly inside of the fuze. The end of the cotter pin is spread where it exits the fuze body to prevent accidental removal. The legs of the cotter pin a spread in such a way as to require 10 to 30 pounds of pull to remove the pin. This much resistance effectively eliminates the Hollywood style of pin pulling with the teeth, unless the operator wants to remove his front teeth rather than the grenade pin.

When the pull ring and cotter pin are removed, hand pressure holds the safety lever down against the body of the grenade which in turn holds back the striker assembly. When the thrower releases his grip, the striker spring rotates the striker on its axis, forcing the safety lever away from the fuze. The striker rotates further and strikes the primer centered at the top of the fuze. The primer ignites the delay element which burns for its prescribed length of time and then initiates the detonator or igniter. The detonator or igniter in its turn sets off the grenade's filler. Overseas, this type of fuze is often called the "mousetrap" fuze from the action of its rotating striker.

The Bouchon type fuze quickly caught on with the US forces as the simplest and safest fuze available. Eighty years later it is still by far the most common grenade fuze used in the US military. Two different types of Bouchon fuze are generally recognized and they are the detonating type and the igniting type. The detonator type of fuze is used in explosive grenades, fragmentation, white phosphorus smoke, and bursting type chemical grenades. Igniter fuzes are generally found in burning type chemical grenades and practice grenades.

Given their effectiveness and convenience, hand grenades have been loaded with a variety of payloads specific for different effects. As new targets developed, new grenades were designed to meet the threat. But in general, all hand grenades fall into five general categories. Two of these categories, Training and Practice grenades are simply either simple inert bodies of the right size, shape, and weight, or have a minor reaction to simulate the actual weapon. Historically, the most important grenade family to the fighting man is the fragmentation grenade. This is the class of grenade that acts as the soldier's personal indirect fire system

The class of fragmentation, also called defensive grenades, are the most common type of grenade used on the battlefield. This class of grenade is designed to produce casualties by the projection of high-velocity fragments. The payload or filler is high explosive and the body of the grenade is intended to shatter in some way and supply the fragmentation. The fragmentation effect will operate well against a scattered group of personnel because the

Grenades

TECHNICAL DATA — Mark 3A2 (Mk 3A1)
TYPE—High explosive blast (concussion) offensive hand grenade
IDENTIFYING COLOR CODE—Black body w/yellow markings and band
BODY—Asphalt-impregnated fiber (cardboard), Mk 3A1s have sheet metal end pieces
FILLER—TNT
FUZE—M206A1 or M206A2 (Mk 3A1- M6A4) Bouchon-type detonating fuze w/pyrotechnic delay, grenade may or may not have an additional safety clip around the fuze body and safety lever
FUZE DELAY—4 to 5 seconds
  WEIGHTS
ROUND—Mk 3A2 - 0.98 lbs (0.44 kg)
  Mk 3A1- 0.69 lbs (0.31 kg)
FILLER—Mk 3A2 - 0.46 lbs (0.21 kg)
  Mk 3A1- 0.43 lb (0.20 kg)
  EFFECTS
EFFECT—Blast
AREA OF EFFECT—2 yds (2 m), secondary missiles and fragments of the fuze may be projected 200 meters from point of detonation
  LENGTHS
LENGTH—Mk 3A2 - 5.43 in (13.8 cm)
  Mk 3A1- 5.35 in (13.6 cm)
WIDTH (DIAMETER)—2.13 in (5.4 cm)
AVERAGE RANGE—Mk 3A2 - 44 yds (40 m)
  Mk 3A1- 50 yds (46 m)

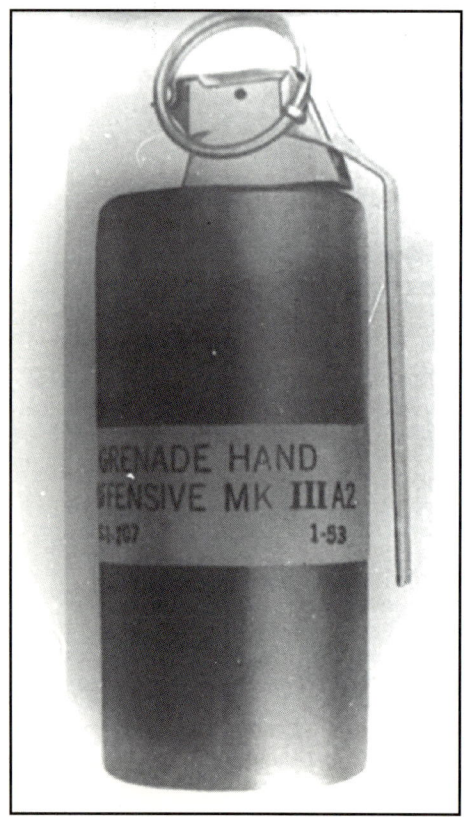

In the Teams, the Mk3A1 was considered a small demolition charge, though as a concussion grenade it also had its uses in after-invasion bunker cleaning.

The fiber-bodied Mark 3A2 offensive grenade. The black body of this grenade is made up from two fiber (cardboard) cylinders slipped one inside the other around a filler of TNT. The seam between the two cylinders is covered by the tape showing the nomenclature on this specimen. The M206 fuze of this grenade was used in a number of additional grenade designs used by the SEALs including the TIARA grenade and Model 308-1 Napalm grenade.
PHOTO CREDIT: US ARMY

Special Weapons

effective range of the high-speed fragments is much greater then the effective radius of the blast alone. The blast effect of the fragmentation grenade may still be used to good effect in small enclosed places even though the fragmentation might not reach the intended target.

Because the fragmentation of a grenade can be projected further than the grenade can be easily thrown, especially in the case of early designs, the fragmentation grenade is also called the defensive type. The defensive type of grenade is employed when the operator is in a defensive position, that is he's protected by cover from the effect of his own weapon. The measurement of the area of effect of a fragmentation is called the effective casualty radius. In the US military, the definition of the effective casualty radius is the radius of a circular area in which at least 50 percent of the exposed personnel will become casualties.

Offensive had grenades are the fourth general type of grenade and they are used to produce blast effects. Fragments of the grenade, especially the fuze body, may be projected over 607 feet (185 m) from the point of the explosion, but this type of grenade is not intended to produce a large number of fragments. Offensive grenades are intended to produce casualties on enemy personnel while minimizing the danger to attacking troops. They are intended for use during offensive movement, where the thrower is not able to take cover during the assault. This type of grenade has also been called a concussion grenade since the main effect of the filler is a concussive blast wave. These grenades are especially useful in built-up areas and fortified positions such as caves or bunkers. Since they tend to stun a target, they are most useful when capture of the enemy is the preferred option. Additionally, the offensive grenade can be used as a small, prepackaged demolition charge.

Chemical hand grenades are the final major category. A very broad category, chemical grenades can cause casualties, start fires, produce irritating gas, make smoke for signaling or screening, or any combination of these effects. This class of grenade is further subdivided into burning-types or bursting-types.

Burning-type chemical grenades cause their effect by creating a cloud of agent, either smoke or gas, by the igniting and burning of their filler. Usually a burning-type grenade is a metal canister with the fuze screwed in at one end and holes drilled into the casing to allow the agent to escape. Since this kind of grenade does not have an instant effect, the burning takes a second or two to build up volume, they are often fitted with a shorter fuze delay than casualty-producing types. Explosive grenades usually have a 4.5 second nominal fuze delay, burning-type grenades usually have a 1.5 second nominal delay.

Bursting-type chemical grenades explode and spread their agent over a wide area. This kind of grenade causes its agent to take effect quickly whether its a chemical agent such as powdered CS or a burning chemical agent such as white phosphorus (WP). The most commonly found loading for this type of grenade is white phosphorus. The bursting of the grenade spreads the WP over a large area where it spontaneously ignites on exposure to air, creating dense white smoke.

Additional grenades come under the heading of Special Purpose. This type of grenade usually has a very specific kind of target or effect and this fact restricts its general issue. Illuminating grenades, stun grenades, and other hand-thrown devices can be included under this category.

The first type of grenade commonly issued in the US military was the Mark II fragmentation grenade, commonly called the "pineapple". The Mark II had a cast iron body with external serrations formed on it, breaking the body up into eight rows of five squares each. This grenade was first issued in October 1918 and remained in the active inventory well after World War II was over.

Though the square serrations on the outside of the Mk 2 gave it a good gripping service for cold or muddy hands, and led to its colorful nickname, they did not act as their designer intended. Instead of breaking up into fragments along the serration lines, Mk 2s tended to shatter into a number of larger pieces and a quantity of iron dust. In an attempt to increase the number of effective fragments, and due to a strategic shortage of TNT in 1941 and 1942, a different explosive filler was experimented with during World War II. Instead of the 2 ounce charge of TNT, the Mk 2A1 was loaded with a 0.74 ounce charge of EC (Explosive Company) Blank powder and fitted with an M10A3 igniter fuze. The EC powder, a nitrocellulose propellant, was expected to break up the body of the Mk 2A1 along the designed lines but failed to meet expectations.

Mk 2 grenades were the most common grenade issued to US forces during World War II and the UDTs and NCDUs were at least generally familiar with the weapon. Though the UDTs were not issued fragmentation grenades during World War II as a matter of course, it is interesting to note just how long the Mk 2 grenade remained in the Navy inventory. SEALs did carry the Mk 2 in Vietnam in limited numbers, usually just because they were available. The other services removed the Mk 2 from their inventories by the late 1960's. In SEAL ammunition manuals dated from the late 1980's, the Mk 2 fragmentation grenade is still listed as being available for issue.

Mk3A2 (Mk3A1) Offensive

The grenade that was issued to the UDTs during World War II, at least in limited numbers, was the Mk3A1 offensive grenade. In the Teams, the Mk3A1 was considered a small demolition charge, though as a concussion grenade it also had its uses in after-invasion bunker cleaning. The shock wave and over pressure produced by the Mk3A1 when it is used in an enclosed area is much greater than the equivalent effect from a fragmentation grenade. Though the blast could drive portions of the metal ends and especially the fuze body for hundreds of yards from the point of explosion, the Mk3A1 had only a 2 yard effective casualty radius. Underwater, the Mk3A1 had a much greater casualty radius against swimmers but this effect was not used in combat during World War II. Later, in Vietnam, the underwater blast effect of the Mk3A2 was used to good effect when defending boats and shipping from enemy sappers in the water.

"The first US issue grenade to make use of the coiled, notched wire system was the M26 fragmentation grenade issued in the early 1950's....(And) because the new style of grenade body was much thinner than the Mk 2 grenade, a larger explosive charge could be used as the filler."

TECHNICAL DATA— M26 (M26A1, M61)
TYPE—High explosive fragmentation hand grenade
IDENTIFYING COLOR CODE—Olive drab body w/yellow markings
BODY—Sheet steel w/inner coil of square cross-section notched steel wire
FILLER—Composition B
　M26A1, M61 Composition B w/tetryl booster
FUZE—M204A1 or M204A2 Bouchon-type detonating fuze w/ pyrotechnic delay
FUZE DELAY—4 to 5 seconds
　WEIGHTS
ROUND—1 lb (0.45 kg)
FILLER—0.36 lb (0.16 kg)
　M26A1, M61 0.34 lb (0.15 kg) Comp B, 0.02 lb (0.01 kg) Tetryl
　EFFECTS
EFFECT—Blast and fragmentation
AREA OF EFFECT—16 yd (15 m) radius
　LENGTHS
LENGTH—3.9 in (9.9 cm)
WIDTH (DIAMETER)—2.25 in (5.7 cm)
AVERAGE RANGE—44 yds (40 m)

　A very special version of the M26 grenade was made for the SEALs in Vietnam for use as a boobytrap. Outwardly, the special M26 was exactly the same as other grenades of the same model but the special fuze had been assembled without a pyrotechnic delay. As soon as the grenade's safety lever was released, it detonated.

　The Mk3A1 is a very simple grenade, not much more than a cylindrical block of explosive surrounded by cardboard and fitted with a fuze. The body of the Mk3A1 had thin metal end caps to secure the cardboard tube and threaded fuze well. Late in World War II a new version of the offensive grenade was designed and issued. The new grenade was the Mk3A2, a larger and improved version of the Mk3A1. In the Mk3A2, the body was made up of two thick, asphalt-impregnated fiber, later fiberglass, cups that would nest one inside the other. The new body material eliminated the need for the metal end caps and could hold a slightly larger change than the earlier grenade. The two cups were water-resistant and were held together at their center seam with a piece of waterproof tape.

　The Mk3A2 grenade proved to be a very popular design and saw long service with all the Teams through the Korean War, Vietnam, and into today where it is still an issue item. In Vietnam, the Mk3A2 was often used during waterborne ambushes where it could be thrown into the water. The underwater blast of the Mk3A2 could stove in the bottom of a sampan or stun a Viet Cong who had fallen into the river. Though the shock wave of the grenade could be very rough on a prisoner, it was far better than a fragmentation grenade landing in the sampan.

　Fragmentation grenades in general saw a great deal of improvement in design following World War II. It had been found that if the serrations were placed on the inside surface of the grenade body, the body would break up along the lines. This was a major step in the direction of controlled fragmentation. Another fragmentation system was to surround the explosive filler with a square cross-sectioned wire, regularly notched along its length. The wire could be formed into a shaped coil and covered with a thin sheet-metal body. The fragmentation could be controlled and the burst radius designed into the system by setting the size of the individual fragments.

M26 (M26A1, M61) Fragmentation

　A larger fragment has more weight and inertia when flying and therefore has a correspondingly longer lethal range, but there can be relatively few of these fragments due to the practical weight limit of a hand-thrown grenade. Smaller fragments lose velocity quickly and have a relatively short lethal range, but there can be many more of them, making a dense pattern near the point of explosion. The first US issue grenade to make use of the coiled, notched wire system was the M26 fragmentation grenade issued in the early 1950's.

　Because the new style of grenade body was much thinner than the Mk 2 grenade, a larger explosive charge could be used as the filler. In addition, advances in explosive technology had come up with more effective explosives for use in fragmentation grenades. The M26 was loaded with Composition B, a mixture of RDX, TNT, and wax. With the Composition B filler, the fragments of the M26 had an initial velocity in the 3200 feet per second range (1000 m/s). The coiled wire fragmentation system gave the M26 nearly 1,000 fragments but because of their low weight and poor aerodynamic qualities, the majority of the fragments were lethal at 16 yards (15 m) and relatively harmless at 33 yards (30 m).

The Composition B filler of the M26 was less sensitive than TNT and in some conditions was not easily set off by just the detonator on the M204 series fuze. To ensure complete and reliable detonation, the M26A1 fragmentation grenade was issued for service beginning in the late 1950's. In the M26A1, a small quantity of the Composition B explosive was removed surrounding the fuze well and pellets of tetryl inserted. The tetryl acts as a booster to the detonator and insures complete detonation of the explosive filler.

One problem arose from the use of the Bouchon-type fuze in US grenades of almost all types. Because the safety handle of the Bouchon fuze stood out from the body of the grenade and was reasonably long, almost everyone who used hand grenades at one time or another carried them by hooking the safety lever to a convenient spot on their uniform. This made for colorful pictures of fighting men going into combat festooned with grenades, but it also led to a lot of lost ordnance. Not only could the grenade easily slip off during movement, the safety of the device was compromised by the habit. If the spoon should break off close to the fuze, there would be nothing for the operator to easily hold down for safety while pulling the pin.

To help eliminate this problem, two actions were taken. The M1956 universal ammunition pouch, which could hold M-14 or M16 magazines, 40mm grenades, or other loose ordnance, had two special holders for carrying hand grenades. The holders were on either side of the pouch and consisted of a long vertical cloth tube for holding the grenade safety lever and a securing strap. The securing strap would be wrapped around the grenade's fuze, through the pull ring, and snapped to the pouch. In this carrying configuration, the grenade is safe from falling off or breaking the safety lever.

The second action taken to help secure the safety of casualty-producing grenades was an addition to the fuze. Beginning with the M26A1 grenade, in 1970 a secondary safety clip was added to the body of the grenade's fuze. The safety clip is intended to retain the safety lever should the pin of the grenade come loose accidentally. The clip is simple in construction, wrapping either around an extension of the fuze below the pull ring, or about the neck of the fuze where it enters the grenade. Not all grenades are fitted with the safety clip, but it is found on almost all modern US manufactured explosive filled hand grenades. The safety clip is easily removed and is usually taken off just before the grenade is used. Nomenclature was changed for grenades that are issued with the safety clip. The M26A1 fragmentation grenade is known as the M61 grenade when fitted with a safety clip, there being no other difference between the two grenades.

Later issue carrying equipment, such as the All-purpose Lightweight Individual Carrying Equipment (ALICE) gear available in the 1970s, has small pockets on the outside of the magazine pouches to safely carry fragmentation grenades. On the ALICE pouches, the grenades are secured in their pockets by a strap across the top of the grenade. The pocket system of carrying fragmentation and other grenades has been retained in the Teams through the 1980's and into the 1990's with new types of carrying gear designed specifically with SEAL missions in mind.

"INSTANT" M26A1

There was one type of fragmentation grenade loaded for the SEALs in Vietnam that could not be made safe for use in any normal sense. Designed by the Special Ordnance Branch of the Naval Weapons Center at China Lake, California, the grenade looked like a normal M26 fragmentation grenade except for one difference, its fuze had no time delay. In the "instant" M26A1 grenade, the delay element had been removed from the fuze so that it could be used as a booby trap. As soon as the safety lever was released, the grenade detonated.

This type of grenade was very useful for the quick and dirty booby trap, such as materials or equipment that had to be left behind. Placing one of the zero-delay grenades under a box, board, or other item would make the VC very wary about going back into an area that the SEALs had just left. Conveniently dropping one as "lost" when a patrol had gone through a known VC area would also make the VC think twice about using recovered US ordnance. Care and SEAL discipline helped keep accidents with the zero-delay grenade to a minimum, only one such accident took place with US troops and that was caused by a non-SEAL. The incident involved the recovery of remote sensors for the replacement of the batteries. SEALs assisted the PBRs conducting the operation.

> "They [SEALs] had booby-trapped one of the sensors before they implanted it with a special zero-delay hand grenade… Recovering a booby trapped sensor was tricky.
>
> The PBR Lieutenant had the grenade in his hand. All he had to do was hold it or tie the spoon down and it would have been safe until we put the pin back in… He threw it. The spoon came up and the thing went off just as it left his hand. He lost a good part of his hand. He had a flak jacket and helmet on, otherwise he really would have been shredded…"

The lesson learned on the sensor recovery mission was a simple one, leave ordnance to the people who understood it. The PBR officer involved did know that the grenade didn't have a delay but he threw it before thinking the situation through. Though the SEALs did not have any other accidents involving the zero-delay grenade, there was the occasional problem with just using hand grenades in combat. Standard operating procedure on an ambush often entailed several members of the unit throwing hand grenades into the kill zone

Grenades

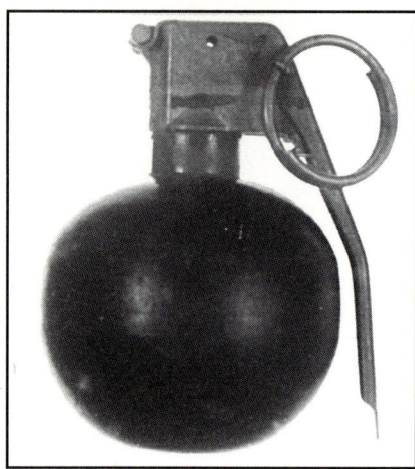

The M67 "baseball" fragmentation grenade. This grenade and variations of it are the standard fragmentation grenades used today by the US military including the SEALs. The simple spherical body shape allows this grenade to be thrown more easily, naturally, and further than earlier models. This specimen of M67 grenade does not have the steel safety clip that goes around the fuze body and neck of the grenade, additionally securing the safety lever. The groove for the safety clip can be seen underneath the fuze body, inside of the safety lever and pull ring. The safety clip is the only difference between the M67 grenade and the earlier M33 grenade used in Vietnam.
PHOTO CREDIT: KEVIN DOCKERY

TECHNICAL DATA— M33 (M67)
TYPE—High explosive fragmentation hand grenade
IDENTIFYING COLOR CODE—Olive drab body w/yellow markings
BODY—Cast steel
FILLER—Composition B
FUZE—M213 Bouchon-type detonating fuze w/pyrotechnic delay (M67 grenade has additional safety clip around fuze body and safety lever)
FUZE DELAY—4 to 5 seconds
  WEIGHTS
ROUND—0.88 lbs (0.40 kg)
FILLER—0.41 lbs (0.19 kg)
  EFFECTS
EFFECT—Blast and fragmentation
AREA OF EFFECT—16 yds (15 m) radius
  LENGTHS
LENGTH—3.53 in (9 cm)
WIDTH (DIAMETER)—2.5 in (6.4 cm)
AVERAGE RANGE—46 yds (42 m)

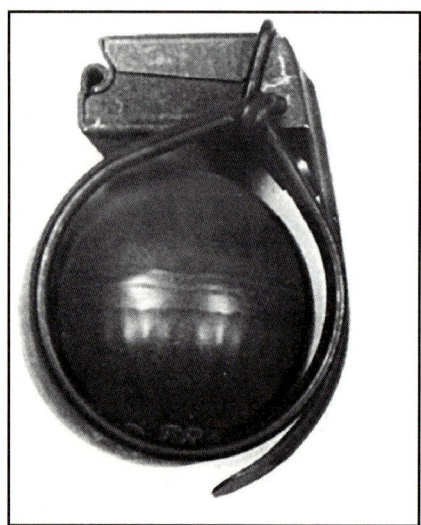

The V40 miniature fragmentation grenade is so small that the pull ring folds down and surrounds the fragmentation body of the grenade. To the right of the pull ring can be seen the small curved safety lever, almost hidden behind the pull ring. Some of the markings identifying this grenade can be seen just around the base of the fragmentation body.
PHOTO CREDIT: KEVIN DOCKERY

TECHNICAL DATA — NWM V-40 mini grenade
TYPE—High explosive fragmentation hand grenade
IDENTIFYING COLOR CODE—Olive drab body w/white markings
BODY—Internally-notched steel
FILLER—Composition B
FUZE—Bouchon-type detonating fuze w/pyrotechnic delay, special locking-type pull ring surrounds grenade body and must be rotated 160 degrees to unlock and be pulled
FUZE DELAY—4 seconds
  WEIGHTS
ROUND—0.26 kg (0.12 kg)
FILLER—0.99 oz (28 g)
  EFFECTS
EFFECT—Blast and fragmentation, produces 400 to 500 fragments
AREA OF EFFECT—5 yds (5 m), some larger fragments may be projected over 27 yds (25 m)
  LENGTHS
LENGTH—2.24 in (5.7 cm)
WIDTH (DIAMETER)—1.78 in (4.5 cm)
AVERAGE RANGE—over 55 yds (50 m+)

Special Weapons

while other SEALs continued firing. This procedure helped ensure full coverage of the target but could backfire on occasion.

"Nobody was sure whose grenade hit the tree.... One of our grenades hit a tree and bounced right back at us, landing in the canal. These weren't old-fashioned Mark II pineapples. They were modern M26A1's lined with notched wire. All of our eyes were huge, watching that grenade bounce back at us. Smacking our faces down, everyone ate mud. The grenade detonated harmlessly in the canal."

CHICOM STICK-TYPE DEFENSIVE

One grenade accident the SEALs never contended with was one caused by using captured enemy ordnance. Though the SEALs were trained as to what the capabilities were and how to use grenades in use by the VC and NVA, combat use of such material was very rare. The Chinese communist pattern of explosive-filled hand grenades were either supplied to or manufactured by North Vietnamese forces along with a number of Soviet designs. The Chicom grenades are among the most dangerous given the variety of materials they are made of and the difficult tropical environment of Vietnam. The general pattern of the Chicom explosive grenade was a short wooden or bamboo handle topped by a cast metal, usually iron, head. The head could be a simple blunt cylinder or egg-shaped with deep serrations. A simple pull-friction fuse was inserted into the head of the grenade and the pull string passed through the handle. Fuse delays ran from 2 to 6 seconds on the average depending on the amount of humidity the grenade had been exposed to and how it had been made originally.

The real danger in the Chicom grenades lay in the explosive filling. Various fillers were used including salvaged explosives removed from dud US ordnance. Picric acid, long discarded as being too dangerous an explosive filling for grenades, was in common use among the NVA and VC forces. The main danger of Picric acid is its tendency to form unstable salts when it comes in contact with metals, including iron. Though their effectiveness was occasionally noted by the SEALs, Chicom grenades were something the Teams scrupulously avoided whenever possible.

M33 (M67) FRAGMENTATION

Though the notched-wire coil was proving itself a successful design in the M26 family of fragmentation grenades, a second method of producing controlled fragmentation was also fielded in quantity for the first time during the Vietnam War. External serrations had been proven not to effect the size of casing fragments in a regular manner, internal serrations were another matter.

As early as World War I, a hand grenade had been produced with internal serrations, the British Number 16 of 1915. But the design of the grenades themselves had proven faulty. During the 1950's, fragmentation control by internal serrations was "rediscovered" and further developed. The M33 fragmentation grenade became the first issue US hand grenade to use the internal serration

> **TECHNICAL DATA**— Chicom Stick-type Defensive grenade
> **TYPE**—High explosive fragmentation hand grenade
> **IDENTIFYING COLOR CODE**—Wooden or bamboo handle, grey cast iron head
> **BODY**—Cast iron
> **FILLER**—Varies, has included TNT, Picric acid, various dynamites, and salvaged explosives from dud US ordnance (Vietcong manufacture only)
> **FUZE**—Pull-friction igniter
> **FUZE DELAY**—2.5 to 6 seconds
>   **WEIGHTS**
> **ROUND**—1.16 to 1.22 lbs (0.53 to 0.55 kg)
> **FILLER**—0.06 to 0.14 lbs (0.03 to 0.06 kg)
>   **EFFECTS**
> **EFFECT**—Blast and fragmentation
> **AREA OF EFFECT**—11 yds (10 m) radius
>   **LENGTHS**
> **LENGTH**—8.0 to 9.7 in (20.3 to 24.6 cm)
> **WIDTH (DIAMETER)**—1.7 to 2.2 in (4.3 to 5.6 cm)
> **AVERAGE RANGE**—33 yds (30 m)

system and was issued to the troops in Vietnam, including the SEALs, in the late 1960's.

The oblate spheroid shape of the M33 grenade is a more natural shaped object for throwing, especially for men from a country where baseball is a prominent sport. In addition to being better balanced for throwing, the rounder shape of the M33 grenade gives the weapon a more regular fragmentation pattern, no matter what its orientation at detonation. The lemon-shaped grenades, such as the M26 family, have their best fragmentation out from their sides but the patterns are much poorer from the bottom and top areas.

The body of the M33 grenade is made up of two formed steel hemispheres welded together at their equator. Each body half is formed with an internal diamond serration pattern pressed into its inside surface. The characteristics of the M33 body allow the grenade to have a larger explosive charge than the M26 family of grenades while still having a good throwing range. The heavy charge of explosive gives the M33 grenade a very dense pattern of high velocity fragments while the shape and weight of the fragments themselves prevent them from having too great a lethal range.

A later version of the M33 grenade, the M67, was produced as an almost identical piece of ordnance but incorporated a safety clip into the design. The M67 fragmentation grenade has proved itself the most successful design of its type coming out of the Vietnam War and it remains the standard issue fragmentation grenade in the US services today.

V-40 MINI GRENADE

Another fragmentation grenade was used by the SEALs in some numbers in Vietnam and it too made use of the internal fragmentation system. The Dutch V40 mini-grenade, manufactured by the Netherlands Weapon & Munition Company (NWM), was one of the smallest fragmentation grenades ever commercially produced and was issued to the Teams beginning in 1968. The

175

Grenades

A selection of grenades and pyrotechnics used by the SEALs in Vietnam. At the far right is a V-40 mini-fragmentation grenade. The second grenade in from the right is an M26 fragmentation grenade. The spherical grenade is an M33 baseball fragmentation grenade. Above the two fragmentation grenades is a Mark 13 day/night signal flare. The fourth grenade in from the right is a M18 burning-type yellow smoke grenade. Next to the M18 grenade is an M7A3 CS tear gas grenade with the covering tape torn off the emission hole at the bottom of the grenade. The center canister grenade is a special China Lake designed TIARA marking grenade. The last canister grenade on the left appears to be a re-marked China Lake Napalm grenade.
PHOTO CREDIT: DARRYL YOUNG COLLECTION

TECHNICAL DATA—M15 WP
TYPE—Bursting-type white phosporus smoke/incendiary hand grenade
IDENTIFYING COLOR CODE—Grey body w/yellow markings and 1 yellow band
BODY—18 gage sheet steel
FILLER—White phosphorus w/RDX burster
FUZE—M206A1 or M206A2 Bouchon-type detonating fuze w/ pyrotechnic delay
FUZE DELAY—4 to 5 seconds
  WEIGHTS
ROUND—1.94 lbs (0.88 kg)
FILLER—0.94 lbs (0.43 kg)
  EFFECTS
EFFECT—Bursting grenade spreads burning particles of phosphorus over the burst area. White phosporus ignites spontaneously on contact with air creating a dense hot cloud of smoke while it burns at over 4800 degrees F.
BURN TIME—60 seconds
AREA OF EFFECT—16 yds (15 m), some particles may be projected over 33 yds (30 m)
  LENGTHS
LENGTH—4.5 in (11.4 cm)
WIDTH (DIAMETER)—2.38 in (6 cm)
AVERAGE RANGE—27 yds (25 m)

The M15 white phosphorus grenade. Identified by touch from the M34 WP grenade by its smooth sides and flat bottom, this was the standard US WP grenade dating from World War II. The smoothly rounded edges visible on the ends of this grenade help keep it from being dangerously mistaken for a standard smoke grenade by touch or at night. The M15 WP grenade has finally been declared obsolete for SEAL use only within the last few years (1996).
PHOTO CREDIT: US ARMY

Special Weapons

round body of the V40 greatly resembles in size and effect the internal explosive ball assembly in the 40mm grenades only fitted with a special Bouchon fuze. The body of the V40 is internally notched into square fragments, ensuring optimum fragment size when the grenade explodes. The design of the V40 is such that the body of the grenade breaks up into about 500 fragments, over 300 of which are in the 2.3 to 3.1 grain (0.15 to 0.2 g) range. The V40's fragments give the weapon a 100 percent casualty rate at 3 meters from the point of burst and an almost 0 percent casualty rate at 25 meters range. This makes the V40 a very good grenade for close-in and house-to-house combat.

The fuze of the V40 has a safety lever than extends halfway around the grenade's body to insure solid gripping of the lever. The pull ring is teardrop-shaped and actually folds around the grenade's body for carrying. To add to the grenade's safety, the pull ring assembly is of the locking type. The pull ring has to be rotated about 120 degrees before an L-shaped extension on the pin can clear the fuze body, allowing the pin to be pulled. In general, the V40 grenade is less than half the size and weight of a regular fragmentation grenade, giving it a much greater throwing range and making it more convenient to carry in numbers.

But for all its apparent advantages, the V40's size also was a drawback. One young SEAL remembered vividly using the little grenade when he and his partner were cut off from the main body of their patrol. A VC had been shot by the two SEALs and lay out of their direct sight. The wounded VC was making considerably noise and drawing the very unwanted attention of a large body of VC near the two SEALs.

"We were carrying a number of mini-grenades with us. These little frags weren't much larger than a golf ball and a man could carry several more minis for every normal-sized grenade. The little grenades (Dutch NWM V-40's) could also be thrown a lot farther than a regular M-26 frag as well, and that was the problem.

…Grabbing a minigrenade from my web gear, I pulled the pin and threw it where the wounded VC lay in the grass. Trouble was, with my heart pumping and the adrenalin flowing from the excitement, I put a little too much arm behind throwing the little 3 1/2 ounce minigrenade.

…We watched the minigrenade whistle well over the horizon… Grabbing another grenade off my rig … I tried again to nail the wounded VC. Again, I was so pumped up that little grenade just sailed off into the distance. By this time, fire was starting up around us and I had enough of these little grenades. Pulling a standard M26 frag off my rig, I lobbed it into the wounded VC's position and his moaning suddenly stopped with the explosion."

The SEALs ceased issuing the V40 during the 1970's. Commercial sales had not developed for the V40 enough to satisfy NWM in Holland and production ceased in 1972.

M15 WP SMOKE

Among the most universally useful grenades carried by the SEALs are the white phosphorus (WP) smoke grenades. The bursting-type "Willy Peter" grenade can be used for signaling, screening with smoke, target marking, incendiary purposes, and causing casualties. The screening effect of white phosporus smoke is limited due to the high heat of burning phosphorus, causing the smoke to rise more rapidly than other types of smoke. In its favor, white phosphorus produces a smoke screen much faster than other smoke grenades. Reactive with oxygen, white phosphorus spontaneously ignites on contact with air. White phosphorus burns at a temperature of about 5000 degrees Fahrenheit and is easily able to set fire to flammable materials as well as cause very severe burns on tissue.

Two WP grenades are used by the SEALs and UDTs, one being a World War II design, circa 1943. The M15 WP grenade was the first white phosphorus smoke grenade to be issued in the US military. Externally, the M15 grenade resembles other canister-style burning-type smoke and gas grenades. To help prevent mix-ups with other types of less lethal grenades, the M15 has a seamless sheet steel body stamped out in one piece with rounded ends. With the rounded-edge end cap in place, the M15 grenade can be easily recognized by touch as being different from the canister-type grenade with its rolled metal edges.

Centered in the top of the M15 grenade is the same powerful M206A2 detonator fuze used in the Mk3A2 offensive grenade. A burster well extends down the center of the M15 grenade, containing the fuze and sealing out the WP filling. A very real danger of fire exists with all WP filled grenades as any leakage of the filler will ignite as soon as it touches the air. This is part of the reason that the sheet steel that makes up the body of the M15 grenade is about twice as thick as the metal used to make up other canister-type grenades.

When the detonator of the M206A2 fuze goes off, it bursts the M15 casing, sending particles of WP streaming

> "Among the most universally useful grenades carried by the SEALs are the white phosphorus (WP) smoke grenades. The bursting-type "Willy Peter" grenade can be used for signaling, screening with smoke, target marking, incendiary purposes, and causing casualties."

Grenades

This is the M34 white phosphorus smoke grenade still in use by the SEALs today. The serrated exterior of the grenade body is to assist in breaking up the body when the grenade is detonated. The conical tapered base and groove in the body just above the base are so that this grenade may be fitted to an M1A2 grenade projection adapter for launching from a rifle.
PHOTO CREDIT: US ARMY

TECHNICAL DATA—M34 WP
TYPE—Bursting-type white phosphorus smoke/incendiary hand grenade
IDENTIFYING COLOR CODE—Light green body w/square serrations, 1 yellow band, light red markings
BODY—18 gage sheet steel
FILLER—White phosphorus w/RDX burster
FUZE—M206A1 or M206A2 Bouchon-type detonating fuze w/pyrotechnic delay, new production has an additional safety clip around fuze body and safety lever
FUZE DELAY—4 to 5 seconds
  WEIGHTS
ROUND—1.7 lbs (0.77 kg)
FILLER—0.94 lbs (0.43 kg)
  EFFECTS
EFFECT—Bursting grenade spreads burning particles of phosphorus over the burst area. White phosporus ignites spontaneously on contact with air creating a dense hot cloud of smoke while it burns at over 4800 degrees F.
BURN TIME—60 seconds
AREA OF EFFECT—27 yds (25 m), some particles may be projected over 33 yds (30 m)
  LENGTHS
LENGTH—5.2in (13.2 cm)
WIDTH (DIAMETER)—2.38 in (6 cm)
AVERAGE RANGE—38 yds (35 m)

The AN-M8 white smoke grenade. Used for both signaling as well as screening purposes, this smoke grenade is marked with a much lighter, light green, body color than the almost identical M18 colored smoke grenade. This light color was often painted or taped over for additional concealment by the camouflage-conscious SEALs. The AN in the designator indicates that this grenade was considered standard issue for both the Army and Navy.
PHOTO CREDIT: KEVIN DOCKERY

TECHNICAL DATA— AN-M8 HC
TYPE—Burning-type white smoke hand grenade
IDENTIFYING COLOR CODE—Light green body w/black markings
BODY—28 gage sheet steel
FILLER—Type C Hexachlorethane (HC) mixture (grained aluminum, zinc oxide, and hexachloroethane)
FUZE—M201A1 Bouchon-type igniting fuze w/pyrotechnic delay
FUZE DELAY—0.7 to 2 seconds
  WEIGHTS
ROUND—1.5 lbs (0.68 kg)
FILLER—1.19 lbs (0.54 kg)
  EFFECTS
EFFECT—Creates large cloud of dense white smoke while burning
BURN TIME—105 to 150 seconds
AREA OF EFFECT—5551 cubic yard (4244 cubic meter) cloud maximum
  LENGTHS
LENGTH—5.7 in (14.5 cm)
WIDTH (DIAMETER)—2.5 in (6.4 cm)
AVERAGE RANGE—33 yds (30 m)

Special Weapons

out in all directions. The WP particles burn through the air with a bright yellow-white light and leave tracks of white smoke behind them. Effectively unchanged since World War II, the M15 remained a standard issue WP grenade with the US forces until recently.

M34 WP SMOKE

Shortly after World War II another type of WP grenade was designed. The M34 WP grenade is also a bursting-type grenade and shares most of the characteristics of the M15 WP grenade. The major difference between the M15 and M34 WP grenades is the size and body shape of the M34 grenade.

The body of the M34 WP grenade is a sheet steel cylinder of the same thickness as the M15 grenade. The body of the M34 grenade is serrated into 60 squares to help facilitate the body bursting and is tapered at its lower end for fitting into the M1A2 Grenade projection adapter. The M1A2 grenade projection adapter allows the M34 WP grenade to be launched from a rifle fitted with a spigot-type rifle grenade launcher. Though the adapter was intended to allow the M34 grenade to replace both the M19A1 WP rifle grenade and the M15 WP hand grenade, in practice the system never worked to everyone's satisfaction. The UDT and SEALs used the M34 and M15 grenades interchangeably, by never fully accepting the rifle grenade adapter concept.

Using the same M206A2 fuze as the M15 grenade, the M34 WP grenade has a larger burst radius due in part to the serrations in the grenade body. The scattered particles of white phosphorus from both grenades burn for about 60 seconds, spreading a thick cloud of relatively non-poisonous phosphorus pentoxide smoke.

The WP grenades were found to have a large number of applications by SEALs operating in Vietnam. The white cloud of phosphorus smoke could readily be seen from aircraft or other support craft and was often used to mark targets for fire support. Even at night, the brilliant flare of the burning phosphorus could be seen though the smoke. This made phosphorus ideal for marking a unit's flanks, as was done in Vietnam by the SEALs.

> "The SOP for this operation called for us to light up our flanks with WP grenades if anything was happening. The [boat] coming in would then be able to suppress any enemy fire on either side of us and know exactly where we were at."

On one operation, the SEALs involved were relative newcomers to direct combat. Mistakes are common during the confusion of war and even the superbly trained SEALs were not immune to making them. During the action, SOP was followed and WP grenades put out to mark the unit's flanks. Only while one SEAL was watching the approach area for possible enemy activity, other SEALs were hiding an Inflatable Boat, Small (IBS) the unit had brought with them as an escape route. When the action took place and the SOP followed, the one SEAL who had been on guard never knew where the rubber boat had been placed. He soon learned his mistake when he was told to go into the brush and retrieve the boat for the units withdrawal.

> "In the bushes?" I thought, "But that's where I threw the grenade." I found the IBS all right, and so had my WP grenade. The grenade had landed right inside the boat and completely destroyed it. The stink of the burning phosphorus had covered the smell of the burning rubber."

AN-M8 HC SMOKE

Other smoke grenades were used by the SEALs that had less destructive potential than the white phosphorus variety. The AN-M8 HC smoke grenade is a canister-style burning type grenade used to produce dense clouds of white smoke for signaling or screening purposes. The M8 grenade uses the standard sized cylindrical sheet metal body found on most of the US burning-type grenades. Designed prior to World War II, the M8 is loaded with Type C, HC smoke mixture, a combination of zinc oxide, ammonium perchlorate, dechlorane, aluminum, and other materials.

When burning, HC mixture produces zinc chloride smoke, a dense white/gray heavy smoke that has excellent obscuring qualities and hugs the ground much better than white phosphorus smoke. Though the M8 grenade does not have the incendiary qualities of a WP grenade, the casing of the M8 becomes very hot while the filling burns, hot enough to ignite any flammable materials it may be in contact with.

The M8 grenade burns for at least several minutes, releasing its smoke through emission holes in the top of the grenade body. White smoke was not used in combat by the SEALs as often as in the other services as their operations generally did not call for it. Several AN-M8 HC grenades would be with a unit of SEALs as they conducted missions, scattered among the men. Though signaling, especially to aircraft and boats, could be done with the AN-M8 grenade, the white smoke could be mistaken for other kinds of explosions or ordnance, adding to the confusion of an already difficult situation. For signaling purposes, the M18 colored smoke grenade was commonly used.

M18 COLORED SMOKE

Developed in a few short weeks in 1942, the M18 colored smoke grenades met the US Army requirement for a colored smoke grenade that would form a smoke visible at a slant range of 10,000 feet (3,050 m) and last about one minute. Issued in four colors: red, green, yellow, and violet, the M18 quickly became and has remained, the most widely used pyrotechnic signaling device in the military. The colored smoke produced by the M18 is not as dense as WP or HC smoke and is intended to have a bright color, easily visible against most natural backgrounds.

A selection of the colors would be carried on a SEAL mission with the colors either being chosen by SOP or simply picked at random. The most common use by far of the M18 grenade was to mark the wind direction and speed for helicopter landing zones in the jungle. By tossing out a colored smoke grenade, the pilot of an

Grenades

Two of the four different types (colors) of M18 smoke grenades. These are the red and green versions of the M18 grenade, identified by their markings and the top of the grenade body being painted the color of the smoke loading. The grenade on the left (red) has had its pull ring removed and replaced on the right side of the fuze. The grenade on the right (green) is as it was removed from the shipping container.
PHOTO CREDIT: KEVIN DOCKERY

TECHNICAL DATA— M18
TYPE—Burning-type colored smoke hand grenade
IDENTIFYING COLOR CODE—Olive drab body w/gray or yellow markings and one 1 inch wide band. The top of the grenade is the same color as the smoke the grenade produces.
BODY—29 gage sheet steel
FILLER—Red, green, yellow, or violet smoke composition
FUZE—M201A1 Bouchon-type igniting fuze w/pyrotechnic delay
FUZE DELAY—0.7 to 2 seconds
   WEIGHTS
ROUND—1.19 lbs (0.54 kg)
FILLER—0.72 lbs (0.33 kg)
   EFFECTS
EFFECT—Produces large cloud of colored smoke
BURN TIME—50 to 90 seconds
AREA OF EFFECT—average 20 x 4 x 2 yd (18 x 4 x 2 m) cloud
   LENGTHS
LENGTH—5.75 in (14.6 cm)
WIDTH (DIAMETER)—2.5 in (6.4 cm)
AVERAGE RANGE—38 yds (35 m)

The M7A1 burning-type (CN) grenade. This grenade is identical in construction to the M18 and AN-M8 smoke grenades, differing only by its filler.
PHOTO CREDIT: US ARMY

TECHNICAL DATA— M7A1 CN
TYPE—Burning-type CN tear gas hand grenade
IDENTIFYING COLOR CODE—Gray body w/red markings and 1 red band
BODY—28 gage sheet steel
FILLER—CN (Chloroacetophenone)/pyrotechnic mixture
FUZE—M202A1 Bouchon-type igniting fuze w/pyrotechnic delay
FUZE DELAY—0.7 to 2 seconds
   WEIGHTS
ROUND—1.16 lb (0.52 kg)
FILLER—0.78 lb (0.35 kg)
   EFFECTS
EFFECT—Burning grenade releases a cloud of CN gas and smoke from the four holes in its top and single hole in its base. CN causes a very heavy flow of tears and strong pain in the eyes and upper respiratory passages within 15 to 30 seconds of exposure. Higher concentrations, such as would be inside a building or bunker, will cause irritation to the skin, especially moist skin, as a strong itching and burning sensation. Symptoms last for 5 to 20 minutes following removal from exposure.
BURN TIME—20 to 60 seconds
AREA OF EFFECT—Approximately 20 x 4 x 2 yd (18 x 4 x 2 m) cloud of dense gas, can cover a much larger downwind area with a less dense, less effective cloud
   LENGTHS
LENGTH—5.7 in (14.5 cm)
WIDTH (DIAMETER)—2.5 in (6.4 cm)
AVERAGE RANGE—38 yds (35 m)

Special Weapons

incoming bird could also locate a hidden group of SEALs calling for fire support. The color of smoke used was not specified soon after combat operations began in Vietnam. The VC soon scrounged or made a sufficient supply of colored smoke that if a specific smoke was known to be used, they would release their own smoke of the same color. Most SEAL uses of M18 grenades followed a general pattern of first contacting the approaching aircraft by radio and then putting out an M18 grenade;

> "Well, you can identify me by this." And one of us would pop a colored smoke grenade. "Tell me what color you see. Yeah, that's me. All right, anybody else you see, you pop 'em."

The procedure was simple, straightforward, and kept confusion to a minimum. Yellow and red smoke were among the most popular loadings carried in Vietnam though the violet smoke, usually reserved for training back in the US, also stood out surprisingly well as did even the green smoke, it being a different shade than the jungle surroundings.

M7A1 CN Tear gas

Other burning-type grenades were carried by the SEALs in Vietnam with a considerably more active filling than colored or white smoke. Tear gas riot control agents were found to be excellent means to empty out bunkers, concealed compartments, and tunnels, without exposing the SEALs to the dangers of having to enter such areas first. Riot control gases could quickly make an enclosure impossible to remain in for unprotected VC troops and when the people did emerge, they were usually in no condition to fight. This allowed the SEALs to conduct their preferred action, the taking of prisoners to gather intelligence. In addition, it gave the Teams a non-lethal way of clearing areas where civilians might be, and often were, encountered.

The first tear gas used to any great extent was chloroacetophenone, widely known under its military designation CN. CN is a colorless solid when pure with a pleasant odor resembling apple blossoms. When mixed with a burning agent for fuel and vaporized, CN smoke has anything but a pleasant effect. Immediate weeping occurs on exposure to even slight concentrations of CN gas. Heavier concentrations quickly cause coughing, and an itching, burning sensation to the body's moist tissues such as the eyes, nose, throat, and lungs. Though non-toxic, it is very difficult for even a trained individual to function in a CN atmosphere. Incapacitation will usually happen within 15 to 30 seconds of exposure to the gas and the painful symptoms can last for 5 to 30 minutes after removal to clean air.

For military use, CN is loaded with a burning fuel mixture into the standard canister-style grenade body. The original M7 grenade had 3 rows of 6 holes down the sides of the canister to release the CN gas. The M7 grenade was prone to "flashing", catching flame and bursting. The later M7A1 grenade was designed to remove the problem of flashing and became widely issued due to its relative safety. The M7A1 CN grenade also has a

---

TECHNICAL DATA — M6A1 CN-DM
TYPE—Burning-type CN-DM tear/vomit gas hand grenade
IDENTIFYING COLOR CODE—Gray body w/red markings and 1 red band
BODY—28 gage sheet steel
FILLER—CN (Chloroacetophenone) and DM (Diphenylaminochloroarsine or Adamsite)/pyrotechnic mixture.
FUZE—M202A1 Bouchon-type igniting fuze w/pyrotechnic delay
FUZE DELAY—0.7 to 2 seconds
  WEIGHTS
ROUND—1.25 lbs (0.57 kg)
FILLER—0.59 lbs (0.27 kg) CN/DM mixture
  EFFECTS
EFFECT—Burning grenade releases a cloud of CN and DM gas and smoke from the four holes in its top and single hole in its base. CN causes a very heavy flow of tears and strong pain in the eyes and upper respiratory passages within 15 to 30 seconds of exposure. DM increases the flow of tears and pain in the repiratory tract as well as causing sneezing and coughing. Symptoms increase with exposure to include severe headache, acute pain, and tightness in the chest. After about 1 minute's exposure, symptoms include nausea and vomiting. DA symptoms last about 30 minutes after removal from exposure. Exposure to heavy concentrations of DM can cause the effects to last for up to 3 hours. DM takes about 1 minute to become effective and the CN is used to increase the immediate effects of the grenade. Exposure to very heavy concentrations of DM, such as in a closed room or bunker, can be toxic as the gas is an arsenic salt.
BURN TIME—20 to 60 seconds
AREA OF EFFECT—Approximately 20 x 4 x 2 yd (18 x 4 x 2 m) cloud of dense gas, can cover a much larger downwind area with a less dense, less effective cloud
  LENGTHS
LENGTH—5.7 in (14.5 cm)
WIDTH (DIAMETER)—2.5 in (6.4 cm)
AVERAGE RANGE—38 yds (35 m)

This is the M6A1 CN-DM burning-type gas grenade. This is the last model of this very toxic gas grenade produced. Though both the M6 and M6A1 grenades were available to the SEALs, they were rarely used. The M6 CN-DM grenade is close to being identical to the M6A1 grenade except for its having several rows of gas vent holes covered with tape along its sides.
PHOTO CREDIT: US ARMY

Grenades

The M7A3 burning-type tear gas (CS) grenade. This grenade is identical in construction to the M18 and AN-M8 smoke grenades, differing only by its filler. A number of other gas grenades, such as the M7A1 CS gas grenade are identical to this specimen except for filler.
PHOTO CREDIT: US ARMY

TECHNICAL DATA — M7A3 CS
TYPE—Burning-type CS tear gas hand grenade
IDENTIFYING COLOR CODE—Gray body w/red markings and 1 red band
BODY—28 gage sheet steel
FILLER—Pelletized CS (O-Chlorobenzalmalononitrile) agent/pyrotechnic mixture
FUZE—M202A1 Bouchon-type igniting fuze w/pyrotechnic delay
FUZE DELAY—0.7 to 2 seconds
   WEIGHTS
ROUND—0.97 lbs (0.44 kg)
FILLER—0.28 lbs (0.13 kg) CS pellets, 0.46 lbs (0.21 kg) burning mixture
   EFFECTS
EFFECT—Burning grenade releases a cloud of CS gas and smoke from the four holes in its top and single hole in its base. CS causes a heavy flow of tears and pain in the eyes and upper respiratory passages almost immediately on exposure. Further exposure causes coughing, difficulty in breathing, and chest tightness, along with an involuntary closing of the eyes, itching and stinging sensation on moist skin, a runny nose, and dizziness. Onset of incapacitation is 20 to 60 seconds. Higher concentrations, such as would be inside a building or bunker, will cause nausea and vomiting in addition to the above effects. Symptoms last for 5 to 20 minutes following removal from exposure.
BURN TIME—15 to 35 seconds
AREA OF EFFECT—Approximately 20 x 4 x 2 yd (18 x 4 x 2 m) cloud of dense gas, can cover a much larger downwind area with a less dense, less effective cloud
   LENGTHS
LENGTH—5.7 in (14.5 cm)
WIDTH (DIAMETER)—2.5 in (6.4 cm)
AVERAGE RANGE—38 yds (35 m)

The canister-style incendiary grenade used in the US Military from World War II to the present day. Primarily used to destroy materials and ordnance, this grenade is filled with formula 3 thermate as indicated by the TH3 marking on the body.
PHOTO CREDIT: US ARMY

TECHNICAL DATA—AN-M14 TH3
TYPE—Incendiary hand grenade
IDENTIFYING COLOR CODE—Blue/gray body w/purple markings and 1/2 inch purple band or olive drab w/black markings (old mfg), Red body w/black markings (new mfg)
BODY—28 gage sheet steel
FILLER—TH3 Thermate w/First—fire mixture VII
FUZE—Bouchon-type igniting fuze w/pyrotechnic delay
FUZE DELAY—0.7 to 2 seconds
   WEIGHTS
ROUND—2.0 lbs (0.91 kg)
FILLER—1.66 lbs (0.75 kg)
   EFFECTS
EFFECT—Intense heat (4000 degrees F.) and brilliant light w/molten iron spray. Can burn through 1.2 inch (1.3 cm) steel plate and will burn underwater after ignition.
BURN TIME—40 Seconds
AREA OF EFFECT—2 yd (2 m) spray/spark radius
   LENGTHS
LENGTH—5.7 in (14.5 cm)
WIDTH (DIAMETER)—2.5 in (6.4 cm)
AVERAGE RANGE—27 yds (25 m)

Special Weapons

cooler surface when burning and this helps limit the grass fires a burning-type grenade can cause.

First issued in 1935, the M7 CN grenade established the usefulness of the tear gas grenade for all of the services in general. Carried by the Teams in Vietnam, the CN grenade in general added a non-lethal weapon to the SEALs' arsenal that increased the number of prisoners captured without a shot having to be fired.

M6A1 CN-DM Irritant gas

A more serious chemical riot control agent was also used by the Teams in Vietnam and remains in the inventory today. Diphenylaminechloroarsine, also called Adamsite or more simply DM, is the only nauseating chemical agent loaded for general use. As the name of the agent type indicates, DM has a far more serious physiological action on the human body than simple tear gas. Initial reaction to even small concentrations of DM gas causes irritation to the eyes, nose, and throat after a few minutes' exposure. Within another minute or two of exposure, sneezing and coughing join the earlier symptoms, increasing in severity until the final stage of symptoms occur. The final stages of DM effects include severe headache, pains in the nose and chest, and finally nausea and violent vomiting. Long exposure is toxic and can result in death, but this is the exception since most people cannot stand being exposed to the earlier symptoms of DM.

The DM agent itself is a crystalline solid and is turned into a gas by burning it with an appropriate fuel similar to that used with CN gas. Since the effects of DM gas take several minutes to build up in severity, the agent is usually employed mixed with CN tear gas. The CN gas takes immediate effect and, if the individual exposed ignores the CN effects, masks the early symptoms of the DM agent. CN and DM are both loaded into a burning-type canister grenade with the same characteristics as the M7 series of CN grenades. The M6A1 CN-DM grenade was used in Vietnam by the SEALs in the same manner as the M7A1 CN grenade, though not in as large a number. The effects of DM lasts for three or more hours and this can make handling a prisoner affected by the agent a messy proposition. On the other hand, DM effects prevent a person from putting up any kind of real resistance at all, no matter what their situation.

M7A2 (M7A3) CS Tear gas

In 1960, the US Army announced the adoption of a new riot control agent in the form of a super tear gas. The agent has the rather daunting chemical name Orthochlorobenzalmalononitrile, but is universally called CS. CS combines the effects of both CN and DM but in a more powerful and safer form. Even low concentrations of CS gas produce its full range of symptoms within 20 to 60 seconds of exposure. Initial reactions include extreme burning of the eyes, a copious flow of tears, and sneezing. Further exposure to higher concentrations increases the severity of the symptoms already being experienced and add irritation of the nose and throat, coughing, tightness in the chest, marked sinus and nasal drip, and difficulty in breathing. Further exposure to even higher concentrations add nausea, vomiting, and vertigo to the

> **"Though the AN-M14 TH3 grenade produced tremendous heat, it was not considered an optimum design for the SEALs use in Vietnam. The desire of the SEALs was for a lighter piece of ordnance..."**

other symptoms as well as increasing difficulty in breathing, to a very frightening level, and an involuntary closing of the eyes.

As fast and violent as the symptoms are of CS gas, they disappear within five to ten minutes of the victim being removed to fresh air. CS is loaded into a standard burning-type grenade canister in much the same way as CN or DM, the agent is mixed with an appropriate burning fuel for use. Issued as the M7A3 CS grenade, the CS agent quickly became the preferred riot control agent in the military and police forces. M7A3 grenades are still being manufactured and stocked since their introduction in the early 1960's.

AN-M14 TH3 Incendiary

An additional burning-type canister grenade is used by the Teams, only the burning effects of this type are extreme. The grenade is the AN-M14 TH3 incendiary grenade loaded with a TH3 thermate filler. World War II issue versions of this grenade were filled with thermite, an mixture of 73 percent iron oxide and 27 percent fine granular aluminum. Thermate TH3 is thermite mixed with 29 percent barium nitrate, sulfur, and binders to make a superior mixture. In both mixtures, the general reaction is the same. Aluminum reacts chemically with the iron oxide when the mixture is heated enough. In the reaction, the aluminum strips the oxygen from the iron oxide resulting in aluminum oxide and free iron. The reaction is so hot and intense that the iron is released in a white-hot molten state.

Thermite reactions reach a temperature of 4,000 degrees Fahrenheit, spraying molten iron over a small area. This reaction makes the AN-M14 incendiary grenade one of the most effective devices for destroying equipment rapidly. The heavy AN-M14 grenade can burn its way through 1/2 inch of homogeneous steel plate and will weld together engine parts or the breech of cannons. Once ignited, the AN-M14 grenade will even burn underwater, the reaction supplying its own oxygen. To the SEALs, the AN-M14 grenade was an good way of destroying caches of rice and other burnable materials too bulky to be carried away. Even the normally hard to burn rice would ignite from the intense heat of a thermate grenade and continue smoldering for hours.

Though the AN-M14 TH3 grenade produced tremendous heat, it was not considered an optimum

Grenades

A top view of a dud Model 308-1 Napalm grenade. This photograph was taken on a SEAL range in Virginia where the grenade had failed to function. The safety lever is missing from the modified M206 detonating fuze and the percussion primer appears to have been removed or blown out. The extended filler neck of the grenade can be seen just below the fuze body. This extended neck is one of the visible distinguishing characteristics of the Napalm grenade. Some of the white markings on the gray body of the grenade are also visible in this photograph.
PHOTO CREDIT: US NAVY

"To meet the SEALs need for a compact flame weapon, China Lake developed their Model 308-1 Napalm grenade."

TECHNICAL DATA— Model 308-1 White Smoke Grenade
TYPE—Burning-type white smoke hand grenade
IDENTIFYING COLOR CODE—Black body w/white markings (prototype)
BURN TIME—120 seconds

This is a standard AN-M8 HC smoke grenade modified at NWC China Lake to have an increased burning rate and maximum smoke output. The general characteristics and operational features are the same as the AN-M8.

TECHNICAL DATA— Model 308-1 Napalm grenade
TYPE—Bursting-type incendiary hand grenade
IDENTIFYING COLOR CODE—Black body w/white markings (prototype). Light grey body w/white markings (limited production)
BODY—28 gage sheet steel
FILLER—Gasoline thickened w/M1 Thickener (Napalm)
FUZE—M206A2 Bouchon-type detonating fuze w/pyrotechnic delay
FUZE DELAY—4 to 5 seconds
 WEIGHTS
ROUND—0.75 lb (0.34 kg)
FILLER—0.52 lb (0.24 kg) Napalm [12 fluid ounces (355 ml)
 EFFECTS
EFFECT—Spreads burning (2200 degrees F.) napalm over burst area.
BURN TIME—20 to 60 seconds
AREA OF EFFECT—3.3 yd (3m) burst radius
 LENGTHS
LENGTH—6.7 in (17 cm)
WIDTH (DIAMETER)—2.5 in (6.4 cm)
AVERAGE RANGE—44 yds (40 m)

TECHNICAL DATA— Model 308-1 TIARA (Target Illumination And Recovery Aid)
TYPE—Bursting-type illuminating/marking hand grenade
IDENTIFYING COLOR CODE—Grey body w/black markings
BODY—28 gage sheet steel
FILLER—TIARA (Dupont chemiluminescent compound PR-155)
FUZE—Modified M206 Bouchon-type detonating fuze w/pyrotechnic delay additional safety clip around fuze body and safety lever
FUZE DELAY—Nominal 3 seconds
 WEIGHTS
ROUND—1 lb (0.45 kg)
FILLER—0.75 lbs (0.34 kg)
 EFFECTS
EFFECT—Spreads glowing TIARA compound over burst area
BURN TIME—20 minutes
AREA OF EFFECT—17 yd (16 m) radius
 LENGTHS
LENGTH—5.7 in (14.5 cm)
WIDTH (DIAMETER)—2.5 in (6.4 cm)
AVERAGE RANGE—44 yds (40 m) hand projected

design for the SEALs' use in Vietnam. The desire of the SEALs was for a lighter piece of ordnance than the issue incendiary grenade that could also cover a larger area with a burning agent. The humid conditions of southeast Asia kept a high moisture content in many natural materials. Bunkers, VC hooches, and caches of burnable materials were all targets for an easy to carry and employ flame weapon. Instead of the high heat in a small area for a short time provided by a thermate grenade, a large amount of heat over a wide area for a longer time was needed to first dry out and then ignite most targets.

MODEL 308-1 NAPALM GRENADE

The Special Operations Branch of the Naval Weapons Center (NWC) at China Lake, California produced a number of limited production, special application materials for the SEALs and UDTs throughout the Vietnam War. The specialty at China Lake, as it was most commonly called, was answering the problems of Naval commands that required unique, quick-reaction, ordnance related support. To meet the SEALs' need for a compact flame weapon, China Lake developed their Model 308-1 Napalm grenade.

To ease manufacturing problems, and shorten production time, many of the items produced at the Special Operations Branch of China Lake were made of standard issue components as much as possible. This policy extended to the Napalm grenade as well. Using a standard-size 18 gage sheet steel canister body, China Lake fitted an extended fuze neck that would accept a modified M206 series detonating fuze. The fuze was sufficient to rupture the grenade body and spread the filling over a reasonably wide area while the modifications insured ignition of the napalm.

Napalm, also called M1 thickener, is a mixed aluminum soap derived from coconut oil, naphthenic, and oleic acids issued as a light tan to brown granular powder. When mixed with gasoline, the napalm powder swells until the entire volume of gasoline becomes a homogeneous gel. The gel varies in consistency from a thick liquid to a rubbery material depending on the amount of napalm used. Allowed to sit, napalm becomes a semirigid jelly. Sudden shock or being squirted through an opening causes the napalm to become almost liquid again. When thickened with napalm, gasoline will stick to a target rather than simply run off, greatly increasing its efficiency as an incendiary agent.

Made available to the Teams in mid-1968, the napalm grenade was issued in kit form. A SEAL unit only had to mix regular gasoline with the powdered napalm supplied with the grenade to prepare the weapon for use. Designed specifically for use in igniting water soaked structures, the napalm grenade was found to be very satisfactory by the SEALs in Vietnam.

MODEL 308-1 WHITE SMOKE GRENADE

To satisfy a SEAL need for the fast production of a thick screening smoke, China Lake modified a standard AN-M8 smoke grenade. Modifications to the grenade did not change the physical or operational features but increased the burning time of the filler. With the faster burning rate, the modified AN-M8 grenade had a correspondingly greater smoke output and proportionally shorter burning time. Instead of having the up to 150 second burning time of a standard AN-M8 grenade, the modified grenade was completely burned out in 120 seconds or less. Issued as the Model 308-1 White smoke grenade, the China Lake grenade could quickly put out a cloud of dense white smoke that would remain close to the ground, giving a SEAL unit cover to break contact or screen their movements.

NWC TIARA MARKING GRENADE

In the early 1960's, a material was developed that has proved to be the most unusual filling for a hand grenade to date. Research was initiated by the Navy in July 1961 on a compound developed by the Dupont Co. identified as PB-155. When exposed to air, PB-155 glows brilliantly with a blue-green light while undergoing oxidation. Different formulations of PB-155 were developed under the name TIARA (Target Illumination And Recovery Aid) for use in a wide variety of applications ranging from emergency lights to marking airstrips. The different formulations of TIARA had a duration of luminescence ranging from several seconds to hours.

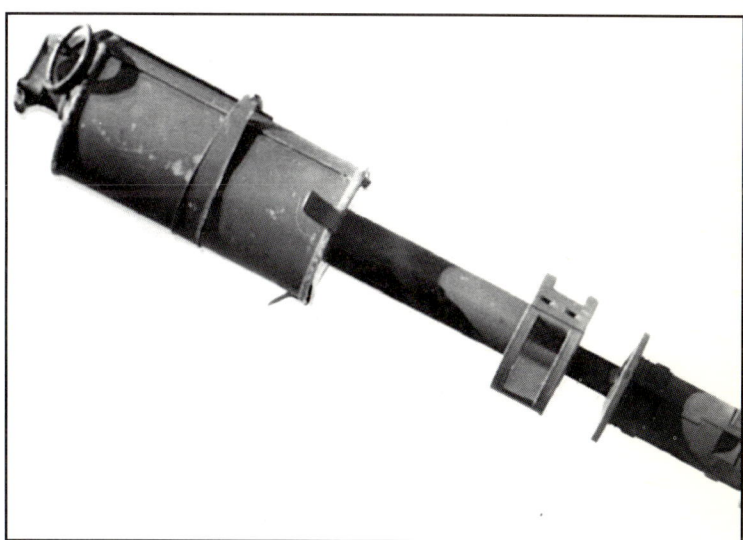

The TIARA Night Canopy Marker in an experimental form. This grenade could be either hand thrown or launched from a rifle. This photograph is of the rifle-launched version with the canister-style grenade fitted onto a standard M2A1 chemical grenade adapter. Of particular note is the small canister behind the fins of the M2A1 adapter. This canister holds a small amount of line that trails out behind the grenade when the device is launched. The line is intended to tangle in the tree canopy, holding the grenade above the leaves. When the grenade detonates, the glowing TIARA would be spread over the tree canopy, marking the area for aircraft. The setback band around the body of the grenade itself would slide back when the device was launched. With the pin pulled, when the setback band released the safety lever, the modified M206 fuze would function, bursting the grenade body several seconds later. For hand-thrown use, the grenade body is simply removed from the M2A1 adapter, the setback band slid off, and the grenade thrown in the normal manner.
PHOTO CREDIT: US NAVY

Grenades

TECHNICAL DATA — Mk 1 Mod 2 Illuminating
TYPE—Illuminating magnesium flare hand grenade
IDENTIFYING COLOR CODE—White body w/black markings or unpainted body w/one white band and black markings or olive drab body w/white markings (most recent manufacture).
BODY—Sheet steel
FILLER—Magnesium flare composition
FUZE—Mk 372 Mod 0 Bouchon-type detonating fuze w/pyrotechnic delay
FUZE DELAY—7 seconds
  WEIGHTS
ROUND—0.58 lbs (0.26 kg)
FILLER—0.22 lbs (0.10 kg)
  EFFECTS
EFFECT—Bright light, 55,000 candlepower
BURN TIME—25 seconds
AREA OF EFFECT—218 yd (200 m) radius
  LENGTHS
LENGTH—4.35 in (11 cm)
WIDTH (DIAMETER)—2.21 in (5.6 cm)
AVERAGE RANGE—44 yds (40 m)

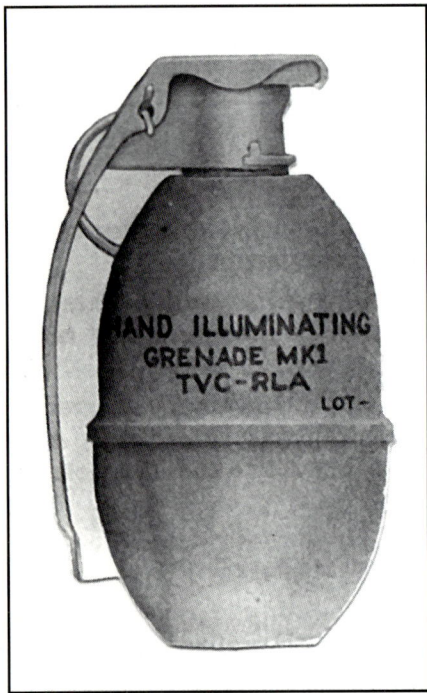

This very light grenade resembles an M26 fragmentation grenade but is instead a hand-thrown flare. The body of this Mod 1 specimen is made of two pressed steel shells, the seam of which can be seen underneath the markings. The top half of the body is empty with only the bottom shell containing the magnesium flare composition.
PHOTO CREDIT: US ARMY

As early as July 1962, 100 hand grenades (EX 1 Mod 0), 300 rifle grenades (EX 2 Mod 0), and Marstick colored crayons had been sent to Vietnam for testing. Results of the original testing samples were encouraging and further development of TIARA munitions continued. By 1968 TIARA-filled ordnance for special operations use had been made at China Lake specifically for the SEALs and UDTs. At least two different methods for the application of TIARA were made available to the SEALs in Vietnam during the war.

An aerosol spray can was filled with TIARA for use by the SEALs as a general marking agent. By spraying buildings or bunkers with TIARA, a glowing spot would be instantly made to indicate a place had been searched or to mark it as a target for air support. Though easily used, the TIARA spray can was not as popular with the SEALs as the other TIARA-filled piece of ordnance they had available, the night canopy marker grenade.

Designed to provide a method of marking a position at night in wooded or jungle areas, the TIARA marking grenade was developed by China Lake specifically for SEAL operations in Southeast Asia. The Night Canopy Marker, as it was officially called, was a gray-painted canister-type bursting grenade loaded with a TIARA filler and marked with black stenciled letters NWC MARKING GRENADE. A modified M206 series detonating fuze was used to burst the body of the grenade, spreading the TIARA agent over a wide area. As soon as it contacted the air the TIARA would begin glowing with a blue-green light that would be visible to aircraft up to 10 miles away on a clear night.

The Night Canopy Marker was issued as a rifle fired or hand thrown grenade. An M2A1 grenade projection adapter would snap over the base of the grenade allowing it to be fired from a rifle grenade launcher or the flash hider of an AR-15/M16 rifle. Rifle launching the marker grenade would put it above the trees before the fuze detonated, spraying the jungle canopy and indicating a specific area to aircraft.

By far the most popular method of employing TIARA by the SEALs was using the marking grenade as a hand-thrown grenade. Having the same handling characteristics as an M18 or AN-M8 smoke grenade, the marking grenade was easily carried as an additional item of ordnance.

By tossing the grenade into a hooch or bunker, everything within the building would be covered with the agent. The harmless, non-toxic TIARA filler of the marking grenade would cause everything it touched to glow in the dark. Anyone inside the area being searched by the SEALs would find it very hard to hide in the dark when they glowed like a giant firefly. Rubbing the TIARA agent to try and get it off would only increase the oxidation rate and cause the TIARA to glow even more brilliantly. Running away through the dark jungle would be next to impossible for a fleeing VC covered with TIARA and, if any of the agent had gotten on the man's feet, even if he did get away momentarily he would leave glowing footprints on the jungle floor.

Special Weapons

Mk 1 Illuminating

There was another hand grenade used to provide combat illumination for the SEALs in Vietnam that was not quite as exotic as the TIARA marking grenade. The Mk 1 series of illuminating grenades act as a hand-thrown flare, brilliantly lighting an area with the blue-white light of burning magnesium. Three Mods of the Mk 1 illuminating grenade exist, all of which can still be found in use until supplies of the earlier mods are exhausted.

The basic Mk 1 illuminating grenade consists of a thin steel shell body made up in two parts. The bottom cup of the Mk 1 body contains the illuminating composition topped with an igniter charge. The illuminating composition is a hot-burning mixture of powdered magnesium, sodium nitrate, and binder agents. As the illuminating charge does not easily ignite from a fuse or quickmatch, it is topped with a first-fire composition that is itself topped with an igniter charge.

The upper half of the Mk 1 body shell is hollow and holds the fuze assembly in place and additionally gives the Mk 1 grenade a reasonably aerodynamic shape. When the fuze of the Mk 1 functions and ignites the main illuminating charge, pressure is rapidly built up inside the grenade casing. The two shells burst apart from the pressure and the burning contents are exposed. To help conceal the direction from which the Mk 1 grenade was thrown, the fuze has a long 7-second delay.

Mods 1 and 2 of the Mk 1 illuminating grenade differ primarily in the way the fuze assembly ignites the illuminating composition. The Mod 2 is a much simple version of the initial Mod 1 design which has been in the inventory since World War II. The Mod 3 version of the Mk 1 uses the same fuze assembly as the Mod 2 version but has a body made from two plastic shells instead of sheet steel and has a slightly longer and thinner profile than the earlier mods.

In addition to acting as short-term illuminating charges, the high burning temperature of the illuminating composition allows the Mk 1 series to be use as an incendiary device for flammable targets.

Kilgore/Schermuly Stun

The most recent type of hand grenades has only come into official existence within the last twenty years or so. With the advent of international terrorism and wholesale hostage taking, a new munition was needed to help give an edge to antiterrorist forces. The idea was to disorient the terrorists while not causing major harm to any hostages or the surroundings. Though the Mk3A2 Offensive grenade has the effect of stunning a target through concussion, it is generally considered far too powerful an explosion for use in a hostage situation, not even considering the danger from fragments of the fuze.

Pyrotechnic training munitions had long been recognized as having a strong effect on troops exposed to them at close range, even when out in the open. The first stun grenade was based closely on a training munition used to simulate hand grenades. The Schermuly training grenade, manufactured in the United States by the Kilgore corporation, is a well known example of the first model of stun grenade.

In the Kilgore/Schermuly grenade, a molded plastic casing makes up the body of the grenade. Shaped somewhat like the M26A1 grenade, the plastic body holds the fuze in place as well as containing a paper-wrapped submunition. The submunition is the heart of the system, containing a charge of pyrotechnic flash powder and bursting with no dangerous fragmentation.

When the safety lever of the Kilgore/Schermuly grenade is released, it ignites a 2-second delay train. At the end of the delay, the submunition is ejected from the base of the grenade with its own 1-second or less delay ignited. When the submunition explodes it does so with a brilliant flash of light and thundering detonation.

Because of the brilliant light flash and loud explosion, a stun grenade can temporarily incapacitate or disorient a target for up to several seconds while causing little or no permanent damage. That stunned delay can give an antiterrorist unit a strong edge as they enter a hostage area and eliminate the terrorists. Drawbacks to the early style of stun grenade, such as the Kilgore/Schermuly, included releasing a large cloud of smoke obscuring the target area and hot paper fragments starting small fires. Constant development of the stun grenade system has largely eliminated these early complaints.

Also called distraction devices, stun grenades of various types are in use with all of the SEAL Teams for several different types of missions. Besides use in antiterrorist operations, stun grenades have proved useful in boarding ops against possible enemy shipping and would be vary valuable in prisoner snatch operations. The exact types of stun munitions used by the SEALs today is not available for public release. One grenade that can be shown is a stun munition originally produced by the using units themselves.

TECHNICAL DATA—Kilgore/Schermuly Stun grenade
TYPE—Stun hand grenade
IDENTIFYING COLOR CODE—Grey body
BODY—Plastic casting
FILLER—Cardboard cylinder (submunition) containing photoflash composition
FUZE—M202A1 Bouchon-type igniting fuze w/pyrotechnic delay
FUZE DELAY—0.7 to 2 seconds
  WEIGHTS
ROUND—0.50 lbs (0.23 kg)
FILLER—0.07 lb (0.03 kg)
  EFFECTS
EFFECT—Blast of 175 db and bright flash, 1,000,000 candela causing 5 to 15 seconds of disorientation when used in an enclosed area (room)
AREA OF EFFECT—5.5 yd (5 m) radius
  LENGTHS
LENGTH—4.29 in (10.9 cm)
WIDTH (DIAMETER)—2.5 in (6.4 cm)

Grenades

This is the "flash-crash" stun grenade used by the SEALs until supplanted by newer, and still classified, models. The flash-crash is a modified M116A1 hand grenade simulator with the burning-type fuse removed and an M201-family fuze screwed in its place into the opening at the top of the body. The cardboard body of the simulator results in little fragmentation but the heavy fuze body could be projected for some distance at a dangerous velocity. These grenades could still be produced by a deployed SEAL group as necessary if the mission demanded.
PHOTO CREDIT: KEVIN DOCKERY

TECHNICAL DATA—Flash/Crash
TYPE—Stun hand grenade
IDENTIFYING COLOR CODE—White body w/olive drab fuze
BODY—Cardboard
FILLER—Photoflash powder consisting of aluminum powder, potassium perchlorate, and barium nitrate
FUZE—M201A1 Bouchon-type detonating fuze w/pyrotechnic delay additional safety clip around fuze body and safety lever
FUZE DELAY—0.7 to 2 seconds
 WEIGHTS
ROUND—0.33 lb (0.15 kg)
FILLER—0.078 lb (0.035 kg)
 EFFECTS
EFFECT—Blast of 175 db and bright flash causing 5 to 15 seconds of disorientation when used in an enclosed area (room)
AREA OF EFFECT—5.5 yd (5 m) radius
 LENGTHS
LENGTH—4.75 in (12.1 cm)
WIDTH (DIAMETER)—1.59 in (4 cm)

FLASH CRASH

The flash crash as it is called, is a modified M116A1 hand grenade simulator. Easily available from existing supply channels, the M116A1 hand grenade simulator greatly resembles the standard stun grenade submunition with its paper body and soft plastic end seals. To make the M116A1 simulator more effective and dependable as a flash crash, the issue pull string igniter and fuse assembly is completely removed from the simulator. In the original fuse's place is a pull-ring Bouchon fuze of the M201 series. The M201 series igniting fuze is the same model as used on the burning-type of chemical grenade such as the M18 colored smoke or the M7A3 CS grenade. The M201 fuze is simply screwed into the enlarged hole at the end of the M116A1 simulator where the original fuse was removed. With the M201 series fuze installed, the flash crash has the same standard pull ring and safety lever as the standard grenades used by the SEALs.

When the safety lever of the flash crash is released, the 1.5 to 2 second delay of the M201 fuze is ignited. When the fuze delay is over, it spits out a flame, igniting the flash powder charge inside the simulator body. The flash composition, a mixture of aluminum powder, potassium perchlorate, and barium nitrate, burns almost instantly with a bright flash, loud noise, and cloud of white smoke.

Though the flash crash has its drawbacks, the cloud of smoke and possible danger from the metal fuze body, the cost of the device is much less than for a standard stun grenade. It can also be made practically on demand when needed and other munitions may not be available. In general, the flash crash has proven itself very useful not only for training, but as an active non-lethal field munition.

TECHNICAL DATA—Mk 40 Mod 1 Depth charge
NSN 1361-00-055-1094
TYPE—Hand-launched high explosive antipersonnel depth charge
IDENTIFYING COLOR CODE—Olive drab body
BODY—Sheet aluminium
FILLER—TNT
FUZE—Electrically fired w/water-activated battery, pressure activated switch and electrical delay detonator, Armed by standard pull ring
FUZE DELAY—6 seconds (initiates at 13 feet), fires at 30 to 35 foot (9 to 11 m) depth
 WEIGHTS
ROUND—3.6 lbs (1.63 kg)
FILLER—3 lbs (1.36 kg)
 EFFECTS
EFFECT—Underwater blast will kill or stun a swimmer
AREA OF EFFECT—Kill 30 ft (9 m), Stun 55 ft (17 m)
 LENGTHS
LENGTH—9.88 in (25.1 cm) w/lid
WIDTH (DIAMETER)—3.59 in (9.1 cm)
AVERAGE RANGE—
 Blast may cause hull damage to a naval vessel within 35 feet (11 m) or a merchant vessel within 70 feet (21 m). Charge sinks about 3 feet every second. Fuse arms at 8 foot (2.5 m) depth. After 6 second delay, the fuze will fire at 30 to 35 foot depth. If fuze fails to fire, the battery will expire after about 30 minutes rendering the device inactive.

 **Special Weapons**

Mk 40 Mod 1 HE Depth charge
(Antipersonnel)

One antipersonnel munition used by the Teams is more of a hand-thrown explosive device then a regular hand grenade. The Mk 40 Mod 1 high explosive depth charge is an antiswimmer device used in much the same manner as a large hand grenade. Designed to be launched from harbor patrol boats when enemy swimmers are suspected, the Mk 40 is an improvement over the use of the Mk3A2 offensive grenade in protecting boats against sabotage in Vietnam. Instead of having a regular delay fuze assembly, the Mk 40 has a pull-ring safety electric firing mechanism with a pressure-activated switch.

To prepare the charge for use, a protective metal cap is removed from over the fuze. In the Mod 0 model, the pull ring is first removed to free a brass plunger at the top of the fuze. The plunger is then driven into the fuze by hand. The Mod 1 version of the Mk 40 charge acts in much the same way except that a spring-loaded striker is released when the pull ring is removed.

Both the plunger and the striker perform the same action, breaking a glass bulb enclosing the battery inside the perforated fuze housing. With the glass bulb broken, either fresh or salt water can enter the battery and activate it.

The charge sinks at a rate of about 3 feet per second. When the charge has reached a depth of about 13 feet (4 meters), the water pressure closes a switch starting a 6-second detonator delay. At the end of the delay time the charge detonates, usually at a depth of about 30 to 35 feet (9.1 to 10.7 meters) given clear water. When the charge is used in water less than 13 feet deep, the fuze will usually not detonate though it could be activated by the over-pressure from another charge going off. The battery in the Mk 40 continues to function for about 30 minutes after activation. When the battery has expired the fuze becomes inactive.

The shock and over-pressure of the Mk 40 charge exploding at a depth of 30 feet (9.1 meters) will stun an underwater swimmer at a radius of about 55 feet (16.8 meters) and will kill a swimmer within a radius of about 30 feet (9.1 meters). Surface swimmers and personnel in small boats are not in danger when 70 feet (21.3 meters) or more from the point of explosion of the Mk 40 charge. This safety distance is part of the reason for the detonator delay built into the fuze of the Mk 40 depth charge.

Basic loads for common hand grenades used by the SEALs in Vietnam usually consisted of several M26-type fragmentation grenades, one or two M18 colored smoke grenades of different colors, and either a WP grenade or a Mk3A2 offensive grenade. Personal taste, and strength, usually determined just how many grenades an individual SEAL would carry. A Chief or Officer might tell a particularly heavily-laden SEAL to leave a number of his grenades off his load to keep him from being too burdened. But after a number of missions were under their belts, most SEALs knew what they wanted immediately available, as well as what the other members of their unit normally carried.

As SEAL operations grew more sophisticated in the 1970's and 1980's, basic loads of ammunition also became more specialized. During VBSS (Visit, Board, Search & Seizure) operations, the average SEAL would carry an M7A3 CS grenade, a Mk3A2 offensive grenade, and four flash crashes. For the same operation a sniper wouldn't carry any hand grenades at all while a breacher, armed with a shotgun and equipped to open locked doors, would carry an M7A3 CS grenade, a Mk3A2 offensive grenade, and only two flash crash stun grenades.

While attending Basic Underwater Demolition/SEAL (BUD/S) training in California, this trainee waits for his turn on the hand grenade range. In his hands are a number of M26A1 fragmentation grenades.
PHOTO CREDIT: US NAVY

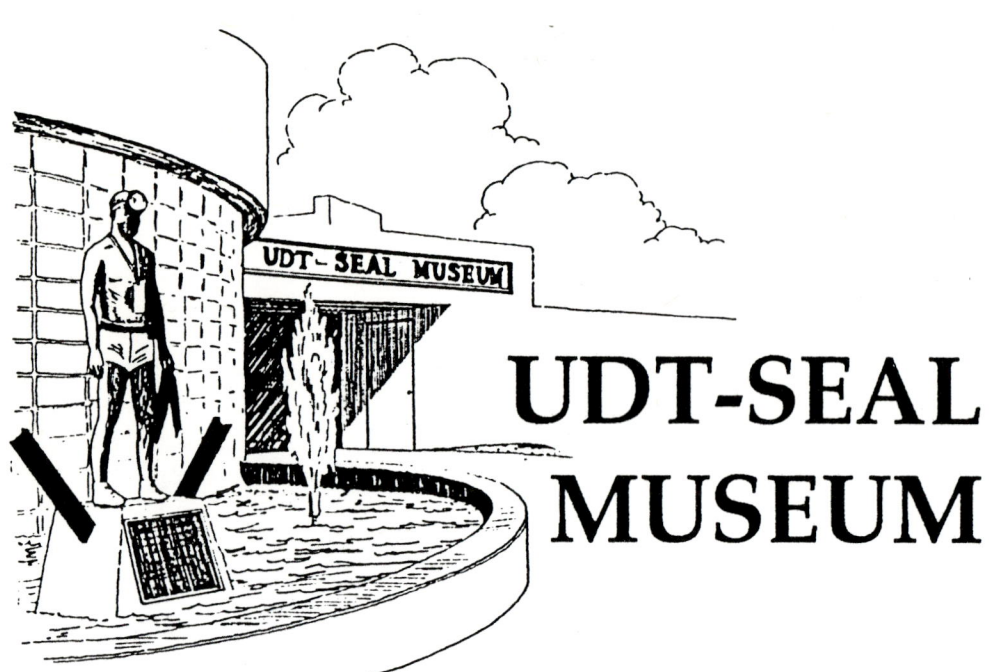

UDT-SEAL MUSEUM

...Located on the Original Training Site of the Navy Frogmen in Fort Pierce, Florida

The UDT-SEAL Museum tells the story of U.S. Navy special warfare from the early days of Naval Combat Demolition Units and Scouts & Raiders to Underwater Demolition Teams—better known as Frogmen—and today's SEALs. Outdoor and indoor exhibits illustrate the unique history of the men who fought in World War II, and those who followed them in Korea and Vietnam. Also part of the exhibits are recent operations in Haiti, Somalia, and Iraq.

The museum, dedicated to preserving the weapons, equipment, artifacts, vehicles, and valor of the country's most secretive fighting men, is operated by the UDT-SEAL Museum Association. For information about becoming an association member, contact the association at the address below, or call (561) 595-1570, or fax (561) 595-1576.

UDT-SEAL Museum
3300 North A1A
North Hutchinson Island
Fort Pierce, FL 34949-8520
(561) 462-3597

INDEX

Items in *italics* have no data bloc attached to them, they are found in captions or separate tables.

A

AAI CAWS	119
AAI Silent Shotgun Shell	107
ALICE Gear	109
AN-M8 Smoke Grenade	178
AN-M14 Incendiary Grenade	182
AN/PRC-25 Radio	98
AN/PRC-77 Radio	114
AN/PRR-9 Receiver	141
AN/PRT-4 Transmitter	141
AN/PVS-2 Starlight Scope	135

B

Beckwith Manufacturing Scabbard	9
Bell Labs M3 Suppressor	61
Beretta M9	44
Beretta M92S-1	40
Beretta M92SB-F	44
Browning Automatic Rifle	122
Browning HP-35	30
Buck Knives Buckmaster	14

C

Caws Requirements	116
Camillus S1760 Pocketknife	13
Camillus Pilot Survival Knife	13
Carl Gustav SMG	66
Chicom Stick Grenade	175
China Lake Special Projects Division	148
C-MAG 100 Round Magazine	164
Colt .380 Automatic	27
Colt AR-15 Model 601	124
Colt CAR-15 Model 605	132
Colt CAR-15 Model 607	138
Colt Detective Special	24
Colt M4 Carbine Model 720	166
Colt M-16 Model 602	131
Colt M-16A1 Model 603	130
Colt M-16A2	163
Colt M1911A1 Government Model	22
Colt Mark 4 Mod 0	156
Colt Carbine Model 653	160
Colt Model 723	164
Colt USSOCOM OHWS	48
Colt XM177E1 Model 609	141
Combat Shotgun Ammunition	106
Compact Laser Designator	134

D

Daewoo USAS-12	118
Dahlgren 50 Round Magazine	147
Delft Optics 3x25 Telescope	133
Draeger LAR-V Rebreather	80

F

F1 Submachine gun	69
Flash/Crash Grenade	188
FN-Browning Shotguns	103
Folding Demolition Knife	20

G

Gerber Mark II Combat Knife	13
Glock Pistols	45
Gyrojet Rocket Gun	51

H

Harrington & Richardson T223	150
Heckler & Koch CAWS	116
H&K Concealment Carriers	85
Heckler & Koch 54A1	84
Heckler & Koch MP5A3	76
Heckler & Koch MP5A5	76
Heckler & Koch MP5K	76
Heckler & Koch MP5KA4	76
Heckler & Koch MP5K-N	96
Heckler & Koch MP5-N	94
Heckler & Koch MP5SD3	76
Heckler & Koch MP5SD6	76
Heckler & Koch MP2000	88
Heckler & Koch P9S	41
Heckler & Koch P9S/Suppressor	38
Heckler & Koch P11 ZUB	54
Heckler & Koch SMG I	88
Heckler & Koch SMG 94054	88
Heckler & Koch USSOCOM OHWS	50
HEL M4 Supressor	144
High Standard Model HD	30

I

Ingram M10	70
Ingram M11	70
Insight Technology LAM	49
Ithaca Model 37	98
Ithaca Model 37 Duckbill	100

J

JSSAP 6.3 SMG	88

K

KAC Mark 2 Blast Suppressor	158
Kalishnikov AK-47	154
Kalishnikov AKS-47	154
Kalishnikov AKM-47	154
Kalishnikov AKMS-47	154
Kilgore/Schermuly Stun Grenade	187
Knight's Armament Co. Suppressor	51

L

Lancejet Underwater Weapon	51
LC-2 Canteen Carrier	109
Leatherman Multiblade Tool	14

M

M-1 Carbine	120
M1A1 Ammunition Can	55
M-2 Carbine	112
M-3 Submachine gun	58
M-3 Submachine gun (Suppressed)	60
M-3A1 Submachine gun	58

Index

M6A1 Gas Grenade	181
M7A1 Gas Grenade	180
M7A3 Gas Grenade	182
M-9 Bayonet	17
M-14	134
M-14 Folding Stock	163
M-60 Machine gun	98
M12 Universal Military Holster	41
M15 W.P. Grenade	176
M17A1 Gas Mask	82
M18 Smoke Grenade	180
M26 H.E. Grenade	172
M26A1 H.E. Grenade	172
M29 Anti-tank Rifle Grenade	62
M33 H.E. Grenade	174
M34 W.P. Grenade	178
M61 H.E. Grenade	172
M67 H.E. Grenade	174
M72 LAW	136
M79 Grenade Launcher	72
M116A1 Grenade Simulator	188
M206 Fuze	170
M228 Fuze	168
M1910 Pistol Belt	120
M1912 Holster	57
M1936 Pistol Belt	7
M1945 Suspenders	25
M1956 Load Bearing Equipment	98
Mac Series Suppressor	73
Mad Dog Knives ATAK	17
Madsen M50	64
Mark 1 Ka-Bar Knife	6
Mark 1 Mod 2 Illum. Grenade	186
Mark 2 Ka-Bar Knife	8
Mark II H.E. Grenade	168
Mark 3 Knife	12
Mark 3 Noise Suppressor	32
Mark III SAS Holster	113
Mark 3A1 Concussion Grenade	170
Mark 3A2 Concussion Grenade	170
Mark VI Breathing Rig	128
Mark 13 Day/Night Signal Flare	11
Mark 23 Offensive Handgun	51
Mark 26 Pistol Accessory kit	32
Mark 40 Mod 1 Depth Charge	188
Mark 59 Projectile	53
Mark 144 Mod 0 Cartridge	35
MAT-49	64
Mauser Broomhandle Pistol	62
Mini-Uzi	75
Mission Knives MPK	18
Model 184 Buckmaster	14
Model 308-1 Napalm Grenade	184
Model 308-1 Smoke Grenade	184
Model 308-1 TIARA Grenade	184
MP 40 Submachine gun	62

N

Nonmagnetic SCUBA Knife	10

O

Olin Co. CAWS Ammunition	109
Ontario Knife Company Mark 3	13

P

Phobis International CUK	16
PRC Type 51	26
PRC Type 56	139
PRO-TEC Helmet	112

Q

QualaTech Suppressor	41

R

Randall Combat Knife	13
Remington 870 Mark 1	112
Remington 870 Mark 6	108
Remington 870 P	113
Remington 1100	105
Remington 7188 Mark 1	102
Ruger Mark II with suppressor	42

S

Samozaridnya SKS	153
Sidewinder Stock	113
Sig-Sauer P226	46
Smith & Wesson K38 Model 15	24
S&W Military & Police .38	22
S&W Model 19 .357 Magnum	23
Smith & Wesson Mark 22 Mod 0	34
Smith & Wesson Mark 23 Mod 0	34
Smith & Wesson Mark 24 Mod 0	63
Smith & Wesson Model 36	26
Smith & Wesson Model 39	26
Smith & Wesson Model 60	26
Smith & Wesson Model 66	38
Smith & Wesson Model 76	68
Smith & Wesson Model 459	39
Smith & Wesson Model 686	42
Smith & Wesson .38 Victory Model	23
SOG Specialty Knives ST2SS	18
SS109 5.56 Ammunition	163
Sten Gun	63
Stoner 63A Machine gun	128
Swedish K	66
SwissChamp Swiss Army Knife	12

T

Thompson M1928A1	56
Tokarev TT-33	28
Type L Drum Magazine	57
Type 51 Pistol	29
Type 54 Pistol	29

U

Underwater Defense Gun Mark 1	52
USSOCOM OHWS Specifications	48
Utility Life Jacket	98
Uzi	74

V

V-40 H.E. Mini-grenade	174
Victorinox Swiss Army Knife	13

W

Walther P-38 (Suppressed)	31
Winchester Model 97	99

X

XM148 Grenade Launcher	128
XM162 00 Buckshot	101
XM257 #4 Buckshot	101
XM855 5.56 Ammunition	147